Gendered Aesthetics of Blackness

SUNY series, Afro-Latinx Futures

_____

Vanessa K. Valdés, editor

Gendered Aesthetics of Blackness

Afro-Cuban Women's Visual Art and Activism

ROSITA SCERBO

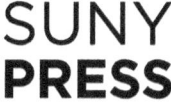

Cover art: Harmonia Rosales, *The Birth of Oshun*, 2017 (used by permission).

Published by State University of New York Press, Albany

EU GPSR Authorised Representative:
Logos Europe, 9 rue Nicolas Poussin, 17000, La Rochelle, France
contact@logoseurope.eu

For information, contact State University of New York Press, Albany, NY
www.sunypress.edu

Library of Congress Cataloging-in-Publication Data

Name: Scerbo, Rosita, author.
Title: Gendered aesthetics of Blackness : Afro-Cuban women's visual art and
    activism / Rosita Scerbo.
Description: Albany : State University of New York Press, [2025] | Series:
    SUNY series, Afro-Latinx futures | Includes bibliographical references
    and index.
Identifiers: LCCN 2024049453 | ISBN 9798855802924 (hardcover : alk. paper) |
    ISBN 9798855802900 (ebook) | ISBN 9798855802917 (pbk. : alk. paper)
Subjects: LCSH: Feminism and art—Cuba. | Art and society—Cuba. | Art,
    Black—Cuba—Themes, motives. | Art, Cuban—Themes, motives.
Classification: LCC N72.F45 S33 2025 | DDC 704/.042089960721—dc23/eng/20250122
LC record available at https://lccn.loc.gov/2024049453

Contents

Illustrations

Acknowledgments

It is a profoundly humbling task to express gratitude in a way that fully captures the breadth of influence and support I have received throughout the journey of writing this book. From my earliest memories to the present moment, countless voices have contributed to the knowledge, inspiration, growth, and resilience that made this work possible. Every interaction, every shared story, and every act of resistance has left an indelible mark on me, shaping both my personal and scholarly path.

In acknowledging those who have directly supported the creation of *Gendered Aesthetics of Blackness: Afro-Cuban Women's Visual Art and Activism*, I am keenly aware that this book is a culmination of collective wisdom and strength. It stands as a testament to the many who have come before me and those who continue to inspire my work every day.

I would like to extend my heartfelt gratitude to Afro-Cuban American artist Harmonia Rosales for her generous contribution to this work. Her permission to feature her painting *The Birth of Oshun* as the cover of this book, along with three additional paintings within its pages, has added profound depth and visual resonance to the themes explored here. I am equally grateful for the time she took to engage in an interview, which is also included in this book, offering invaluable insights into her artistic process and vision.

I also wish to thank Spelman College Museum of Fine Art for hosting the *Master Narratives* exhibition, which opened on August 18, 2023, and featured Harmonia Rosales's remarkable work. I am especially grateful for the invitation to the VIP private opening, where I had the opportunity to meet Harmonia Rosales in person after years of working on her art. This meeting was a significant moment for me, allowing us to connect, converse, and even capture a photograph of us together in front of *The*

Birth of Oshun—the very piece that now graces the cover of this book. The photograph, a cherished memento of that encounter, is included in the interview I conducted with the artist.

Special thanks to María Magdalena Campos-Pons, the Cuban-born artist now based in Nashville, Tennessee, for allowing the inclusion of three of her art pieces in this manuscript. Her work continues to inspire and challenge conventional narratives within the Afro-Cuban and broader Afro-diasporic communities.

I also wish to express my deep appreciation to Susana Pilar, Afro-Cuban visual artist who remains rooted in Havana, Cuba, for permitting the use of three of her evocative and thought-provoking pieces. Her work is a powerful testament to the resilience and creativity of Afro-Cuban women.

I am equally indebted to the Belkis Ayón Estate for granting me access to three of the late artist's iconic works, ensuring that her legacy continues to resonate within the pages of this book.

A special thanks to Diarenis Calderón Tartabull, an Afro-Cuban queer activist, curator, and cultural promoter, for her willingness to share her knowledge and insights through an interview that has greatly enriched the content of this book.

I also wish to acknowledge the invaluable support of the Co-PIs of the grant *Global Education Initiative/Afro-Brazilian Studies Abroad Program*, funded by the Fulbright-Hays Group Project Abroad (GPA) and the Department of Education Grant Award. The time I spent at the Steve Biko Institute in Salvador, Bahia, Brazil, during the summer of 2024, along with the pre- and postdeparture lectures, workshops, and seminars, provided me with critical perspectives not only on Afro-Brazilian studies but also on Afro-Cuban productions and the broader aesthetic studies of the African Diaspora.

Additionally, my sincere gratitude goes to the Georgia State University HRC Faculty Fellow Maymester 2024 grant, sponsored by the Humanities Research Center. This grant afforded me and a small group of faculties the dedicated time to write, share our work-in-progress, and gather strategies and tools for writing productivity, which were crucial in the completion of this book.

I would also like to thank the organizers and participants of the "Afro-Cuban Legacies: Visual Arts, Literature, Theatre, Music, and Religion" conference, held at the University of Missouri, Columbia, in April 2024. The opportunity to present portions of this book and receive feedback from fellow Afro-Cubanist scholars, artists, and activists significantly shaped the final manuscript.

To my mentors, advisers, colleagues, and friends, your unwavering support and commitment to racial and social equity in Latin America and the Caribbean have been instrumental in both the content and spirit of this work. A special acknowledgment goes to my comrades and fellow community organizers, especially the members of the Black Land Working Group at Georgia State University. Your dedication to justice and equity continues to inspire me.

To my husband, Matt—thank you for being my rock, the steady force in my life that grounds me. Your unwavering support and belief in me have been my anchor throughout this journey. Without you, this book would not have been possible.

And to my fierce little feminist, Sol—at just five years old, you've already taught me so much about empathy, generosity, and the power of standing up for what is right. Your spirit inspires me every day, and I am so proud to be your mother.

I would also like to extend my thanks to Rebecca Colesworthy, my senior acquisitions editor at SUNY Press, for her insightful guidance and support throughout the publication process. Her keen editorial eye and steadfast support have been invaluable in bringing this project to fruition. Last, my deepest appreciation goes to the three anonymous reviewers whose critical feedback and suggestions have been instrumental in refining and improving this book.

As I end these acknowledgments, I am reminded that the journey of creating this book has been one of deep reflection and active resistance. It is a testament to the enduring power of Afro-Cuban women's visual expression and the Decolonial AfroARTivism that continues to challenge and dismantle oppressive narratives. This book, like the many voices and works it highlights, is an act of defiance against the erasure and marginalization that Black women have faced for generations.

In a world where the forces of inequity are relentless, our collective resistance becomes not just a means of survival, but a path to liberation. The stories, art, and wisdom shared within these pages are a celebration of that resistance—a refusal to be silenced, a commitment to preserving and honoring our cultural identities, and a steadfast belief in the transformative power of art.

Introduction

Afro-Cuban Women as Bridges Between Worlds, Custodians of the Past, and Weavers of Alternative Futures

I still smell the foam of the sea they made me cross.
The night, I can not remember it.
The ocean itself could not remember that.
But I can't forget the first gull I made out in the distance.
High, the clouds, like innocent eyewitnesses.
Perhaps I haven't forgotten my lost coast,
nor my ancestral language.
They left me here and here I've lived.
And, because I worked like an animal,
here I came to be born.
How many Mandinga epics did I look to for strength.

— Nancy Morejon, "Mujer Negra/Black Woman"[1]

Cuba's cultural landscape has long been shaped by the complex interplay of African and Afro-Caribbean identities. From the early twentieth century to the present day, modern and contemporary artists have created a remarkable body of work that reflects these intricate dynamics. They engaged deeply with African traditions, acknowledging their centrality in Cuban national culture, and produced art that underscored the ongoing influence of Africa and the Caribbean as vital forces shaping what it means to be Cuban. This vision, articulated by Afro-diasporic artists, placed African practices at the forefront of Cuban identity, insisting on their importance in the formation of the nation. At the heart of this discourse was the Afrocubanismo movement, which emerged in the 1920s as a significant

1

artistic and social force. As part of this movement, Black-themed Cuban culture was brought to the fore, marking an era when white intellectuals, for the first time, openly acknowledged the significance of African culture in shaping the nation (Ortiz 1950). Fernando Ortiz, a cultural anthropologist and key figure in Afrocubanismo, was instrumental in establishing the legitimacy of Black identity in Cuban society, culture, and art. The movement arose during the interwar period, following decades of tense racial dynamics between Black and white Cubans, which had persisted even after the abolition of slavery in 1886 (Arnedo-Gomez 2012). This intersection of race, art, and national identity in Cuba set the stage for a broader discussion of Blackness in Cuban visual culture, a discussion that continues to evolve as new generations of artists grapple with their heritage and redefine what it means to be Afro-Cuban today.

Building on the legacy of Afrocubanismo, Afro-Cuban women have played a pivotal role in shaping the visual art landscape, contributing to a rich and evolving narrative that foregrounds their unique experiences and perspectives. Through their work, these women have not only participated in the broader dialogue about Cuban identity but have also expanded it, offering nuanced interpretations of race, gender, and cultural heritage. One of the most significant contributions by Afro-Cuban women artists is their reimagining of Black female identity and spirituality. By drawing on Afro-Caribbean religious practices such as Santería, also known as Lucumí, Regla de Ocha, or Regla Lucumí, these artists invoke the Orishas, or deities, as powerful symbols of strength, resilience, and ancestral connection. In doing so, they elevate Afro-Cuban religious iconography into the realm of contemporary art, blending tradition with innovation. This will be evident in the works of the artists analyzed in this book. The art of Afro-Cuban women also reclaims the visibility of Black bodies, particularly Black women's bodies, which have historically been marginalized or misrepresented in visual culture. Their work resists colonial and patriarchal gazes by asserting agency over how Black womanhood is portrayed. These artists challenge the legacies of slavery, migration, and displacement, engaging with themes of memory and diaspora through multimedia works that blend photography, video, painting, and performance. These Afro-Cuban women artists do more than represent; they actively construct spaces for dialogue, resistance, and healing. They use visual art as a form of decolonial praxis, disrupting historical narratives that have silenced or erased the contributions of Black women in Cuba. By centering their own lived experiences and cultural histories, they challenge both the Cuban art establishment and global art markets to reckon with the complexities of Blackness and gender in the Cuban context. Through their works, Afro-Cuban women redefine the contours of Cuban national culture, positioning themselves not only as artists but as cultural bearers of a lineage that is both personal and collective. Their contributions to visual art continue to push boundaries, creating a powerful visual language that speaks to the multiplicity of identities within Afro-Cuban society, while offering transformative perspectives on race, spirituality, and gender. In their hands, art becomes a tool for empowerment, self-expression, and cultural affirmation, adding new layers to the ever-evolving narrative of Blackness in Cuba.

Through their visual expressions and engagement with what I call Decolonial AfroARTivism, Afro-Cuban women articulate a critical discourse on identity, gender, and race. In this framework, AfroARTivism refers to the intentional convergence of artistic production and political activism within the Afro-Cuban community, reflecting the conscious efforts of Afro-Cuban women to utilize their art as a medium for challenging dominant social norms, advancing decolonial perspectives, and fostering dialogue on issues of identity, race, and gender. This concept captures the intricate relationship between art and activism, highlighting how visual culture functions as a potent instrument for social and cultural critique. This study engages with the interdisciplinary intersections of Afro-Cuban women's art and activism, focusing on the ways in which cultural production, aesthetics, and resistance are interwoven. It seeks to illuminate the complexities of gender and Blackness within Cuba's sociocultural landscape, examining how art serves as a vehicle for both personal expression and political resistance. The term *Afro-Cuban women*, as used throughout this work, encompasses not only artists residing in Cuba but also those in the diaspora, including second-generation Afro-Cuban women born in the United States and Afro-Cuban women currently living in exile. This expansive definition allows for a comprehensive exploration of the diverse experiences and artistic practices of Afro-Cuban women across multiple geographies and cultural contexts. This inclusive approach acknowledges the fluidity of identity and the transnational connections that shape the lives and works of these artists. The diverse backgrounds of the selected artists provide a rich spectrum that holds considerable promise for illuminating the complexities of racial, identity, and gender dynamics in contemporary Cuba from a comprehensive standpoint. Afro-Cuban women have historically been at the forefront of efforts to challenge established norms, deconstruct oppressive systems, and redefine the narrative surrounding Black female identity within a society marked by historical inequities. Utilizing a diverse range of artistic mediums, encompassing painting, performance art, multimedia installation, and photography, these women have crafted a body of work that transcends conventional categorization. In *Gendered Aesthetics of Blackness*, I explore the complex visual expressions crafted by Afro-Cuban women in both Cuba and the United States. This study critically analyzes how their art subverts dominant conventions, actively reconfiguring the intersections of gender, race, and identity. Through their artistic practices, I demonstrate the capacity of art as a tool of resistance, one that interrogates deeply embedded power structures and serves as a catalyst for transformative social and cultural change. The scope of this inquiry includes Afro-Cuban women in their homeland as well as those in the diaspora, highlighting the transnational dimensions of their work. The inclusion of these diverse groups is pivotal, as it highlights the transnational dimensions of Afro-Cuban identity and reveals the impact of varied cultural and social contexts on their artistic production. The selection of subjects residing in both Cuba and the United States underscores the shared and distinct experiences that shape their creative practices. This approach not only enriches the discourse on identity, resistance, and transformation but also provides a comprehensive understanding of the diasporic connections and the influence of migration on cultural expression. Beyond analyzing the visual works, I present to the audience, this manuscript highlights and amplifies the work of understudied and underrepresented artists from the intersectional standpoint of gender and race. This work is valuable to several fields in the humanities and the arts because I use the academic platform to make visible the most vulnerable and marginalized artists, who often struggle to gain recognition in the art industry. These artists frequently go unrecognized by national and international networks, making it difficult to study them within academia. My research demonstrates that it is possible to produce intellectual work from a decolonial perspective within academia, by utilizing various outlets and reaching out to artists who may not be discoverable through traditional web or library searches. Thus, the contribution of this monograph is twofold: it covers visual arts from an understudied angle and sets a precedent for conducting decolonial academic research. In my work, I deliberately incorporate scholars from Latin America and the Caribbean, particularly women of Afro-descendant and Indigenous origin, as a fundamental component of a decolonial approach to knowledge production. This framework is central to the aims of my project. By foregrounding scholars from the Global South, I actively contest the prevailing Eurocentric and North American–centric paradigms that often marginalize these critical perspectives. This methodological choice not only broadens the academic discourse but also fosters a more equitable and representative process of knowledge production. Through this decolonial lens, I seek to disrupt entrenched power structures within academia, cultivating a more inclusive and comprehensive understanding of Afro-Cuban women's visual expressions and Decolonial AfroARTivism.

This book extends beyond the field of art; it constitutes a celebration of Afro-Cuban women as agents of change. It amplifies their voices, examines their struggles, and commemorates their triumphs. It scrutinizes the ways in which their artistic creations serve as acts of resistance, reclamation, and reimagining. As you navigate the pages of *Gendered Aesthetics of Blackness*, you will encounter Afro-Cuban women who challenge us to interrogate our presuppositions and envision a world where the confluence of gender and Blackness does not signify oppression but rather symbolizes resilience and fortitude. Their narratives and artistic expressions motivate us to engage in the perpetual struggle for justice, parity, and emancipation, not only within the bounds of Cuba but also across the expanse of the African diaspora. In recent years, a notable shift has occurred in recognizing and celebrating the profound contributions of Afro-Cuban women to both Cuban and international culture. A remarkable milestone in this evolving narrative is the recent planned inclusion of the legendary Afro-Cuban singer, Celia Cruz, on US currency scheduled for release in 2024 (Gómez, 1). This significant gesture symbolizes a broader acknowledgment of Afro-Cuban women's indelible impact and legacy, not only within the United States but also globally. Celia Cruz, often referred to as the "Queen of Salsa," was far more than just a remarkable vocalist and performer. She stood as a symbol of resilience, creativity, and unyielding cultural pride. Born in Havana in 1925, Cruz's journey to international fame was characterized by her extraordinary talent, unwavering determination, and deep connection to her Afro-Cuban heritage. Her unique voice, dynamic stage presence, and vibrant personality captivated audiences worldwide, transcending borders and breaking down racial barriers. Celia Cruz's legacy extended beyond her musical prowess; it encompassed a broader message of Afro-Cuban pride and cultural inclusivity. Her bold and unapologetic embrace of her African heritage paved the way for future generations of Afro-Cuban women to assert their identities and make their voices heard. The decision to feature Celia Cruz on US currency is a powerful testament to her enduring impact. It signifies a departure from the historical erasure and marginalization of Afro-Cuban contributions and represents a significant step toward recognizing the vital role of Afro-Cuban women in shaping cultural identities. This recognition of Celia Cruz on American currency is not an isolated event but rather part of a larger trend of honoring the legacies of Afro-Cuban women. It serves as a symbol of shifting societal attitudes toward acknowledging and celebrating the diversity and richness of cultural contributions influenced by the African diaspora. As we delve deeper into the exploration of Afro-Cuban women's visual expressions and ARTivism in this book, it is essential to recognize that the inclusion of Celia Cruz on US currency symbolizes a broader cultural shift. It signals an increasing awareness of the need to uplift and honor the voices, experiences, and contributions of Afro-Cuban women who have played an integral role in shaping not only Cuban but also international cultural landscapes. This recognition stands as a testament to the enduring legacy of Afro-Cuban women and their profound influence on society, both past and present. Afro-Cuban women continue to shape national and international dialogues and restlessly keep making significative contributions in each field and professional areas of our society. While the recent acknowledgment of Afro-Cuban women's contributions marks a pivotal moment in history, it is essential to underscore that this recognition represents only a starting point in the broader narrative. Despite the significant strides made in recent years, challenges persist, and much remains to be done. The challenges faced by Afro-Cuban women are multifaceted and deeply rooted in social disparities. These challenges encompass unequal representation in various spheres, limited access to resources, and the enduring struggle against deeply ingrained stereotypes. The intersectionality of race and gender plays a significant role in shaping these challenges, as Afro-Cuban women experience compounded discrimination and marginalization. Moreover, the hypervisibility of Afro-Cuban women in cultural contexts, such as music and tourism, intersects with identity politics and resistance, reflecting the complex dynamics of representation and marginalization (Bishell 2021; Babb 2018). These challenges underscore the need for comprehensive efforts to address the intersecting forms of discrimination and inequality faced by Afro-Cuban women, recognizing the systemic and deeply entrenched nature of these social disparities. The journey toward a comprehensive appreciation and understanding of Afro-Cuban women's contributions, both past and present, is ongoing. Even as we celebrate milestones like the inclusion of Celia Cruz on US currency, we must also confront the systemic biases and underrepresentation that Afro-Cuban women continue to face in many spheres. Their stories, voices, and experiences still require amplification and advocacy, reminding us that the path toward genuine acknowledgment and equality is one that demands sustained effort and commitment.

Black Visions:
Theorizing Afro-Cuban Women's Decolonial AfroARTivism

The theoretical concept I propose in this book is the one of Decolonial AfroARTivism, a theoretical framework that seeks to challenge dominant narratives, power structures, and systems of oppression that have historically marginalized Black Latin American and Caribbean women. AfroARTivism stands at the intersection of decolonial aesthetics and Black feminism,[2] weaving together powerful narratives that challenge historical injustices and amplify the voices of Afro-Latina artists. In art history, "aesthetics" refers to the philosophical and theoretical study of the principles governing beauty, taste, and artistic appreciation. It encompasses the examination of how visual elements, such as form, color, composition, and style, contribute to the overall perception of artistic works. Aesthetics delves into the subjective and cultural aspects of artistic expression, exploring the ways in which individuals and societies interpret and respond to visual stimuli. This field of study seeks to understand the nature of artistic experience, the criteria for evaluating artistic merit, and the broader cultural implications of aesthetic choices in art. Framing AfroARTivism as a decolonial aesthetic emphasizes that this art is reassessing and redefining prevailing artistic norms, dismantling Eurocentric perspectives to reclaim Indigenous, Afro-descedant, and other marginalized voices. Decolonial aesthetics, rooted in decolonial theory, seeks to deconstruct the enduring legacies of colonialism and imperialism. It critiques the Western-centric gaze that has historically dominated art, perpetuating harmful stereotypes. It seeks to challenge and dismantle the structures of power, knowledge, and cultural dominance that have been imposed by colonial forces. Decolonial theorists in Latin America, like Aníbal Quijano, María Lugones, Sylvia Marcos, and Yuderkys Espinosa Miñoso, have made significant contributions to this field, with specific attention to the experiences and perspectives of Indigenous and Afro-descendant women. Simultaneously, positioning AfroARTivism within Black feminism highlights that this art recognizes and confronts the unique struggles faced by Black women, embracing intersectionality to address the intricate web of race, gender, class, and other identity categorizations.

Four integral elements define Decolonial AfroARTivism: narrative redefinition, cultural reappropriation, intersectional empowerment, and community engagement. Narrative redefinition constitutes a central tenet, employing various artistic modalities to challenge and reconstruct prevailing misrepresentations of African and African diasporic cultures. Concurrently, cultural reappropriation emphasizes deliberate reclamation, employing artistic expression to restore cultural authenticity and pride, countering historical distortions. Intersectional empowerment underscores AfroARTivism's commitment to recognizing and empowering individuals within intersecting social dimensions such as race, gender, and sexuality. This principle fosters inclusivity in artistic narratives, authentically reflecting the nuanced experiences of diverse communities. Finally, community engagement is integral, positioning AfroARTivism as a collaborative force addressing systemic issues. Through dialogues and cooperative efforts, it serves as a catalyst for collective identity, resilience, and solidarity within historically marginalized communities. These elements serve as guiding principles that echo through the Afro-Cuban women art productions analyzed in this manuscript.

Decolonial AfroARTivism is a form of activism and resistance that recognizes the intersectionality of race, gender, class, and sexuality in shaping diasporic experiences and identities. The application of this framework involves the creation of art that centers Black Latin American identities and experiences, utilizing decolonial methodologies that challenge Eurocentric notions of art and culture. This involves the rejection of the notion that art must be apolitical or detached from social issues, as well as the rejection of the idea that only certain forms of art are considered "high art." The benefits of this theoretical perspective are numerous. First, it allows for the elevation of marginalized voices and perspectives that have been excluded from mainstream art and culture. By centering Black Latin American and Caribbean voices, it offers a more inclusive and diverse understanding of visual expressions. Additionally, it offers a critical lens through which to view existing power structures and systems of oppression, enabling us to challenge and dismantle these structures. Finally, it promotes greater self-awareness and understanding of identity, aiding in the development of a more nuanced and empathetic view of the world. Decolonial AfroARTivists, such us the Afro-Cuban women explored in this book, create art pieces that draw on traditional African and Latin American art forms, challenging the dominance of Eurocentric art traditions. They also incorporate elements of social commentary or political critique into their work, highlighting issues that Afro-descendant communities are facing.

Art can be a powerful form of activism because it has the ability to convey political or social messages and raise awareness about important issues in a creative and impactful way. It can evoke emotions, challenge beliefs and attitudes, and spark public discourse and action. In this context, Afro-Cuban women's visual expression represents a form of decolonial aesthetic. Decolonial aesthetics refers to the study of the relationship between aesthetics (the philosophy of beauty and art) and colonialism. It is concerned with the ways in which colonialism has impacted the production and reception of art, as well as the ways in which aesthetics has been used to perpetuate colonial power and oppression. Decolonial aesthetics seeks to challenge the Eurocentric and colonial biases that have dominated the field of aesthetics and to bring to light the aesthetics of colonized and marginalized peoples. This may involve reclaiming and valuing Afro-diasporic artistic traditions or creating new forms of art that resist colonial narratives and celebrate the experiences and perspectives of historically oppressed communities. The ultimate goal of decolonial aesthetics is to promote a more equitable and diverse appreciation of beauty and art across cultures and to challenge the ongoing effects of colonialism in the production and reception of art. Black diasporic art is often shaped by a unique history of colonialism, slavery, and migration, as well as ongoing struggles for social, political, and economic justice. More specifically, Afro-Cuban artists draw on a rich history of African influence in Cuba, which dates back to the colonial era when large numbers of enslaved Africans were brought to the island. Their work often reflects themes related to race, identity, and Afro-Cuban culture, and can be seen as a way of preserving and promoting this important cultural heritage. When approaching art produced by Afro-Cuban women, a Black decolonial feminist perspective can be useful in understanding its numerous layers and meanings. While Black feminism is pivotal in formulating an "understanding of interlocking oppressive systems" (Roth 2003, 46–47), it is decolonial feminism that stands out for scrutinizing the lack of acknowledgment, within dominant feminism, of the intersectional analysis focusing on the varied forms of oppression impacting nonwhite women.

Decolonial feminism seeks to rectify the ongoing historical and theoretical sidelining encountered by nonwhite women within hegemonic feminism. This mainstream branch of feminism has long overlooked the intricate intertwining of race, class, gender, and sexuality. It has failed to recognize the extensive implications of these factors, especially considering that women of color have experienced victimization stemming from both the coloniality of power and the coloniality of gender (Lugones 2008). María Lugones, with her groundbreaking work in 2008 and 2010, ushered in the notion of the "modern/colonial system of gender." This concept served to dismantle the entrenched binary beliefs found within modern Western thought processes. To truly comprehend the essence of Western logic and its gendered structure requires an intricate understanding of gender as a racialized system of power. This system facilitates the dehumanization and subjectification of marginalized individuals and underscores "the attempt to turn the colonized into less than human beings" (Lugones 2010, 745). Decolonial feminist scholars have emphasized the imperative need to broaden the modern/colonial analytical framework, traditionally dominated by male perspectives, in order to unravel how power imbricates within gender norms (Lugones 2008) and the "everyday practices of racialized violence" (Fabricant & Postero 2013, 205). This expansion aids in elucidating the multifaceted ways in which power intersects with gender norms and racialized violence, thus providing a more encompassing and nuanced understanding of oppression and marginalization. The criticisms lodged by Black women and women of color are directed at Western or white feminisms, particularly for their propensity to overshadow and distort the experiences and realities of nonwhite women. These criticisms spotlight the persistent inadequacies and biases of mainstream feminism in addressing the unique and layered struggles faced by nonwhite women, revealing a pressing need for a more inclusive and equitable feminist discourse that acknowledges and incorporates diverse perspectives and experiences. By exploring these deeper, nuanced intersections of identity and oppression, decolonial feminism offers a more holistic and inclusive approach, addressing the inadequacies in hegemonic feminism and pushing for a more equitable representation and understanding of all women's experiences and struggles.

Art has always been a powerful tool for expressing ideas, emotions, and experiences that are often marginalized or excluded from mainstream discourse. My proposed theoretical concept of Decolonial AfroARTivism builds also on the rich legacy of Afrocentric art and activism while it incorporates the insights of contemporary Black feminist and decolonial theories. It challenges us to move beyond traditional approaches that focus solely on representation or aesthetic value and instead embrace more collaborative and participatory practices that center on the voices of marginalized communities. At its core, Decolonial AfroARTivism is about using art as a means of resistance and reclamation. It seeks to create spaces in which those who have historically been silenced, excluded, or oppressed can speak their truths and tell their own stories. By creating alternative narratives and images, it challenges dominant power structures and offers hope for a more equitable world. Within this intertwining of intricate oppressions and intersectionalities, the concept of Decolonial AfroARTivism emerges as a beacon of expression, resistance, and decolonization. It amalgamates the aesthetic vigor of art with the rebellious spirit of activism, all underpinned by an Afro-centric and feminist decolonial framework. This convergence aims to challenge, dissect, and ultimately deconstruct the colonial legacies and narratives that have persistently marginalized and oppressed individuals of Afro-descent. The principle introduced by María Lugones regarding the "modern/colonial system of gender" forms an integral component of this conceptual framework, portraying how the colonial and modern Western paradigms have perpetuated racialized power systems, leading to the dehumanization and subjugation of the colonized. Decolonial AfroARTivism, thus, strives to augment the analytical matrix of decolonial studies, integrating artistic mediums to articulate the everyday practices of racialized violence and the nuanced interplays of power within gender norms. It seeks to bring forth the voices, experiences, and histories of Afro-descendant individuals, promoting a comprehensive understanding of the racialized, gendered, and classed dimensions of coloniality. This aesthetic framework propels forward the discourse initiated by Black and decolonial feminists, offering not merely a critique of the hegemonic structures but also a creative and revolutionary pathway to illuminate, resist, and subvert the enduring impacts of coloniality on Afro-descendant individuals. The artistic expressions within Decolonial AfroARTivism serve as potent reminders and narrators of the unrepresented and distorted stories, providing a platform for the silenced to articulate their experiences, reclaim their narratives, and contribute to the broader struggle against all forms of oppression.

The methodology of AfroARTivism varies depending on the artist or collective involved, but it always involves using a range of visual and performative techniques, such as painting, sculpture, graffiti, photography, dance, and theater, to convey political messages and spark dialogue. At its core, Decolonial AfroARTivism draws on a rich legacy of resistance and resilience in Black and Afro-Latinx communities, while also pushing the boundaries of what art can do and be. It is an approach to art that seeks to challenge and dismantle colonial and Eurocentric norms that have historically marginalized and oppressed Black and Afro-diasporic individuals and communities. It aims to consciously disrupt these dominant narratives through creating new artistic practices and representations that center and celebrate Afro-diasporic experiences, voices, and perspectives. This approach recognizes the historical and ongoing impact of colonization on the lives and identities of Afro-descendant individuals, and actively works to counteract such systemic oppression through the medium of art. It is an approach to art that is grounded in feminist and decolonial theory[3] and seeks to challenge and dismantle the intersections of patriarchy, colonialism, and Eurocentrism that shape the experiences, in the specific case of this book, of Afro-Cuban women. Feminist and decolonial theory serve as a framework that enables us to analyze the power dynamics at play when exploring the meanings of an art piece. It involves critically examining an image within the contexts in which it originated and circulates. This entails studying the image itself, the individuals who engage with it, the motivations behind its creation, and the specific locations where it is exhibited (Cannella, 276). Moreover, Decolonial AfroARTivism can also be used as a tool to break racial and gender stereotypes and historical misrepresentations. Hazel Carby (2007) argues convincingly that the perceptions and portrayals by white feminists of the life experiences and struggles faced by Black women have been significantly skewed and misconstrued. Black women have been often reduced to mere "objects of research," or they have been depicted as "passive recipients of colonial oppression," bereft of agency or voice. This oversimplified representation fails to encapsulate the complexity and multifaceted nature of their lived experiences and ongoing battles. Additionally, Carby asserts that the prevalent frameworks in "contemporary feminist theory do not begin to adequately account for the experience of black women" (111), highlighting a profound gap in understanding and acknowledging the unique challenges and perspectives of Black women within the broader feminist discourse. This issue is not confined to the experiences of Black women alone; indeed, women of color, including Asians, Latinas, and others, have vocally "criticized Western feminism for being racist and overly concerned with White, middle-class women's issues" (Collins 2000a, 5). Such criticisms underscore a long-standing discontent and highlight the limitations inherent in Western feminist frameworks that seem to prioritize certain experiences and struggles over others. Therefore, this criticism sheds light on the apparent self-centeredness of Western or white feminist discourse, where the representations are predominantly, if not exclusively, reflective of the perspectives and issues of white, middle-class women (Carby 2007; Collins, 2000b). The emphasis on their own experiences and struggles results in a kind of myopia, obscuring the diverse range of experiences, struggles, and perspectives of women from different ethnic, racial, and class backgrounds. To develop a more equitable and inclusive feminist discourse, it's imperative to interrogate these biases and actively work toward incorporating a multitude of voices, experiences, and struggles, transcending racial, ethnic, and class boundaries. By doing so, the richness and diversity of women's experiences can be acknowledged and addressed in a more holistic and nuanced manner, allowing for a more comprehensive understanding of the myriad ways in which different forms of oppression intersect and manifest.

Decolonial AfroARTivism is a powerful tool for liberation, resistance, and healing for Black and Afro-Latina women who have been systematically silenced and erased in dominant cultural narratives. In particular, through their work, Afro-Cuban women artists have explored themes such as identity, history, and cultural heritage, bringing attention to the rich diversity of their experiences. They have also challenged the stereotypes and misconceptions that have often been associated with being both Black and Latina and have helped to create a more nuanced understanding of this complex identity. Decolonial AfroARTivism as a framework aims to address a wide range of social issues through art, including racism, economic and social inequality, gentrification, environmental degradation, colonialism and imperialism, and the marginalization of Black and Afro-Latinx communities within mainstream society. These issues are often interconnected and intersect with other forms of oppression, such as patriarchy, ableism, and heterosexism. Through their artistic practice, Decolonial AfroARTivists seek to raise awareness of these issues and challenge dominant narratives and power structures that reinforce systemic injustice. They use a variety of media, from painting and sculpture to performance and digital art, to create provocative and socially conscious works that engage audiences in critical reflection and dialogue. In addition to creating artwork that addresses specific issues, Decolonial AfroARTivists work to build networks and coalitions with other artists, activists, and community members to effect change at the grassroots level. They view art as a tool for mobilizing people and catalyzing social movements and believe that collective action is necessary to achieve lasting social transformation. My aim in this book is to highlight the transformative power of art in promoting social justice and equity, particularly in the context of the Black experience. Decolonial AfroARTivism is a dynamic approach that builds on the legacy of Afrocentric art and activism, while also recognizing the challenges of contemporary struggles for justice. This approach offers a unique perspective on how art can be used to educate, inspire, and mobilize others toward a common goal of social transformation.

Given this backdrop, it is also useful to refer to Nelson Maldonado-Torres who vehemently proposes that prevailing culture and the realms of knowledge creation have been complicit in sculpting subaltern women as "subjects without the capacity for autonomy and self-determination" (17). This portrayal erases the agency and autonomy of subaltern women, painting them as passive entities within the broader sociopolitical landscape. In stark contrast to this imposed narrative, Black and Indigenous women have historically stood as bastions of resistance within the Americas. These women, despite being "who simultaneously face multiple oppressions," have showcased the inherent ability to reconceptualize emancipatory politics, to be the embodiment of unique differences, and to innovate and experiment with the formation of novel subjectivities (Seppälä 2016, 4). Their resilience and resistance, while navigating through multifarious layers of oppression, position them as transformative figures capable of redefining political landscapes and creating profound, enduring changes. It is crucial to underline the discrepancy between the theoretical construction of subaltern women and their lived realities and historical roles. The characterization of these women as lacking autonomy and self-determination starkly contrasts with their long-standing roles as proactive agents of change, resistance, and re-imagination within their respective communities and beyond. These women have not only resisted and survived amid multiple oppressions but have also been instrumental in shaping new visions for emancipatory politics and cultivating diverse subjectivities. In light of this, it becomes imperative to challenge and dismantle the prevailing narratives and constructions that seek to undermine the capacities and contributions of Black and Indigenous women and to acknowledge and elevate their roles as pivotal figures in reimagining and restructuring sociopolitical and cultural paradigms. The bodies of Black women in art have long been sites of meaning-making, representation, and activism. From the earliest depictions of Black women in European art as exotic objects of desire or subservient laborers, to contemporary works by Black women artists that challenge and transform those stereotypes, the representations of Black women's bodies in art have always carried social, cultural, and political significance. One way to understand the significance of Black women's bodies in art is to view them as archives of memories. As scholar and artist Deborah Willis (2002) has argued, Black women's bodies are repositories of personal and collective histories, memories, and experiences that can be read and interpreted through their physical features, gestures, and expressions. For example, the scars, wrinkles, and stretch marks on a Black woman's body can tell a story of resilience, survival, and resistance against the forces of racism, sexism, and colonialism that have shaped her life, while the twists, curves, and angles of her body can embody a sense of pride, power, and beauty that defies mainstream beauty standards and Eurocentric ideals. Moreover, Black women's bodies in art can be seen as archives of collective memories that connect them to broader traditions and legacies of Black resistance, creativity, and imagination. For instance, the Black female body has been central to many artistic movements and genres, such as jazz, blues, hip-hop, poetry, and visual arts, that have emerged from Black communities as means of expressing their struggles, joys, and aspirations. Within these frameworks, Black women's bodies serve as vessels of cultural memory that transmit and transform the stories, myths, and rituals of their ancestors and contemporaries. The fact that Black women's bodies in art can be conceived as archives of memories highlights the richness, complexity, and diversity of their experiences and identities. It emphasizes their agency, creativity, and resilience in the face of oppression, while also recognizing their connection to broader histories of Black struggle and liberation. By foregrounding Black women's bodies in art as sources of memory and meaning, we can challenge and disrupt dominant narratives and representations that erase or distort their contributions to society and culture and celebrate their unique and essential role in shaping our world. Through various forms of art, Black women have challenged dominant narratives and created spaces for their voices and stories to be heard. They have used their bodies as sites of resistance, transformation, and affirmation, reclaiming and redefining their identities in the face of social and cultural oppression. At the same time, Black women's bodies in art have been objectified, fetishized, and exploited, perpetuating harmful stereotypes, and perpetuating systemic inequalities. Engaging with different perspectives on this topic has taught me the importance of listening to and centering the voices of Black women themselves. It has also highlighted the need for ongoing and critical reflection on our own biases and assumptions, and the ways in which we contribute to or challenge systems of oppression. Ultimately, I believe that understanding and appreciating the significance of Black women's bodies in art requires ongoing learning, listening, and active engagement with diverse perspectives and experiences.

The paradigms of Black and decolonial feminist theories and practices underscore the vital need to avert essentialism regarding Black, indigenous, and other nonwhite women. These theories stress the imperative to comprehend the multifaceted manners in which these women leverage their subjectivities—politically, strategically, discursively, and textually (Collins 2000a; Crenshaw 1991; hooks 1992a; Lugones 2008; 2010; May 2015). The focus on the lived, experiential epistemologies of Black women (Collins 2005) within Black/decolonial feminist frameworks acts as a catalyst in reinforcing Black women's capacities for self-definition and self-determination. This acknowledgment and affirmation pave the way for the development and articulation of situated "oppositional knowledge" (Collins 2000a; Crenshaw 1991; hooks 1992b; Roth, 2003)—a form of knowledge that is inherently resistant and does not seek or require validation from male perspectives. It is a form of knowledge that emerges from the lived experiences and struggles of Black and nonwhite women, offering a counternarrative to the predominant discourses. When these theories are put in conversation with the art created by Afro-Cuban women, a rich tapestry of resistance, expression, and self-determination unfolds.

The artwork of Afro-Cuban women serves as a vibrant manifestation of their subjectivities, utilized both discursively and textually to communicate their experiences, aspirations, and critiques of the societal structures that encircle them. Their artistic expressions are not only reflective of their individual and collective experiences but also serve as strategic and political tools to challenge, subvert, and reshape the narratives surrounding their identities and existence. Afro-Cuban women artists, through their innovative creations, give visual and tangible form to the "oppositional knowledge" delineated by Black and decolonial feminist theories. The interplay of colors, forms, and themes in their art encapsulates their unique epistemologies, resonating with their histories, struggles, and hopes. These artistic endeavors act as a conduit for affirming their self-definition and self-determination, providing an insightful lens to view and understand their multifaceted subjectivities. Moreover, these works of art serve as a testament to the political and strategic utilization of subjectivities by Afro-Cuban women. They traverse beyond the aesthetic realm, engaging with the viewers on intellectual and emotional levels, prompting reflections, conversations, and even actions aimed at acknowledging and addressing the diverse experiences and oppressions faced by Black, Indigenous, and other nonwhite women. In essence, the art of Afro-Cuban women and the intricate weave of Black and decolonial feminist theories construct a symbiotic relationship, enriching and illuminating each other. The coalescence of these elements fosters a deeper understanding of the lived experiences, resistant knowledge, and expressive subjectivities of these women, enabling the exploration of uncharted territories in both artistic and theoretical realms. This intersectionality offers a vibrant and potent platform for dialogue, reflection, and transformation in the ongoing quest for equity, justice, and self-determination.

Building on the insights of bell hooks (1992a), I formulate the struggles encountered by Afro-Cuban women as embodying a form of radical and oppositional consciousness. This perspective provides a framework that facilitates the strategic contestation, negotiation, and questioning of prevailing power dynamics. Delving into the nuanced activism of Black women and exploring their diverse modalities of resistance (May 2015) illuminate our understanding of the long-standing exclusion and marginalization of Black Latina women as creators of culture and art within the predominantly recognized art sphere. This conceptualization of Afro-Cuban women's struggles as exercises of radical and oppositional consciousness unfolds an intricate tapestry of resilience and defiance. It allows for a meticulous examination of how these women navigate, confront, and disrupt established power structures, employing tactical maneuvers to challenge the status quo. By doing so, they are actively redefining spaces and narratives, asserting their agency and autonomy in domains that have historically attempted to silence and invalidate them. Understanding the patterns and intricacies of Black women's activism sheds light on the systemic and pervasive dismissal of Black Latina women in their roles as cultural contributors and art producers. This insight opens up pathways to critically assess and address the entrenched biases and barriers that have perpetuated their erasure and underrepresentation within mainstream artistic circles. Such a perspective prompts reflective engagement with the histories and contexts that have shaped the experiences and responses of Afro-Cuban women, enabling a more nuanced and enriched comprehension of their journeys and aspirations.

Hegemonic discourses have always reduced Afro-descendant women to invisible beings and erased their contributions to history accounts. The obliteration of this specific part of history predominantly arises from the systematic execution of hegemonic epistemological initiatives. Within these frameworks, the elite are typically represented as the solitary proprietors of historical narratives, effectively rendering 'Others' unseen and unacknowledged within the annals of history (Scott 2012). This selective portrayal orchestrates a homogenized historical discourse, marginalizing diverse experiences and voices, particularly those that challenge or disrupt the established narratives dominated by elite perspectives. The pursuit of Decolonial AfroARTivism by Afro-Cuban women emerges as a transformative response to such historical erasures. It aligns with and contributes to "the demand to decolonize feminism" (Seppälä 12), addressing and countering the systemic invisibility imposed on marginalized communities within mainstream historical and feminist discourses. Afro-Cuban women's Decolonial AfroARTivism embodies a powerful amalgamation of art and activism, serving as a conduit for reconstructing and reclaiming erased histories and identities. By intertwining artistic expression with decolonial feminist perspectives, they create spaces for dialogue and reflection, challenging the prevailing exclusivity and bias inherent in historical and feminist discourses. Their endeavors contribute to the broader decolonial movement, fostering an environment where feminism is inclusive, diverse, and reflective of the myriad experiences and struggles of women from different backgrounds and communities. Decolonial AfroARTivism becomes an agent of change, not only demanding the decolonization of feminism but also actively participating in the reshaping of historical narratives. It disrupts the hegemonic epistemological projects that have long monopolized the portrayal of the past, offering alternative narratives that acknowledge and celebrate the existence, resilience, and contributions of those who have been rendered invisible in history. Through their artistic and activist practices, Afro-Cuban women are at the forefront of redefining and reconstructing a more equitable and inclusive understanding of history and feminism. Black feminism firmly posits that individual experiences are inherently political, stemming from the understanding that the bodies and day-to-day experiences of Black women are deeply entrenched in historical frameworks characterized by both marginalization, exclusion, and consequential resistance and struggle (Combahee River Collective, 2014). It underscores the interconnectedness of personal experiences with broader political and societal structures, highlighting the unique positioning of Black women at the intersections of multiple forms of oppression and struggle. Expanding on this, Black Decolonial feminism emerges as a transformative paradigm, offering innovative pathways for comprehending the lives of Afro-Cuban women based on their specific historical and geopolitical contexts. It acts as a revolutionary instrument for re-envisioning the world and contesting prevailing power dynamics, racism, patriarchy, sexism, violence, and classism. Beyond mere theoretical postulations, it embodies a profound political dedication and serves as a rebellious approach to generating knowledge, particularly through artistic mediums. The visual art created by Afro-Cuban women becomes a powerful mechanism for the cultivation of alternative liberatory practices and the development of feminist Afro-epistemologies. Their artistic expressions transcend aesthetic boundaries, serving as conduits for the propagation of liberation ideologies and the construction of knowledge frameworks rooted in African diaspora culture. These art forms are instrumental in fostering a sense of identity and belonging within Afro-Cuban communities, imbuing them with meaning and connection to the broader tapestry of the African diaspora. These artistic endeavors align with the principles of Black Decolonial feminism to challenge and reshape the existing narratives and structures of power, providing spaces for the articulation and manifestation of resistance, identity, and liberation. The integration of art and decolonial feminist perspectives opens dialogues and reflections, enabling the exploration and recognition of diverse epistemologies and experiences within the global African diaspora. In essence, the confluence of Black Decolonial feminism, articulated through the visual art of Afro-Cuban women, elucidates the intricate interplay of personal experiences, historical contexts, political commitments, and artistic expressions in the pursuit of liberation, knowledge production, and the dismantling of oppressive structures. It is a multidimensional approach that enriches our understanding of Afro-Cuban communities' contributions and their relentless pursuit of equality, justice, and self-determination within the encompassing sphere of Afro-diasporic epistemologies.

Mapping the Scholarly Terrain

The interplay between Afro-Latin American art and the experiences of Black women in Latin America and the Caribbean weaves a rich tapestry of historical narratives. Despite the wealth of insights it harbors, the scholarly exploration of this domain is still unfolding. The recent momentum in the literature around Afro-diasporic visual cultures is exemplified by works like Thompson (1981, 1983), Blier (1995), Lawal (2004), and Martínez-Ruiz

(2010, 2012, 2013). As societies evolve, art emerges as not just an expression, but a formidable medium of resistance against racial oppression. De la Fuente (2018) affirms this, suggesting that art has consistently been a lever for societal transformation, shaping discourses on racial justice. Echoing these sentiments, Movsky (2016) posits that visual culture, while being pivotal in constructing dominant narratives, can also be a potent realm for counternarratives and resistance. However, as de la Fuente (2018) points out, the field is nascent, with many areas remaining untapped. The experiences of Black women, especially, find limited representation in scholarly discourses. The uniqueness and often overlooked experiences of Afro-Cuban female artists are, therefore, crucial threads in this tapestry. The erasure of much of the art produced by Afro-descendants, particularly before the twentieth century, underscores the systemic sidelining of Latin America's Black history. Hence, contemporary Black female artists bear the onus not just of voicing current struggles but resurrecting a history often muted. De la Fuente (2018) further enriches this perspective, highlighting the intricate exchanges—not just between Africans and Europeans, but among Africans of diverse origins in colonial settings. Such insights pave the way for an engaged, critical, and informed approach to the multifaceted art forms discussed in subsequent chapters.

My exploration in this book intricately examines the lived experiences, cultural contexts, and personal narratives of Afro-Cuban women artists, many of whom have been overlooked in mainstream art discourse. By centering their voices and stories, this manuscript offers a lens that contrasts with generic art narratives, allowing readers to witness the richness and complexity of Afro-Cuban contributions. Instead of a mere appreciation of art techniques and aesthetics, readers are invited on a journey that interweaves history, identity, resistance, and empowerment. Through this perspective shift, the themes of the visual arts are no longer just about the finished piece but about the stories, the struggles, and the triumphs embedded within every brushstroke and artistic choice. This manuscript ventures beyond mere acknowledgment of Afro-Cuban women in visual arts, plunging deep into the nuances of their artistic expressions, an area that existing literature merely skims. The significance of addressing this "gap" extends beyond academic fulfillment; it challenges prevailing mainstream narratives, actively reshaping our understanding of Afro-Cuban art, its influences, and the broader impacts it holds on to cultural discourse. By delving into the works of overlooked artists like Harmonia Rosales and Susana Pilar, who have yet to grace the pages of academic publications, this book offers readers a fresh, enriched perspective. It paints a vivid picture of the unique blend of cultural, historical, and personal experiences that shape their artistry. By engaging with this text, readers won't just fill a knowledge void; they'll be equipped to appreciate the layers, textures, and depths of Afro-Cuban women's contributions to the visual arts world. Addressing the gap surrounding the visual arts of Afro-Cuban women is essential for several reasons. First, it rectifies a significant omission in our understanding of global art history. Second, by learning about their unique perspectives, we are granted a window into the intersecting challenges and triumphs of race, gender, and culture in Cuba, enriching our comprehension of sociocultural dynamics. By filling this gap, readers will not only gain knowledge about these artists and their works but will also develop a more holistic appreciation of the broader art landscape and the myriad forces that shape it.

In the context of the literature published on Black women in Cuba there is the collection of essays *Afrocubanas: History, Thought, and Cultural Practices* (2020), which stands as a pivotal contribution. Originally published in Spanish and curated by Cuban historian Daisy Rubiera Castillo and dramatist/theater critic Inés María Martiatu Terry, this groundbreaking anthology is a trailblazer in its field. Beyond being a mere compilation of narratives, the collection strategically places the experiences and stories of Black and mulatta women at the forefront of Cuban historical discourse. The contributors to *Afrocubanas* not only bring together but also critically examine the voices of Black Cuban women. They delve into the multifaceted contributions made by these women across political, cultural, social, and ideological realms throughout the nation's history. It's noteworthy that, following the 1991 dissolution of the Soviet Union, Cuba's principal trading partner, various organizations emerged to confront the racial inequality exacerbated by the nation's ensuing economic challenges. However, the Afrocubanas Project, established in the mid-2000s, distinctly confronts both racism and sexism. Its members, originating from diverse professional backgrounds, ages, and sexual orientations, unite under a shared ambition to contest detrimental stereotypes about Black women.

Afro-Cuban women's visual art is also analyzed in two of the eight chapters of my recently published book *The Afro-Descendant Woman in Latin American Diasporic Visual Art* (2024). The Black Latin American women featured in the various chapters, spanning multiple artistic mediums and originating from various Latin American and Caribbean nations, including Mexico, Colombia, the Dominican Republic, Puerto Rico,

Brazil, and Cuba, collectively pursue the central aim of foregrounding the Afro-descendant woman's experience. Simultaneously, they strive to enhance the visibility and acknowledgment of gendered Afro-diasporic culture within the Latin American context. Afro-Cuban women's cultural contribution is one of the themes analyzed in the book *Guarding Cultural Memory* (2006) by Flora González Mandri. In this work, the author delves into the vibrant and distinctively enlightening cultural expressions of Afro-Cuban women in the post-Revolutionary era, addressing the ways in which cultures of the African diaspora engage in practices of remembrance. The author unveils the multifaceted methods these women employ to re-create the clashes between tradition and modernity, providing a platform for reimagining and reformulating cultural narratives. González Mandri scrutinizes the contributions of poet and cultural analyst Nancy Morejón, poet Excilia Saldaña, filmmaker Gloria Rolando, and artists María Magdalena Campos-Pons and Belkis Ayón. Through their diverse representations, these women merge the artistic, historical, and personal realms to craft transformative depictions of Black women as architects of Cuban culture. When talking about highlighting the voices of Black Latina women, it is important to mention the book *Women Warriors of the Afro-Latina Diaspora* (2012), edited by Marta Moreno Vega, Marinieves Alba, and Yvette Modestin, a collection of eleven essays and four poems in which Latina women of African descent share their stories in the form of testimonios and address issues such as inequality, racism, and social justice in their respective countries. Some portions of the book *Black Social Movements in Latin America: From Monocultural Mestizaje to Multiculturalism* (2012), edited by Jean Muteba Rahier, also attest to Black Latina strength and leadership in the modern era.

The two most recent books published on the experience and cultural heritage of Black Latina women are the edited volumes *AfroLatinas and LatiNegras* (2022), edited by Rosita Scerbo and Concetta Bondi, and *Black Women in Latin America and the Caribbean* (2023), edited by Melanie A. Medeiros and Keisha-Khan Y. Perry. In *AfroLatinas and LatiNegras* the unwavering focus on Afro-Latinas' agency throughout every chapter is both empowering and meticulously cognizant of the challenges inherent in exercising such agency, as well as of the extensive array of forms this agency can assume. The authors advocate for the conceptual strength of intersectionality, considering the hegemonic influences on AfroLatinidad and the pivotal capabilities an intersectional perspective offers in circumventing, countering, and opposing power structures. The edited volume *Black*

Women in Latin America and the Caribbean utilizes an intersectional and interdisciplinary lens as well to explore the multifaceted experiences of Black cisgender women across the social, cultural, economic, and political landscapes of Latin America and the Caribbean.

While the contributions of Afro-descendant or Black women artists with identities rooted in Latin America are significant, they have remained conspicuously absent from much of academic scholarship. This oversight is more than a mere gap in the literature; it's a reflection of the broader erasure faced by these communities in national dialogues and historical narratives. Recognizing this lacuna, *Gendered Aesthetics of Blackness* endeavors to be more than just an acknowledgment; it's an analytical exploration into the depth of their impact. The undeniable influence of the African diaspora and its descendants on the cultures and modern nations of the Americas and the Caribbean challenges monolithic perspectives, introducing complex layers of identity, artistry, and history. Reintroducing these voices is not merely a matter of inclusion; it's a profound recalibration. By amplifying these voices, the goal is not only to restore justice to marginalized artists but to fundamentally transform and enrich our collective comprehension of the broader sociocultural dynamics at play. Specifically, this exploration aims to reshape our understanding of the history of art by challenging traditional narratives and expanding the scope of Latin American identity beyond conventional frameworks. It seeks to spotlight the nuanced contributions of Afro-descendant and Black women artists, providing a more comprehensive and accurate representation of the diverse voices shaping the cultural landscape of Latin America.

In recent years there has been a renewed interest in recovering and reclaiming the forgotten histories and voices of the Afro-Latin population, both historic and contemporary. As a result, a growing body of scholarship on the topic has expanded the scope of research and led to the development of a concentrated field of study. These works offer significant counternarratives that challenge stereotypes and destabilize dominant hegemonic narratives surrounding the African diaspora in the New World. Their subject matter ranges from the re-evaluation of historical documents including Royal Archives and colonial texts to the analysis of contemporary expressions of diasporic cultural production. Though early investigations focused on examples from specific national contexts, several contemporary studies take a more holistic approach that extends physical borders. In this new critical space, some distinct branches of study can be defined, including those with a historical focus, those focusing on the experience of

Blackness, and the celebration of the contributions of the African diaspora and their descendants. Here I provide a brief review of some fundamental contributions to the field that bring to light the lived experience of the African diaspora. This review of the existing literature does not intend to represent an exhaustive list, but rather a selective one outlining some pieces of work and concepts that inform my methodology. Echoing the diversity of the geographic region itself, the identities and experiences of Afro-Latin populations both past and present are difficult to synthesize without running the risk of overgeneralizing; Gwendolyn Midlo Hall has noted, "Nothing in the realm of slavery stood still. Patterns changed over time and place in both Africa and the Americas." In part, this diversity is rooted in the regional nature of the transatlantic slave trade and the vast ethnic and geographic origins of this population. Though early forced migrations initiated along the coast of West Africa, Congo, and Angola, as the trade system expanded, it expanded into parts of Central Africa. The arrival of millions of people to the New World with distinct linguistic, cultural, and ethnic backgrounds created new alliances and divisions among these groups. In colonial Spanish and Portuguese society, these distinctions were amplified within a complex hierarchical caste system that ensured European superiority and placed those of Indigenous and African descent at the bottom. As McKnight and Garfalo note, this caste system was not only race-based but also distinguished between generation and birthplace, as well as social status, religious affiliation, language, profession, cultural and social practices, and even marital status. Complex and porous, they go on to note that "race and ethnicity operated as social constructions rooted in a particular place at a particular historical moment." Among the most prominent works to trace the history of the Afro-Latinx population in the Americas and Caribbean from the early fifteenth century to the present is Leslie Rout Jr.'s *The African Experience in Spanish America: 1502 to the Present Day*. Originally published in 1976, it is considered one of the founding texts of African diaspora studies. The first general history on the people of African descent in the Spanish Americas, it examines the history of slavery in each country. Rout also interrogates perceptions of Spanish America as a "racial paradise" and the idea that "we have no discrimination in our country." Other influential texts on this topic include the ones by authors such as Klein and Vinson III (1986) or George Reid (1980, 1991, 2004, 2010, 2016).

Contemporary studies continue to expand the scope of Afro-Latin American studies, many examining how this population has helped shape the modern nations of the Americas and the Caribbean. Early research on the topic had focused to a great degree on its contribution to artistic and cultural production in music, dance, and theater. Since then, several authors have sought to address gaps in established anthologies by mapping out the work of Afro-Latin American culture producers from a wide range of mediums. For example, in the case of literary production, notable examples include Margaret Lindsay Morris's *The Afro-Latino Voice in World Literature*. Other notable contributions to this field include: *Daughters of the Diaspora: Afra-Hispanic Writers* (2003), *Literary Passion, Ideological Commitment: Toward a Legacy of Afro-Cuban and Afro-Brazilian Women Writers* (2008), *Voices Out of Africa in Twentieth Century Spanish Caribbean Literature* (2009), and *Writing the Afro-Hispanic: Essays on Africa and Africans in the Spanish Caribbean* (2012); the latter presents a collective view of Afro-Latinx literature that pays tribute to the significant contributions of Black female voices. Among them, Afro-Cuban poetry reciter and actress Eusebia Cosme (1911–1976)—the only Cuban woman to participate in the art of declamation, performing poetry on the topic of Black racialized identities internationally—along with Nancy Morejón (1944–) who wrote on the use of culture as commodity from an African-centered perspective. The recent period has seen the publication of new synthetic texts that bring innovative approaches to the study of contemporary Afro-Latin American cultural production; notable examples include López Oro's "Refashioning Afro-Latinidad: Garifuna New Yorkers in Diaspora" (2021) and *Being La Dominicana: Race and Identity in the Visual Culture of Santo Domingo* (2021), or Jerome Branche's edited collection, *Black Writing, Culture, and the State in Latin America* (2015) presents an important contribution to the field. The chapters examine poetry and narrative alongside film and popular theater and even a segment of rap and hip-hop. Often absent from history books, other recent publications have explored the untold histories of Afro-Latin American communities and their contributions to the intellectual, social, and political realms of Latin American society. Among the examples, *Afro-Descendants, Identity, and the Struggle for Development in the Americas* (2012) includes a discussion on activist organization and mobilization in the Afro-Colombian population in the quest for independence and equality. *The Afro-Latin Diaspora: Awakening Ancestral Memory, Avoiding Cultural Amnesia* also focuses on the contributions of Afro-descendants in political and cultural work. Taking a comparative approach, the study examines Afro-Latin communities in over twenty-two Latin American countries and the United States; its chapters highlight the stories of Afro-Latino leaders and freedom fighters, while dialoguing with issues of ethnic, cultural, and linguistic identity.

Another body of literature have chosen to shed light on these silenced voices and histories in specific cultural and national contexts—for example, *Finding Afro-Mexico: Race and Nation After the Revolution* (2020), *Colonial Blackness: A History of Afro-Mexico*, and *Afro-Mexico: Dancing Between Myth and Reality* (2009) explore both Afro-Mexican identity and influence. Others have instead opted to go beyond material borders and draw transnational connections; among the notable examples are *Afro-Latin@s in Movement: Critical Approaches to Blackness and Transnationalism in the Americas* (2016), *The Afro-Latin@ Experience in Contemporary American Literature and Culture: Engaging Blackness* (2016), *The Afro-Latin@ Reader: History and Culture in the United States* (2010), *Afro-Latinx Digital Connections*, and *Afro-Latinos in the U.S. Economy*, which explores the economic impact and status of the US Afro-Latinx population. Though this list of works is far from comprehensive, the above-mentioned studies provide valuable findings that have expanded the scope of Afro-Latin American research and have allowed us to rethink the ways in which the African diaspora and their descendants have helped shape contemporary cultures in the Americas.

Introducing the Artists and Exploring Key Analytical Themes

The dynamic and multifaceted cultural history of Cuba provides a distinctive framework for examining the visual expressions of Afro-Cuban women. At the core of this complex narrative lies the evolving identity of Black Cubans, a trajectory marked by episodes of systemic oppression interspersed with powerful moments of cultural resurgence. Embedded within this journey, Afro-Cuban feminism has played a critical role in addressing the unique challenges confronted by Black women, positioning itself as a pivotal force in their ongoing struggle for agency and representation. The inaugural chapter, titled "Tracing Black Identity and Afro-feminism in the Cuban Historical Context," delves into the historical backdrop of Cuba, illuminating the intricate dance between Black identity and Afro-feminism. As I traverse key events, figures, and societal shifts, the visual expression of Afro-Cuban women emerges as a poignant testimony to their resilience, creativity, and activism. Through this exploration, I aim to offer a richer understanding of how these visual expressions have not only been reflective of their identity and struggles but also instrumental in shaping the larger narrative of Afro-feminism in Cuba and its diaspora. This foundation sets the stage for the subsequent chapters, where I will examine the visual expressions of Afro-Cuban women and showcase their indomitable spirit and the artistry born from their experiences. In the subsequent four chapters of this book, I explore the artistry of Afro-Cuban women artists Harmonia Rosales, María Magdalena Campos-Pons, Susana Pilar, and Belkis Ayón. I aim to highlight how their works powerfully challenge and counter the long-standing stereotypes associated with Black femininity.[4] In chapter 2, "Black Femininity Reimagined: Bridging AfroARTivism and Black Decolonial Aesthetics in the Visionary Artistry of Harmonia Rosales," I examine the world of Harmonia Rosales, an artist who boldly reinterprets classical works of art, replacing traditionally white and male figures with Black women. This chapter examines how Rosales's paintings undermine conventional representations of Black women, transforming them from figures often sexualized and marginalized to embodiments of nobility, strength, and divinity. Through a detailed analysis of her works, I discover the innovative ways Rosales encourages audiences to reevaluate and dispel ingrained stereotypical imagery associated with Black femininity. In chapter 3, "Decolonizing Trans-Generational Memories of Slavery, Spirituality, and Exile: The Multicultural Artistic World of María Magdalena Campos-Pons," I turn my focus on María Magdalena Campos-Pons, a multidisciplinary artist who merges history, memory, and identity in her visual narratives. This chapter dissects Campos-Pons's intricate ability to narrate the expansive story of the Afro-Cuban diaspora using elements from her personal history, crafting a rich and layered portrayal of Black femininity that transcends restrictive stereotypes. Through her art, Campos-Pons facilitates a dialogue that reveres the depth, history, and complex identities of Black women, offering a counternarrative to the narrow portrayals that have historically dominated. In the chapter 4, "Susana Pilar's Self-Portrayal of Black Womanhood: A Visual Chronicle of Diasporic Femininity, the Trauma of Separation, and the Legacy of Enslavement," I explore the provocative world of Susana Pilar, whose art stands as an evocative critique of history and its lingering, oppressive impacts. This chapter reveals Pilar's courageous confrontation with history, where she uses her own body as a platform to question and challenge stereotypes associated with Black femininity. Her powerful installations and performances act as a form of protest, reclaiming the narrative and promoting a discourse that seeks to dismantle deep-seated prejudices. In chapter 5, the last analytical chapter, "Unveiling Symbolic Silence: Cultural Syncretism and Archetypal Allegory in Belkis Ayón's Visual Expression," I examine the remarkable work of Belkis Ayón. Ayón's distinctive monochromatic prints delve deep into Afro-Cuban mythology,[5] presenting complex narratives that rise above simplistic and derogatory representations. This chapter elucidates Ayón's meticulous craftsmanship, where she elevates Black women to powerful figures in religious mythology, thereby fostering a narrative that respects the multifaceted experiences of Black women and rejects limiting representations. In the two concluding chapters of the book, I bring forth the personal journeys and philosophical insights of Afro-Cuban women artists Harmonia Rosales and Diarenis Calderón Tartabull, as narrated by them in two separate interviews. These intimate interviews offer a glimpse into the minds of artists at the forefront of challenging and reshaping the representation of Black femininity in contemporary art. Their voices echo the transformative power of art as a tool for fostering inclusivity and respect in the discourse surrounding Black women's representation. Chapter 6, "Empowering Through Art, Shaping Cultural Narratives, and Celebrating Afro-Cuban Heritage: An Interview with Harmonia Rosales," explores Rosales's creative process, the cultural influences that shape her art, and her dedication to centering Afro-Cuban heritage in her work. Her reflections highlight the role of art in reclaiming narratives and fostering a deeper appreciation for Black femininity and cultural identity. Chapter 7, "Transcending Boundaries: Art, Activism, and Afro-Cuban Identity: An Interview with Diarenis Calderón Tartabull" delves into Calderón Tartabull's intersection of artistic expression and activism. Her narrative provides insights into the challenges and triumphs of addressing systemic inequalities through art, as well as her vision for transcending cultural and social boundaries to amplify Afro-Cuban identity. The book concludes with "Resonating Echoes: Toward a Liberated Aesthetic Future," in which I reflect on the transformative power of these artists' works and their potential to inspire a more inclusive and liberated future in the discourse surrounding Black women's representation in art.

Through the perspectives offered by these artists, this book aspires to initiate a transformative shift, envisioning a future where the portrayal of Black Cuban women is not only enriched and nuanced but authentically mirrors the multifaceted range of their experiences and resilient spirit. In my manuscript, I extend beyond the traditional boundaries of Cuban

Studies, Caribbean, and Latin American Studies, making a significant contribution to these fields while introducing new layers from an international, global, transnational, and diasporic perspective—a departure not commonly found in academic literature on Cuba. The interview with Rosales complements the chapter dedicated to her artistry by engaging in a dialogue with her subject of study, a rarity in academic texts that enhances its scholarly value. The inclusion of the interview with Diarenis Calderón Tartabull is crucial due to her contemporary perspective as a Black queer woman in her forties, born, raised, and still residing in Havana's marginalized neighborhood of San Miguel del Padrón. Calderón Tartabull's influential work in arts and culture, particularly within the Black and LGBTQ+ communities, sheds light on the current challenges faced in Cuba—such as frequent power outages and inadequate access to basic necessities—experienced predominantly by Black Cubans in poorer areas. Providing a platform for Calderón Tartabull enriches my project with contemporary insights into the realities of living and creating in Cuba today. This endeavor not only aligns with my decolonial approach on a theoretical level but also underscores my commitment to integrating decolonial methodologies into my writing and research practices. In organizing the volume, the arrangement of the chapters is not based on a chronological order of the artists' lives or careers, but rather on the thematic depth and evolution of the discourse surrounding Black femininity as interpreted by each artist. The intention behind this narrative journey is to guide the reader from the transformative reimagining of classical art in Harmonia Rosales's work to the multidisciplinary approaches of María Magdalena Campos-Pons, where history, memory, and identity seamlessly meld. This deliberate progression enables me to examine how Afro-Cuban women artists have actively revisited and reclaimed historical narratives. Susana Pilar's chapter then introduces a more introspective exploration of Black womanhood, using the artist's own body as a platform, before delving into the rich symbolic world of Belkis Ayón, rooted in Afro-Cuban mythology. By organizing the chapters thematically, the book seeks to underscore the myriad ways in which these artists have confronted, deconstructed, and ultimately transcended the entrenched stereotypes associated with Black femininity. Each chapter, in its unique focus, builds on the previous one, adding layers of complexity to our understanding of Black Cuban women's representation in art. The concluding interviews with Harmonia Rosales and Diarenis Calderón Tartabull then serve to provide a personal touch, grounding the analytical in the lived experiences of these artists, thereby offering a holistic view of the artistic and personal journeys of these trailblazing Afro-Cuban women.

In *Gendered Aesthetics of Blackness*, the study of Afro-Cuban women artists extends across a wide range of temporal and spatial contexts, encompassing those who reside in Cuba, the diaspora, Black Cuban women in exile, second-generation immigrants in the United States, and both modern and contemporary periods. This deliberate choice allows for a multifaceted analysis that enriches the primary argument by presenting it through various lenses. The study includes Afro-Cuban American artists such as Harmonia Rosales, who navigate the complexities of identity and cultural heritage in the United States. The experiences of these artists are markedly different from those of their counterparts in Cuba, as they negotiate their Afro-Cuban identity within the broader context of American racial dynamics. The inclusion of diaspora artists like María Magdalena Campos-Pons further broadens this perspective, showcasing how migration and transnational experiences shape artistic expressions. Conversely, the works of Afro-Cuban artists still residing in Cuba, such as Susana Pilar and Diarenis Calderón, offer a direct insight into the contemporary cultural and political landscape of the island. These artists provide a lens through which to view the unique challenges and influences that arise from creating within the Cuban sociopolitical environment. The inclusion of Belkis Ayón, who tragically committed suicide in the 1990s, a historically significant decade for Cuba, adds a crucial historical dimension to this study. Ayón's work, produced during a time of immense socioeconomic upheaval, reflects the intense pressures and profound cultural shifts occurring within the island during the Special Period. The diversity of these artists' backgrounds is not incidental but foundational to the project's analytical depth. By juxtaposing the experiences of Afro-Cuban women in Cuba with those in the diaspora, and by comparing contemporary artists with those from pivotal historical moments, the study underscores the heterogeneity within the Afro-Cuban female artistic community. This approach allows for a comprehensive understanding of how different environments and temporal contexts influence artistic production and thematic focus. Afro-Cuban women artists in Cuba face distinct challenges compared to those in the diaspora. In Cuba, their work is shaped by the island's unique cultural, economic, and political conditions, which include state support for the arts juxtaposed with limited access to international markets and materials. In contrast, diaspora artists often grapple with issues of cultural identity, assimilation, and racial dynamics in their host countries. These artists are influenced by both their Cuban heritage and their experiences within the broader Afro-diasporic context, which can lead to a richer, more hybrid-ized form of artistic expression. The historical context is also crucial. The 1990s, a decade marked by economic crisis and significant cultural shifts in Cuba, produced a distinct artistic response characterized by themes of struggle, identity, and survival. Contemporary artists, working in a post–Special Period Cuba, address a different set of realities, including globalization, technological advancements, and evolving social norms. By explicitly voicing the differences among Afro-Cuban women artists in Cuba and the diaspora, and by contextualizing their varied temporal and spatial realities, this study aims to avoid a superficial and generic analysis. Instead, it seeks to provide a nuanced understanding of how these artists' unique circumstances influence their visual productions. This approach not only enhances the project's analytical depth but also highlights the diverse ways in which Afro-Cuban women navigate and articulate their identities through art.

While each Afro-Cuban woman artist brings her unique style and perspective, they all share several common elements in their artistic endeav-ors. One of the most poignant of the elements shared by the artists studied is their unified front in challenging the deeply entrenched stereotypes and misrepresentations surrounding Black femininity. Through their potent artworks, they vehemently counter the historically distorted narratives that have persistently cast Black women in a narrow, lascivious light, epitomized by derogatory labels such as "Jezebel." These artists confront and dismantle the age-old depictions that have unjustly characterized Black women as seductive, alluring, or lewd, stereotypes that are rooted deeply in history, juxtaposing white women as models of modesty and purity. Through their creative prowess, they reclaim the narrative, presenting Black women as embodiments of dignity, strength, and complexity, far removed from the simplistic, offensive categorizations of the past. In 1993, sociologist K. Sue Jewell outlined her perception of the Jezebel stereotype, describing it as a "tragic mulatto" characterized by "thin lips, long straight hair, slender nose, thin figure and fair complexion" (46). However, this delineation is markedly limited. While it is acknowledged that the narratives of the "tragic mulatto" and "Jezebel" converge in depicting sexual seductiveness, contrasting sharply with the desexualized portrayal seen in the Mammy caricature, it erroneously narrows its scope to primarily fair-skinned black women, overlooking the broader spectrum of objectification experienced by Black women in society. Indeed, since the early 1630s up until now, Black women across a diverse range of complexions have been subjected to the reductive and demeaning hypersexual "bad-black-girls" stereotype. During the period of slavery, many Black individuals who were sold into prostitution were indeed mulattoes. Moreover, it was not uncommon for freeborn light-skinned Black women to become consensual companions to affluent white men in the south.

This practice, known as placage, required the white patron to provide financial assistance to the Black woman and her offspring in return for sustained sexual relations. These encounters often commenced at "Quadroon Balls," a form of genteel sexual commerce. The inception of the Jezebel stereotype has its roots deep in history, predating even the establishment of slavery. When European explorers arrived in Africa, they encountered locals who wore minimal clothing, which was misconstrued as an indication of promiscuity. Trapped in the seventeenth-century mindset characterized by racial ethnocentrism, white Europeans interpreted African polygamous practices and tribal dances as demonstrations of unrestrained sexual desire. This fascination with African sexuality was well documented by Europeans of the time. William Bosman characterized the women of the Guinea coast as being "fiery" and "warm," displaying a passion that surpassed that of the men. Similarly, William Smith depicted African women as ardently pursuing love interests, continually devising plans "to gain a lover" (White, 29). This period saw the birth of harmful sexual stereotypes about Black individuals, painting Black men as potential brutes and rapists, and Black women as Jezebel-like figures. In the harrowing era of slavery, the Jezebel stereotype was systematically employed as a cunning pretext to validate the sexual exploitation that occurred between white men and Black women, with particular emphasis on the coerced unions where enslavers took advantage of those they enslaved. This stereotype, deeply entrenched in the sociocultural narrative of the time, caricatured Black women as inherently sexually voracious, a depiction that was wielded as a form of "justification" for the heinous acts of sexual violence perpetrated by white men. By fabricating a scenario where Black women were perceived as willing, even eager, participants in these unions, the true nature of the abuse and exploitation was obscured, allowing white men to evade responsibility for their actions. Moreover, the widespread dissemination and acceptance of this stereotype fortified the existing racial and gender inequalities, giving white men perceived dominion over the bodies of Black women, and thereby facilitating a pervasive culture of sexual coercion and abuse. The Jezebel stereotype acted as a malignant force that stripped Black women of their dignity and agency, relegating them to mere objects for sexual gratification, rather than acknowledging them as human beings with rights and autonomy. The literature on race, slavery, and discrimination in Latin America and the Caribbean provides a rich and complex understanding of the historical and contemporary dynamics of racial ideologies and their impact on social structures. Blackburn's work *The Making of New World Slavery: From the Baroque to the Modern 1492–1800* (1999) offers a comprehensive analysis of the historical evolution of slavery in the New World, shedding light on the complex interplay of race, colonialism, and labor. The book provides critical insights into the ways in which people thought about race and slavery during this transformative period, emphasizing the enduring impact of slavery on the social and economic fabric of Latin America and the Caribbean. Telles's article "Who Is Black, White, or Mixed Race? How Skin Color, Status, and Nation Shape Racial Classification in Latin America" (2014) delves into the complexities of racial classification and identity in Latin America, offering valuable insights into the fluidity and nuances of racial categories. The work examines the intersection of skin color, social status, and national context in shaping racial classification, highlighting the evolving ways in which people have thought about race in the region. Wade's book *Race and Ethnicity in Latin America* (2010) provides a critical analysis of the historical and contemporary discourses on race and ethnicity in Latin America, challenging essentialist notions and emphasizing the diverse and dynamic nature of racial identities in the region. The book underscores the need to contextualize the historical legacies of slavery and discrimination within the complexities of Latin American and Caribbean societies.

Enslaved Black women were habitually found to be pregnant, a bleak testament to the oppressive demands placed on them during the era of slavery. The perpetuation of this institution significantly relied on the forced fertility of Black women to produce successive generations of individuals destined for a life of servitude and exploitation. This persistent cycle of enforced pregnancies served as a critical pillar in sustaining the vile structure of slavery, demonstrating the ruthless extent to which these women were manipulated and abused. Slaveholders, eager to expand their labor force, resorted to all conceivable measures to pressure these women into continual reproduction. In an explicit display of their dehumanizing and commodifying perception of enslaved people, they formulated a series of depraved incentives aimed at stimulating higher birth rates within the enslaved community. For instance, the birth of a new child in a slave family was sometimes "rewarded" with a new pig, a shocking and clear representation of the way the slaveholders equated human lives to mere property or livestock. Further, to coax more births, slaveholders would promise a new piece of clothing to the mother for every infant that managed to survive the harsh conditions of infancy, a grim and exploitative tactic that leveraged the dire circumstances these women were enmeshed in to spur further reproduction. Additionally, the prospect of brief respites from the relentless labor was dangled as an incentive, offering a day off work on Saturdays to those who could bear as many as six children, an appalling exploitation of the natural maternal instinct to create a perverse motivation to meet the oppressive demands set by the slaveholders (Rawick 1972, 228; Gutman 1976, 77). This relentless and brutal focus on reproduction not only underscores the depth of cruelty and dehumanization that defined the institution of slavery but also highlights the instrumental role that the forced fertility of Black women played in the expansion and maintenance of this vicious system. Their bodies, seen as mere vessels for the creation of more slaves, were exploited without remorse, illustrating a dark period in history where human dignity and individual rights were blatantly disregarded in favor of sustaining a morally reprehensible economy. These deeply entrenched stereotypes, rooted in slavery and cultivated over centuries, have pervasively permeated various avenues of popular culture, including movies, photography, literature, and more. The media, both past and present, often play a significant role in perpetuating these derogatory images, thus fostering a continuous cycle of prejudice and discrimination. In the world of cinematography, these stereotypes have been historically depicted through characters that emphasize hypersexualization and objectification, especially of Black women. Throughout the decades, numerous films have showcased Black women in roles that strictly adhere to the Jezebel stereotype, a woman with an unquenchable sexual appetite, thereby reinforcing the wrongful association of Black femininity with promiscuity and moral laxity. Some specific films have been criticized for perpetuating the Jezebel stereotype. *Birth of a Nation* (1915), for instance, depicted Black women as sexually aggressive and promiscuous. *Gone with the Wind* (1939), based on Margaret Mitchell's 1936 novel, while a classic film, it has faced criticism for its portrayal of Mammy, a character seen by some as conforming to the Jezebel stereotype. *Monster's Ball* (2001), though praised for Halle Berry's performance, has been criticized for reinforcing certain stereotypes about Black women's sexuality. Another example is *Precious* (2009), which while addressing important social issues, has faced criticism for its portrayal of the protagonist, Precious, and the depiction of her relationships. This misrepresentation not only misshapes the perception of Black women but also detracts from the rich tapestry of stories that encompass the real experiences of Black women throughout history. Photography, too, has been a medium through which these stereotypes have been relentlessly echoed. Historically, photographs have often featured Black women in derogatory and submissive poses, sometimes scantily clad to emphasize the false narrative of their supposed inherent lascivious nature. Such imagery serves to cement the distorted view of Black femininity, reducing these women to mere objects of desire, devoid of depth, complexity, or individuality.

These stereotypes have also seeped into literature, where the depiction of Black women often oscillates between the hypersexualized Jezebel or the desexualized Mammy caricature, both of which serve to dehumanize and objectify Black women. This binary representation restricts the portrayal of Black women to these limited and disparaging narratives, overshadowing the diverse, nuanced, and rich experiences of them in reality. Moreover, in various forms of art and advertisements, these stereotypes have been visually represented, further entrenching the harmful ideologies surrounding Black femininity. Often, the artistic representations have been exploited to emphasize exaggerated physical features, thus reinforcing the fetishization and objectification of black women. In addressing these issues, it's pivotal to foster a culture that challenges and critiques these damaging representations, encouraging a shift toward more accurate, respectful, and multidimensional portrayals of Black women in popular culture. This would not only help in dismantling the long-standing stereotypes but also promote a more inclusive and empathetic understanding of the diverse narratives that define Black womanhood. When talking about stereotypes is also useful to refer to the theoretical categories proposed by Stuart Hall in his essay "The Spectacle of the 'Other.'" Stuart Hall defines stereotyping as a significant practice that reduce people "to a few, simple, essential characteristics, which are represented as fixed by Nature" (257). Moreover, he explains that stereotypes act "a splitting strategy," that is, they divide what is "normal" and acceptable from what is "abnormal" and unacceptable. In other words, "stereotyping . . . symbolically sets boundaries and excludes everything that does not belong." Furthermore, stereotypes are often used when there are big power inequalities (258). Stuart Hall's insights have shed on the process and implications of stereotyping. Stereotyping, according to him, is not just a simplification of characteristics but a form of societal othering, wherein specific groups are marginalized by categorizing them as "abnormal" or "unacceptable," thereby fostering inequality and discrimination. In the context of the stereotypes associated with Black women, this theoretical framework can be extensively applied. Historically, Black women have been subject to numerous stereotypes, a process deeply rooted in colonial histories and perpetuated by existing sociopolitical structures. They have often been portrayed through a limited and harmful lens, ascribing them characteristics that are generalized, derogatory, and deeply entrenched in racist and sexist narratives. These stereotypes range from depicting them as overly aggressive, hypersexualized, to nurturing matriarchs, each essentially serving to undermine their complex individualities and reduce them to mere caricatures. Applying Hall's theory to this context, we find that these stereotypes, as a form of "splitting strategy," function to maintain power imbalances. By marking Black women as "other," it alienates them, essentially delegitimizing their experiences and excluding them from narratives of normalcy and acceptability. This not only restricts them in sociocultural spheres but also has real and tangible effects on their economic opportunities, healthcare access, and overall societal treatment.

Furthermore, the stereotypes surrounding Black women are perpetuated and magnified by media representations, which have a significant role in shaping public perception. They are often portrayed through a narrow lens, reinforcing existing stereotypes and fostering new ones. This amplifies the exclusionary tactics, as mentioned by Hall, setting boundaries that are difficult to dismantle, thereby cementing their position in a cycle of marginalization and discrimination. To challenge and reframe these existing narratives, it is imperative to foster dialogue and education, which emphasize the diversity and richness of Black women's experiences, and this is exactly what the Afro-Cuban artists analyzed in this book are doing. It is through dismantling these stereotypes, as Hall suggests, that we can begin to break down the divisive barriers and foster a society that embraces diversity and inclusivity. Promoting representations that are varied and authentic can serve as a counternarrative to the existing stereotypes, paving the way for a more equitable society.

Another common thread found among the Afro-Cuban women artists analyzed in *Gendered Aesthetics of Blackness* is the employment of visual storytelling[6] as intersectional feminist practice. Visual storytelling refers to the practice of conveying narratives, ideas, and experiences through visual mediums such as photography, film, painting, illustration, or any other visual art form. It involves using images, symbols, colors, and composition to communicate messages, evoke emotions, and engage the viewer in a narrative or concept. Visual storytelling holds significant importance in feminist indigenous and Afro-descendant communities for several reasons, such as amplifying marginalized voices. This means that visual storytelling provides a platform for individuals from these communities to share their unique perspectives, challenges, and aspirations. It allows them to reclaim their narratives and challenge dominant representations that have historically silenced or misrepresented their experiences. It can also be applied as a practice for cultural preservation and revitalization. Visual storytelling enables Indigenous and Afro-descendant communities to document and preserve their cultural practices, traditions, and knowledge. It becomes a tool for intergenerational transmission of cultural heritage, revitalization of ancestral wisdom, and celebration of cultural diversity. It can also be seen as a form of resistance and empowerment. Through visual storytelling, feminist indigenous and Afro-descendant communities can challenge oppressive structures, stereotypes, and narratives. It becomes a means of reclaiming agency, resisting colonial legacies, and asserting their identities on their own terms. Moreover, it is undoubtedly, an intersectional feminist method as visual storytelling allows for the exploration and representation of intersectional experiences of gender, race, culture, and other aspects of identity. It facilitates the understanding and highlighting of the unique challenges and strengths faced by women within these communities, creating space for discussions on gender equality and social justice. Healing and empathy are other keys components of this medium of storytelling that can serve as a powerful tool for healing and building empathy. It creates spaces for individuals to share their personal stories, trauma, resilience, and hopes. By engaging with these visual narratives, viewers from diverse backgrounds can develop a deeper understanding, empathy, and solidarity with feminist Afro-descendant communities.

Another common aspect evident among the artists and that it will accompany each chapter, is the legacy of African religions in the visual art of Afro-Cuban women. The rich and vibrant cultural heritage of Afro-Cuban women encompasses a complex tapestry of traditions, beliefs, and artistic expressions. At the heart of this heritage lies the profound legacy of African religion, which has played a pivotal role in shaping the visual art created by Afro-descendant women. Rooted in ancestral wisdom and spiritual practices, this art form serves as a testament to the enduring influence and resilience of African religious traditions in Cuban society. It is fundamental to explore the legacy of African religion in Afro-Cuban women's visual art, shedding light on the profound connections between spirituality, cultural identity, and artistic expression. By delving into the works of prominent Afro-Cuban women artists and examining the themes, symbolism, and artistic techniques employed, we can gain a deeper understanding of the ways in which African religious practices continue to shape and inspire their art. African religion, brought to Cuba through the transatlantic slave trade, forms the foundation of the religious syncretism[7] that characterizes the island's cultural landscape. By examining the themes of spirituality, cultural memory, identity, and resistance, I aim to unravel the intricate layers of meaning embedded in these artistic creations. Drawing from diverse African traditions such as Yoruba, Congo, and Arara, Afro-Cuban women artists infuse their works with elements of myth, spirituality, and ancestral knowledge. These artistic expressions serve as visual narratives, encapsulating stories of resistance, survival, and resilience in the face of adversity. It is also helpful to turn to the theoretical work of bell hooks (1992a), who delved into the construction of agency and subjectivity within the realm of visual culture. She conceptualized the act of gazing as a practice that is influenced by racial dynamics, characterized by systems of domination and fear. The visual art created by Afro-Cuban women reflects their deep connection to the spiritual realm and the intricate rituals and ceremonies that are central to African religious practices. We will see how by vibrant colors, intricate patterns, and powerful symbolism, artists pay homage to deities, spirits, and ancestors, evoking a sense of reverence and spiritual connection. This art serves as a medium through which Afro-Cuban women reclaim and celebrate their cultural heritage, asserting their presence and agency within a society that has often marginalized their contributions. Furthermore, African religious influences in Afro-Cuban women's visual art extend beyond individual artistic expression. They form an integral part of collective memory and cultural identity, fostering a sense of belonging and community among Afro-Cuban women. By engaging with ancestral traditions, artists create spaces for cultural preservation, resistance, and cultural continuity. Their art becomes a vehicle for storytelling, communication, and empowerment, allowing the narratives of African religion to transcend time and permeate contemporary society. Throughout this book, I will explore specific examples of Afro-Cuban women's visual art and analyze the ways in which African religious traditions manifest in their work.

From an historical standpoint, despite the implementation of various redistributive social policies during the Cuban Revolution, the Special Period crisis had profound effects on Afro-Cubans, who are disproportionately represented in the lower socioeconomic sectors of Cuban society. Simultaneously, the emergence of increased social competition and social benefits has exacerbated existing racial prejudices. Notably, Cuban visual arts, among other cultural expressions, have initiated a public dialogue surrounding the escalating social divisions caused by the collapse of the Soviet Union and the subsequent rise of racial inequalities. Moreover, the loss of social benefits and heightened social competition exacerbated latent racial prejudices. By the mid-1990s, it became evident that Afro-Cubans encountered numerous barriers beyond the perceived glass ceiling that hindered their access to high-status positions. Historically, Cuban visual artists like Belkis Ayón, Alexis Esquivel, Juan Roberto Diago, and René Peña have not only been adamant in their denunciations of racism, but they also carefully examined the intricacies of what it means to be of African descent in contemporary Cuba (West-Durán, 207).

Art exhibits like Queloides have showcased the works of several artists who are currently focusing their artistic endeavors on issues of race and racism. By incorporating elements from Afro-Cuban religious practices, which were previously marginalized or diminished, these women artists utilize the Afro-Cuban legacy to challenge processes of racialization in society. Their artwork aims to contest and redefine the significance of identity markers such as race, gender, and ethnicity. Within this context, the artwork becomes a platform for reinvention, where identity markers are restructured and redefined, and subjectivity plays a pivotal role in informing the artistic process (Martín Sevillano 2011, 136). In the spring of 2010, the Wifredo Lam Centre for Contemporary Art in Havana showcased the exhibition titled *Queloides: Raza y racismo en el arte cubano contemporáneo (Keloids: Race and Racism in Contemporary Cuban Art)*. This exhibition's title was not unexpected for those familiar with the Cuban art scene, as it established a connection to previous exhibits with the same title held in 1997 (curated by Alexis Esquivel and Omar Pascual Castillo) and 1999 (curated by Ariel Ribeaux). The 1997 *Queloides* exhibition marked a significant moment in Cuba, being the first art exhibition specifically aimed at addressing the issue of racial discrimination on the island (137). Moreover, the 2010 exhibition featured the artworks of three female artists who had not previously participated in the earlier shows: Belkis Ayön, María Magdalena Campos-Pons, and Maria Pérez Bravo. These three artists bring a compelling perspective to the discourse surrounding race and gender. Similar to the other artists in the *Queloides* series, Ayön, Campos-Pons, and Pérez Bravo belong to the generation born immediately after the revolution and were raised within its political, cultural, and social framework. They received their education within Cuba's reformed educational system, which emphasized strong secondary and postsecondary levels of education, including renowned institutions like the Escuela Vocacional (138). The 2010 Queloides exhibition, curated by renowned racial studies scholar Alejandro de la Fuente[8] and artist Elio Rodriguez, represented a significant advancement compared to its previous iterations. The exhibition extended its reach beyond Havana, traveling to the Mattress Factory Museum in Pittsburgh, Pennsylvania, and the eighth-floor gallery in New York in 2011. Despite months of negotiations and preparations by the curators, a surprising turn of events unfolded when de la Fuente discovered he was not welcomed at the Havana opening and later learned of his official ban from the island. While the Cuban government has acknowledged the persistence of racial inequality since 1985, alternative discourses and critical perspectives, including de la Fuente's, have been met with official unease (137). Martín Sevillano accurately points out how "the use of the Afro-Cuban legacy enables women artists to reflect on the consistency of identity markers such as race, gender, and ethnicity" (138). The critic also finds communality in their artwork, stating that: "A main trait of their artwork is the presentation of a specific Afro-Cuban aesthetic, which they achieve through the depiction of ritual elements and symbolic objects from the syncretic cults, through references to their mythology and cosmology, and through the inclusion of actual references to the African visual and material culture" (139). The above statement highlights a significant characteristic of the artwork created by Belkis Ayön, María Magdalena Campos-Pons, and Maria Pérez Bravo, which is the embodiment of a distinct Afro-Cuban aesthetic. This aesthetic is achieved through various artistic techniques employed by the artists, including the portrayal of ritual elements and symbolic objects from syncretic cults, references to Afro-Cuban mythology and cosmology, and the incorporation of visual and material references to African culture. One key aspect of their artwork is the depiction of ritual elements and symbolic objects from syncretic cults. The references to Afro-Cuban mythology and cosmology further enrich the artists' work. Additionally, the inclusion of actual references to African visual and material culture strengthens the Afro-Cuban aesthetic in their artwork. By incorporating elements such as traditional clothing, patterns, or objects with cultural significance, the artists establish a visual connection to the African roots that underpin Afro-Cuban culture. This inclusion serves as a powerful reminder of the enduring legacy of African traditions and their impact on contemporary Afro-Cuban identity. Through their art, Afro-Cuban women not only celebrate and preserve Afro-Cuban cultural heritage but also challenge prevailing narratives and stereotypes. Their use of the Afro-Cuban aesthetic disrupts dominant discourses that have historically marginalized Afro-Cuban voices and experiences. It serves as a means of asserting agency, reclaiming identity, and fostering a sense of pride and belonging among Black Cuban communities.

Chapter 1

Tracing Black Identity and Afro-feminism in the Cuban Historical Context

Approximately 130 million Afro-descendants reside in Latin America, significantly contributing to its cultural and historical landscape (Telles 2014). Countries like Brazil, Cuba, the Dominican Republic, and Colombia are home to the majority of this Afro-descendant population (Gonzalez-Barrera & Gustavo Lopez 2016). Even in the United States, the Afro-Latinx community is not a recent addition. Their history intertwines with the colonial era (McKnight & Garofalo 2009). Yet, Román and Flores (2010) depict Afro-Latinos in the US as a dynamic but often overlooked group. Their identity frequently gets conflated with African Americans (Busey & Cruz 2015); a phenomenon Hernández attributes to the unfamiliarity of Latinos with Blackness (2003, 153). Indeed, in both the US, Latin America, and the Caribbean, Afro-descendants experience marginalization. The darker skin tone leads to their sidelining in Latin America, while in the US, it's often their racial identity that pushes them to the fringes (Bucholz 2005). This peripheral status impacts their socioeconomic and political well-being. As highlighted by Gonzalez-Barrera and Gustavo Lopez (2016), Afro-Latinos in the US often have lower educational attainment, reflected in the fewer numbers who pursue college education, and typically earn lesser income. The marginalization of Afro-descendants in both the US and Latin America is not merely a product of contemporary biases but has deep historical roots that continue to shape their experiences today.

In Latin America, the legacy of colonialism and the transatlantic slave trade has left indelible marks on societal structures and cultural attitudes. Despite the significant contributions of Afro-descendants to the culture, politics, and economics of many Latin American nations, they remain underrepresented in positions of power and influence. Discriminatory practices, often rooted in colonial-era caste systems, persist, relegating many Afro-Latinos to lower socioeconomic statuses. An overview of the experiences of Afro-Latinos across the Americas is essential to contextualize the specific experiences of Afro-Cuban women artists. This broader perspective is necessary to understand the pervasive and systemic nature of racial and socioeconomic discrimination that Afro-descendants face throughout the region. By situating Afro-Cuban women within this larger framework, we can better appreciate the unique cultural and historical dynamics that shape their artistic expressions. In a following section, a closer understanding of race in Cuba will be explored, providing a crucial context for examining the works and experiences of the Afro-Cuban women artists under study. Afro-descendant's cultural contributions in music, dance, cuisine, and other areas often face appropriation without due credit, further erasing their prominence in the region's heritage. In the US, the experiences of Afro-Latinos intersect with both anti-Black racism and xenophobic sentiments. The long history of racial segregation, discriminatory policies, and institutional racism toward African Americans extends, in many ways, to Afro-Latinos. Moreover, as part of the Latinx community, they also grapple with issues related to immigration, language barriers, and stereotypes related to Latin American identities. These combined biases lead to a unique form of marginalization for Afro-Latinos in the US. Gonzalez-Barrera and Gustavo Lopez's (2016) findings underscore the material consequences of this marginalization. Reduced access to quality education, limited job opportunities, and systemic discrimination contribute to the economic disparities faced by Afro-Latinos. Furthermore, this socioeconomic marginalization often translates to political disenfranchisement, with Afro-Latinos having less representation and voice in policy making and governance.

The label "Afro-Latino" has been the subject of significant discussions about its definition and who falls under this categorization. Being Afro-Latino isn't solely about having a darker skin tone relative to other Latinx individuals; it's more about an individual's choice in connecting with their ancestral roots (Román & Flores 2010). Hordge-Freeman and Veras (2020) define Afro-Latinos as "individuals with discernible or self-recognized African ancestry who link their lineage to Spanish- or Portuguese-speaking Latin America" (146). Freire et al. (2018, 56) note that in Latin America, there are 138 million people who recognize themselves as Afro-descendants. Meanwhile, a 2016 Pew Research report indicates that 25 percent of Latinx in the US identify as Afro-Latinos (Pew Research Center 2016). While the term *Afro-descendant* has gained some recognition, it has not been universally accepted in either Latin America or the US. Its association with historical prejudices and discrimination hinders its complete acceptance. A 2019 Pew study found that Latinx individuals with darker skin tones were more prone to experiencing racism and prejudice than their lighter-skinned counterparts (Gonzalez-Barrera 2019). In many Latin American nations, categorizing people based on skin shade is more prevalent than categorizing them based on the descriptor "Afro-descendants." Common terms used in these regions include *morenos*, *negros*, *pardo*, *preto*, *creole*, and *zambo*, to name a few. In Brazil, Telles (2017) notes three primary racial categorizations for Afro-descendants: those used in census data (like *preto*, *indigena*), those in everyday language (such as *moreno*), and those championed by Black activist groups pushing for equality (like the embrace of the term *negro*). Afro-descendants are a diverse group, and the terms used to describe them vary significantly across Latin American and Caribbean nations. For example, in countries like Nicaragua, Honduras, and Belize, they are known as the Garifunas. These people trace their lineage to escaped enslaved individuals from St. Vincent who mingled with the Amerindian population in the Caribbean. In contrast, Brazil has the Cafuzos, while in Haiti, they are called Marabou, and in the Andes and Central America, they are known as the Zambos. Additionally, Colombia houses Afro-Latinos in remote areas such as the Palenque de San Basilio. In countries like Honduras and Nicaragua, the Miskito represent an Afro-Amerindian community descending from the Macro-Chibchan Indigenous groups and runaway enslaved individuals (Smith 2008). Over in Mexico's Veracruz, there exists a group named Cimarrones, believed to be related to the Chicanos in the US southwest. Numerous maroon societies also emerged in places like Jamaica, Cuba, Puerto Rico, Haiti, and other Caribbean regions (Menchaca 2001).

In order to fully appreciate the significance of Afro-Cuban women's visual expressions that will be analyzed in this book and their impact on challenging societal norms, it is essential to delve into the historical context that has shaped their experiences. Historically, Cuba has grappled with patriarchal and racist structures that have marginalized and silenced Afro-Cuban women. Initially driven by intellectuals, musicians, writers, and artists, since the late 1990s, the Afro-Cuban movement has been successful in breaking the official silence that covered the racial issue in

Cuba while sheddinglight on the experience of Black women (de la Fuente " 'Tengo una raza oscura y discriminada," 92). The emergence of the Afro-feminist movement has provided a powerful platform for these women to express themselves and challenge these oppressive norms through various artistic mediums. By examining the historical struggles and resilience of Afro-Cuban women, we can better understand the transformative power of their art and its role in sparking social change. In this chapter, I delve into the historical context surrounding the visual expression of Afro-Cuban women. By exploring the evolution of Afro-Cuban identity in the island and the development of Afro-feminism, I aim to provide a comprehensive understanding of the challenges, triumphs, and artistic contributions made by Cuban women of African descent. To fully appreciate the significance of Afro-Cuban women's visual expressions, it is crucial to acknowledge the historical events and social conditions that shaped their experiences. Understanding the evolution of Afro-Cuban identity in Cuba allows us to grasp the unique struggles faced by this community, as well as the resilience and strength they have demonstrated throughout history.

Furthermore, examining the evolution of Afro-feminism in Cuba provides valuable insights into the intersectionality of gender and race within the country's social fabric. Afro-feminism emerged as a response to the systemic oppression experienced by Afro-Cuban women, and it embodies a powerful movement that seeks to dismantle patriarchal and racist structures. By offering historical context on Afro-Cuban identity and Afro-feminism in Cuba, we can better comprehend the significance of the visual media used by Afro-Cuban women. Photography, installation, performance, and painting serve as mediums through which Afro-Cuban women express their lived experiences, challenge societal norms, and advocate for social change. Through this exploration, readers will gain a deeper understanding of the multifaceted narratives and artistic expressions of Afro-Cuban women. By recognizing their contributions as agents of change, we can appreciate not only their artistic talents but also their role in shaping communities and challenging societal norms. By providing a foundation rooted in historical context, this chapter aims to foster appreciation for the visual expressions of Afro-Cuban women. It is my hope that readers will engage with their stories, empathize with their struggles, and acknowledge the broader sociocultural significance of their artistic contributions. The evolution of Afro-feminism has had a profound impact on the visual expressions of Afro-Cuban women. Afro-feminism emerged as a response to the intersectional oppression experienced by Afro-Cuban women, and it seeks to dismantle patriarchal and racist structures. This movement has provided a platform for Afro-Cuban women to express their lived experiences and challenge societal norms through various artistic mediums. By utilizing these artistic mediums, Afro-Cuban women not only challenge societal norms but also actively shape and influence communities. Their work fosters dialogue, raises awareness, and highlights the importance of intersectionality in understanding and addressing social issues. Their visual expressions serve as a means of empowerment and resistance against the systemic oppression they face.

The origins of Africans in the Americas remain ambiguous, yet evidence suggests their presence predates the infamous slave trade. Notably, Africans journeyed alongside Christopher Columbus in 1492, serving pivotal roles during the Spanish conquest, functioning as servants, soldiers, seamen, settlers, and even warriors. These individuals bore the moniker "negros ladinos." The influx of Africans in Spanish America escalated with the inception of the transatlantic slave trade (Pew Research Center 2016). These Africans filled the void left by the dwindling Indigenous populace, casualties of warfare and disease. Over the course of the 400-year slave trade, an estimated twelve million individuals, hailing from regions such as Nigeria, Ghana, and Angola, were forcibly relocated to the Americas (Postma 2003). In territories like Brazil and parts of the Caribbean, these enslaved individuals comprised the population majority. While many succumbed to illnesses or the dire conditions, others fled their captors, establishing independent settlements across countries like Colombia and Honduras. Even as some slaves gained freedom, others were continually trafficked from Africa. This persisted until the abolition of slavery in most of Latin America around the 1820s, in the US by 1865, while Cuba and Brazil abolished it in 1886 and 1888, respectively (Postma 2003).

The suppression of these historical ties between slavery and ongoing racial prejudice contributes to the continued marginalization of Afro-Latinos (Godreau et al. 2008). This dark legacy seeps into every facet of Afro-Latinx socioeconomic existence. Andrews (2004) contends that contemporary Afro-Latin Americans grapple with the economic shadows cast by plantation agriculture (5). Furthermore, he suggests that in Latin America, skin color remains a profound indicator of one's social standing. The dark complexioned often endure lingering class-based biases and alienation, remnants of the late fifteenth-century New Spain caste system (Rochin 2016). Consequently, Afro-Latin Americans typically occupy a lesser socioeconomic position relative to their white or mestizo counterparts in the region (Telles 2014; Telles, Flores, & Urrea-Giraldo 2015). The journey of Africans to the Americas, woven through trials, resilience, and cultural amalgamation, forms the intricate tapestry on which the visual expressions and activism of Afro-Cuban women can be comprehended. At the heart of this narrative is not just the story of survival but also the story of transformation and reclamation. Afro-Cuban women, through the centuries, have not only been witnesses to these historical shifts but active participants and creators within them. From the early days of their arrival, Africans brought with them diverse cultural, artistic, and spiritual practices that became foundational to many Latin American cultures, Cuba being no exception. This rich heritage was a springboard for visual and artistic expression, blending African traditions with Indigenous and European influences. Within this melting pot, Afro-Cuban women found their voice and means of expression, often using art as a medium to navigate and negotiate their identity, rights, and place in society. Furthermore, the legacy of slavery and subsequent racial discrimination, especially the attempt to marginalize and erase Afro-Latinx contributions, made activism a necessary companion to artistic expression for Afro-Cuban women. Their artwork, be it through paintings, sculptures, performances, or other visual mediums, often carried potent messages challenging societal norms, questioning racial hierarchies, and celebrating Afro-Cuban heritage. The visual became a form of resistance, a way to counteract erasure, and a method to assert presence. In a society where colorism and racial hierarchies persisted beyond the slavery era, Afro-Cuban women's activism was not just a fight for equality but also a struggle for recognition and respect of their African heritage. Their visual expressions became both a mirror reflecting their lived experiences and a window into the aspirations and dreams of a community yearning for acknowledgment and respect. Thus, when we dive deep into the visual expression and activism of Afro-Cuban women, we are not just exploring artworks or isolated acts of defiance; we are journeying through a rich historical narrative of identity, resistance, and cultural evolution. This history informs and enriches every brushstroke, every performance, and every act of activism, making the story of Afro-Cuban women an essential chapter in the broader saga of the African diaspora in the Americas.

To fully comprehend the marginalization of Afro-descendant individuals, it's crucial to delve into the racial ideology prevalent in Latin America. This is of utmost importance since North American racial categories, like Black and white, don't align with those in Latin American contexts. Instead, in Latin America, race is more intricately associated with nuances like skin shade, physical features, and hair types (Busey & Cruz 2015; Duany 2005). Central to this discourse is the concept of *mestizaje*, which encapsulates the racial and cultural intermingling primarily of Spanish and Indigenous groups in Latin America, rooted in the nineteenth century (Telles & Garcia 2013). This principle championed the fusion of various races to establish a genuine national persona and a cohesive state, sidelining specific ethnic identities. It was a reaction against ideologies fueled by the concept of white supremacy and scientific racism. Essentially, mestizaje was perceived as an avenue to elevate the societal standing of Indigenous and African communities in Latin American territories (Burke 2008). Mestizos were often regarded as the ideal representation of citizenship, embodying a constructed standard of cultural and racial hybridity that aligned with national narratives of unity and progress. This perception positioned mestizos as the epitome of societal belonging, while simultaneously marginalizing individuals and communities who did not conform to this idealized racialized identity (Telles & Garcia 2013). Yet, the embrace of mestizaje varied across Latin American nations based on their racial demographics. In countries like Peru, Bolivia, and Guatemala, the idealized mestizaje was the blend of Spanish and Indigenous lineages, conveniently sidelining African heritage. Conversely, nations like Brazil and the Spanish Caribbean saw it as the amalgamation of African and Spanish ancestries (Paschel 2010). This led to the emergence of diverse racial classifications including mulattoes (white and Black mix), mestizos (white and Indigenous blend), and pardos (a fusion of Black, white, and Indigenous lineages), among others. Wade (2018) postulated that while mestizaje did pave the way for transcending social divisions, fostering a new mestizo generation, it simultaneously perpetuated the hierarchical inferiority assigned to Blacks and Indigenous communities, juxtaposed against the loftiness of white identity (Wade 1993). This ideology manifested a spectrum where Afro-descendants and Indigenous communities languished at the bottom, mestizos occupied the middle, and those aligning with or claiming European descent reigned supreme. Intricately linked to mestizaje is colorism, where lighter skin hues are favored over darker ones within the same racial group (Hunter 2005). Consequently, Latinos with a lighter complexion are perceived superior to their darker-skinned counterparts, while traits akin to white Europeans are prized over those of African or Indigenous origins (Perez Lopez 2017). Furthermore, mestizaje subtly obscures the prevailing racial prejudices against Blacks and Indigenous groups in Latin America. This ideology cloaks the stark realities of racial disparities and discrimination by projecting an illusion of a racially neutral and just society. A case in point is Mexico's assertion that everyone belongs to the mestizo fold, effectively denying the presence of racial biases (Harris 2008).

The Afro-descendant community in Latin American countries has long faced a multifaceted issue of invisibility and exclusion. Many racial minority groups, including the Afro-Latinxs, grapple with a confluence of factors that shape their distinct experiences. As Ray articulates, "Race connects cultural rules to social and material resources through organizational formation, hierarchy, and processes" (27). Supporting this notion, the Economic Commission for Latin America, and the Caribbean (2021) discovered that the majority of the impoverished in areas where Afro-Latinxs reside are, in fact, Afro-Latinx. They also tend to have diminished access to economic opportunities and are more frequently victimized compared to their white Latino counterparts. The realm of education isn't exempt from these challenges, where Afro-Latinx students face biased portrayals, a dearth of educational resources, and a shortage of educators equipped to navigate racial diversity (Freire et al. 2018). There's a silver lining, however. Over recent years, several Latin American nations have started acknowledging these disparities, taking steps to recognize and uplift their Afro-descendant citizens. A notable example is Brazil, which pioneered the initiative of introducing quotas to ensure Afro-Latinx representation in governmental roles (Ribando 2005). In a similar vein, 2019 saw Chile formalizing the acknowledgment of its Afro-descendant tribal communities in its laws. Guatemala too, in 2016, legislated the recognition of its Afro-descendant Creole demographic (Economic Commission for Latin America and the Caribbean 2021).

Legislative actions are just one part of the larger puzzle. Efforts are also being made to rectify the historical oversight in census data. Initiatives in this direction have led countries like Panama and Costa Rica to introduce Afro-descendant categories in their 2010 and 2011 censuses, respectively. Mexico followed suit in 2015, marking a shift in acknowledging its Afro-Mexican or Black populace (Gonzalez-Barrera 2016). Yet, challenges remain, as some South American nations continue to negate the presence of Black communities, often linking Black identity to poverty and socioeconomic disadvantage (Telles & Garcia 2013). The advocacy isn't restricted to Latin America alone. In the US, there's a growing movement to enhance the visibility of Afro-Latinos. A testament to this is the US census, which, for the first time, introduced categories allowing Afro-Latinos to identify as Afro-Latinx, Afro-Caribbean, or Afro-Latin.

According to 2019 census data, 5 percent of Latinx individuals identified with these categories, with the majority residing in New York (23%), California (15%), and Florida (12%) (Gonzalez-Barrera 2016). Given the broader context of the invisibility and marginalization faced by the Afro-descendant community in various parts of Latin America, this book focusing on the visual expression and activism of Afro-Cuban women becomes even more significant. The issues surrounding Afro-Latin representation, as detailed from the general Latin American context, offer a foundational backdrop against which Afro-Cuban women's experiences can be understood. Knowing that Afro-descendants have historically been marginalized in socioeconomic and political spheres underscores the importance and urgency of their activism and self-expression. With the pervasive invisibility and systemic biases against these communities, visual expression becomes a powerful tool for Afro-Cuban women to reclaim their narrative. The art, photography, painting, or any form of visual medium can be seen as an act of resistance, carving out space in public consciousness and challenging predominant stereotypes.

A Chronicle of Heritage:
Exploring the Evolution of the Afro-Cuban Cultural Identity

The consequences of colonization and slavery in Cuba have been far reaching and deeply impactful, shaping the island's history, culture, and society in significant ways. The legacy of slavery has resulted in deep-seated racial inequalities and discrimination in Cuban society, with Afro-Cubans often facing disadvantages in areas such as employment, education, and political representation. The enduring scars of slavery in Cuba have interwoven to craft a narrative marked by sustained economic disparities between Afro-Cubans and other community segments (Aimes 1907; Allahar 1988; Franklin 2012; de la Fuente 2012; Murray 1999). This lingering legacy has not only cemented profound economic inequalities but has also intertwined with a troubling history of cultural erasure, where the rich cultural heritage of Afro-Cubans—including their music, dance, religion, and oral traditions—has been marginalized and stifled, a silent victim of the shackles of colonialism and slavery. Afro-Cubans find their voices and stories suppressed, their vibrant cultural tapestry at risk of fading into the shadows of disregard and neglect, a consequence of the lingering imprints of colonial exploitation and the continuous devaluation of their cultural expressions. The echoes of these silenced voices are met with a parallel narrative of political exclusion, where Afro-Cubans, marginalized and often ignored, struggle against the prevailing currents of political power and decision-making processes. This exclusion perpetuates a cycle of underrepresentation and unacknowledged needs and concerns, reinforcing barriers to addressing the unique challenges faced by the Afro-Cuban community.

Beyond the realm of cultural and political landscapes, the shades of colonialism extend their reach to the natural environment. The ruthless exploitation of Cuba's natural resources during the colonial period has left indelible marks on its environment, leading to extensive degradation and the irrevocable loss of pivotal ecosystems. The interplay between economic inequality, cultural erasure, political exclusion, and environmental degradation sketches a profound and complex panorama of the multifaceted struggles faced by Afro-Cubans, each aspect amplifying the others, entwined in a continuous dance of resilience and quest for recognition and equality. The Cuban Revolution, which took place in 1959, and resulted in the overthrow of Fulgencio Batista's regime, brought about profound changes in the culture and politics of Cuba. Led by Fidel Castro, the revolutionaries embraced socialist ideology, sparking a transformation that permeated every aspect of Cuban society. To explore the multifaceted effects of the revolution on culture and politics, highlighting key areas where its influence was most evident. The Cuban Revolution marked the rise of socialist ideology as the guiding principle of the newly established government. Inspired by Marxist–Leninist ideals, the revolutionaries sought to eradicate social inequality and class distinctions. They implemented policies promoting egalitarianism, collectivization of agriculture, and the nationalization of industries, aiming to redistribute wealth more equitably. The socialist framework became deeply ingrained in the political structure, shaping policies and decision-making processes for decades to come. Central to the revolution was a powerful sense of Cuban nationalism. The revolutionaries sought to free Cuba from the shackles of foreign domination, particularly that of the United States. This newfound nationalism was rooted in a desire to assert Cuban independence and sovereignty. The revolution became a symbol of resistance against imperialism, inspiring a collective identity among the Cuban people and fostering a sense of pride in their country's history, culture, and values. The revolution brought about significant changes in cultural policies, promoting, and nurturing a distinctly Cuban cultural identity. The government aimed to dismantle cultural imperialism and celebrate the rich cultural heritage of Cuba (Guerra 2012). It supported cultural expressions that aligned with revolutionary values, emphasizing Afro-Cuban culture, and rejecting oppressive influences. Nationalization of cultural institutions and the establishment of new ones facilitated the promotion of revolutionary cultural initiatives, encouraging artistic and literary creativity that reflected the ideals of the revolution. The impact of the Cuban Revolution extended beyond the island itself. Cuba emerged as a symbol of anti-imperialism and a source of inspiration for leftist movements and governments worldwide. Cuba actively supported and assisted revolutionary movements in Latin America and Africa, providing military aid, education, and healthcare professionals. The country's involvement in international affairs bolstered its global standing, influencing political dynamics in the region and demonstrating its commitment to solidarity and social justice. The Cuban Revolution's influence on the culture and politics of the island cannot be overstated. Its embrace of socialist ideology, promotion of Cuban nationalism, and implementation of policies in education, healthcare, and agrarian reform reshaped the fabric of Cuban society. While the revolution brought about positive changes, it also resulted in limitations on political freedoms. The ongoing US embargo and other external factors have also influenced the trajectory of Cuba's culture and politics. Nonetheless, the Cuban Revolution remains a defining moment in the nation's history, leaving an indelible mark on its cultural identity and political landscape. As Rodríguez Mangual points out, "The revolution converted the small island into a real foe of the ideological apparatus of North America capitalism, altering U.S. policy for many years, while Cuba became a paradigm for leftist political groups in Latin America" (3).

The Cuban Revolution's impact extended far beyond the borders of the island, transforming Cuba into a formidable adversary of the ideological apparatus of North American capitalism and serving as a paradigm for leftist political groups in Latin America. The revolution's influence on the political dynamics of the region and the response it elicited from the United States had long-lasting effects. First, the Cuban Revolution challenged the dominance of North American capitalism in Latin America. By successfully overthrowing a US-backed dictator and establishing a socialist state just 90 miles from the shores of the United States, Cuba became a symbol of resistance against imperialism and a beacon of hope for leftist political groups throughout the region. The revolution demonstrated that an alternative to capitalism was not only possible but also achievable, inspiring leftist movements across Latin America to challenge the status quo and pursue their own paths of revolutionary change. The revolution's success also had a profound impact on US policy toward Cuba. Prior to the revolution, Cuba had been a close ally of the United States, particularly in economic and strategic terms. However, the revolutionary government's socialist orientation and its nationalization of US-owned properties directly challenged American interests in the region. In response, the United States imposed an economic embargo on Cuba, severed diplomatic ties, and supported numerous attempts to overthrow the Cuban government, including the failed Bay of Pigs invasion in 1961. Cuba's transformation into a socialist state with close ties to the Soviet Union during the Cold War further intensified tensions between Cuba and the United States. The Cuban Missile Crisis of 1962 brought the world to the brink of nuclear war and highlighted the significance of Cuba as a geopolitical flashpoint. The revolution's defiance of US hegemony in the Western Hemisphere fundamentally altered US policy toward Cuba for many years, resulting in a protracted period of hostility and isolation.

Moreover, Cuba's revolutionary model and the government's support for leftist movements in Latin America solidified its status as a paradigm for political groups across the region. The Cuban Revolution offered a tangible example of successful revolutionary change, inspiring leftist political organizations and guerrilla movements to pursue similar strategies in their own countries. Cuba provided military training, ideological guidance, and material support to various groups, such as the Sandinistas in Nicaragua and the Revolutionary Armed Forces of Colombia (FARC). The Cuban government's solidarity with leftist movements and its anti-imperialist stance resonated with those who sought to challenge the political and economic structures that perpetuated inequality and dependency on foreign powers. The Cuban Revolution's transformation of Cuba into a foe of North American capitalism and its influence as a paradigm for leftists in Latin America cannot be understated. The revolution's success in establishing a socialist state close to the United States challenged the dominance of North American capitalism in the region and triggered a significant shift in US policy toward Cuba. Cuba's support for leftist movements in Latin America further solidified its position as a symbol of resistance and inspired political groups to pursue their own paths of revolutionary change. The Cuban Revolution remains a pivotal moment in the history of Latin America, with its effects continuing to shape regional politics and ideologies. In this context, the Cuban intellectual Lydia Cabrera (1900 to 1991) worked to redefine the identity of marginalized Afro-Cubans and reinsert their story into the broader understanding of Cuban identity, especially after four decades of Revolution and a massive emigration that has divided the nation (Rodríguez Mangual, 3).

To understand Afro-Cuban cultural identity, it is also fundamental to refer to the studies of Fernando Ortíz (1881 to 1969) who was a prominent Cuban intellectual, anthropologist, and essayist. He is widely regarded as one of the most influential figures in the development of Cuban cultural studies and the study of Afro-Cuban culture. Ortíz's work focused on understanding and documenting the cultural and social dynamics of Cuba, particularly the Afro-Cuban experience. He coined the term *transculturation* to describe the process of cultural exchange and transformation that occurs when different cultures come into contact. His research aimed to shed light on the complex racial and cultural dynamics in Cuba and challenge racial stereotypes. Ortíz's studies and writings had a significant impact on various fields, including anthropology, sociology, history, and literature. He played a crucial role in promoting the recognition and appreciation of Afro-Cuban culture within the broader Cuban society. His work highlighted the African roots of Cuban culture, the contributions of Afro-Cubans to Cuban society, and the importance of cultural diversity in shaping the nation's identity. In addition to his scholarly pursuits, Ortíz was actively involved in Cuban public life. He was a founding member of the Cuban Academy of Sciences, and he served as a senator in the Cuban Parliament. Ortíz's contributions to academia, his advocacy for cultural diversity, and his efforts to combat racism in Cuba make him an important figure in both Cuban and Latin American intellectual history. His book, *Hampa Afro-Cubana*, explores the marginalized Afro-Cuban subculture in Cuba. Ortíz delves into the lives of Afro-descendants in the impoverished neighborhoods of Havana and other Cuban cities, focusing on aspects such as music, dance, religion, and survival mechanisms within these communities. The term *hampa* refers to crime and marginality, and Ortíz analyzes how these realities intersect with the Afro-Cuban experience. The author explores the social and economic dynamics that lead some Afro-descendants to engage in illegal activities or live in precarious conditions. The book also highlights the significance of Afro-Cuban culture within these marginalized contexts. Ortíz examines Afro-Cuban cultural practices, such as Afro-Cuban music and Afro-Caribbean religious rituals, and how these cultural expressions are maintained and adapted in the marginalized neighborhoods. *Hampa*

Afro-Cubana provides a deep and critical insight into the Afro-Cuban subculture and its relationship with marginality and crime. The book seeks to challenge stereotypes and promote a more comprehensive understanding of the Afro-Cuban experience, emphasizing its cultural richness and its contribution to Cuban identity. The author points out that the total number of enslaved Africans brought to Cuba was extremely high. He estimates that from the year 1517, when King Carlos I of Spain issued the first license for the introduction of Black enslaved individuals in the Antilles, until 1800, a time in which slavery was definitely prohibited, thousands and thousands of Africans were taken from their native country (19–20). To fully acknowledge and appreciate the creative endeavors and societal contributions of Afro-Cuban women artists, it is crucial to comprehend these historical events and their long-standing impacts.

Charting the Journey and Influence of Afro-Feminism in Cuba

The sixties and seventies were undoubtedly decades of high theoretical production and new political practices in feminism in many countries. By then, feminist claims and demands were no longer about the right to vote or merely entering masculinized institutions; other logics and political proposals were enriching feminism. Afro-descendants, feminist lesbians, postcolonialists, multiculturalists, among others, broadened the spectrum of analysis with new perspectives concerning women's subordination (Curiel 2007, 1). Latin America and the Caribbean is a continent that has been marked by colonialism and economic dependence, embedded in free-market capitalism but with weak markets and limited capacity to compete internationally, which keeps it in a situation of widespread poverty. The political thought in Latin America and the Caribbean has been framed within this context, determined by colonization and conquest that imposed Indigenous and African slavery, a form of enslavement that has extended and had repercussions in the lives of a vast majority of the population, with women being greatly affected. Women's political action has taken place in response to discriminatory economic and social policies, dictatorships, and authoritarian leadership, sexism, and racism. The construction of the critical political subject has been built on a notion of liberation in response to these phenomena (11). It was in 1983, during the second *Feminist Encounter of Latin America and the Caribbean*, that the issue of racism was collectively and continentally addressed as a notably absent topic from political debates. Even when introduced with hesitancy and a somewhat essentialist identity vision, Afro-descendants, and subsequently, Indigenous people, began to organize discussion spaces within the encounters. One of the first Afro-feminists in the context of Latin America and the Caribbean was Afro-Brazilian Leila González. With her internationalist vision of the antiracist struggle, she formulated a concept to define the common experience of Afro-descendants in the Americas: "Amefricanity." This concept is based on rejecting the Latin identity of the Americas by considering the preponderance of Indigenous and Black cultural elements (12). Afro-descendant women in Latin America and the Caribbean have begun to embrace a political identity, initially identifying as *negras* and more recently as afrodescendiente. Embracing Black womanhood has been one of the political priorities of the movement, highlighting the need to forge a reaffirmed femininity in the face of the onslaughts of racism and its impacts on women. Thus, Blackness was and continues to be the starting point for political articulation (15). In the national context of the island of Cuba, due to their "skin color," Black women experienced the misfortune of the remnants of slavery. The various problems to which they were exposed are linked to the undeniable flaws of racist ideologies that corroded Cuban society (Fernández Robaina 2012). The early feminist movements in Cuba spurred the birth of the magazine *Minerva* (1888 to 1889). This biweekly publication was dedicated to "women of color" and, throughout its year of existence, it focused on three main areas: poetry, the advocacy of education and instruction, and notes related to morality. Within its pages, a considerable group of Afro-descendant women expressed themselves, and several of the most prominent Black and mestizo intellectuals of the time also contributed (Pichardo 2016, 181–82). Cuban Black women bore the historical social origin on their backs, to which gender and "skin color" were added as points of confrontation within the rigid socio-racial structures of nineteenth-century colonial Cuba (Zeuske 2008; Montejo 1998; Stoner y González 1998). It is also worth mentioning the creation of women's clubs among immigrants, mostly gathered around the People's Republic of China. According to research by González Pagés (2006), three of these clubs had Black and mestizo women on their respective boards: Club Céspedes y Martí (New York), Club José Maceo (New York), and Club Mariana Grajales de Maceo (Key West). With the arrival of the twentieth century, Cuba experienced the long-awaited creation of the first Republic in 1902, fraught with nuances that promoted various changes (Pérez 1986). These changes occurred at the ideological level, intrinsically linked to the enactment of universal male suffrage, which was protected by the support of a myth of racial equality (De la Fuente 2001). Within this framework, the feminist movement in Cuba saw a rapid rise, and to some extent, the myth of racial equality was noticeable within it, especially considering that the overwhelming majority of its positions focused exclusively on the struggle of Cuban women, as they still remained foreign to full participation, with equal rights, within society as a whole (Pichardo 2016, 186). The initial debates posed by the feminist movement in the early decades of the twentieth century were focused on state instances and women's rights, on the creation of feminist associations, and consequently, on the opening of spaces for confrontation and dialogue, materialized with the holding of the National Women's Congress in 1923, 1925, and 1939 (Stoner 2003). Significant goals were achieved through the Parental Authority Law of 1917 and the Divorce Law of 1918. One of the most significant achievements was also the Women's Universal Suffrage in 1934 (Pichardo 2016, 187). The relaunch of the magazine *Minerva* in the new republican context is significant, where it re-emerged in a second stage (1910 to 1915) as a universal illustrated publication. In the pages of the new *Minerva*, we find a very particular section called "Páginas Feministas" (Feminist Pages) where, as some of its illustrations indicate, many of its writings came from the pen of Black and mestizo women (Pichardo 2016, 187). Another important event was the third National Women's Congress (1939). This preceded the legislative reforms that were outlined for the new Constitution (1940), and the virtually null role that Black and mestizo women played in Cuban society was one of the essential axes of discussion (Keosha 2011), alluding to one of the issues in question, the access of these women to the labor market under equal conditions compared to white women (Rubiera 2011).

In contemporary Cuba, the recent establishment of a public platform for discussions encompassing issues related to race, gender, and sexuality has paved the way for the emergence of new Afro-Cuban feminisms. Within the Cuban chapter of the Articulación Afrodescendiente en América Latina y el Caribe (ARAAC), women have taken on prominent leadership roles, offering a counterbalance to the predominantly male critics within the organization. An exemplar of this growing movement was the release of the collection *Afrocubanas* in 2013, which was met with enthusiastic reception, bearing witness to the increasing interest in Black feminism within Cuba. Concurrently, there has been a notable public advocacy for the rights of sexual diversities, spearheaded by Mariela Castro, the daughter of the president. This advocacy has created an enabling environment for Afro-Cuban lesbian feminists to voice their concerns, emphasizing the intersections of racism, sexism, and homophobia as essential aspects of their call for a more profound and revitalized Cuban liberation project (Laó-Montes 2016, 12).

In *Afrocubanas: Historia, Pensamiento y Prácticas Culturales* (2013), authors Daisy Rubiera and Maria Inés Martiatu embark on a profound exploration of Afro-Cuban feminisms, reaching back to the nineteenth century. Led by Daisy Rubiera Castillo and Inés María Martiatu Terry, their meticulous study reveals a striking reality: the marginalized presence of Afro-descendant women within Cuba's intellectual and cultural landscapes. This scholarly journey is a captivating voyage through history, unearthing the multifaceted experiences and perspectives of AfroCuban women.[1] The authors trace the origins of Afro-Cuban feminisms, demonstrating that these movements have deep historical roots, often obscured by prevailing societal narratives. A central tenet of their research is the enduring social conceptualization that has relegated Afro-descendant women to the periphery of Cuban intellectual and cultural life. Rubiera and Martiatu argue that this relegation has stifled the recognition and representation of Afro-Cuban women's contributions and perspectives, leaving them with limited space to voice their experiences and ideas. Through a rigorous examination of historical documents, personal accounts, and cultural artifacts, the authors bring to the forefront the voices, struggles, and achievements of Afro-Cuban women who have been historically marginalized and silenced. The authors' nuanced exploration prompts a reevaluation of established perspectives, offering a deeper understanding of the complex interplay between race, gender, and cultural identity in Cuba.

A significant offering originating from Afro-Cuban feminism is also the blog *Negra Cubana Tenia Que Ser*, curated by the blogger Sandra Torres. Sandra initially began her blogging journey in Cuba and has since relocated to Germany. Her blog has evolved into a forum for discussion, encompassing not only topics related to racial politics in Cuba but also serving as a virtual, critical public space for Black feminisms across the broader global African diaspora. This platform, particularly influential in Latin America and the Caribbean, facilitates the exchange of information, analytical perspectives, and meaningful dialogues among Black feminists (Laó-Montes 2016, 12). What was once a personal blog has transformed into a digital platform that extends far beyond its Cuban origins. Today, *Negra Cubana Tenia Que Ser* serves as a thriving virtual space for dialogue and engagement, addressing not only the intricate nuances of racial politics in Cuba but also functioning as a critical public sphere. This expansion has had a profound effect, particularly within the realm of Black feminisms, reaching out to individuals and communities throughout the global African diaspora. In the vast virtual corridors of this blog, Black feminists from various corners of the world come together to share insights, information, and analyses. It provides a unique opportunity for these voices to unite, transcending geographic boundaries and cultural differences. The platform has emerged as a nexus for collaboration, fostering a sense of solidarity among Black feminists who often face similar challenges and experiences in their respective regions. One of the blog's most compelling attributes is its capacity to bridge the gaps between Latin America, the Caribbean, and the broader African diaspora. By doing so, it helps create a more interconnected and informed network of Black feminist thinkers and activists. These individuals engage in rigorous debates, discussions, and collaborations that have the potential to bring about meaningful change and progress, not only in the realm of feminism but also in addressing broader social issues related to race, gender, and sexuality. *Negra Cubana Tenia Que Ser* is more than just a blog; it is a testament to the power of digital platforms in amplifying marginalized voices and fostering international solidarity among Black feminists. Sandra Torres's work transcends borders, fostering a global community dedicated to dismantling systems of oppression and advocating for a more just and equitable world.

Afro-Cuban lesbian feminisms are increasingly making their mark on the political landscapes of the African diaspora, with a notable example being the rap group Las Krudas. Originally hailing from Cuba, Las Krudas have since relocated to the United States and are now taking their incisive critique of capitalism, racism, and heteronormativity to a global audience. In the spring and summer of 2016, Las Krudas embarked on their first tour in Colombia, where they were warmly embraced by Afro-Colombian feminists. Following this, they extended their tour to Europe. The title of Las Krudas's concert, "Retumbe de Cimarronas contra la violencia racista, sexista, capitalista y colonial" ("Resonance of Cimarronas Against Racist, Sexist, Capitalist, and Colonial Violence"), encapsulates the essence of their decolonial practice and mission. This name symbolizes their commitment to challenging and dismantling oppressive systems, advocating for social justice, and promoting decolonization as a central part of their artistic and political project. In essence, Las Krudas exemplify the global impact of Afro-Cuban lesbian feminisms, transcending borders, and boundaries to engage with issues of systemic inequality and injustice on a worldwide scale. Their music and activism serve as a powerful force for change and solidarity, resonating not only with Afro-Cuban and Afro-Colombian feminists but also with individuals and communities throughout the African diaspora and beyond (Laó-Montes 2016, 13). In this contemporary landscape, the Afro-Cuban women artists featured in this book are integral to the new wave of the Afro-Cuban feminist movement.

Chapter 2

Black Femininity Reimagined

Bridging AfroARTivism and Black Decolonial Aesthetics
in the Visionary Artistry of Harmonia Rosales

In the expansive realm of visual arts, where creativity intricately intertwines with identity and resistance, influential voices emerge to challenge
entrenched narratives and introduce new perspectives. This chapter examines the work of Harmonia Rosales, a prominent contemporary artist
whose oeuvre serves as a catalyst for exploring the intersections of Black
feminism, decolonial aesthetics, and what I term *Decolonial AfroARTivism*.
Rosales's art invites viewers into a vibrant and provocative universe that
subverts the conventions of a society steeped in racism and sexism. She
stands as a dynamic and courageous voice, illuminating the importance of
embracing and celebrating the experiences and resilience of Black Latina
women. This chapter aims to analyze Rosales's visual expressions as a
form of Afro-descendant artistic activism. I will scrutinize how her work
challenges and subverts prevailing aesthetic canons, exposing the systemic
oppression and exclusion faced by Black women for centuries. Through
her decolonial approach, Rosales invites us to reimagine and reconstruct
narratives that exalt the beauty and power inherent in racial and gender
diversity. I will examine how her art serves as a tool to question and redefine
the historical representations of Black women in Western art, establishing
a critical dialogue with stereotypes and imposed constructions of beauty.

Through the lens of Black feminism, this chapter explores how
Rosales's work encourages a reassessment of our perceptions of femininity
and Blackness. Her art confronts us with the need for introspection and

challenges the patriarchal and racist structures deeply rooted in our society. Afro-diasporic artists have always created historically valuable art pieces that became graphic and symbolic testimonies of their history, traditions, and struggles. Afro-descendant visual culture represents a privileged space where Black artists, and particularly Black women, can renegotiate their identities and give form to their agency. In the Latin American and Caribbean context, the effects of conquest and colonization have played an especially significant role in shaping social and cultural histories and identity representations. In the world of art, there are few female artists as innovative and thought provoking as Afro-Cuban American female artist Harmonia Rosales. Her work challenges societal norms and highlights the struggles of marginalized communities, all while exploring the complex nuances of identity and representation. Through her vibrant and powerful paintings, Rosales has become a force to be reckoned with in the contemporary art world, carving out a space for underrepresented voices and making a bold statement about the importance of diversity and inclusion. This chapter offers an exploration of the captivating and dynamic art of Harmonia Rosales, delving into her inspirations, techniques, and impact on the art world. From her stunning portraits to her powerful reinterpretations of classic works of art, we will take a closer look at this groundbreaking artist's unique perspective and artistic vision. Harmonia Rosales, born and raised in Chicago by a Cuban father and a Jewish Jamaican mother, reimagines classic works with Black femininity and deconstructs traditional ways of thought. Her multicultural background profoundly influences her art, allowing her to address complex themes of identity, race, and gender with a nuanced and richly informed perspective. By delving into the specificities of Rosales's heritage and experiences, this text aims to dismantle the monolithic perception of Afro-Cuban identity and highlight the diverse and multifaceted nature of her artistic expression. Through a postcolonial feminist analysis of three of her paintings, this analysis attempts to answer the following research questions: How does Harmonia Rosales employ visual elements and symbolism in her paintings to convey messages related to social justice, and how effective are these strategies in engaging diverse audiences both within and outside her cultural context? In what ways does Harmonia Rosales's artistic practice contribute to or challenge the existing discourses on Afro-Latina activism, freedom-making, and decolonial feminist practices, and what implications does this have for the broader sociopolitical landscape? Can we discern distinct patterns or themes in Rosales's work that align with or deviate from traditional narratives within the Afro-Latina activism movement, and how do these choices impact the potential for her art to foster dialogue and instigate social change?

Engaging with Harmonia Rosales's Decolonial AfroARTivism invites us on an analytical journey that delves into the dynamics of discovery and resistance, where visual forms serve as vital agents for societal transformation and psychological healing. Rosales's oeuvre, grounded in decolonial aesthetics, fosters a profound commitment to equality and social justice. In recent decades, an emergent artistic and cultural movement has attracted significant scholarly, artistic, and activist attention on a global scale. I have coined the term *Decolonial AfroARTivism* as part of a theoretical framework to encapsulate the synergistic integration of art and activism that foregrounds the lived experiences and struggles of Afro-descendant communities. Decolonial AfroARTivism seeks to dissect and comprehend the transformative potential of art in advancing social justice, fostering racial consciousness, and asserting Afro-descendant identity. Through diverse artistic modalities such as music, dance, poetry, painting, and theater, Decolonial AfroARTivists challenge systemic inequalities, address racial discrimination, and celebrate the cultural wealth of Afro-descendant populations. This concept transcends the realm of artistic production, establishing itself as a movement dedicated to cultivating critical dialogue, creating safe and inclusive spaces, and advocating for social change. Decolonial AfroARTivists leverage their creative talents to educate, inspire, and mobilize communities while deconstructing pervasive stereotypes and dominant narratives that sustain the marginalization of individuals of African descent. As an academic concept, it endeavors to deepen our understanding of how art functions as a powerful instrument for resistance, healing, and societal transformation. By analyzing Afro-descendant artistic practices and investigating their historical roles in confronting racial discrimination, Decolonial AfroARTivism enriches the disciplines of cultural studies, women's studies, racial studies, and activism studies.

This chapter aims to explore and scrutinize Decolonial AfroARTivism as an emergent field of inquiry and a pivotal cultural movement. Fundamentally, it represents a theoretical lens that invites rigorous exploration of the intersection between art, activism, and the Afro-descendant experience. Through this research, I hope to shed light on the ways in which art can catalyze social change, foster collective healing, and build a more inclusive and equitable future for Black Latinx communities and society at large. Decolonial aesthetics, Black feminist thought, and the practices that I will call here "Decolonial AfroARTivists" are intrinsically linked, as movements that aim to challenge and dismantle oppressive systems while centering the experiences and perspectives of marginalized communities, particularly those of African descent. By exploring the intersections of these concepts, we can better understand how Decolonial AfroARTivists utilize decolonial aesthetics to disrupt dominant narratives, reclaim cultural heritage, and promote social transformation. Decolonial aesthetics, rooted in decolonial theory, seek to deconstruct the enduring legacies of colonialism and imperialism. It critiques the Western-centric gaze that has historically dominated art, perpetuating harmful stereotypes and erasing the voices of marginalized communities. Decolonial aesthetics emphasize the importance of recognizing diverse knowledges, histories, and ways of being, challenging the hierarchies imposed by colonial powers. Decolonial AfroARTivists, on the other hand, utilize artistic practices to resist and reimagine oppressive narratives related to race, identity, and power. Through their art, they confront and subvert dominant representations of Blackness and challenge Eurocentric beauty standards. These artists create spaces for healing, celebration, and empowerment within their communities by highlighting the richness of African cultural heritage and reclaiming agency over their own narratives. In their artistic endeavors, they often draw inspiration from decolonial aesthetics by incorporating elements such as symbolism, cultural references, and visual narratives that challenge colonial legacies. They reclaim and reinterpret historical images, traditions, and iconography, offering counternarratives that disrupt colonial and racist frameworks. By employing decolonial aesthetics, these ARTivists reclaim the power to define their own identities and challenge the monolithic narratives that have historically marginalized and erased their experiences. Moreover, Decolonial AfroARTivists often engage in collaborative and community-oriented practices that align with decolonial principles. They actively seek to challenge and transform power dynamics within artistic spaces, with other marginalized communities. They promote inclusivity, intersectionality, and collective healing by fostering dialogues, organizing workshops, and creating spaces for marginalized voices to be heard and celebrated. Their practices and the utilization of decolonial aesthetics are crucial for disrupting oppressive systems, addressing racial inequalities, and promoting social justice.

Historically, the Black woman's body has been a site of struggle, exploitation, and resistance. In visual arts, Black femininity has often been objectified, fetishized, and exoticized, perpetuating harmful stereotypes and reinforcing power dynamics embedded in colonialism and slavery. As discussed in the introduction, this problematic history forms the backdrop against which artists like Harmonia Rosales navigate their creative expressions. Amid this troubling legacy, there is a burgeoning movement seeking to reclaim the Black woman's body as a powerful site of resistance and memory. In this context, the body can be seen as an archive, storing memories and histories of colonialism and slavery, as well as the resilience, strength, and resistance of Black women. Visual artists are exploring new ways of representing the Black woman's body, moving beyond the narrow stereotypes and tropes that have dominated traditional representations. Through their work, they are expressing the complexity and diversity of Black women's experiences, honoring their legacies, and giving voice to their struggles and triumphs. One example is the work of Harmonia Rosales, who critiques the limited representation of Black women in art and media by placing them in powerful positions, subverting dominant narratives and celebrating Black womanhood. One way to celebrate the richness of Black culture is through the use of visual storytelling and mythology to create new narratives and images that center the experiences and perspectives of Black women. For example, Rosales draws on traditional African mythology and creates new myths and stories that reimagine the role of Black women in history and culture. Rosales is also challenging the visual language and symbols that have been used historically to represent the Black woman's body, such as the exotic or hypersexualized "Other." Instead, they are creating new visual vocabularies that prioritize agency, complexity, and diversity. The artist is using her work to explicitly confront and critique the impact of colonialism and slavery on the Black woman's body. This might involve exploring the legacy of violence, exploitation, and objectification that Black women have experienced throughout history, or unpacking the ongoing intersections of racism, sexism, and other oppressive systems that continue to shape the lives of Black women today. Black Latina artists are acutely aware of the ways in which harmful stereotypes have historically been perpetuated through art, media, and popular culture. As a result, they often approach their work with a deep sense of responsibility and purpose.

Despite her profound impact and the compelling nature of her work, Harmonia Rosales has long been underrepresented and rendered invisible in peer-reviewed academic publications. In recent years, however, I have sought to address this oversight through several publications that analyze her craft from various perspectives. One of the eight chapters in my book,

The Afro-Descendant Woman in Latin American Diasporic Visual Art, titled "Reimagining Mythical Spaces: Spiritualized Afro-feminism and Decolonial Aesthetics in the Visual Expression of Afro-Cuban Painter Harmonia Rosales" (2024), explores Rosales's spiritualized Afro-feminists aesthetics and practices. Additionally, the chapter "Reimagining Black Femininity: Afro-Latina's Decolonial Aesthetics and AfroARTivism" in *Introduction to Women's, Gender and Sexuality Studies: Interdisciplinary and Intersectional Approaches* (2024) delves into her decolonial feminist practice and AfroARTivism, making her work accessible to undergraduate and graduate students entering the field of women's and gender studies. Furthermore, my articles in *PerspectivasAfro* ("El arte visual como práctica feminista decolonial: feminidad negra y ARTivismo afrocubano en las pinturas de Harmonia Rosales" [2024]), *Confluencia* ("Centering Black Women, Challenging Latinidad: Harmonia Rosales' Black Decolonial Aesthetics and AfroARTivism" [2024]), and *Hispanic Journal* ("Bridging the Gap Between Literature and Visual Art: Reimagining Black Femininity Through an Ekphrastic Analysis of Harmonia Rosales' Decolonial Feminist Aesthetics" [2023]) further explore her work, contributing to the academic discourse surrounding Rosales's significant contributions to art and activism. This current chapter, however, represents the most in-depth and comprehensive analysis of Harmonia Rosales's artistry to date, both in terms of the quantity of artworks scrutinized and the analytical approaches employed.

When analyzing Afro-Latina's art productions, it is essential to refer to Afro-Latina scholars, theorists, and activists who have shaped the modern and contemporary postcolonial theory and theoretical perspectives on race, class, and gender. Therefore, my theoretical approach aims to put at the center the work of Black Latina intellectuals, professors, and human rights activists who often go unrecognized in the academic world. Black Latina's art is then analyzed here through the lenses of Black Latina scholars such as Ochy Curiel, Caridad Souza, Karina L. Cespedes, among others. In the context of the afterlife of slavery (Hartman 2008), Afro-Latina epistemologies and cultural productions, negotiate their space and sense of belonging amid the ramifications of the Spanish colonial caste system, centuries of enslavement, and the consequences of the whitening period in Latin America and the Caribbean. As Souza and Cespedes point out, Afro-Latinas "experience constant diaspora, the persistence of not belonging, of being *ni de aquí, ni de allá* as well as being unclaimed and unrecognized" (32). This phrase, *ni de aquí, ni de allá*—"neither from here nor from there"—captures the dual marginalization Afro-Latinas face, highlighting their liminal existence both within their own cultural spaces and in broader societal contexts. Afro-Latina scholars Souza and Cespedes introduced the theoretical term *AfroLatinx decolonial feminism*, putting emphasis on the fact that this approach sits adjacent to, but in its form, independent from, both Chicana and Black feminism (26). These three feminist approaches share a common goal of addressing the ways in which gender, race, and class intersect and impact the lives of women of color.

However, there are some important differences in their perspectives. AfroLatinx feminism recognizes the experiences of Afro-Latinas, who occupy a unique space in the intersections of race, ethnicity, and gender. Afro-Latinas are often marginalized within both the Black and Latinx communities, and their experiences are often overlooked in feminist and racial justice movements. As a result, AfroLatinx feminism centers the experiences of Black women from Latin America and the Caribbean, and recognizes the importance of intersectional analyses that account for both race and ethnicity. Chicana feminism[1] emerged from the experiences of Mexican American women in the United States, and often centers on issues related to immigration, language, and cultural identity. Chicana feminism also has a strong emphasis on collective struggle and community organizing. As Souza and Cespedes point out, "while much of Afro-Latina/x feminist scholarship recognizes the constant state of diaspora, Chicana/x feminists have historically and geographically been 'at home' in the Southwestern territories" (55). Black feminism arose in the United States in response to the ways in which mainstream feminist movements ignored the specific experiences of Black women. It emphasizes the intersection of gender, race, and class in the lives of Black women and recognizes the importance of a global perspective on issues of oppression and resistance. This framework is particularly insightful when analyzing the art of Harmonia Rosales, as it provides the tools to explore how her work addresses and challenges systemic inequities, reclaims narratives, and centers Black femininity in both historical and contemporary contexts. The two Afro-descendant authors mentioned above ground themselves in what Amalia Dache (2021) defines as the "guerreras," or women warriors, of the Lucumí Orisha. Rooted in Maria Lugones's decolonial feminist praxis (2010) Souza and Cespedes recognize that this form of resistance means engaging the living cosmology that survived various forms of violence from enslavement, colonialism, and coloniality[2] (28). Afro-Latinas constantly battle with defining their identity and belonging in a binary world overwhelmed with dichotomies that do not leave space for individuals who occupy the so-called place of *ni de aquí, ni de allá* (Jiménez Román 2001; Lopez Oro 2016) having to negotiate relentlessly between their Blackness and Latinidad. Drawing from both Gloria Anzaldúa (1987) and her theorization of a mestiza consciousness that emerges from multiple forms of oppression and the psychosocial space of *ni de aquí, ni de allá* (Jiménez Román 2001), my analysis of Rosales's art also benefits from the concept of "Fronterisleña" introduced by Eliana Rivero (1994).

Visual Art as Decolonial Feminist Practice

The Afro-Cuban American artist under analysis, Harmonia Rosales, was born in 1984 in Chicago, where she was also raised, and she currently resides in Los Angeles, California. According to her official website, Rosales self-identifies as Afro-Cuban American. Since the inception of her career, her primary artistic focus has been on Black female empowerment within Western culture, with a particular emphasis on depicting and honoring the African diaspora. This chapter seeks to interpret some of her most iconic artworks, acknowledging how her artistic expressions serve as exemplars of decolonial feminist practice. *Decolonial feminism* is a term that refers to a theoretical and practical framework that seeks to challenge and transform the structures of power and knowledge that have been shaped by colonialism and imperialism. It recognizes that the histories and experiences of colonized people, especially women, have been marginalized and erased, and it seeks to center their voices and perspectives in the struggle for justice and liberation. Ochy Curiel is an Afro-Dominican lesbian, feminist, antiracist, decolonial scholar and activist who has contributed to the development of decolonial feminist thought. She has written extensively on issues related to gender, race, and class, and has sought to build bridges between different feminist and anticolonial struggles (Curiel 2005, 2007, 2010). One of Curiel's key contributions to decolonial feminism has been her insistence on the importance of intersectionality. She has argued that any analysis of oppression must take into account the ways in which different forms of oppression intersect and reinforce one another. For example, she has highlighted the ways in which racism and sexism intersect to produce a specific form of violence against Black women and has emphasized the importance of recognizing the specific struggles and experiences of Afro-descendant women. Curiel has also been critical of mainstream feminist movements that have failed to address the ways in which colonialism and imperialism have shaped the global distribution of power and resources. She has argued that these movements often reproduce the same hierarchies and exclusionary practices that they claim to challenge, and has called for a more radical, decolonial feminism that can challenge these structures at their root. Ochy Curiel's work has contributed to the development of decolonial feminist thought and has helped to highlight the importance of centering the perspectives and experiences of colonized women in the struggle for liberation and justice. Ochy Curiel's work is highly relevant to understanding Harmonia Rosales's art. Curiel's concept of decolonial feminism provides a valuable framework for analyzing Rosales's use of Yoruba iconography and mythology to challenge dominant Eurocentric notions of beauty and power. By centering African cultural heritage and subverting traditional Eurocentric aesthetic norms, Rosales's art embodies this decolonial perspective and offers a powerful alternative vision of beauty and identity. Furthermore, Curiel's ideas about the intersections of race, gender, and power are also relevant to understanding Rosales's art. Through the representations of powerful Black women and feminine-appearing Orishas,[3] Rosales opposes both racial and gendered power structures and creates space for alternative forms of identity and empowerment.

In this context, there are a multitude of reasons why it is important to analyze and study Harmonia Rosales's art. One of the key reasons is that her work resists dominant and exclusionary representations of beauty, identity, and representation. Just as an example, we will see how Rosales uses the skin condition vitiligo as a means of celebrating difference and diversity and showcasing the beauty and strength of those who are often marginalized or oppressed. By studying Rosales's art, we can gain a deeper understanding of the ways in which art can be used as a tool of resistance and social critique. Her work highlights the power of representation and self-expression and invites us to rethink our perceptions of what is "normal" or contributes to a broader conversation about the role of women and people of color in art and society. Her representations of strong and confident Black women challenge patriarchal norms and celebrate the resilience and strength of women who have often been overlooked or silenced in history. Rosales's art encourages empathy and compassion. Through her depictions of diverse individuals, she invites viewers to understand and connect with those who may be different from themselves. This, in turn, fosters a more inclusive and compassionate society, one in which all people are valued and respected. The relationship between visual media and the creation of empathy is a topic that has been analyzed by many critics. Significant is the book *Empathy: Philosophical and Psychological Perspectives*, edited by Amy Coplan and Peter Goldie. This volume brings together eighteen essays that reflect on empathy-related issues from the appreciation of works of art, the concept of morality, and interpersonal understanding. In the case of Rosales, her paintings are known for their powerful and emotional impact on viewers, particularly in terms of encouraging empathy for Black women. In many traditional artworks, Black women have been depicted in subservient or stereotypical roles, often portrayed as exotic or sexualized objects rather than fully realized human beings. By contrast, Rosales's paintings place Black women front and center, depicting them as powerful and dignified figures who command respect and admiration. This approach defies established norms and encourages empathy by helping viewers see these women in a new light. Instead of being reduced to stereotypes or caricatures, they are depicted as complex and multifaceted individuals with unique personalities, experiences, and perspectives. By inspiring empathy for Black women, Harmonia Rosales's paintings promote greater understanding and appreciation for the diversity and richness of human experiences, ultimately working to break down barriers and foster a more inclusive and compassionate society. In this context, the book chapter "An Empathic Eye," written by Dominic McIver Lopes, is particularly useful here. In this chapter, the author states that what you see can shape how you feel, and the route from seeing to feeling sometimes involves empathy. McIver Lopes underlines the fact that empathy also comes from what you see in pictures, paintings, drawings, prints, and photographs. It is explained that episodes of empathy triggered by images can help build up a person's capacity for empathic response. They do so by fortifying the link between seeing and empathy in a distinctive way (118–133).

Ultimately, the significance of studying Harmonia Rosales's art lies in its ability to inspire and empower. Through her bold and dynamic representations, Rosales encourages us to see the world in new ways, to challenge dominant narratives, and to celebrate the beauty and strength of difference. By analyzing her work, we deepen our understanding of these themes and contribute to a broader conversation about the power of art to shape our perceptions of ourselves and the world around us. In general, studying the visual art of Black Latina artists is crucial to recognize and appreciating the diverse cultural and historical contributions of

Afro-Latinas to the world of art. This recognition allows us to challenge the dominant narratives that often neglect or erase the experiences of marginalized communities. The study of Black Latinas' art provides an opportunity to explore and understand the intersectional experiences of race, gender, class, and nationality. By analyzing how these female artists express and navigate these intersecting identities in their artwork, we gain a deeper understanding of the complexity and diversity of the Afro-Latina experience. Moreover, as scholars, we could think of the numerous benefits related to the inclusion of Black Latina art in our research and teaching practices. The inclusion of Afro-Latina's art in academic curricula disputes existing biases and encourages diversity in learning. By exposing students to different perspectives, we can foster critical thinking skills and promote a more inclusive learning environment. In terms of benefits for the academic field, the study of Afro-Latina's art contributes to the development of new and innovative research methodologies. Scholars can use interdisciplinary approaches to explore the relationship between art, culture, politics, and identity. Furthermore, this study can also expand the canon of art history and provide alternative narratives that challenge Eurocentric perspectives. This intentional focus can also contribute to the larger cultural and social conversations about equity and social justice. By highlighting the work of Afro-Latina artists, we bring attention to social issues and amplify the voices of underrepresented communities.

As I will demonstrate in the following sections of this chapter, the study of the Yoruba religion is essential for understanding the artwork of Harmonia Rosales, as it offers critical insights into the cultural and spiritual influences that shape her creative vision. Centering Yoruba[4] traditions and cultural practices is undeniably one of the key factors that make Rosales's art a perfect example of decolonial feminist practice. The Yoruba religion is an ancient African belief system that originated in what is now Nigeria and has spread throughout the African diaspora. It is a complex system of beliefs that encompasses a wide range of spiritual practices, including ancestor worship, divination, and herbal medicine. One of the key aspects of Yoruba religious belief is the concept of Orishas, which are spiritual entities that represent different facets of the natural world and human experience. Each Orisha has its own distinct personality and characteristics, and is associated with specific colors, symbols, and rituals. The Orishas are often depicted in Yoruba art and mythology and play a central role in Harmonia Rosales's work. In her art, Rosales draws on the visual language and symbolism of the Yoruba religion to create powerful and evocative images that explore themes of identity, spirituality, and social justice.

Her use of Afrofuturist imagery[5] and iconography reflects a deep engagement with Yoruba cosmology, as well as her own personal experiences as an Afro-Latina woman living in the United States. Rosales's art challenges traditional Eurocentric notions of beauty and aesthetics and offers a bold new vision of Afro-Latinx identity and culture. Furthermore, the incorporation of Yoruba religion in Rosales's art also speaks to a larger cultural and political context, one that highlights the intersectionality between race, culture, and history. The Yoruba religion is a powerful symbol of African resistance and resilience in the face of colonialism and slavery. By emphasizing the importance of Yoruba cultural heritage in her art, Rosales not only celebrates the rich diversity of African culture but also affirms the ongoing struggle for social justice and equality. This is why the study of the Yoruba religion is critical in understanding Harmonia Rosales's art and its significance within the broader landscape of contemporary artistic expression. By exploring the spiritual and cultural dimensions of her work, we gain insight into the complex web of relationships that inform her creative vision and discover new possibilities for artistic and cultural expression. Rosales's incorporation of Yoruba religion in her art is rooted in her personal experiences and cultural heritage. As we learn by exploring her official webpage, Rosales grew up with a strong connection to her African roots and was inspired by the resilience and resistance of her ancestors in the face of colonialism and slavery. Through her study of Yoruba religion, which originated in West Africa and was brought to the Americas through the transatlantic slave trade, Rosales found a powerful symbol of African cultural heritage and resistance. The spiritual beliefs and practices of the Yoruba people, including their veneration of ancestors and the deities known as Orisha, resonated with Rosales's own experiences and provided a rich source of inspiration for her art. By incorporating Yoruba iconography, symbolism, and mythology into her paintings, Rosales seeks to celebrate the diversity and richness of African culture and challenge traditional Eurocentric notions of beauty and aesthetics. Ultimately, her art serves as a testament to the ongoing struggle for social justice and equality and invites us all to explore the complex intersections of race, culture, and history that inform our understanding of identity and community.

The Birth of Oshun

Focusing on Harmonia Rosales's career as a visual artist, in 2017, she was presented with the opportunity by Simard-Bilodeau Contemporary, a Los Angeles–based art gallery, to debut her first solo exhibition. Among the works featured in this inaugural show was *The Birth of Oshun* (figure 2.1), an oil-on-canvas painting that reimagines Sandro Botticelli's iconic work, *The Birth of Venus*. In this reimagining, Rosales replaces Botticelli's white Venus, the goddess of love, beauty, and fertility, with Oshun, the Yoruba goddess of fertility, sensuality, and prosperity. Oshun is depicted in a seashell, surrounded by what it appears to be Black angels, in stark contrast to the traditional depiction where Venus is encircled by white mythological figures. This painting exemplifies Rosales's practice of reinterpreting classic artworks by centering Black and Brown women. In this

Figure 2.1. *The Birth of Oshun*, Harmonia Rosales, 2017, 55 × 67. *Source:* Courtesy of Artist.

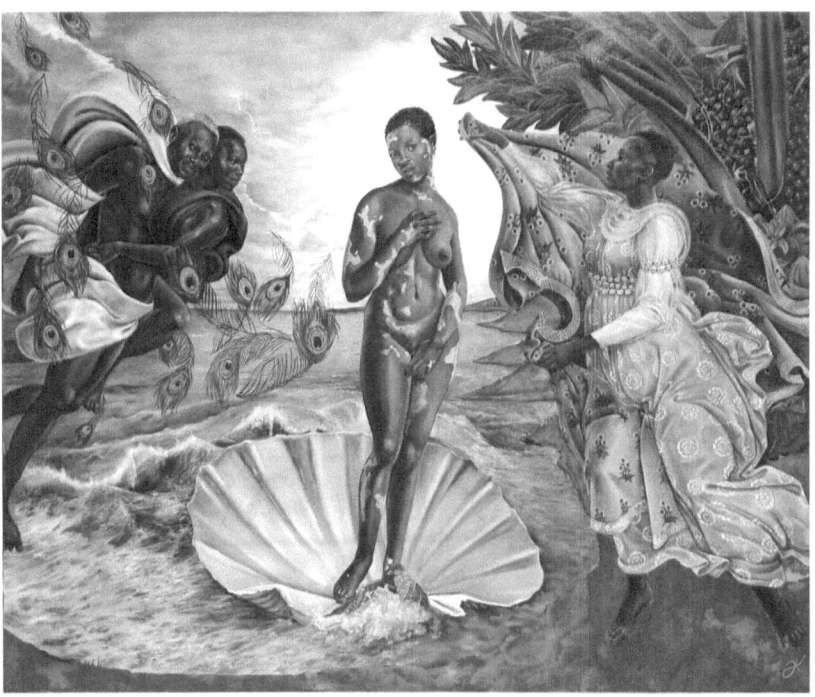

reinterpretation, Oshun is portrayed with vitiligo, with gold patches that are rooted in traditional Nigerian storytelling traditions (Dazed 2018). What appears at first glance to be Black angels are, in fact, other Orishas. To the left, Oya, the goddess of winds and storms, dressed in red, supports Obatalá, the creator of all humans, who is dressed in white. Yemayá, the Orisha of the ocean, identified by her cowrie shells, stands ready to welcome her sister Oshun, the goddess of rivers, to the shore with a golden robe decorated with sunflowers, which are Oshun's signature color and floral attribute. Oshun's golden markings, suggestive of vitiligo, symbolize a traditional pataki, or story, in which she saves humanity by transforming into a peacock and flying to Olodumare to beg for rain during a severe drought. Her arduous journey into the sun burned the feathers from her head, represented by her sheared hair, while the swirling peacock feathers in the painting hint at her sacrifice. Rosales cloaks the piece in classical mythology and Renaissance motifs to challenge Eurocentric ideals of beauty, making space for Black female empowerment and a broader representation of beauty. Oshun is one of the Orishas, Yoruba deities from West Africa, each of whom presides over one or multiple aspects of human existence. As Helen Morales points out: "The worship of *Orishas* survived the brutal trafficking of millions of Yorùbá people from West Africa (the southern part of present-day Nigeria) to the Americas via the Atlantic slave trade route known as the Middle Passage. Approximately 750,000 Yorùbá people were enslaved and taken to Cuba, where they became known as the Lucumí. The Cubans forced the Lucumí to be baptized into the Catholic Church. However, the Lucumí continued to worship *Orishas* by identifying them with Catholic saints" (9). The painting references traditional Yoruba religious beliefs and symbolism, with Oshun representing the goddess of love, fertility, and beauty. Rosales's depiction of Oshun as a Black woman fights against traditional Western depictions of beauty.[6] Historically, Western beauty standards have favored features commonly associated with people of European descent, such as fair skin, straight or wavy hair, narrow facial features, and specific body proportions. This Eurocentric bias has influenced perceptions of beauty and led to the marginalization of other racial and ethnic features. In many Western societies, there has been a strong emphasis on thinness as an ideal body shape, particularly for women. The idealized female body has often been portrayed as slim, toned, and possessing certain body measurements, which can contribute to body dissatisfaction and unhealthy body image issues. Western beauty standards often prioritize youthfulness, associating it with attractiveness and desirability. This can lead to ageism and pressure to maintain a youthful appearance through various cosmetic and anti-aging practices. Symmetrical facial features and balanced body proportions are often considered markers of beauty within Western depictions. Deviations from these ideals may be viewed as less attractive or even stigmatized. *The Birth of Oshun* is a powerful representation of Black womanhood and spirituality, challenging traditional narratives and power structures within art and religion. Beside Oshun stands the majestic figure of Yemaya, a powerful deity revered as the mother of all Orishas in certain narratives and considered to be Oshun's elder sister in others. Yemaya's presence in the artwork is a juxtaposition of the calm sea and the nurturing force of a mother or protective sister. She is depicted wearing a blue dress, a color that resonates with her association with the sea, moon, and maternity. This chromatic choice not only offers a soothing contrast to Oshun's golden glow but also metaphorically envelops the scene in a comforting embrace, akin to the embrace of the sea that Yemaya represents. Yemaya's act of holding out the cloak to Oshun can be perceived as a symbolic gesture of passing down wisdom, protection, and the nurturing force she embodies. This action transcends mere presentation, evolving into a sacred ritual that signifies Oshun's coming into her full power and grace. It portrays a moment of divine union and familial bond, a depiction of sisterhood or mother-daughter relationship that is steeped in deep respect and mutual acknowledgment of each other's strengths and roles in the cosmic narrative. The painting speaks to the importance of representation and the need to elevate marginalized voices and experiences in the art world. The painting is highly detailed, with intricate patterns and textures throughout the composition. Oshun is depicted standing naked on a seashell, similar to the position of Venus in Botticelli's painting. However, in contrast to Venus's demure expression, Oshun appears serene and confident, gazing out at the viewer with quiet strength. The surrounding elements in the painting also reference Oshun's Yoruba mythology. The water around her is depicted with a range of blue hues, which evoke the idea of fertility and abundance, both qualities often attributed to Oshun. Additionally, the gold leaf in the background is a nod to the wealth and opulence that Oshun represents. Rosales uses a variety of artistic techniques to capture the essence of Oshun and the power of her birth. One of the most striking aspects of the painting is its use of contrast, both in terms of light and dark and in the contrasting colors of gold and blue. The figure of Oshun herself is depicted in shades of gold, which creates a sense of warmth and radiance, while the background is a rich shade of blue that evokes the cool serenity of the water. It is a powerful and stunning reimagining of a classic artwork that centers on a Black woman and a deity often overlooked in Western art history. The painting speaks to Rosales's ongoing exploration of issues related to identity, power, and representation, and offers a thoughtful and nuanced perspective on the intersection of art and spirituality.

Another fundamental element in this piece is Rosales's use of the skin condition of vitiligo. Oshun is represented with golden patches typical of this condition which is more notable in people with darker skin complexions. In this way, Rosales continues to challenge traditional notions of beauty and representation by portraying subjects with features that are often considered unconventional or stigmatized. In the mesmerizing artwork by Rosales, Oshun embodies an epitome of both beauty and resilience, evident from the visual narrative detailed on her skin—the golden patches of vitiligo that seem to weave a story as old as time itself. These markings not only highlight her ethereal beauty but also serve as a visual narration of a revered *pataki*,[7] where she becomes the savior of humanity, showcasing her altruistic and nurturing essence. This pataki narrates a time of immense crisis—a severe drought that threatened to engulf life as known. It was during this perilous time that Oshun transformed into a resplendent peacock, her feathers capturing the ethereal grace that she is renowned for. With an unwavering resolve, she embarked on a celestial journey, soaring high up to reach Olodumare,[8] the supreme deity overseeing the cosmos. Her plea was one of desperation, a plea for the merciful heavens to unleash heavy rains, to quench the parched earth and save the beings residing on it. In the artwork, Oshun's transformative journey is not without sacrifice. Her close encounter with the mighty sun resulted in a fierce battle that left her once lush feathers scorched and burned, representing a tangible manifestation of her sacrifice. The resultant sheared hair stands as a stark testament to the harsh conditions she endured—a journey marked with arduous trials. It speaks volumes, narrating a tale of undying perseverance and a willingness to give oneself for the greater good. And as if painting a poetic verse in the canvas, Rosales portrays the peacock feathers swirling gracefully in the wind, each feather carrying a tale of Oshun's undying commitment and formidable courage. They flutter as silent witnesses to Oshun's grandeur and her remarkable sacrifice, a testament to her formidable will and boundless love for humanity. The golden markings on Oshun's skin seem to echo across time, a reminder of a journey fraught with challenges yet marked by a profound triumph. Each marking is a golden verse that sings praises of a deity who embraced her vulnerability, turning it into a beacon of hope and a source of inspiration for generations to behold. Through Rosales's adept hands, the artwork transforms into a living scripture, a dynamic canvas that invites viewers to immerse themselves into a narrative that reverberates with elements of sacrifice, resilience, and an unfathomable love that seeks to preserve and nurture life in its many forms. Vitiligo has historically been associated with shame, embarrassment, and social isolation, particularly for people of color who may already face discrimination on the basis of their race or ethnicity. However, Rosales reclaims vitiligo as a source of empowerment and beauty, highlighting the unique and distinctive qualities of individuals who have this condition. In many of Rosales's paintings, vitiligo serves as a symbol of individuality and self-expression. Through her use of vitiligo, Rosales encourages viewers to challenge mainstream standards of beauty and embrace diversity and inclusivity. She celebrates the unique qualities that make each person special, regardless of whether those qualities conform to conventional norms or not. By doing so, Rosales reminds us of the power of art to challenge our perceptions and inspire us to see the world in new ways. Through her art, Rosales invites us to reconsider our perceptions of identity, representation, and self-expression, inspiring us to see the world through a more inclusive and compassionate lens. Her art is a testament to her commitment to representing marginalized communities and challenging conventional notions of beauty. By depicting individuals with vitiligo as strong, confident, and beautiful, she encourages us to embrace diversity and celebrate what makes us unique. *The Birth of Oshun* is a masterful work of art that combines technical excellence with deep emotional resonance. Through her use of color, composition, and symbolism, Harmonia Rosales captures the essence of one of the most beloved deities in the Yoruba pantheon and reminds us of the power and beauty of the natural world.

Moreover, the portrayal of Oshun as a curvy and not a skinny woman challenges the prevailing Western beauty standards that prioritize thinness. Oshun, an Orisha in Yoruba religion, is traditionally associated with beauty, love, and fertility. In many Yoruba and African diasporic traditions, beauty is often depicted in a way that celebrates diverse body types and embraces natural curves. By representing Oshun as a curvy woman, Rosales's artwork challenges the narrow and limited portrayal of beauty often found in Western societies. It offers an alternative vision of beauty that embraces and celebrates different body shapes and sizes.

The curvaceous depiction of Oshun highlights the idea that beauty is not limited to a specific body type but can be found in the uniqueness and diversity of individuals. The artwork by Rosales contributes to the broader movement of body positivity and challenges the harmful effects of unrealistic beauty ideals. It disrupts the narrative that equates beauty solely with thinness and invites viewers to reconsider their perceptions of beauty. By portraying Oshun in this way, the artist celebrates the beauty of Black women's bodies and challenges the Eurocentric beauty standards that have historically marginalized and excluded them. This portrayal also aligns with the cultural and spiritual significance of Oshun within the Yoruba tradition. Oshun is revered for her feminine energy and sensuality, and her portrayal as a curvy woman reflects her association with fertility and abundance. It reaffirms the value and beauty of diverse body types and celebrates the natural and inherent beauty found in women who do not conform to conventional Western beauty standards. The depiction of the goddess Oshun, who is revered in Yoruba religion as the embodiment of beauty, love, and fertility, adds another layer of cultural significance to the artwork. By using gold, black, and indigo-blue colors, and Yoruba mythological symbols, Rosales not only celebrates and honors Afro-Caribbean culture but also confronts the dominant narratives and Eurocentric standards in the art world. This approach emphasizes the importance of adopting diverse perspectives and amplifying marginalized voices in contemporary art. Another artistic choice worth analyzing here is the fact that Rosales decided to depict Oshun with extremely short hair, in opposition to the flowing long hair found in the original artwork depicting Venus. Therefore, this choice reverses the traditional notion of beauty that often prioritizes long, straight, or wavy flowing hair. Instead, Rosales celebrates the natural beauty and uniqueness of Black women, while also incorporating cultural symbols and themes into her artwork. Oshun's short hair represents a form of resistance to Eurocentric beauty standards suggesting that the short, Afro-textured hair should be celebrated in the process of affirming the natural beauty and uniqueness of Black women. Harmonia Rosales's decision to depict Oshun with short hair raises important questions about the role of beauty standards in society and the ways in which they can limit and marginalize certain groups. In advertisements, film, and television, light-skinned women with straight hair are often prominently depicted in positive roles, which reinforces the notion that short, kinky, or curly hairstyles are unacceptable (Patton 2006). Folola also argues that in Yoruba traditions "cut hair is usually associated with widows, while disheveled hair could signify a mad woman or a woman in mourning. These hairstyles are not manifestations of beauty, but their beauty-opposing and repudiating states manifest the symbolic power of their anti-aesthetic nature" (409).

Another key element found in this work of art is the peacock feathers. In particular, the two angels flying to the left side of Oshun are surrounded by flowing colorful peacock feathers. The peacock feathers in *The Birth of Oshun* are a key element of the composition and carry important symbolic meaning. Peacock feathers have been associated with various deities throughout history, and in this painting, they are used to represent Oshun's connection to the natural world and her status as a powerful and regal figure. The feathers themselves are intricately rendered, with each individual barb and eye meticulously detailed. Additionally, the colors of the peacock feathers, iridescent blues, greens, and gold complement the warm hues of Oshun's skin, adding to the overall harmony of the composition. Feathers are also considered symbols of *aché*[9] (West-Durán 206). Aché is a concept that originates from the Yoruba language and is also found in various Afro-Cuban and Afro-Brazilian religious traditions, such as Santeria and Candomble. The term *aché* encompasses a complex and multifaceted meaning, encompassing spiritual power, life force, and divine energy. In these traditions, aché represents the vital energy or spiritual power that flows through all living beings and the universe itself. It is considered a divine force that sustains and animates life. Aché is often associated with blessings, good fortune, and the manifestation of positive outcomes. Therefore, beyond their aesthetic value, the peacock feathers also carry layered symbolic meaning in the context of the Yoruba religion. In some interpretations, the eyes on the feathers are said to represent the all-seeing nature of the gods, while in others, they symbolize the interconnectedness of all things. Either way, their presence in *The Birth of Oshun* underscores the idea that Oshun is not just a powerful force of nature, but a divine entity with connections to the spiritual realm. As we learn in the book *Symbols in Arts, Religion and Culture* by Farrin Chwalkowski, "peacocks are a symbol of openness and acceptance. The peacock is also associated with the mind and is often a symbol of pride. The stunning tail, famous in the peacock's courtship display, heavy and conspicuous, makes the peacock vulnerable to predators and also to moralizers who judge this display to be an example of pride and a fall from grace" (475). In this book, Chwalkowski also references Oshun as one of the African goddesses of the Yoruba Orisha where she rules over love, intimacy, wealth, beauty, and dance. The author explains that

> Oshun represents the colors of the peacock and the parrot, her two primary bird companions, who both radiate beauty and joy in their colorful plumage. In the Yoruba, as well as in the Cuban, religious view Oshun is associated with the color yellow, the important metals gold and copper, peacock feathers, mirrors, and anything relating to charm, lightness, beauty, and sweet taste. Like these birds, beauty belongs to Oshun and reminds us of our ability to create beauty for its own sake. (475)

Therefore, the peacock feathers in this painting are a visually striking and symbolically rich element of Harmonia Rosales's masterful artwork. Their use underscores the importance of Oshun's connection to the natural world and her status as a transcendent figure worthy of awe and reverence. Peacock feathers then hold significant symbolic meaning. They are seen as a representation of spiritual power, protection, and divine connection. The eyes on the feathers are believed to represent the omniscience of the gods, while the colors of the feathers symbolize different aspects of nature and spirituality. In some interpretations, the blue represents the heavens and divinity, the green represents life and growth, and the gold represents wealth and prosperity. Moreover, peacock feathers are often used in religious ceremonies and rituals, where they are believed to attract positive energy and ward off negative energies. They are also used as offerings to deities and ancestors, as a way to honor and seek their blessings. It is then fundamental to point out how this symbolic element holds great spiritual significance in the Yoruba religion and is seen as an important tool for connecting with the divine and accessing spiritual power. The use of color and composition in the painting is also significant. The vibrant blues and yellows in the painting create a sense of warmth and energy, while the swirling lines and shapes give the painting a dynamic and fluid quality. The central figure of Oshun is positioned in the center of the painting, drawing the viewer's eye toward her and emphasizing her importance to the composition. It defies traditional representations of Black femininity by celebrating the power and beauty of Black women. Its message of hope and renewal makes it a particularly timely and resonant work of art in today's world.

This artwork represents an uncommon standpoint that just a few Afro-Latina artists embrace by identifying themselves as believers of cosmologies that fall outside the mainstream Christian faith that is practiced by the majority of the Latinx community (Souza 2022, 28–29). Centering Oshun in this artwork means challenging the Catholic history of oppression and the primordial fear of rejection and persecution that comes from the centuries of colonial imposition of Christianity.[10] Rosales's piece calls out the historical processes that outlawed and condemned non-Western spiritual traditions in Latin America and the Caribbean. *The Birth of Oshun* can also be seen as a visual representation of spiritualized feminism, carefully delineated over the years by feminist scholars of color such as Gloria Anzaldúa and Cherríe Moraga (1981), and Akasha Gloria Hull (2001). At the same time, the painting can be perceived as a medium of spiritualizing intersectionality (Méndez 2018, Facio & Lara 2014). This painting also represents the power of Black women to create life and bring beauty into the world. Rosales's painting is also notable for its use of color and composition that reflects the importance of the next generation in continuing and building on the traditions of the past.

The Creation of God

Another renowned piece by Rosales is *The Creation of God* (figure 2.2). In 2017, Rosales posted this image on her official Instagram page as her first completed work for her solo exhibition *Black Imaginary to Counter Hegemony*. This painting is also an oil-on-canvas piece in which Rosales re-creates Michelangelo's original *Creazione di Adamo*, which translated into English is *The Creation of Adam*. In this image, Rosales displays both God and Adam as Black women, challenging the traditional portraiture of white subjects and deconstructing the traditional way of thought. The composition of the painting is striking. One of the most remarkable features of Rosales's painting is the use of vibrant colors and patterns. The background is represented by a gray cloudy sky and God appears in a pink flowing dress that is inspired by traditional African textiles. God is surrounded by Black angels, further highlighting the artist's emphasis on diversity and representation. The pink flowing dress creates a sense of movement and dynamism that contrasts with traditional religious art's static and rigid poses. The color pink is often associated with femininity, love, and compassion. By dressing God in pink, Rosales may be

Figure 2.2. *Creation of God*, Harmonia Rosales, 2017, 48 × 60. *Source:* Courtesy of Artist.

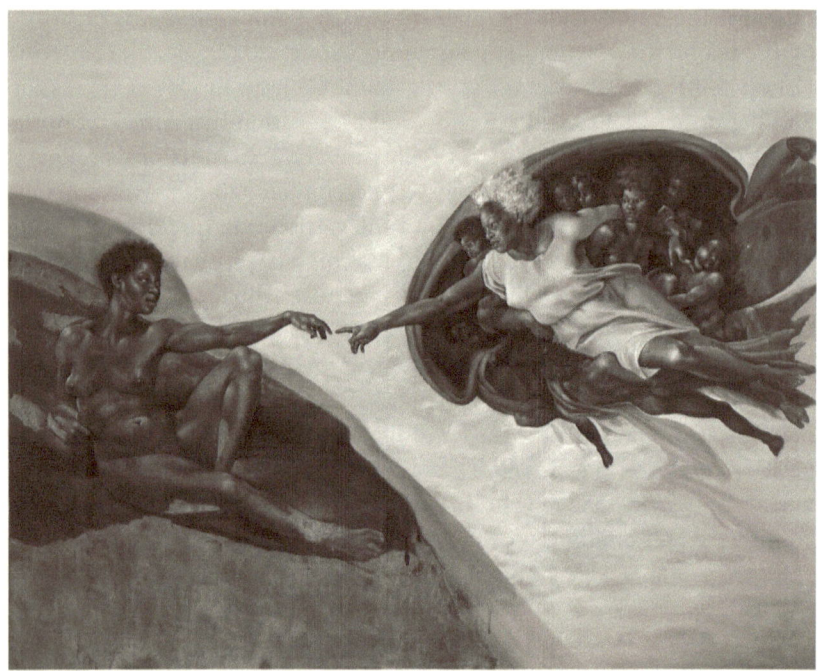

emphasizing the nurturing and compassionate aspects of divinity and highlighting the importance of empathy and care in our spiritual lives. Additionally, the pink dress may serve as a symbol of creation and fertility. The pink color can be associated with new beginnings and growth, which could be interpreted as a reference to the act of creation described in the biblical story of Genesis. In terms of symbolism, there is much to unpack in *The Creation of God*. By depicting God as a Black woman, Rosales defies traditional notions of spirituality. She highlights the fact that people of color and women have historically been excluded from positions of power and authority, even in religious contexts. By placing Black women at the center of creation, Rosales celebrates their strength and resilience. The figure of Eve as a Black woman also carries symbolic weight. In the Bible, Adam and Eve are portrayed as the first man and woman, and as such, they represent all of humanity. By depicting Eve as a Black woman, Rosales calls attention to the fact that people of color and women are often overlooked or erased from history. It can also be seen as a deliberate attempt to reclaim and rewrite history, particularly in light of the ongoing struggles for Black people to assert their voices and visibility in various aspects of modern society. Regarding Eve's appearance, it might be argued that the fact that she is depicted as completely naked is significant as it highlights the vulnerability and objectification that Black women have faced throughout history. In the biblical story, Eve is often portrayed as the source of sin and temptation, and her nakedness might be seen as symbolizing her shame and guilt.

However, Rosales's portrayal of Eve as comfortable and confident in her nudity could be interpreted as a subversion of traditional patriarchal narratives that seek to control and shame women's bodies. Furthermore, the depiction of Eve as a naked woman with short hair and vitiligo is also a deliberate artistic choice made by Harmonia Rosales. It is important to note that this is not a traditional representation of Eve in religious iconography, which often portrays her with flowing hair, perfect skin, and covered in fig leaves. The decision to depict Eve with short hair may be a nod to contemporary notions of gender and beauty standards. Short hair is often associated with a more masculine appearance, and so Rosales's decision to portray Eve in this way may reflect her desire to oppose traditional gender roles and stereotypes. Similarly, the depiction of Eve with vitiligo may be interpreted as a commentary on current societal values and attitudes toward physical difference and diversity. Vitiligo is a skin condition that causes patches of skin to lose pigment, and it can be stigmatized and marginalized in some cultures. By portraying Eve with vitiligo, Rosales may be drawing attention to the importance of embracing and celebrating diversity in all its forms. The platform on which Eve is shown lying is a significant element in the artwork, as it may have important symbolic connotations. The colors used in the platform, red and gold, are often associated with wealth, power, and luxury. In many cultures, these colors have been used to represent royalty or divinity, and they are often used in religious and ceremonial contexts. The use of these colors in Rosales's artwork could be interpreted as a nod to the biblical story of Adam and Eve, in which Eve is often depicted as a powerful and seductive figure who tempts Adam into sin. The red and gold platform on which she is shown lying may symbolize her power and allure, as well as her connection to the material world and its luxuries. Moreover, by placing Eve on this platform, Rosales may be highlighting her connection to nature, fertility, and the divine. The glittering platform may also symbolize the abundance and richness of life in the Garden of Eden before the fall. The colors and design of the platform serve to enhance the visual impact of the artwork and underscore its thematic significance. The choice of red and gold as the dominant colors of the platform may also reflect Rosales's own artistic style and sensibility, as she often uses bold, bright colors to create striking visual effects. Through her masterful use of composition, color, and symbolism, Harmonia Rosales invites viewers to rethink and question their own assumptions about gender, race, and the stories that shape our collective histories.

The image of God as a Black woman is a concept that has roots in various religious and spiritual traditions but is most commonly associated with African diaspora religions and feminist theologies. This image represents a challenge to dominant, patriarchal representations of God that are often seen as exclusively male, white, and Eurocentric. The image of God as a Black woman represents a way of connecting with the divine that is more inclusive and culturally relevant. It can be seen as a way of affirming the experiences and perspectives of Black women, who have often been marginalized and oppressed both within society and within religious institutions. By reimagining the image of God to reflect their own experiences, Black women are able to access a sense of spiritual empowerment and connection to the divine that may have been previously unavailable to them. The image of God as a Black woman is then seen as a way of reclaiming and valuing the experiences, knowledge, and wisdom of Black women, who have often been erased from religious narratives and history. By affirming the divine presence in Black women, communities are able to recognize and celebrate their own inherent worth and dignity. In the artist's words,

> Replacing the white male figures—the most represented—with people I believe have been the least represented can begin to recondition our minds to accept new concepts of human value. . . . If I can touch even a small group of people and empower them through the power of art, then I've succeeded in helping to change the way we see the world. . . . And when you consider that all human life came out of Africa, the Garden of Eden and all, then it only makes sense to paint God as a black woman, sparking life in her own image. (Rosales in Ruiz 2018)

In the process of analyzing the symbolism of God portrayed as a Black woman, it is worth mentioning the recently published book *God Is a Black*

Woman (2022) by activist, theologian, and social psychologist Christena Cleveland. Cleveland like Rosales re-imagined a new God she could relate to and advocate for. In the book, she recompiles her spiritual and intellectual journey of rediscovering of the ancient symbols of Black Madonnas, while affirming how she found healing in this process of transformation and liberation. The author talks about the Sacred Black Feminine by offering an exploration of the white patriarchal Christianity religion and culture. The term *sacred Black feminine* is used in popular culture and it refers to a spiritual concept that honors the divine feminine energy present in Black women. It recognizes and celebrates the unique cultural and historical experiences of Black women, who have often been marginalized and oppressed throughout history. The sacred Black feminine means embracing the power and wisdom of Black women as vessels of strength, resilience, creativity, and spirituality. It is a way of acknowledging the deep roots of Black women's culture, traditions, and spiritual practices and recognizing their contributions to society as mothers, healers, teachers, leaders, and activists. The sacred Black feminine is also about reclaiming and affirming the beauty and worth of Black women's bodies, which have been objectified and dehumanized by mainstream media and society. It is a way of empowering Black women to stand in their truth, honor their ancestry, and cultivate a deep sense of self-love and self-respect. Cleveland's point of view applies an intersectional approach when describing the reality of Black women, referring in various sections of the book to interlocking systems of oppression: "whitemalegod's toxic trifecta of racism, sexism, and classism landed on my Black female body and kept me on his plantation" (174), "The liberation of all Black women requires the dismantling of all systems of oppression—white supremacy, patriarchy, capitalism, Islamophobia, homophobia, transphobia, and more" (223) or "more than anything, we must eradicate the transphobia within ourselves and our communities. For if God is a Black woman, then She's a Black trans woman. Obviously" (232). Rosales's work challenges traditional notions of God's identity and the way that it has been represented in Western art history. By utilizing a Black female figure, Rosales highlights the need for greater representation and inclusivity in not just religious iconography, but in art as a whole. *The Creation of God* is a powerful work of art that resists our preconceptions about race, gender, and faith. It encourages us to examine the ways that art can be used to promote social change and to embrace a more inclusive and diverse worldview. This artwork prevents the historically white, male-dominated depictions of biblical scenes, which has sparked debate about the role of art in shaping religious beliefs and traditions. It cannot be denied that Rosales has brought important issues to the forefront of the conversation about religion and representation. Her work encourages us to question the status quo and to think critically about the ways in which we depict and understand religious stories and traditions.

Building on the conceptualization by Souza and Cespedes of "testimonios as ritual" (55), it is important to point out how the body of the Black Latina woman in artistic works by Afro-Cuban female artists like Rosales represents also a form of visual archive and *testimonio*. Souza and Cespedes describe the *testimonios* as ritual as the practice used to "merge the multiple feminist pathways we traverse towards the creation of our own decolonial perspective" (57). As Zamora points out, our bodies are archives that serve to preserve and collect collective and personal memories and re-create and disseminate knowledge. In the author's words: "Our bodies are central to that remembering. Memory is embodied" (1). As the two Afro-Latina scholars Souza and Cespedes confirm, "Our lives provide a history, and via the use of testimonio, we unpack the living archive that brings to the women of color kitchen table an AfroLatinx decolonial feminism that contributes to the ongoing political work of feminist theorizing" (43). In her book *Body of Writing: Figuring Desire in Spanish American Literature*, René Prieto argues that the body can be seen as an archive of cultural and historical experiences in Spanish American literature and cultural productions. According to Prieto, the body functions as an archive in several ways. First and foremost, it works as a site of memory. The body serves as a repository of personal and collective memories, including experiences of trauma, violence, and oppression. These memories are often repressed or silenced, but they are inscribed in the body and can be retrieved through acts of remembrance and (visual) storytelling. They can be a record of social and political history: The body can also be read as a historical document that reflects the social and political contexts in which it exists. For example, the body can reveal the effects of colonialism, nationalism, and globalization on individuals and communities. Ultimately, and more connected to the scope of this analysis, it can be seen as a medium of artistic expression. Prieto argues that the body can be a source of inspiration for artists and writers, who use it as a canvas or a tool to express their creative visions. Through visual art, Afro-Cuban American artists such as Harmonia Rosales can explore the body's potential for transformation, resistance, and liberation. These ideas are rooted in the conception that cultural productions can help us to reimagine our relationship with the body, reclaiming it from dominant cultural narratives and affirming its potential as a site of agency, creativity, and empowerment. Rosales's multicultural background, being born and raised in Chicago by a Cuban father and a Jewish Jamaican mother, provides a unique lens through which she re-imagines beauty, resistance, and liberation. This background allows her to draw from a rich tapestry of cultural influences, making her artistic expressions distinctly multifaceted. Examining how these reimaginings might differ for an Afro-Cuban woman living in Cuba today offers a critical comparative perspective. An artist residing in Cuba would navigate different sociopolitical and cultural landscapes, potentially leading to variations in themes and methods of artistic expression. The distinct experiences of Afro-Cuban women in Cuba, shaped by the island's unique cultural, economic, and political conditions, might result in different interpretations of resistance and empowerment. This comparative analysis enriches our understanding of how cultural and geographical contexts influence the articulation of identity and liberation in visual art.

Particularly useful for my interpretation of the work of Harmonia Rosales is also the feminist and Caribbean articulation of geographical and metaphorical borders by Eliana Rivero in her essay "Fronterisleña" (1994). The *Borderlands* identity she describes brings forth the imaginary of the coastline of an island, where the ocean and the water meet the land in a never-ending exchange and motion (340). This constant movement and negotiation evoke the multiplicity of Afro-Latina's consciousness and epistemology in continued dialogue with various systems of racialization, discrimination, gendering, and stereotyping. The theoretical notion of Fronterisleña fits perfectly with the geographical and political location of Cuba and the cultural and spiritual geographies of Afro-Cuban female artists. A Fronterisleña reading allows us to create alternative ways of being distinct from the North American and Anglophone hemisphere and empower Afro-Latinas to be able to connect with multiple continents and ancestors. In this context, it is worth mentioning that other Black Latina scholars have centered the experience of Afro-Latinas through the lenses of a decolonial feminist perspective that focus on Afro-Caribbean women and that create philosophical and intellectual bridges between Africa, the Americas, and the Caribbean (Coco Fusco 2001, Miriam Jiménez Román 2007, Angela Jorge 2010, and Figueroa 2020).

Harmonia Rosales's artwork has certainly sparked important conversations about representation and diversity within religious communities.

Her reimagining of biblical scenes with Black women as the central figures challenges the dominant narrative and traditional depictions of these stories. This has led to discussions about the importance of inclusivity and representation in religious art and the need for diverse voices and perspectives in the creation and interpretation of these works. Rosales's work has had a significant impact on the representation of people of color and women in religious art. By depicting religious figures and stories through a lens that is inclusive and diverse, Rosales has challenged traditional representations of these subjects that often privilege white, male perspectives. Her vibrant, colorful depictions of biblical scenes featuring people of color and more specifically Black women encourage a more inclusive and diverse understanding of religious history and traditions. This has helped to broaden the representation of marginalized communities in religious art and contribute to a more equitable and just society. Therefore, Rosales's work has been an important contribution to the ongoing struggle for diversity, inclusivity, and representation in contemporary art and culture.

The Virgin

The last art piece by Rosales analyzed in this chapter is *The Virgin* (figure 2.3), another artwork included in the Series *B.I.T.C.H. Black Imaginary to Counter Hegemony* (2017). In this image, we observe the Virgin Mary holding baby Jesus and depicted again as a Black woman. The Virgin is a pivotal work that reinterprets traditional religious iconography through the lens of Afro-diasporic spirituality. The painting presents a novel fusion of the Virgin Mary and Eve as a single Black figure, which highlights the origins and spiritual principles of the Lucumí religion. This portrayal is particularly significant in the context of Yorubaland, where women were historically revered as life-givers and protectors of sacred forces. The female Orishas such as Yemayá and Oya, who govern the oceans and winds respectively, embody the divine empowerment and safeguarding associated with female spirituality. Rosales's depiction is a groundbreaking synthesis of iconographic traditions, uniting the Virgin and Eve into one entity. The figure is illuminated in a cool, ethereal light, with intricate Orís patterns serving as the sole decoration. This minimalist approach emphasizes the figure's spiritual significance and directs the viewer's focus to the Virgin/Eve's direct gaze, which invites deep engagement and reflection. Encircled by red cloth, the figure represents the cyclical nature of life, symbolizing

Figure 2.3. *The Virgin*, Harmonia Rosales, 2018, 24 × 24. *Source:* Courtesy of Artist.

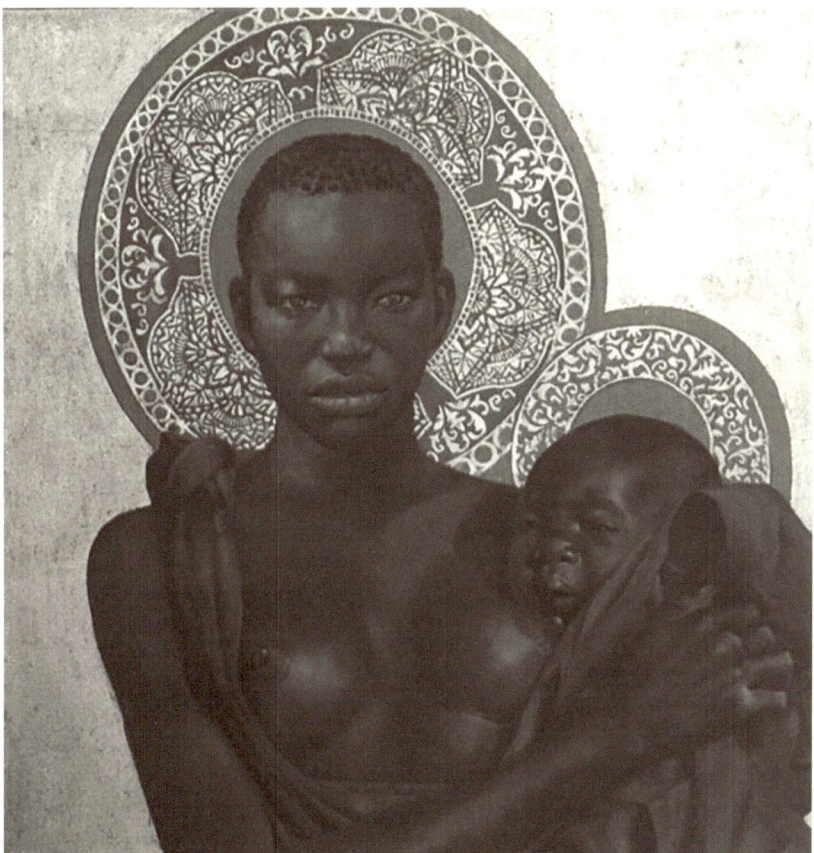

both continuity and transformation. Additionally, the painting's 24-karat gold leaf background and half-length portrait design draw on elements of Byzantine iconography. This choice situates Rosales's contemporary work within a historical framework, underscoring the enduring power of art to provide comfort and facilitate spiritual healing. Through this piece, Rosales reclaims and recontextualizes sacred symbols, extending the tradition of art as a transformative medium that bridges cultural and spiritual realms. In my analysis, I aim to explore how *The Virgin* redefines and revitalizes these sacred images, affirming the ongoing relevance of Afro-diasporic perspectives in global artistic discourse. It is fundamental to point out that the Black Virgin Mary holds significant cultural, spiritual, and political significance for many communities, especially among African American and Afro-Caribbean people. The image of the Black Virgin Mary is often seen as a representation of strength, hope, and resilience in the face of oppression and discrimination. The Black Virgin Mary serves as a symbol of hope and liberation and is a representation of the divine feminine that is accessible and relevant to Afro-diasporic experiences and identities. In terms of political significance, the Black Virgin Mary can be seen as a way of reclaiming religious imagery and symbolism that has been co-opted by dominant cultures and used to enforce cultural assimilation. It also represents a challenge to the notion that the divine can only be represented in the form of a white, European body. Furthermore, the veneration of the Black Virgin Mary has been used to promote social and political activism, especially in the fight against racial discrimination and injustices. The Black Virgin Mary serves as a source of empowerment and inspiration, reminding communities of their own strength and resilience in the face of adversity. This imaginary holds significant cultural, spiritual, and political significance for many communities and continues to play an important role in shaping their beliefs, values, and experiences.

The Virgin is a rich and complex work of art. At first glance, it appears to be a traditional depiction of the Virgin Mary, with her gentle gaze and flowing robes. However, on closer inspection, it becomes clear that Rosales has infused the image with a sense of contemporary urgency. One way to approach an analysis of this piece is through the lens of decolonial feminism (Lugones 2010; Curiel 2010). By placing the Virgin in a modern context and imbuing her with agency and strength, Rosales confronts the traditional role of women in Christian iconography[11] as passive and submissive. The Virgin Mary has often been used as a tool of colonization and cultural imposition. By reclaiming the iconography of the Virgin and infusing it with the spirit of resistance, Rosales subverts these oppressive structures and offers a vision of empowerment for communities that have been historically marginalized and oppressed. Moreover, the depiction of the Virgin Mary as a Black woman with naked breasts holding a Black baby Jesus is innovative and revolutionary because it challenges the traditional representation of the Virgin Mary in Christian art. Traditionally, the Virgin Mary has been depicted as a white, European-looking woman with a demure expression on her face, dressed in a modest, long-sleeved gown. By portraying the Virgin Mary as a Black woman with naked breasts, Harmonia Rosales subverts these traditional expectations and creates a new, powerful image that is both empowering and challenging.

The inclusion of a Black baby Jesus also serves to challenge traditional depictions of Jesus as a white, European-looking baby or man. We cannot forget that traditional representations of the Virgin Mary in Western art have upheld white Eurocentric beauty standards and have often been used to reinforce patriarchal power structures.

The choice to depict the Virgin Mary with naked breasts also reflects a broader trend toward celebrating and normalizing breastfeeding in public spaces, which can help to break down taboos and promote greater gender equity. While the concept of a naked-breasted virgin may be challenging for some, it is ultimately a strong statement of inclusivity and empowerment, promoting a more expansive understanding of femininity and motherhood. Furthermore, the use of this kind of iconography can serve to uplift marginalized communities who may not see themselves represented in mainstream religious imagery. It can provide a sense of empowerment and healing for communities that have historically been excluded from or oppressed within religious institutions. Ultimately, *The Virgin* is a remarkable work of art that speaks to important issues of race, gender, and power. By breaking down traditional boundaries and creating a new, unique image of the Virgin Mary, Harmonia Rosales invites us to rethink our assumptions about representation, identity, and agency in contemporary society. *The Virgin* is a powerful example of how contemporary artists can engage with historical traditions to create new forms of meaning and resistance. Moreover, by blurring the lines between past and present, Rosales invites us to rethink our assumptions about identity, power, and agency in today's world.

Another relevant aspect of Rosales's artistic technique that can be observed in *The Virgin* as well as all her creative pieces is the intentional employment of dark-skinned Black women. The consistency of this method of representation speaks to the histories of colorism[12] that affect BIPOC communities all around the world. The decision to represent all the figures in Rosales's painting as Black people with dark complexions can be interpreted in a number of different ways. One possible interpretation is that it is a deliberate act of reclaiming and celebrating Blackness, which has historically been stigmatized and devalued in many societies around the world. Moreover, the existing body of literature that underscores the importance of an intersectional approach to colorism and skin-tone trauma primarily focuses on the differential experiences between African American men and women with varying skin tones. Referred to as "gendered colorism," scholars have generally reached a consensus that African

American women bear a disproportionate burden of colorism compared to their male counterparts (Hill 2002, 78; Landor et al. 2013; Hunter 2007). Within a society that highly esteems lightness of skin as a dimension of beauty, dark-skinned African American women face inherent disadvantages. While both males and females encounter colorism, the psychological consequences, such as self-esteem (Thompson & Keith 2001) and body satisfaction (Glenn 2008; Hughes & Hertel 1990; Keith & Herring 1991), are more likely to negatively impact dark-skinned women (Nittle 2021; Hall & Fields-Smith 2019; Hunter 2007; Keith & Herring 1991). In this context, by celebrating Blackness and representing all of the figures in her painting as Black people, Rosales is making a bold statement about the beauty and power of Black identity. She is challenging the dominant cultural narratives that have historically portrayed Black people as inferior or less desirable, and instead presenting them as deserving of respect, admiration and recognition. Furthermore, the decision to depict the figures in the painting as dark-skinned may be seen as a nod to the rich and diverse cultural heritage of the Black community. In many parts of Africa, for example, dark skin is traditionally associated with beauty, strength, and spiritual power. By depicting the figures in her painting with dark complexions, Rosales is tapping into this tradition and celebrating the unique cultural identity of Black people around the world. The decision to represent all of the figures in Rosales' painting as Black people with dark complexions is a powerful affirmation of Black identity, culture, and history. It highlights the resilience and creativity of Black people in the face of systemic oppression and marginalization and celebrates the beauty and richness of their cultural heritage.

Colorism is an issue that has long plagued the Black community, both within and outside of the United States. This is the idea that individuals with lighter skin tones are viewed as more desirable or valuable than those with darker skin tones, perpetuating a hierarchy based on skin color. Rosales chose to depict all of the figures as dark-skinned individuals. This could be seen as a powerful statement against colorism, as it suggests that all shades of Blackness are equally beautiful and valuable. By avoiding the use of lighter-skinned individuals, Rosales challenges the notion that Black beauty is only achievable through proximity to whiteness. It is important to note that even within the Black community, there are still hierarchies based on skin color. Dark-skinned individuals may still face discrimination and stereotyping, particularly in media representation and certain social settings. By depicting the figures in her painting as very dark-skinned, Rosales may be making a statement about the importance of celebrating and affirming those who have historically been marginalized within the Black community itself. The use of dark-skinned women in Rosales's painting is multifaceted and thought provoking. While it could be seen as a celebration of Blackness and a rejection of colorism, it also highlights the ongoing complexities and hierarchies that exist within the Black community itself. The concept of colorism has had a significant impact on the representation of Black individuals in media and popular culture. Historically, lighter-skinned individuals have been favored in media representation over their darker-skinned counterparts. This preference for lighter skin has led to the underrepresentation and marginalization of dark-skinned individuals in mainstream media. Lighter-skinned individuals have been seen as more desirable and attractive and have therefore been more likely to be cast in leading roles and portrayed as successful and intelligent. Meanwhile, darker-skinned individuals have often been relegated to supporting roles or depicted as criminals or villains. This type of stereotyping reinforces the idea that lighter skin is superior and perpetuates harmful beauty standards that contribute to colorism.

The influence of colorism can also be seen in the beauty industry, where products designed to lighten skin tone are often marketed to Black consumers. This perpetuates the notion that lighter skin is more desirable and reinforces the idea that dark skin is something to be fixed or improved upon. The impact of colorism goes beyond media representation and has real-world consequences. Studies have shown that individuals with lighter skin tones receive more favorable treatment in the workplace, education, and health-care systems. This privilege can lead to unfair advantages and opportunities that are not available to their darker-skinned counterparts.

Conclusion

Through the analysis of three of Harmonia Rosales's most acclaimed artworks, it becomes evident that the artist deliberately creates work that challenges and subverts stereotypes rather than perpetuates them. She employs a range of artistic techniques and forms of subversion to disrupt dominant narratives and expectations. One of her key strategies involves applying a critical lens to her own identity and experiences, thereby acknowledging the complexity and diversity of her community. By grounding her work in her lived realities as a Black Latina in the United States, Rosales reflects on and challenges harmful stereotypes while also celebrating the richness and diversity of her multicultural identity. Rosales's art is deeply rooted in authenticity and empowerment, offering a counternarrative to the harmful stereotypes that have long constrained the representation of Black Latina women. Her work interrogates traditional gender roles by depicting Black women in positions of power and agency, often as central figures rather than as objects or supporting characters. In subverting conventional portrayals, she presents Black women as protectors and providers, challenging the gendered expectations commonly imposed on women, particularly women of color. Moreover, Rosales's work explores themes of identity and self-determination, portraying Black women as complex, multifaceted individuals with unique experiences and perspectives. In doing so, she contributes to dismantling narrow and limiting stereotypes about race and gender. Rosales's oeuvre offers a compelling critique of dominant narratives and representations of Black women, advancing a more inclusive and representative art world that better reflects the full diversity of human experience.

The three paintings analyzed demonstrate that it is possible to subvert patriarchal and sexist expectations and present women of color as complex, multifaceted individuals with their own agency and power. Rosales's emphasis on Black women as protectors and providers, rather than mere caregivers or nurturers, is especially powerful. By presenting women in these roles, she is showing that women have the capacity to be strong and capable leaders, rather than just supporting characters. Her artistic expressions also encourage other artists to explore themes of identity and self-determination and to present their subjects as complex individuals rather than one-dimensional stereotypes. This can be especially important for artists who belong to marginalized groups, as it allows them to challenge narrow and limiting representations of themselves and their communities. On her official website, we can read how Rosales was inspired by her own experiences as a woman of color to challenge traditional gender roles and stereotypes in her artwork. She has expressed frustration with the way women of color are often portrayed as one-dimensional and subservient in mainstream media and art, and wanted to create works that would challenge these representations. Rosales has also talked about how she draws inspiration from her Afro-Cuban heritage, and the traditions and stories of her ancestors. She sees her work as a way to honor these traditions and to celebrate the strength and resilience of Black women. In addition, Rosales has cited a desire to inspire other artists to explore similar themes in their own work, and to encourage viewers to see women of color in a new light. She believes that art has the power to shape perceptions and shift cultural narratives and sees her work as an important part of this process.

In conclusion, Harmonia Rosales visually embodies the AfroLatinx decolonial feminist position articulated by Souza and Céspedes, who describe it as "a third space that is multiple, relational, and differential," promoting the "racialized othering that captures the complexity of an identity that borders Blackness and Latinidad" (36). As survivors and archives of both enslavement and colonization, Afro-Latina artists like Harmonia Rosales resist binary categorizations and geographical limits, existing simultaneously in multiple worlds. In the words of Agustin Lao-Montes, "The multiple streams of Afro-Latina feminism . . . boom and bloom in the belly of the beast . . . explicitly seeking to decolonize the empire from within . . . Afro-Latina feminisms cross borders of multiple kinds (north/south, national, gender, sexual, linguistic) thus setting the stage for trans-local feminist solidarity and decolonial coalition-building for intersectional politics of liberation" (14). The visual art of Rosales fluctuates and resembles the constant state of diaspora, a diasporic identity suffering from multiple displacements and episodes of migration that unify while at the same time separating continents and regions.

This chapter has demonstrated how art can serve as a potent form of activism, possessing the unique ability to convey political and social messages while raising awareness about critical issues in a creative and impactful manner. ARTivist work, such as that of Harmonia Rosales, has the capacity to evoke emotions, challenge prevailing beliefs and attitudes, and catalyze public discourse and action. Throughout history, feminist artists like Rosales have employed various forms of artistic expression—including painting, sculpture, music, performance, and film—to address social and political issues, thereby driving change. Through her paintings, Rosales draws attention to pressing social and political issues, inspires transformative change, and mobilizes communities. Her art functions as a form of resistance against oppressive systems, amplifying the voices of marginalized communities. Moreover, Rosales's work transcends borders and cultures, fostering understanding and empathy on a global scale. She views her craft as a means of expressing dissent, challenging dominant ideologies, and advocating for those who have been historically marginalized. In this way, art emerges as a powerful vehicle for social justice and a formidable force for promoting positive change. This analysis also highlighted how

Rosales's art raises awareness about the ways in which Black women are frequently objectified and marginalized in Western society. Through her work, she advocates for greater representation and inclusion in the mainstream art world, challenging the exclusionary practices that have long dominated the artistic canon. Rosales's work not only critiques existing power structures but also envisions a more inclusive and equitable future, making her a pivotal figure in contemporary Decolonial AfroARTivism.

Chapter 3

Decolonizing Trans-Generational Memories of Slavery, Spirituality, and Exile

The Multicultural Artistic World of María Magdalena Campos-Pons

In analyzing Afro-Cuban femininity, it is crucial to incorporate perspectives that address the lived experiences of exile and migration, as these experiences often play a significant role in shaping the identities and artistic expressions of Afro-Cuban women. Exile offers a unique lens through which to understand the intersection of identity, culture, and displacement. Artists in exile navigate between multiple worlds, grappling with notions of belonging, memory, and loss, while maintaining ties to their cultural roots. This transnational existence enriches their work, providing a broader scope for understanding the complexities of race, gender, and identity across geographical borders. By including the perspective of exile, we gain a deeper understanding of how displacement impacts the creation of art, particularly as it relates to Afro-Cuban women whose experiences are marked by both the legacies of colonialism and the realities of migration. This approach also highlights the resilience and adaptability of these artists, showing how they use their art as a tool to negotiate their fragmented identities, bridge cultural divides, and offer new narratives of belonging that transcend the limitations of nationhood. María Magdalena Campos-Pons is a contemporary artist whose work exemplifies this intersection of identity and migration.

María Magdalena Campos-Pons is a contemporary artist whose work is as diverse and complex as her own background. Born in Cuba in 1959 and now based in Nashville, Tennessee, Campos-Pons draws inspiration from her Afro-Cuban heritage, as well as her experiences living in both the Caribbean and the United States. Her art spans a wide range of mediums, including photography, installation, sculpture, and performance, and explores themes such as identity, memory, migration, and spirituality. With a career spanning over three decades, Campos-Pons has exhibited her work around the world and is recognized as one of the most important contemporary artists of her generation. Through her art, she invites viewers to explore their own identities and experiences and to engage in a dialogue about the complexities of culture, history, and belonging. María Magdalena Campos-Pons is an artist whose work speaks to the soul, transporting viewers to a world that is at once surreal and grounded in reality. Her multidisciplinary approach results in a body of work that is both stunningly beautiful and deeply thought provoking. Her work often incorporates personal stories and experiences, inviting viewers to reflect on their own connections to history and culture. Through her art, Campos-Pons invites us to explore the complexities of our world and to connect with the humanity that binds us all. Her work is a testament to the power of art to heal, to inspire, and to challenge us to see the world in new and meaningful ways.

Through her art, she subverts hegemonic narratives of Western history, especially the ones surrounding the history of slavery and monotheistic religions. Campos-Pons possesses a multicultural identity rooted in her Cuban, Chinese, and Nigerian heritage, which is a significant influence on her artwork. She was born in Cuba to a Chinese-Cuban father and a Nigerian-Cuban mother, and her work often explores themes of cultural identity, memory, and the legacies of slavery and colonialism, drawing from her experiences growing up in Cuba and her connections to her ancestral roots. In her photography and video installations, Campos-Pons incorporates symbolic imagery and references to her multicultural background. Campos-Pons's sculptures also reflect her multicultural identity, often incorporating traditional African and Chinese materials and techniques. Through her art, Campos-Pons seeks to bridge cultural divides and explore the complex layers of identity that shape our lives. Her work stands as a powerful testament to the diversity of human experience and the ways in which art can connect us to our shared humanity. The element of water accompanied by the ocean and the color blue are prominent in many of her works, reminding us of the trauma of separation from the transatlantic slave trade, histories of exile, and visual narratives around the

Yoruba religion. Starting from the late 1980s, her paintings have attracted international attention with her work being exhibited throughout the world, including at documenta 14 in Kassel and Athens, the Museum of Modern Art in New York, the Venice Biennale, the Dakar Biennale, the *In the Mind's Eye: Landscapes of Cuba* at the Patricia & Phillip Frost Art Museum in Miami, and the Sharjah Biennial. At the Rencontres in Bamako, viewers were able to discover works that evoked stories about the transatlantic slave trade, indigo and sugar plantations, religious practices, and revolutionary uprisings, including *When I'm Not Here/Estoy Allá* (1997), *Abridor de Caminos* (Pathfinder) (1997), *Nesting* (2000), *Dreaming of an Island* (2008), and *Replenishing* (2001). The last two mentioned pieces together with the piece *De las dos aguas* (2007) will be the center of my analysis in this chapter.

Among the Afro-Cuban female artists analyzed in this book, Campos-Pons is undoubtedly the creator who has caught more attention from scholars and critics with several journal articles and book chapters published about her multimedia artistic work. This is probably also due to the fact that Campos-Pons had a long and prolific career already in the visual arts if compared with other emerging Afro-Cuban artists analyzed in this book. For instance, Casamayor-Cisneros (2013) explores new expressions of the Afro-diasporic experience in the Americas by examining the work of María Magdalena Campos-Pons and Puerto Rican writer Mayra Santos Febres. The author studies particular processes of gender, race, and national identification in the Caribbean and its diaspora. Body, performance, erotics, and ritual articulate the main axes of her inquiries (138). Other relevant studies include the ones by Salah Hassan (2004), David Hammons (2008), Michael Harris (2011), Joyce Beckenstein (2016), Alan West-Durán (2013), and an interview conducted with her at Vanderbilt University (Campos-Pons & Luis 2011). West-Durán in particular discusses how Campos-Pons's aesthetic concerns are deeply imbued with the aquatic and cosmological qualities of Yemayá and Ochún (198), citing works such as *I Am a Fountain* (1990), *The Seven Powers* (1992), *The Seven Powers Come by the Sea* (1992), *When I'm Not Here/Estoy Allá* (1994), *When I'm Not Here/Estoy Allá* (1997), *Susurro* (1997), *Spoken Softly with Mama* (1998), *Replenishing* (2001), and *Elevata* (2002), and many others. María-Magdalena Campos-Pons's skin-themed photography is analyzed by Frédéric Lefrançois. The author investigated how the piece called *The Right Protection, Lithograph, and Paper Pulp* (1999) depicts eyes with varying iris complexion and how these are "interspersed on a photograph of the artist's back skin: there are blue eyes, brown eyes, black eyes all over her body. So much so that the picture creates the impression that she finds herself surrounded, even immersed in a sea of eyes" (8). In the same essay, Lefrançois briefly mentions the piece *Replenishing* (2003), in which we find "the larger narrative of transgenerational diasporic connectedness which is often symbolized by the presence of stylized umbilical cords" (8). In this artwork, the Afro-Cuban woman's body ceases to be a posing object and becomes a looking agent that challenges the spectator's traditional role (Cheryl and Hassan 2008, 73). Casamayor-Cisnero in her study, "Cuando Las Negras Se Desnudan: La Experiencia Inasible Del Cuerpo Caribeño y Afro-diaspórico En La Creación Plástica de María Magdalena Campos-Pons y La Narrativa de Mayra Santos Febres," investigates Afro-Caribbean culture and its diaspora, delving into the artistic endeavors of two esteemed Black women from the region: María Magdalena Campos-Pons, a visual and performative artist from Cuba residing in the United States, and Mayra Santos Febres, a Puerto Rican writer. By exploring these artists' work, the author aimed to uncover fresh perspectives on the Afro-diasporic experience in the Americas, focusing on examining the interplay of gender, race, and national identity, with a particular emphasis on the body, performance, eroticism, and ritual as key elements that shape her inquiries. All these previous works are testimony of the enormous significance of Maria Magdalena Campos-Pons's work that is also powerfully autobiographical. As Sally Berger stated, "It encompasses a larger story. It reveals a history of survival—of a culture, a religion, and a people—from the oceanic voyage from Africa during the slave trade in the 18th century, to its aftermath in Cuba on the sugar plantations, to the present day in the United States. It is a felt history—not one of the rhetorical facts and figures told through non-spoken, fragmented narratives" (122).

Replenishing

Replenishing, 2001 (figure 3.1) features seven large-format Polaroids, resembling a modern altarpiece, and depicts the artist and her mother looking straight at the camera/viewer like two goddesses. A particular biographical detail about this piece is that when the image was shot, the two Afro-Cuban women had not seen each other since 1991, the year when the Campos-Pons left the Cuban island for the US. As we take in the striking image, we observe that both figures are adorned with strings

Figure 3.1. *Replenishing*, María Magdalena Campos-Pons, 2001. Composition of seven Polaroid Polacolor Pro 20 × 24 in. photographs. Framed: approximately 88.5 × 66 in. overall. *Source:* Courtesy of Artist.

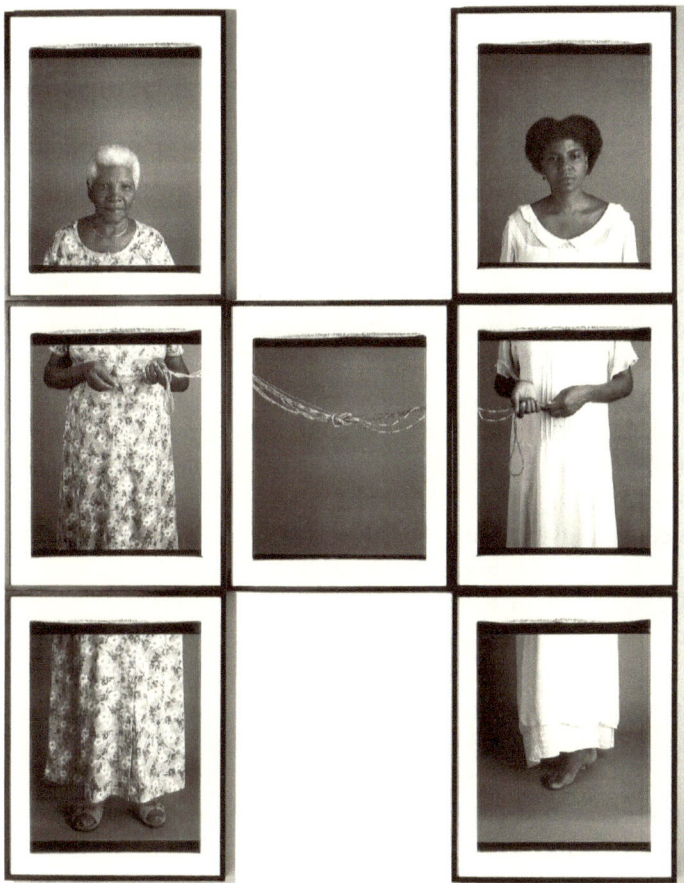

of multicolored pearls, each hue symbolizing a distinct Yoruba deity. In the mother's hands, the light-blue pearls signify Yemayá, the powerful and nurturing goddess of the sea, who is often associated with motherhood and protection. Campos-Pons herself is draped in flowing white garments reminiscent of those worn by initiates in Santería rituals, a visual homage to her spiritual and cultural heritage. She holds strands of gold and amber pearls speckled with crimson, colors intimately tied to Oshun, the Yoruba goddess of love, fertility, and feminine power. Together, the pearls and garments create a vivid tableau that intertwines personal and communal histories, while evoking the spiritual depth and cultural resilience embedded in Yoruba cosmology. More specifically, Yemayá, in the geographical context of Cuba is considered the Virgin of Regla, a port city near Havana. She is the Orisha of all waters and particularly the ocean. In this respect, Lydia Cabrera writes, "Yemayá is the Universal Queen because she is Water, fresh and salty, the Sea, the Mother of all that is created. She nourishes all, since the World is earth and sea, earth and all that lives on earth, and thanks to Her the earth is nourished. Without water, animals, humans, plants would all die" (20–21). Lydia Cabrera, a renowned Cuban ethnographer and folklorist, highlights the significance of Yemayá as the Universal Queen, emphasizing her essential role as the embodiment of water in its various forms and her crucial contribution to the sustenance of all life on Earth. Cabrera describes Yemayá as encompassing both fresh and salty water, representing the duality and vastness of the seas. As the Sea and the Mother of all creation, Yemayá holds a central position within the pantheon of Orishas. She symbolizes the nurturing and life-giving qualities of water, which is fundamental to the existence of all living beings. Water is a universal necessity, and Yemayá's association with it positions her as a pivotal figure in the cosmology of Afro-Cuban religious beliefs. Cabrera's words convey the vital role that Yemayá plays in the ecological balance, ensuring the fertility and abundance of the Earth. The recognition of water's indispensable role in sustaining life extends beyond its physical properties. Yemayá embodies the spiritual and symbolic significance of water, representing emotions, intuition, and purification. Water is seen as a conduit for spiritual energy and a source of cleansing and renewal. Yemayá's domain over water encompasses these aspects, reflecting her ability to guide and heal not only the physical world but also the spiritual well-being of individuals. By acknowledging the essential nature of water, Cabrera highlights the inherent vulnerability and dependence of all living beings on this precious resource. Without water, life as we know it would cease to exist. Through her words, Cabrera emphasizes the profound interconnectedness between humans and the natural world, reminding us of our responsibility to protect and cherish the environment. On closer examination of the central focus of the piece, one observes that the two necklaces are intricately knotted together, both physically and metaphorically linking the two generations depicted. In *Replenishing*, the use of lighting and contrasts accentuates the striking resemblance between the two women. Campos-Pons effectively narrates her own story of separation, emphasizing the profound bond between herself and her mother—a connection that transcends physical borders, including the ocean. Her work frequently assumes an autobiographical character, exploring themes such as the complex relationship with her mother, the experience of exile, the legacy of the slave trade in her hometown of Matanzas, Cuba, and broader topics of family and motherhood.

The artwork above is rich in symbolism and allusions to the Afro-Cuban religious traditions, specifically the Yoruba pantheon, where each color and type of bead represents a particular Orisha, or deity.[1] The blue and clear beads held by the older woman signify Yemayá, the two-headed goddess of the sea, while the pearls represent Obatalá, the creator god, indicating serenity. The younger woman, dressed in white clothing, holds the red-spotted yellow and amber beads associated with Ochún, who is associated with sexuality and motherhood. This chapter will explore the relevance of the representation of these two generations of Afro-Cuban women in the artwork, highlighting their cultural and spiritual heritage, and the complexities of their experiences as Black women in Cuba. The religious and cultural heritage of the Afro-Cuban people is deeply intertwined with the Yoruba tradition, brought to Cuba by enslaved Africans during the colonial era. The Yoruba religion, also known as Santería, is a syncretic blend of African spirituality, Catholicism, and Native American beliefs, developed as a way for the enslaved Africans to preserve their religious practices and customs under the guise of the Catholic Church. The religion is centered on the belief in Orishas, or deities, each with their own colors, symbols, and personalities, and devotees seek their guidance and blessings through offerings, rituals, and divination. In *Replenishing* the two women hold strings of beads that are particular to their respective Orishas. Yemayá, the goddess of the sea, is associated with motherhood, nurturing, and fertility, and her blue and clear beads represent the colors of the ocean and sky, as well as her dual nature as a fierce and protective mother figure. Obatalá, the creator god, is associated with wisdom, purity, and peace, and his pearls indicate his serene and tranquil nature, as well as his role as a source of guidance and clarity. Ochún, the Orisha associated with love, beauty, and sensuality, is represented by the red-spotted yellow and amber beads held by the younger woman, indicating her playful and seductive qualities, as well as her connection to the natural world and its cycles of life and renewal. Moreover, as West-Durán reveals when analyzing the work of Campos-Pons, "the combination of Yemayá and Ochún is not uncommon, they are known as sister Orishas and are associated with salt water and fresh water, respectively" (201). Through her art, Campos-Pons explores the interconnectedness and spiritual resonance of these sister Orishas, creating a visual dialogue that transcends cultural boundaries.

Yemayá and Ochún hold important roles in Afro-Cuban religious traditions, specifically within the practice of Santería. While they are associated with different types of water, their complementary natures make them natural counterparts and allies within the spiritual realm. Their relationship is characterized by a sisterhood, emphasizing their shared origins and the synergy between salt water and fresh water. By incorporating these deities in her visual art, Campos-Pons explores the complex and multifaceted aspects of water as a symbol of life, spirituality, and cultural heritage. In the context of coloniality, water is also a medium of remembrance and resistance against the attempt to erase the past. As M. Jacqui Alexander points out, "Rocks hold memory. Land holds memory," and referring to the mystical element of water the author asserts that it "will call you by your ancient name, and you will answer because you will not have forgotten. Water always remembers" (274). Through her artistic expression, she brings forth the profound symbolism and significance of Yemayá and Ochún, bridging the gap between spirituality, aesthetics, and cultural identity. The combination of Yemayá and Ochún in Campos-Pons's work also serves as a representation of the syncretism found in Afro-Cuban religious practices. Santería, which originated from the blending of Yoruba traditions brought by enslaved Africans and Catholicism, embodies a fusion of diverse beliefs and symbolism. This syncretic approach to spirituality allows for the harmonious integration of various cultural elements, creating a unique and vibrant artistic expression. It is also fundamental to clarify the multidimensional aspect of an Orisha. West-Durán does exactly that when he states the following:

> Many well-intentioned researchers have called them divinities or gods, which is not exactly accurate. Orishas are the varied and multifaceted manifestations of all the divine energies in the universe that together would constitute God, which is too vast for our human capacities to comprehend, so we give names and attributes to these manifestations. It is the proliferation of names and orishas that erroneously gives the impression that Ocha is polytheistic. Others have characterized the orishas as guardian angels or saints (here both show Catholic influences), as well as representing natural forces (water, wind, lightning, fire, earth,

herbs, etc.), the latter not surprising for a religion born in rural surroundings and intricately entwined with nature. Still others see the orishas as a metaphysical principle or as an archetype. As archetypes they are viewed as people, like ancestral spirits, but more powerful. They are described as personifications of certain personalities. An orisha materializes in the life, actions, and the personality of a person. They are role models: parent, sibling, public defender, psychologist, botanist, healer, spiritual advisor. This view is common because believers develop a definite personal relationship with their tutelary orisha, and the orisha becomes a member of the family. (2011, 296)

West-Durán intervention delves into the complexity and diverse interpretations of the Orishas, challenging simplistic characterizations of them as gods or divinities. Instead, the Orishas need to be depicted as multifaceted manifestations of divine energies that collectively constitute a higher power, referred to as God, which surpasses human comprehension. His quote emphasizes that the proliferation of names and attributes associated with the Orishas can lead to misconceptions about the nature of the religion. It clarifies that the multitude of Orishas does not imply polytheism within the practice of Ocha, but rather signifies the various manifestations of the divine within the universe. This concept aligns with the understanding that the Orishas represent different facets of existence, such as natural forces and archetypal principles. The influence of Catholicism is acknowledged in the characterization of the Orishas as guardian angels or saints, illustrating the syncretism present in Afro-Cuban religious practices. This syncretic blend of Yoruba traditions and Catholicism has led to the incorporation of certain Catholic elements, which are used as reference points to describe the Orishas. Furthermore, the Orishas are associated with natural forces, reflecting the religion's rural origins and its deep connection to the natural world. West-Durán point of view highlights the Orishas as metaphysical principles or archetypes, portraying them as powerful ancestral spirits with distinct personalities. It suggests that Orishas manifest in the lives of individuals, influencing their actions, personalities, and roles within society. They are regarded as role models, embodying characteristics such as parental figures, siblings, defenders, psychologists, botanists, healers, and spiritual advisers. This perspective emphasizes the personal and familial relationships that practitioners develop with their tutelary Orisha, considering them as integral members of their spiritual family.

The representation of Afro-Cuban women in *Replenishing* is multifaceted, reflecting the complexities of the two women's experiences in Cuba, as well as their resilience and creativity in the face of oppression and marginalization. The two women in the artwork embody different generations, with the older woman representing the traditional values and customs of the Yoruba religion, passed down through generations of women, while the younger woman represents the contemporary realities and aspirations of Afro-Cuban women in the present day. The representation of two generations of Afro-Cuban women holds immense cultural and historical significance. The art piece speaks to the shared experiences of the mother and daughter and the connections they hold to their heritage and spirituality. The use of multicolored beads, their colors, and their association with different Orishas in the Yoruba pantheon, highlights the importance of African traditions in the lives of Afro-Cubans. In many ways, *Replenishing* serves as a celebration of the resilience and strength of Afro-Cuban women. The artist herself share with the Brooklyn Museum a feminist artist statement in which she states,

> I am a sculptor, installation artist, videographer, and photographer. My work renders elements of personal history and persona that have universal relevance. I exploit a variety of photographic means, portraiture, landscape, and documentary photography. In an effort to create historical narratives that illuminate the spirit of people and places, past and present. My subjects are often my Afro-Cuban relatives as well as myself. My themes are cross cultural, and cross generational; race and gender expressed in symbols of matriarchy and maternity are thematic ideas. The salient tie to familiar and cultural history vastly expands for me the range of photographic possibilities.

Maria Magdalena Campos-Pons's statement reveals several key aspects of her artistic practice and themes. We learn that she engages with a diverse range of mediums, including sculpture, installation, videography, and photography. She also employs various photographic techniques such as portraiture, landscape, and documentary photography. This demonstrates her versatility and willingness to experiment with different artistic forms and methods. The artist emphasizes the importance of personal history and persona in her work, but also highlights their universal relevance. By drawing from her own experiences and exploring her Afro-Cuban heritage, Campos-Pons seeks to create art that resonates with a broader audience and addresses themes that transcend individual narratives. The artist aims to construct historical narratives that shed light on the spirit of people and places, both past and present. Through her artistic endeavors, she strives to capture the essence of individuals and communities, and by doing so, she contributes to a broader understanding of history and culture. Campos-Pons frequently portrays her Afro-Cuban relatives and herself as subjects, reflecting her personal connections and experiences. By incorporating themes of race, gender, matriarchy, and maternity, Campos-Pons explores identity and representation in her work. This indicates her commitment to addressing and challenging social and cultural constructs through art. She expands the boundaries of photography by incorporating familiar and cultural histories into her work. By integrating personal and collective narratives, she broadens the scope and potential of the medium, allowing for new ways of understanding and representing diverse experiences. Campos-Pons's feminist statement highlights her multifaceted approach to art, her exploration of personal and universal themes, and her commitment to creating historical narratives that challenge traditional representations and expand the possibilities of photography.

In the first image analyzed here, Campos-Pons—wears a dirty white dress, indicating her status as an initiate in the Santería religion. Her mother floral and light blue dress evokes the connection to the sea, as represented by Yemayá and speaks to the importance of water and the natural world in Afro-Cuban traditions. The pearls associated with Obatalá indicate serenity and peace, suggesting that the older woman has found a sense of calm and clarity in her life. In contrast, the younger woman, the artist herself, holds the red-spotted yellow and amber beads associated with Ochún, a deity connected to sexuality and motherhood. The colors of these beads, and the fact that they are held by the younger woman, suggest a sense of vitality and vibrancy. The fact that Ochún is connected to motherhood is also significant, as it speaks to the continuation of traditions and the passing down of knowledge from one generation to the next. Together, the two women in *Replenishing* embody the cyclical nature of life and the importance of passing down knowledge and traditions from one generation to the next.

The title *Replenishing* is significant because it speaks to the idea of renewal and restoration. The two figures in the artwork appear to be replenishing themselves, both physically and spiritually. Furthermore, the choice of the title *Replenishing* may also allude to larger themes of replenishment and restoration in the natural world especially in relation to the Orishas celebrated in the art piece. Yemayá, the goddess of water is also seen as a symbol of life and renewal, and by placing this deity symbolically in the art piece, Campos-Pons may be suggesting the need for us to reconnect with the natural world to find healing and restoration. The chosen title adds an additional layer of meaning to the artwork, suggesting themes of self-care and restoration, while also invoking the larger concepts of rebirth and renewal in the natural world. It invites viewers to contemplate their own need for replenishment and restoration and to connect with the deeper meanings behind the artwork. Another significant aspect of the image is the way in which it highlights the connections between spirituality, identity, and heritage. The use of multicolored beads, each associated with a specific Orisha, speaks to the richness and diversity of Afro-Cuban traditions. Each bead has its own significance and meaning, and together they form a complex tapestry of beliefs and practices. The fact that the two women in the painting hold different sets of beads speaks to the individuality and uniqueness of each person's spiritual journey. At the same time, the fact that they are both initiates in the Santería religion speaks to the shared experiences and connections that bind them together. In many ways, *Replenishing* can be seen as a response to the erasure of African traditions in Cuba. Throughout history, Afro-Cubans have faced discrimination and marginalization, and their cultural heritage has often been suppressed or erased. The use of multicolored beads in the painting, and their association with different Orishas, speaks to the persistence of African traditions despite these challenges. The fact that the two women in the painting are Afro-Cuban also speaks to the resilience and strength of this community. The representation of two generations of Afro-Cuban women speaks to the importance of passing down knowledge and traditions from one generation to the next. Yemayá is the mother of all Orishas, and she is often associated with fertility and creation. The pearls that the older woman is holding are a reminder of the importance of serenity and wisdom in the lives of Afro-Cuban women. The artwork also represents the way in which spirituality can provide a sense of peace and calm in the midst of chaos and turmoil.

María Magdalena Campos-Pons's artwork *Replenishing* speaks to the trauma of separation between the mother who remained in Cuba and the daughter who migrated to the United States. The artwork represents the way in which the two women have been separated by distance and time, yet they remain connected through their shared cultural heritage and spirituality. The younger woman, who is the artist herself, migrated to the United States, while the older woman, who is the artist's mother, remained in Cuba. The artwork represents the way in which migration can create a sense of displacement and disconnection from one's cultural heritage and spiritual roots. The artwork also speaks to the trauma of separation between the mother and daughter. The fact that the two women are holding onto strings of beads represents the way in which they are holding onto their cultural heritage and spirituality as a way of coping with the trauma of separation. The artwork is a representation of the resilience and strength of Afro-Cuban women who have had to endure the trauma of separation and displacement. As Verene and Beckles point out, Cuba, together with all the islands of the Caribbean "share the legacies of European colonialism, the transatlantic slave trade, and forced migration" (25). This previous quote highlights the historical and cultural interconnectedness of Cuba and other Caribbean islands, emphasizing the common legacies they share. It draws attention to the deep-rooted historical events and processes that have shaped the region and continue to influence its social, economic, and cultural dynamics. European colonialism played a pivotal role in shaping the Caribbean islands, including Cuba. Starting in the late fifteenth century, European powers, primarily Spain and later Britain, France, and the Netherlands, established colonies in the region. These colonial powers exploited the natural resources, established plantations, and enforced systems of labor, particularly through the transatlantic slave trade. The transatlantic slave trade, one of the darkest chapters in human history, brought millions of Africans to the Caribbean as enslaved individuals. The trade not only caused immense human suffering but also profoundly impacted the cultural fabric of the Caribbean islands. African traditions, languages, religions, and culinary practices were forcibly transplanted and mixed with Indigenous and European cultures, resulting in the rich and diverse cultural heritage seen in the Caribbean today. Forced migration is another significant legacy of colonialism. Recognizing these shared legacies of historical injustices and their ongoing implications, such as economic disparities, social inequalities, and cultural hybridity, is key for understanding diasporic visual art. Understanding and addressing these legacies is crucial for a comprehensive analysis of the Caribbean's past and present. It allows for a more nuanced understanding of the region's complexities and challenges. Furthermore, recognizing shared legacies can foster a sense of unity and solidarity among Caribbean nations' artists, promoting cooperation and collective efforts to address common issues and pursue shared goals.

Diasporic artists like Campos-Pons deal with one of the legacies of colonialism that is forced relocation. Visual artists have the ability to withdraw themselves from the colonial matrix of power and relocate to alternative spaces, a method theorized by art theoretician René Louise as "conceptual marooning" (64–65). Antonio Benitez-Rojo explains that we often see those spaces where the subaltern finds alternative and resistant methods of expression "as inhabited by desire, sexuality, power, nationalism, violence, knowledge, or culture" (150–51) but they are as legitimate and valuable as the ones that constitute mainstream narratives or official history. Benitez-Rojo highlights the importance of recognizing and valuing alternative forms of expression found within spaces occupied by marginalized and subaltern groups. This perspective challenges the tendency to overlook or dismiss these spaces, often associated with desire, sexuality, power, nationalism, violence, knowledge, or culture, by emphasizing their legitimacy and value. The concept of the subaltern refers to groups or individuals who are socially, politically, and economically marginalized within a society. These groups may have limited access to mainstream platforms and face systemic oppression and silencing. Benitez-Rojo's assertion challenges the notion that mainstream narratives or official history are the sole repositories of truth and legitimacy. It encourages a more inclusive and diverse approach to knowledge production and interpretation. Alternative expressions emerging from subaltern spaces offer valuable perspectives, counternarratives, and critiques that can shed light on hidden histories, marginalized voices, and underrepresented experiences. By valuing and engaging with these alternative expressions, we promote social justice, inclusivity, and the democratization of knowledge. We recognize the agency and resilience of subaltern groups in shaping their own narratives and contesting dominant power structures. This recognition paves the way for a more equitable society that appreciates the diverse ways in which individuals and communities navigate and negotiate their existence. As Lefrançois Frédéric accurately states "Caribbean diasporic art frequently highlights the re-appropriation of traumatic history encoded in collective memory" where "history may indeed be seen as the archive that stimulates the visual aesthetics" (5). Lefrançois's perspective suggests that history acts as an archive that serves as a catalyst for the visual aesthetics present in different forms of art. Caribbean diasporic art refers to artistic expressions created by individuals from Caribbean backgrounds who have migrated to other parts of the world. These artists often carry with them a deep connection to their cultural heritage and the historical experiences of the Caribbean region. Lefrançois argues that within this artistic context, there is a prevalent tendency to explore and reinterpret traumatic histories that are ingrained in the collective memory of Caribbean communities. Traumatic history refers to the experiences of colonization, slavery, indentured labor, displacement, and other forms of oppression that have had a profound impact on the Caribbean region. These historical events have left deep scars and imprints on the collective consciousness of Caribbean communities. By re-appropriating traumatic history in their artwork, Caribbean diasporic artists engage with the complex and often painful aspects of their cultural heritage. History, in this context, serves as an archive that informs and inspires the visual aesthetics of Caribbean diasporic art. History acts as a source of inspiration and raw material that artists draw on to create their works. By delving into the historical narratives, these artists engage with the collective memory, bringing forth marginalized stories, challenging dominant narratives, and reclaiming their cultural identities. Through their art, Caribbean diasporic artists aim to shed light on the experiences, struggles, and resilience of Caribbean communities, making visible what may have been marginalized or erased in mainstream narratives. They recontextualize traumatic histories, offering alternative perspectives and interpretations. Furthermore, the act of re-appropriation in Caribbean diasporic art signifies a form of resistance and empowerment. By reclaiming and reinterpreting traumatic history, artists assert their agency and challenge the ways in which history has been constructed and portrayed. It becomes a way to reclaim and reconstruct narratives that have often been distorted or silenced.

Moreover, the body of Afro-diasporic female artists becomes a vehicle for reconstruction and self-preservation, recalling Foucault's conception of the body as "a text upon which social reality is inscribed" (Schildkrout, 319). By drawing a parallel to Michel Foucault's conception of the body as a text on which social reality is inscribed, I suggest that Afro-diasporic artists such as Campos-Pons use their bodies to challenge and reshape societal norms and narratives. These artists, through their creative expressions, reclaim their identities and experiences, often addressing the intersections of race, gender, and cultural heritage. Their bodies become a powerful medium through which they engage in processes of reconstruction and self-preservation. My reference to Foucault's conception of the body as a text suggests that the body itself is not merely a physical entity but also carries symbolic and cultural meanings. Foucault argued that the body is inscribed with social norms, power structures, and ideologies, making it a site of social control and regulation. In this context, this implies that Afro-diasporic female artists use their bodies as a canvas to challenge and subvert these inscriptions, reclaiming agency and asserting their own narratives. By utilizing their bodies in their artistic practice, these artists bring attention to the lived experiences and struggles of Afro-diasporic women. They may engage in performances, visual representations, or other forms of artistic expression that showcase the resilience, beauty, and complexity of the Black female body. Through their art, they challenge stereotypes, confront systemic oppression, and redefine notions of beauty, identity, and empowerment. The act of using the body as a vehicle for reconstruction and self-preservation is a form of resistance and a means of asserting autonomy. By reclaiming their bodies and the narratives associated with them, Afro-diasporic female artists challenge societal norms and structures that have historically marginalized and objectified them. Through the transformative power of art, they reclaim their agency, shape their own representations, and contribute to a broader discourse surrounding race, gender, and identity.

In the image, the act of holding the beads together can be seen as a representation of the bond between mother and daughter. The way in which the beads intertwine and intersect between the two women suggests a connection between the two generations and the passing down of spiritual and cultural traditions from mother to daughter. The fact that the artist is barefoot while her mother wears shoes can be interpreted in different ways. One possible interpretation is that the artist's bare feet symbolize a connection to the earth and nature, which is often associated with spiritual practices. In many cultures, being barefoot is considered a sign of humility and a way to feel grounded and connected to the earth. By contrast, shoes can symbolize the separation from nature and the physical world. Therefore, the artist's bare feet may suggest a closer connection to the spiritual realm and the natural world. Another possible interpretation is that the artist's bare feet represent her youth and innocence. The artist is portrayed as a younger woman, while her mother is depicted as an older woman. By showing the artist barefoot, the artwork may be highlighting her vulnerability and relative inexperience compared to her mother. The shoes worn by the mother may represent the wisdom and experience that comes with age and may be a sign of her authority and knowledge. The contrasting footwear worn by the artist and her mother may be interpreted as a representation of their differing life experiences and stages of life. The fact that the artist is barefoot while her mother is wearing shoes may suggest that the artist is still in a state of flux and transition, while her mother has already gone through this process and is more settled in her life. Bare feet can represent a state of vulnerability and openness, as well as a connection to nature and the earth. In contrast, shoes can symbolize a sense of protection, stability, and the ability to move forward.

Therefore, the barefoot artist may be seen as being in a more vulnerable and open state, while her mother's shoes suggest that she has already established herself and has a greater sense of stability. Another interpretation could be that the barefoot artist represents the younger generation, still learning and growing, while her mother, with her shoes represents the older generation who has already gained knowledge and wisdom through her life experiences. *Replenishing* speaks also about the intergenerational trauma that came from slavery, and how this is transferred through generations. Intergenerational trauma refers to the trauma that is passed down from one generation to the next as a result of historical events that have affected the community. In the case of Afro-Cuban people, this intergenerational trauma is rooted in the transatlantic slave trade, where millions of Africans were forcibly brought to the Americas and subjected to brutal conditions of slavery. The trauma of slavery has had a lasting impact on the Afro-Cuban community, and it is evident in this art piece. The multicolored beads that the two women are holding represent the spiritual practices that were developed by enslaved Africans as a way of preserving their cultural heritage and spirituality in the face of oppression. These practices were passed down from generation to generation, as a way of coping with the trauma of slavery and the ongoing oppression that followed. The intergenerational trauma that came from slavery is also evident in the clothing that the two women are wearing. The flowing white clothes that are befitting Santería initiates are symbolic of purity and represent the way in which the Afro-Cuban community has had to preserve its cultural heritage and spirituality in the face of ongoing oppression. The trauma of slavery is transferred through generations through various mechanisms. One of the most significant ways in which intergenerational trauma is passed down is through family and community narratives. The stories of slavery and oppression that are told within families and communities can have a lasting impact on the way that subsequent generations view themselves and their place in the world. Another way in which intergenerational trauma is transferred is through epigenetics, which is the study of changes in gene expression that occur as a result of environmental factors. Studies have shown that trauma can cause changes in gene expression that are passed down through generations, which can lead to an increased risk of mental health issues and other health problems. Epigenetics is a field of study that explores how environmental factors, such as trauma or stress, can influence gene expression without altering the underlying DNA sequence. Epigenetic changes can be passed down from one generation to the next, potentially leading to an increased risk of mental health issues and other health problems. Epigenetic studies typically involve the analysis of DNA methylation patterns, which is a process where a methyl group is added to DNA, altering the way that genes are expressed. DNA methylation is one of several epigenetic mechanisms that can influence gene expression, and it is often used as a biomarker of environmental exposures. Researchers have used epigenetic studies to investigate the impact of trauma on gene expression and mental health outcomes. Epigenetic studies provide insight into how environmental factors can influence gene expression and increase the risk of mental health issues and other health problems. These studies have the potential to inform the development of new treatments and interventions for individuals who have experienced trauma and other adverse experiences. In this context, art can be a powerful tool for individuals to cope with and overcome the effects of epigenetic trauma. While epigenetic changes can be passed down through generations, it is important to note that they do not necessarily determine an individual's destiny. With the right support and resources, individuals can learn to manage the symptoms of trauma and live fulfilling lives. Art therapy, in particular, has been shown to be an effective treatment for individuals who have experienced trauma. Art therapy is a form of therapy that uses creative processes to improve an individual's physical, mental, and emotional well-being. It is a nonverbal form of therapy that can be especially helpful for individuals who have difficulty expressing themselves through words. Art therapy can improve mood, reduce symptoms of anxiety and depression, and increase self-esteem and self-awareness. It can also help individuals to process traumatic experiences and develop new coping skills. Creating art can also be a way for individuals to connect with their cultural heritage and spirituality, which can be an important factor in overcoming the effects of epigenetic trauma. For example, in the case of Afro-Cuban individuals, engaging in cultural practices, such as the spiritual practices represented in *Replenishing* can be a way to connect with their cultural heritage and spirituality, and promote healing. While art may not be a cure for epigenetic trauma, it can be a valuable tool for individuals to manage the symptoms of trauma and develop new coping skills. Art therapy, in particular, has been shown to be an effective treatment for individuals who have experienced trauma. Additionally, engaging in cultural practices and connecting with one's cultural heritage and spirituality can be an important factor in overcoming the effects of epigenetic trauma.

Dreaming of an Island

The title of the second art piece investigated here *Dreaming of an Island*, 2008 (figure 3.2) delves into the idea of longing, nostalgia, and the yearning

Figure 3.2. *Dreaming of an Island*, María Magdalena Campos-Pons, 2008. Composition of nine Polaroid Polacolor Pro 20 × 24 in. photographs. Framed: approximately 85.5 × 74.75 in. overall. *Source:* Courtesy of Artist.

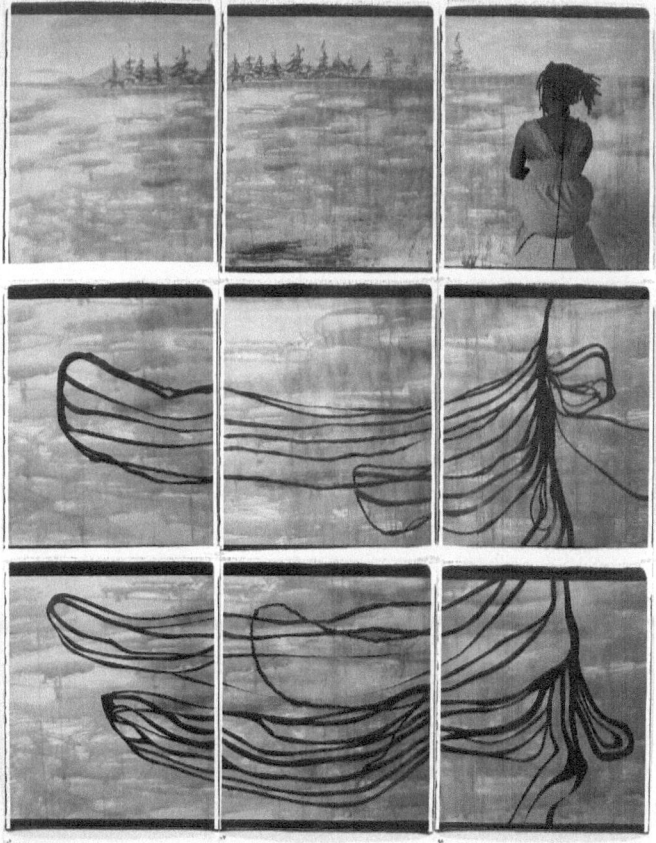

for a sense of belonging. Campos-Pons explores the relationship between personal dreams and aspirations and the collective consciousness tied to her Afro-Cuban heritage and cultural background. *Dreaming of an Island* is a nine-panel Polaroid grid that offers insights into the artist's experiences as an exile living in the United States. The artwork balances a sense of independence and self-assurance with feelings of isolation and loneliness. The composition of the nine-panel grid suggests a narrative or a sequential exploration of the artist's emotions and thoughts. The presence of multiple panels allows for a fragmented visual storytelling, potentially reflecting the complex and layered nature of the artist's experience as an exile. The focal point of the piece is the artist herself, portrayed sitting on a reeflike rock at the top right side of the composition. This positioning draws attention to her as the central figure, indicating her personal perspective and the significance of her gaze. The act of staring at the distant island of Cuba symbolizes a longing for a place of belonging, nostalgia for her homeland, and a yearning for a connection to her cultural roots. This piece suggests that despite the artist's independence and self-assurance, she still experiences a sense of longing and emotional distance from her homeland. The juxtaposition of the distant island and the artist's presence on the rock highlights the contrast between the desired destination and the reality of her current circumstances. The use of Polaroid photography, with its distinctive aesthetic and immediate nature, adds a sense of intimacy and vulnerability to the artwork. The visual quality of Polaroid images, often characterized by soft tones and nostalgic appeal, may evoke a sense of memory and reflection. *Dreaming of an Island* reflects Maria Magdalena Campos-Pons's exploration of her own identity, experiences as an exile, and the complex emotions associated with longing and isolation. The composition and visual elements provide a glimpse into her personal narrative, inviting viewers to contemplate themes of displacement, belonging, and the human longing for connection to one's roots.

The symbolism of the word *dreaming* suggests that the artist may not physically visit the island but rather connects with it through her dreams and childhood memories. Dreams often carry symbolic and subconscious elements, allowing individuals to explore their desires, emotions, and aspirations. In this context, the act of dreaming about the island represents a longing for a connection to her cultural roots, homeland, or a sense of belonging that may not be fulfilled in her current reality as an exile residing in the United States. By framing the artist's relationship with the island through the lens of dreams, it suggests that her connection to it is deeply rooted in her psyche and personal experiences. Childhood memories, as mentioned, also play a role in this symbolism. Memories of the island from her formative years may hold a sense of nostalgia and innocence, further fueling her longing and desire to reconnect with her cultural heritage. While the artist may not be able to physically visit the island, the act of dreaming allows her to experience a form of escapism and transport herself mentally and emotionally to that place. It becomes a way for her to maintain a connection, even if only in her imagination and inner world. The symbolism of dreaming in this context highlights the power of imagination, memory, and the emotional significance of the island in the artist's life. It reflects the complex interplay between reality and fantasy, longing and fulfillment, and the role of dreams in shaping one's sense of identity and belonging. The fact that the artist is turned away from the viewer while maintaining a confident posture adds an intriguing layer of interpretation to the artwork.

This positioning suggests a sense of independence and self-assuredness on the part of the artist, even in the face of her longing and isolation as an exile. By turning away from the viewer, the artist may be symbolically turning toward her own inner world, introspectively engaging with her thoughts, memories, and dreams. It indicates a level of self-contemplation and personal exploration as she navigates her experiences of distance and longing. The strand of hair descending from the artist, stretching into each of the prints below, is a visually striking element. It serves as a connecting thread, symbolizing the artist's ongoing link to her memories and cultural heritage despite physical separation. This imagery suggests that memory plays a vital role in her experience as an exile, shaping her sense of identity and belonging. The focus on memory in relation to the freshness of exile highlights the tension between the present reality of being distanced from her homeland and the lasting impact of her memories. It suggests that the artist's perception of her cultural identity and personal history is shaped by the distance and displacement she experiences. The act of revisiting and engaging with memories becomes a way for her to maintain a sense of connection and preserve her cultural heritage. Moreover, the strand of hair that stretches across the six bottom panels can carry multiple symbolic meanings and evoke various connections within the artwork. Hair holds significant cultural and symbolic associations, often representing personal identity, femininity, and heritage. In this context, the strand of hair can be seen as a metaphorical link between the artist and her Afro-Cuban heritage, emphasizing the importance of cultural identity and ancestral ties. The connection between the strand of hair and the ocean can be interpreted in several ways. The ocean holds deep historical significance, particularly in relation to the transatlantic slave trade. It serves as a symbol of both separation and connection, representing the immense distance that the enslaved African diaspora had to traverse, and the deep wounds inflicted during that historical period. The strand of hair stretching into the ocean may signify the artist's acknowledgment of her African roots and the lasting impact of the transatlantic slave trade on her cultural identity. It can also be seen as a poignant visual representation of the enduring presence and resilience of African heritage within the waters surrounding Cuba. Additionally, the connection between the strand of hair, the ocean, and the island of Cuba can evoke a sense of longing, loss, and ancestral ties. Cuba, being a significant hub in the transatlantic slave trade, has a complex history deeply intertwined with the African diaspora. The artist's gaze toward the distant island and the presence of the hair strand can symbolize her yearning for a connection to her roots, a desire to reclaim and honor her heritage despite physical separation. It underscores the artist's exploration of memory, heritage, and the complex emotions associated with forced displacement. The strand of hair can also be seen as the depiction of roots resembling algae that originated from a lock of hair and are traveling down the artist's spine. This observation introduces additional layers of symbolism and contrasts within the artwork. This imagery suggests a connection to nature, growth, and organic life. The roots are presumed to be a continuation of her hair, reinforcing the link between personal identity and cultural heritage. The hair serves as a visual representation of the artist's roots, both figuratively and literally. However, the depiction of the roots in black ink resembling oil introduces a contrasting element. This contrast between the inky substance of the roots and the watery blue pigment describing the water emphasizes the tension between natural elements and human intervention, particularly in relation to environmental concerns. The black ink resembling oil can symbolize the impact of human actions, such as the exploitation of natural resources or the consequences of the transatlantic slave trade. It serves as a metaphor for historical and ongoing systems of oppression, drawing attention to the lasting effects on cultural identities and the environment. The orientation of the installation, being unambiguously vertical, adds to the significance of the roots. The vertical arrangement emphasizes the idea of growth, resilience, and rootedness, despite being submerged or hidden. The artist, represented by her confident posture and gaze, stands above the submerged roots, suggesting a sense of resilience and personal agency in the face of historical and environmental forces. The juxtaposition of the submerged roots with the nonsubmerged artist further highlights the theme of identity and heritage. It suggests that while the artist acknowledges and is influenced by her cultural roots and history, she also remains separate from the submerged aspects, maintaining a level of agency and individuality. Overall, the portrayal of roots resembling leaves or algae, the use of black ink resembling oil, and the vertical orientation of the installation contribute to the complex symbolism within "Dreaming of an Island." The contrast between natural elements and human intervention, the exploration of cultural heritage, and the assertion of individual agency are key themes that emerge from these visual elements.

The color blue and the ocean are again central topics in this piece. As West-Durán reminds us "Cubans have an intimate, loving, and troubled relationship with the sea. As an island, we have little choice except to know it, embrace it, and reckon with it" (West-Durán 2013, 197) West-Durán in his studies encapsulates the complex and multifaceted connection that the Cuban people have with the sea. It reveals the profound impact that the geographical reality of being an island nation has on Cuba's cultural, emotional, and societal fabric. The author's assertions take on a profoundly poignant dimension when considering the experiences of Afro-Cubans who perished at sea during the transatlantic slave trade. It unveils a layer of historical pain, injustice, and loss that is intertwined with Cuba's relationship with the sea. The phrase "intimate, loving, and troubled relationship" takes on new meaning when we reflect on the countless lives of Afro-Cubans lost in the treacherous waters of the Atlantic. For them, the sea became a site of terror and anguish, as they were forcibly transported from their homelands, subjected to the horrors of slavery, and often met their tragic end in the vastness of the ocean.

The term *intimate* resonates differently here, underscoring the deep connection between the African diaspora and the sea, marked by suffering, displacement, and profound grief. As an island nation, Cuba's geographical reality forced Afro-Cubans to confront the sea under the most harrowing circumstances. The phrase "have little choice except to know it, embrace it, and reckon with it" gains new significance when we consider the coerced journeys of enslaved Africans across the Middle Passage. They were forcibly introduced to the sea as a conduit of their oppression, where they were stripped of their freedom, their dignity, and their lives. The sea became a haunting backdrop to their collective trauma, forever etched in the historical memory of Afro-Cubans. In this context, the word *know* takes on a profoundly tragic meaning.

Enslaved Africans were thrust into a terrifying encounter with the sea, experiencing its merciless waves, its cramped and suffocating conditions, and the relentless brutality of the transatlantic voyage. They intimately knew the sea's capacity for both destruction and deliverance, as they desperately clung to hopes of survival and liberation. While the phrase "embrace it" may seem incongruous in this context, it can be seen as an acknowledgment of the resilience and strength displayed by Afro-Cubans in the face of unimaginable adversity. Despite the sea being a site of profound suffering, Afro-Cubans have inherited a legacy of survival and resistance, drawing strength from their ancestors who endured the horrors of the Middle Passage. The embrace symbolizes the enduring spirit of Afro-Cubans, their cultural resilience, and their determination to reclaim their history and heritage. M. Jacqui Alexander in her book *Pedagogies of Crossing* remind us that "the body thus become a site of memory, not a commodity for sale, even as it is simultaneously insinuated within a nexus of power. Body and memory are lived in the same body, if you will, and this mutual living, this entanglement, enables us to think and feel these inscriptions as process, a process of embodiment" (298, 299). The quote above encapsulates the intricate relationship between the body, memory, and power dynamics. It highlights the significance of the body as a site of memory, emphasizing that it should not be treated as a mere commodity to be bought and sold. Instead, the body carries within it the lived experiences and memories that shape an individual's identity and sense of self. It suggests that the body is not a passive vessel but an active participant in the construction and expression of memory. It implies that memory is not solely a mental or cognitive process but is deeply intertwined with the physical and sensory experiences of the body. Our memories are not detached from our embodied existence; rather, they are stored, felt, and recalled through the very physicality of our being. At the same time, the quote acknowledges that the body is not separate from power dynamics. It acknowledges that power operates on and within the body, shaping and influencing how we experience and remember events. The body becomes inscribed with power relations, social norms, and systemic inequalities, which impact our understanding of the world and ourselves. By recognizing the mutual living and entanglement of body and memory, Jacqui Alexander highlights the importance of understanding memory as a process of embodiment. It suggests that memory is not static or fixed but continually evolving and shaped by our lived experiences. The process of embodiment involves both the internalization of external influences and the active negotiation and reinterpretation of those influences within the body. This perspective challenges the idea of memory as purely individual and highlights its social and collective dimensions. It suggests that our memories are not only personal but also shaped by broader sociocultural forces and collective histories. Memory, therefore, becomes a way to navigate and understand our place within larger social contexts, connecting us to shared histories, struggles, and identities. Ultimately, this perspective encourages us to explore the complex interplay between memory, embodiment, and power dynamics in our individual and collective lives. Jacqui Alexander refers to the explanations she received from Kia Bunseki Fu-Kiau,[2] her Bakongo[3] teacher, stating the following:

> The same force that gave shape to the universe is the same force which resides within us. This force is Kalunga, a complete force by itself, the principle of God, the principle of change, vitality, motion, and transformation. . . . There was nothingness, into which came this source of life, this energy, expressed as heat, cosmic fire after which there was a cooling that produced rivers, oceans, and mountains. The world floated in Kalunga, endless water within subcosmic space, half emerging for terrestrial life, half submerging for marine life and the spiritual world. Kalunga is the ocean door between two worlds. (301)

The above statement offers a profound perspective on the interconnectedness of the universe and the inherent force that resides within all living beings. It introduces the concept of Kalunga as a fundamental force that encompasses the principles of God, change, vitality, motion, and transformation. Kalunga is described as a complete force, representing the principle of God. It is associated with energy, expressed through heat and cosmic fire, which signifies the initial creative spark that sets the universe into motion. This energy then cooled, giving rise to the formation of rivers, oceans, and mountains, representing the diverse elements and landscapes that make up the Earth. The concept of Kalunga also encompasses the idea of dual worlds—the terrestrial and the marine, as well as the spiritual. It acts as an ocean door, connecting these realms and serving as a bridge between different dimensions of existence. This suggests a belief in the interplay and interconnection between the physical and spiritual realms, blurring the boundaries between them. We can discern a deep reverence for the natural world and a recognition of the divine or cosmic forces that govern its existence. It points to a worldview that sees the universe as a dynamic and ever-changing entity, with constant motion and transformation. This understanding invites contemplation on the cyclical nature of life, where elements emerge and submerge, representing the ebb and flow of existence. Furthermore, this quote reflects a holistic perspective that emphasizes the importance of maintaining a balance between different realms and dimensions. It acknowledges the significance of the spiritual and marine worlds, alongside the terrestrial, in shaping the human experience. It implies that by recognizing and honoring these different dimensions, individuals can cultivate a deeper connection to the forces that sustain life. Jacqui Alexander continues by affirming that "in one sense the body's water composition seals our aquatic affinity with the Divine" (301). This perspective suggests that the human body's composition of water establishes a profound connection or affinity between humanity and the divine. By recognizing the presence of water within our bodies, the author implies a symbolic and spiritual link to the fundamental elements of life and creation. Water has long been associated with various symbolic and spiritual meanings across cultures and religions. It is often seen as a purifying and life-giving force, representing renewal, fertility, and spiritual cleansing. In this context, it suggests that our bodies' water composition serves as a reminder of our inherent connection to the divine and the larger cosmic order. Furthermore, the mention of an "aquatic affinity" implies a deeper connection between humans and the realms of water. Water is a ubiquitous element on Earth, covering a significant portion of its surface, and is crucial for sustaining life. This affinity with water underscores the interdependence between humanity and the natural world, highlighting our reliance on water for survival and emphasizing the sacredness and divine essence within nature. The concept of the divine, which varies across different religious and spiritual traditions, often encompasses notions of transcendence, ultimate reality, and interconnectedness. The statement suggests that the presence of water within our bodies serves as a reminder of our spiritual essence and our inherent connection to a larger cosmic or divine order. It implies that our physical bodies, with their water composition, are vessels through which we can experience and connect with the divine. We can interpret it as an invitation to reflect on the inherent sacredness within ourselves and the natural world. It encourages us to recognize the divine presence within us and to honor the interconnectedness of all life.

By acknowledging the water composition of our bodies, we can develop a deeper sense of reverence for the elements that sustain life and foster a greater appreciation for our place within the larger tapestry of existence. Ultimately, the statement serves as a reminder of the profound connection between humanity and the divine, emphasizing the significance of water as a symbol of life, purification, and spiritual connection. It invites contemplation on our relationship with the natural world, our shared origins, and our inherent divinity. Jacqui Alexander also reflects on the strict connection between the making of beauty that artists practice and the Sacred or Divine: "There is no dimension of the Sacred that does not yearn for the making of beauty, an outer social aesthetic of expression whether in written or spoken word, the rhythm of the drum, the fashioning of an altar, or any of the visual arts. The Sacred is inconceivable without an aesthetic" (323). The author makes us reflect on the divine role of visual artists. She suggests that the dimension of the Sacred, or the divine, is intrinsically linked to the creation of beauty and the expression of aesthetics. She argues that there can be no understanding or experience of the Sacred without the presence of an aesthetic dimension, which manifests in various forms such as written or spoken word, rhythmic music, artistic visuals, and the crafting of sacred spaces. By emphasizing the importance of beauty and aesthetics in relation to the Sacred, the statement implies that aesthetics plays a significant role in human spirituality and religious experiences. It suggests that the act of creating beauty through artistic expression and aesthetic practices is not merely a superficial pursuit but an integral aspect of engaging with the divine. The inclusion of various forms of expression, such as written or spoken word, rhythmic drumming, and visual arts, highlights the diversity and multiplicity of aesthetic languages through which the Sacred can be experienced. It suggests that different individuals and communities may connect with the Sacred in unique ways, utilizing different artistic mediums to express their spirituality and engage with the divine. We can read it as an affirmation of the importance of art, creativity, and aesthetics in religious and spiritual contexts. It suggests that aesthetic practices and expressions are not separate or peripheral to the Sacred but are essential components that enhance and deepen our understanding and connection to the divine. Moreover, Jacqui Alexander implies that the pursuit of beauty and aesthetics is a way of honoring and reflecting the divine presence in the world. She suggests that through artistic endeavors and the creation of beauty, humans participate in the ongoing process of cocreation with the Sacred, bringing the divine into tangible and sensory forms. This perspective aligns with the idea that art and aesthetics can evoke profound emotions, inspire contemplation, and provide a means of transcendence. By engaging with the aesthetic dimension of the Sacred, individuals may find solace, inspiration, and a deeper connection to their spirituality and the world around them. This perspective underscores the significance of beauty and aesthetics in religious and spiritual practices, highlighting their role in deepening our understanding, connection, and engagement with the divine. It suggests that through various artistic forms, individuals can partake in the cocreation of beauty and actively participate in the manifestation of the Sacred in the world. In the prayer poem that Jacqui Alexander composed in praise of Yemayá Achaba, Mediator of the Crossing, the author in a stanza asserts,

> In the Vastness of Ocean surrounded by your treasures
> Which passion alone could not
> coax you to reveal
> Inle
> Wash me . . . mother of life
> of water
> One in the beginning when there was no beginning No time
> Take me to that underground home on top of the sand To
> your mirror turquoise jade. (330)

In the Yoruba religion, Yemayá Achaba (also known as Yemọja, Yemaja, or Yemoja) is a prominent and revered deity, often considered the mother of all Orishas (divine beings). Yemayá Achaba is associated with water, motherhood, fertility, and the ocean. She is seen as the nurturing and protective mother figure, embodying the qualities of compassion, wisdom, and resilience. Yemayá Achaba is believed to be the goddess of the salt water, ruling over the vast oceans and bodies of water. She is associated with the Yemọja River in Nigeria, but her influence extends far beyond geographical boundaries. As the deity of the ocean, she holds the power to bring life and sustenance, as well as the ability to unleash destructive forces in the form of storms and tidal waves. In Yoruba religious practices, Yemayá Achaba is often depicted as a regal and majestic figure, adorned in blue-and-white garments, symbolizing the colors of the ocean and purity. She is often depicted with a flowing dress, holding a fan, and crowned with a diadem or a crescent moon. Offerings to Yemayá Achaba typically include items associated with the ocean, such as seashells, fish, and other marine symbols. Devotees of Yemayá Achaba seek her blessings for various aspects of life, including fertility, protection, emotional well-being, and the healing of physical and spiritual ailments. She is revered as a compassionate and understanding deity who listens to the prayers and concerns of her devotees, offering guidance and support. Yemayá Achaba holds a significant place in Yoruba cosmology and is celebrated in various festivals and ceremonies, such as the annual Odun Ijèbú festival in Nigeria and the New Year festival in Cuba known as Fiesta de las Aguas (Festival of the Waters). These celebrations serve as opportunities to honor and connect with Yemayá Achaba, expressing gratitude for her blessings and seeking her continued protection and abundance. Her presence and influence extend beyond the Yoruba community, with her worship and reverence spreading to other regions and cultures influenced by Yoruba traditions.

Moreover, in the Afro-Cuban and Afro-Caribbean traditions that incorporate elements of Yoruba religion, Yemayá takes on a specific role as the protector and mother of those who were forcibly transported across the Atlantic Ocean during the transatlantic slave trade. This belief reflects the historical context of African enslavement, and the immense suffering endured by enslaved individuals during their journey across the treacherous waters. According to these traditions, Yemayá is seen as the guardian of the waters and the deity who oversees the safe passage of those who cross the ocean. As the ocean symbolizes both life and death, Yemayá is believed to embrace and care for the souls of those who lost their lives during the Middle Passage, the harrowing voyage across the Atlantic. Yemayá's association with motherhood and nurturing extends to encompass the enslaved Africans who perished at sea. She is regarded as their spiritual mother, embracing and guiding their souls in the afterlife. Her maternal qualities of compassion, protection, and healing are invoked to provide solace and support to the spirits of those who suffered and died during the brutal transatlantic journey. In ceremonies and rituals dedicated to Yemayá, devotees honor and remember the ancestors who were lost at sea. Offerings are made, including flowers, fruits, and symbolic representations of the ocean, as a way to show respect and gratitude to Yemayá for her care and guidance over these souls. This belief in Yemayá as the mother of those who crossed the ocean not only recognizes the profound loss and trauma experienced by enslaved Africans but also provides a spiritual connection and sense of belonging for their descendants. It is a way to honor their heritage, acknowledges their resilience, and seek healing and empowerment through their connection to Yemayá and the broader African diaspora.

De las dos aguas

The third and last piece by Campos-Pons analyzed is *De las dos aguas*, 2007 (figure 3.3), a photographic installation where two female figures, images of and by the artist María Magdalena Campos-Pons herself are joined by the hair in front of a blue background and holding between them a boat with four carved sailors, each representing Yoruba deities. The hair in

Figure 3.3. *De las dos aguas (Of the Two Waters)*, María Magdalena Campos-Pons, 2007. Composition of twelve Polaroid Polacolor Pro 20 × 24 in. photographs. Framed: approximately 80 × 90 in. overall. *Source:* Courtesy of Artist and Gallery Wendi Norris.

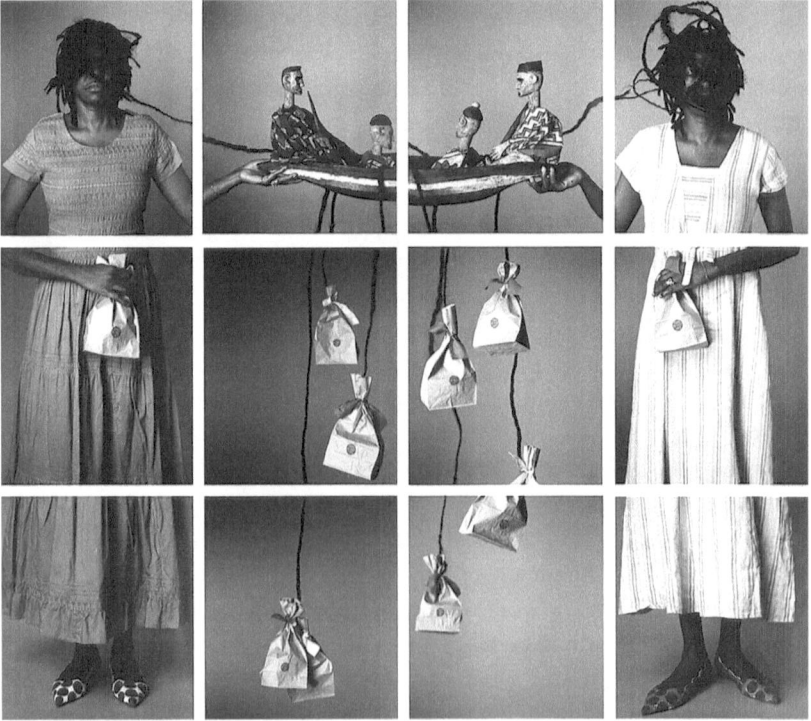

this piece physically and metaphorically becomes a bridge between the two regions of the transatlantic slave trade, America and Africa. Hair in this way also becomes a vehicle for historical reconstruction and a way to reconnect with the ancestors. This art installation is a thought-provoking photographic piece that presents a visually striking representation of the transatlantic slave trade and its enduring legacies. Through the use of the two female figures, the artist explores the themes of cultural heritage, historical reconstruction, and the significance of hair as a bridge connecting Africa and the Americas. Here I aim to provide a comprehensive analysis of the artwork, examining its symbolic elements, artistic techniques, and the broader sociocultural and historical implications it embodies. In this section of the chapter, I analyze how the omnipresence of blue colors in Campos-Pons's artistic practice acts as a binding and unbreakable metaphor of the sea/ocean/body of water as the transmitter of collective memory as well as investigate how hair becomes a spiritualized element for Afro-descendant resistance practices.

The artistic practice of María Magdalena Campos-Pons is imbued with a recurring motif, the omnipresence of blue colors. Through her extensive use of this hue, Campos-Pons skillfully weaves a metaphorical tapestry, binding the sea, ocean, and body of water to the transmission of collective memory. My interpretation explores how Campos-Pons employs the symbolism of blue to evoke a sense of interconnectedness, the fluidity of memories, and the enduring impact of the sea as a carrier of history and cultural identity. As Frédéric Lefrançois precisely describes, on the left-hand side of this artwork we observe a campesina (*guajira*) clothed in a simple blue cloth dress, holding a brown bag in her right hand while her left hand sustains a migrant boat carrying four individuals. On the other side of the photograph, we see standing the same artist who has put on an upper-class dress. Lefrançois describes the bag as a pack of memory stating that "wherever it is transported, it carries the weight of the ocean's trans-personal, inclusive, connectedness thanks to the agency of skin memory" (9). The most visually striking element of the piece is the interweaving of hair that joins the two female figures in the foreground. This physical connection of their hair acts as a metaphorical bridge, symbolizing the historical link between the continents of Africa and the Americas shaped by the transatlantic slave trade. The blue background against which the figures are presented suggests the vast expanse of the ocean, further accentuating the concept of crossing and movement between these two regions. The inclusion of the migrant boat carrying four carved sailors, each representing Yoruba deities, adds a profound layer of meaning to the artwork. The Yoruba religion originated in West Africa and was carried by enslaved Africans to the Americas during the transatlantic slave trade. By depicting these deities in the context of the artwork, Campos-Pons highlights the resilience, spiritual connections, and cultural continuity that survived the traumatic journey of the Middle Passage.[4]

Blue, often associated with water, holds diverse symbolic meanings across cultures. It embodies notions of depth, tranquility, spirituality, and contemplation. In the context of Campos-Pons's work, the color blue acts as a visual thread that interconnects different aspects of her artistic exploration, notably the sea, ocean, and collective memory. The sea has long served as a conduit for migration, trade, and cultural exchange, particularly in the Caribbean region. Campos-Pons taps into this historical significance, employing blue hues to evoke the vastness and boundless nature of the sea. By doing so, she emphasizes the role of the sea as a transmitter of collective memory, carrying stories, experiences, and cultural heritage across generations. The concept of the sea as the transmitter of collective memory takes on a particularly poignant and somber meaning when examined in relation to the transatlantic slave trade[5] and the countless bodies of enslaved Africans that perished during the horrific journey of forced transportation. The sea, which served as the conduit for this brutal trade, not only witnessed the immense suffering and loss of life but also carries the weight of collective memory, becoming a powerful symbol of remembrance and resilience. The Middle Passage, the voyage across the Atlantic, was a treacherous and harrowing journey that resulted in the deaths of countless enslaved Africans due to overcrowding, disease, malnutrition, and physical abuse. The sea, which served as the pathway for this brutal trade, bears witness to the stories of suffering and resistance. The vastness of the ocean echoes the magnitude of the tragedy, and its perpetual motion mirrors the enduring legacy of the transatlantic slave trade. Just as the sea is in constant flux, so too is the collective memory of this traumatic history, persistently shaping the narratives of African diaspora communities. The bodies of the enslaved Africans who perished during the transatlantic crossing form a haunting reminder of the human toll exacted by the slave trade. These bodies, lost at sea, are a testament to the horrors endured and a poignant reflection of lives extinguished. The sea, in this context, becomes a grave for those whose names were erased, a solemn resting place for the memories that were denied proper acknowledgment. Yet, despite the immense tragedy and erasure, the sea also serves as a carrier of resilience and remembrance. The collective memory of the transatlantic slave trade, transmitted through generations, refuses to be silenced. It finds expression in cultural practices, oral traditions, artistic representations, and historical scholarship. The sea, with its vastness and interconnectedness, acts as a conduit for the transmission of these memories, linking African diaspora communities across time and space. Through various artistic forms and cultural expressions, the sea becomes a symbol of resistance, survival, and resilience. It inspires works of literature, visual arts, and music that bear witness to the history of enslavement and commemorate the lives lost. By acknowledging and engaging with this memory, we honor the lives lost and seek to confront the lasting legacies of slavery while working toward a more just and inclusive future. Through her use of blue, Campos-Pons conveys the fluidity and ever-changing nature of memories. Like the shifting tides, memories ebb and flow, sometimes receding and other times crashing onto the shores of consciousness.

The oceanic hues in her work evoke a sense of constant movement and transformation, reminding viewers that collective memory is not static but dynamic and subject to reinterpretation. Blue serves as a metaphorical conduit, connecting the diasporic experiences and histories of Afro-Caribbean communities. Campos-Pons represents the interconnectedness of different cultures and identities through the symbolism of water. Just as the sea knows no borders, the artist suggests that collective memory transcends geographical boundaries, bridging gaps between people and fostering a shared sense of cultural heritage. Blue colors in Campos-Pons's artwork also carry a sense of timelessness and permanence. The enduring presence of the sea throughout history parallels the lasting impact of collective memory. Memories, like the ocean's depths, remain preserved beneath the surface, waiting to be explored and remembered by future generations. Campos-Pons's use of blue serves as a reminder that collective memory persists, shaping identities and providing a sense of rootedness in an ever-changing world. Through her visual exploration of blue, she invites viewers to reflect on the deep connections between personal and shared memories, emphasizing the significance of collective memory as a source of cultural preservation and identity formation.

Another symbolic element worth analyzing is that of hair, constantly present in Campos-Pons's visual practice. As West-Durán points out "Hair . . . not only does it have aesthetic value but also multiple purposes: a link between different worlds or realities, a bridge to her past, an emotional bond to her mother and family, a strand of memory, a diasporic concatenation of exile, wandering, and historical turmoil" (206). West-Durán's assertion about the symbology of hair in the art of Maria Magdalena Campos-Pons encapsulates the rich and multifaceted significance of this artistic element. By highlighting the various purposes and meanings attributed to hair, West-Durán sheds light on the deeper layers of Campos-Pons's work. The quote emphasizes that hair possesses not only aesthetic value but also serves as a conduit between different worlds or realities. It acts as a bridge, connecting Campos-Pons to her past and linking her to her ancestors, heritage, and cultural roots. This notion of hair as a connection to one's history and ancestry underscores the importance of personal and collective memory in Campos-Pons's artistic exploration. Furthermore, the author's perspective suggests that hair represents an emotional bond to Campos-Pons's mother and family. It symbolizes familial ties, nurturing relationships, and the continuity of generations. In this sense, hair becomes a tangible representation of love, care, and intergenerational connections within Campos-Pons's artistic expression. The phrase "a strand of memory" evokes the idea that hair carries memories within its fibers. Hair can serve as a physical repository of personal experiences, cultural traditions, and historical narratives. It embodies the lived experiences and stories of individuals and communities, becoming a tangible thread that weaves together diverse histories and narratives. Additionally, it is worth highlighting the diasporic aspect of hair in Campos-Pons's art. Hair becomes a symbol of displacement, exile, and historical turmoil, embodying the experiences of those who have migrated or have been forced to leave their homes. Through the representation of hair, Campos-Pons explores themes of identity, displacement, and resilience, weaving together individual stories and collective histories of diaspora. It is then fundamental to analyze the symbology of hair in the art of Maria Magdalena Campos-Pons and underscores the complexity and richness of its meaning. Hair serves as a powerful symbol that encapsulates personal, familial, cultural, and historical narratives. It becomes a medium through which Campos-Pons explores themes of identity, memory, love, loss, and the interconnectedness of diverse experiences. The interconnected hair of the two figures can be interpreted as the Sacred interconnectedness and interdependence of the Universe. As Jacqui Alexander clearly points out: "In Kitsimba's[6] universe, the principle is quite simple: You human beings have this fancy word—syncretism-for something quite simple: everything in the universe is interconnected! Interconnectedness, interdependence, and intersubjectivity as constructs or desire do not necessarily provoke resistance within shared canon of materialist modernity. Indeed, we count on this for the making of successful political movements" (323). In order to comprehend the intricate politics surrounding Black hair, it is imperative to contextualize it within its historical and socioeconomic dimensions. Examining the multifaceted nature of Black hair requires a comprehensive understanding of how historical and social factors have shaped its significance and influenced societal perceptions (Mercer 1987; Synnott 1987; Hunt 1994). Black hair carries profound cultural, social, and political implications that have evolved over time. Throughout history, African diaspora communities have developed unique and diverse hairstyles as expressions of identity, creativity, and cultural heritage. These hairstyles often reflect a connection to ancestral roots, symbolize resistance against oppression, and foster a sense of community and pride. However, it is crucial to acknowledge that the history of Black hair is intertwined with a legacy of colonialism, slavery, and systemic racism. The transatlantic slave trade, for instance, not only uprooted millions of Africans from their homelands but also sought to denigrate and suppress their cultural practices, including traditional hairstyles. Enslaved individuals were often forced to adopt Eurocentric beauty standards, which entailed conforming to Western hairstyles and textures that deemed their natural hair as "unprofessional" or "unacceptable." These deeply ingrained prejudices against Black hair persist in contemporary society, manifesting in various forms of discrimination and bias. Black individuals continue to face unequal treatment in workplaces, schools, and even legal settings due to their natural hair texture or styles such as braids, dreadlocks, or Afros. This bias is rooted in societal perceptions that have been perpetuated by media, beauty standards, and cultural biases, which often prioritize Eurocentric ideals of beauty and professionalism. According to bell hooks (2007), the natural hairstyles prevalent during our time serve as defiance against white supremacist culture, projecting a powerful image that could evoke fear in white individuals.

Nonetheless, hooks also contends that Black women themselves could internalize that fear. "The extent to which we are comfortable with our hair usually reflects our overall feelings about our bodies" (8). Understanding the politics of Black hair necessitates an exploration of these historical and socioeconomic factors. By recognizing and challenging the systemic inequalities and biases that persist, society can strive for inclusivity, respect, and equal treatment for all individuals, regardless of their hair texture or style. It is crucial to point out that "Black hair is fundamentally connected, through history and social norms, to identity" (Cannella 274), and it "has the power to dictate how others treat you, and in turn, how you feel about yourself" (Thompson 2). Moreover, from an intersectional perspective, Black women's hair historically had "significant impacts on their economic, social, and emotional lives" (Jacobs-Huey 213). In this context, we saw how Campos-Pons's art often incorporates her own body and hair as central elements, emphasizing the spiritual and cultural significance of hair within the Black community. By doing so, she symbolically connects with her ancestors and their experiences, bridging the gap between past and present. As Cannella (274) reminded us, there is a profound connection between Black hair and identity. Campos-Pons's work echoes this sentiment by placing Black hair as a central aspect of her visual narratives. Through her deliberate focus on hair, she acknowledges the historical and social significance it carries for Black individuals, particularly Black women. In doing so, she emphasizes the agency of hair in shaping one's sense of self and how it influences external perceptions. Additionally, the connection between Black hair and self-perception is emphasized in Thomson's work (2009). Campos-Pons's use of her own hair in her artwork suggests that hair holds power not only in how others treat Black individuals but also in how they perceive themselves. Her visual narratives invite viewers to consider the emotional impact of societal norms and expectations placed on Black hair, and the potential for self-empowerment and self-love in reclaiming one's natural beauty. Moreover, the intersectional perspective highlighted in the work of Jacobs-Huey (2006) resonates with Campos-Pons's artistic exploration of the multifaceted experiences of Black women. By weaving her hair into her visual narratives, she acknowledges the economic, social, and emotional dimensions that Black women historically faced in relation to their hair. Through her art, Campos-Pons provides a platform for these narratives to be seen and heard, challenging the oppressive forces that have sought to control and dictate Black women's experiences with their hair.

Conclusion

María Magdalena Campos-Pons's multicultural artistic world is a rich tapestry of narratives that resonates with themes of African ancestry, black women empowerment, connection to Yoruba spirituality, and the continent of Africa. Through her thought-provoking pieces such as *Dreaming of an Island* and *Replenishing*, and *De las dos* aguas, Campos-Pons delves deep into the complexities of identity, longing, and the search for a sense of belonging. In this chapter, we have explored the deep symbology of these three of María Magdalena Campos-Pons's powerful art pieces. *Replenishing*, with its grandeur and symbolism, captures the profound bond between mother and daughter while embodying the strength and divinity of black women. The use of multicolored strings of pearls, representing unique Yoruba deities, not only pays homage to Afro-Cuban culture but also underscores the connection to Yoruba spirituality and the wider African diaspora. Campos-Pons positions her subjects as goddesses, reclaiming their power and emphasizing the importance of recognizing and celebrating the strength and resilience of Black women throughout history. In *Dreaming of an Island*, Campos-Pons explores the universal human experience of longing and nostalgia, intertwining it with her own personal journey as an exile. Through this piece, she opens a window into the emotional landscape of displacement, inviting viewers to reflect on their own yearnings for a place of origin or a deeper connection to their cultural heritage. In doing so, Campos-Pons speaks to the broader diaspora experience and highlights the significance of embracing one's roots. With the piece *De las dos aguas* we have investigated the connotations of the color blue and its connections with the bodies of waters that remind us of the transatlantic slave trade, Yoruba spiritual practices, and venerated Orishas. We also saw how Campos-Pons's use of hair as a spiritualized element in her artwork serves as a visual testament to the resilience, strength, and ancestral connections of Black women. The deliberate incorporation of her own hair encourages viewers to reflect on the profound historical and cultural significance that hair holds within the Black community. Maria Madalena Campos-Pons's visual art serves as a powerful embodiment of the significance of Black hair in shaping identity and influencing the lives of Black women. Through her work, Campos-Pons invites viewers to engage in a meaningful dialogue about the complexities of Black hair and its role in self-perception, societal treatment, and the collective experiences of Black women.

The relevance of Campos-Pons's work lies in its ability to transcend cultural boundaries and evoke a deep sense of interconnectedness. By exploring multicultural and spiritual themes her art becomes a powerful platform for dialogue and understanding. It challenges existing narratives and invites viewers to engage with the complexities of race, identity, and heritage. Through her artistic vision, María Magdalena Campos-Pons amplifies marginalized voices, celebrates cultural diversity, and invites viewers to embrace the beauty and strength of African traditions in the Caribbean diaspora. Her work serves as a testament to the resilience of Black Cuban women, the power of ancestral connections, and the importance of recognizing and honoring the multifaceted tapestry of identities that make up our Latinx community. In a world where narratives are often dominated by mainstream Western culture, Campos-Pons's artistic contributions offer a counterpoint, reminding us of the richness and significance of diverse cultural expressions that come from exile, multicultural identities, and gender, as well as racial marginalization.

Chapter 4

Susana Pilar's Self-Portrayal of Black Womanhood

A Visual Chronicle of Diasporic Femininity, the Trauma of Separation, and the Legacy of Enslavement

In this chapter, I turn my focus to an artist whose work has remained largely invisible in academic discourse yet offers a profound contribution to our understanding of Afro-Cuban identity and visual expression. While the visibility of Black Cuban women artists continues to grow, many still operate on the margins of both national and international art scenes. One such artist is Susana Pilar, a Cuban-born artist who still resides in her homeland and whose body of work remains relatively underexplored in scholarly circles. By examining artists like Susana Pilar, we confront the limitations of visibility in the academic field and art history, which often prioritize diasporic narratives or artists with more access to global art circuits. However, the inclusion of artists who remain in Cuba allows for a more nuanced understanding of how local experiences of race, gender, and colonial history manifest in artistic production. Pilar's work provides an essential counterpoint to artists living in exile, emphasizing the importance of examining those whose artistic practices remain rooted in their Cuban context, despite facing significant sociopolitical and economic barriers.

As demonstrated in the preceding chapters examining Decolonial AfroARTivism among Black Cuban women, the field of art is inhabited by those exceptional artists who transcend conventional modes of expression, engaging deeply with the intricate fabric of human experience. Susana Pilar, an innovative artist from Havana, Cuba, stands out as a notable figure in this regard. Pilar employs her artistic talents to explore and illuminate the complex narratives of Black femininity[1] and the traumatic legacy of enslavement. Through her use of her own body and visual self-narration, she constructs a narrative that bridges temporal divides, offering viewers an insight into the steadfast spirit and unspoken histories of marginalized and forgotten communities. Pilar's investigation of Black femininity, gender, race, and social issues represents a deliberate challenge to prevailing norms that sustain discrimination and inequality. Motivated by personal experiences and a profound curiosity, she delves into the struggles faced by women worldwide, meticulously revealing the layered complexities of their lives. Particularly, her focus on the physical violence suffered by Cuban women—a topic often obscured by silence and insufficient discourse—aims to unearth and highlight this concealed aspect of reality. Through her work, she seeks to bring this hidden suffering to light, amplifying the voices of those who have been historically silenced. What sets Pilar's artistic journey apart is her audacious use of her own body[2] as a conduit for storytelling.

By constructing photographic scenes drawn from her own memories, she forges a profound connection between her personal experiences and the collective consciousness of those she seeks to represent. The raw vulnerability and unflinching honesty captured in her self-narration transcend mere aesthetics, becoming a compelling visual testament to the resilience and strength of Black femininity throughout history. Inextricably linked to Pilar's exploration of self is her fascination with death—an exploration that defies societal norms and encourages viewers to reconsider their own perceptions. By extracting symbolic interpretations from the concept of death, she challenges the notion of finality, viewing it instead as a transformative force, an everlasting thread that weaves through the fabric of existence. In this uncharted territory, she unearths the physical history and processes of the human body, creating a tableau where the public becomes an active participant, engaging with her work as a collective witness to the eternal cycle of life. Central to Pilar's artistic oeuvre is her unwavering dedication to representing what is real and what society deems as real. Recognizing the constructed realities perpetuated by societal tools of obfuscation and control, she employs art as a potent instrument for dismantling these barriers and accessing the essence of hidden truths. Pilar challenges the viewer to confront their preconceived notions and embark on a transformative journey toward a deeper understanding of the human experience. In exploring Susana Pilar's profound artistic vision, the analysis will navigate the intricate and nuanced landscapes she meticulously constructs, where Black femininity and the history of enslavement intertwine. Through her visual self-narration, Pilar invites us to witness the resilience, struggles, and triumphs of those whose stories have been silenced.

The artistic realm has long been a sanctuary for marginalized voices, a space where the silenced stories of individuals and communities can find resonance and empowerment. Within this realm, Susana Pilar Delahante stands as an artist who weaves a tapestry of disconnection, resilience, and reclamation, breathing life into the narratives of Afro-Cuban women. As we embark on this chapter, we delve into the intricate nuances of Pilar's work, exploring how her artistic expressions transcend mere representation to become vehicles of empowerment, challenging historical erasure, and igniting conversations within the intricate sociopolitical tapestry of Cuba. The exploration of Susana Pilar Delahante's captivating artistic pieces begins with a profound analysis of *Dibujo intercontinental/Intercontinental Drawing* (2017). The performance reveals how Pilar draws the viewer into a visual narrative that transcends both time and space. The act of dragging a boat tethered to her waist emerges as a potent metaphor for the trauma of separation, vividly evoking the historical rupture experienced by Afro-Cuban women. By positioning her body at the core of this performance, Pilar channels the emotions of longing, dislocation, and resilience inherent to the African diaspora experience. This piece not only captures a profound yearning for historical recognition but also functions as a tangible bridge, linking the present to the deeply resonant echoes of the past. The subsequent focus shifts to *El tanque*, a performance that examines the intricate dynamics between identity, beauty standards, and reclamation. In this piece, Pilar adeptly navigates the paradoxes faced by Afro-Cuban women as they balance societal expectations with the assertion of their authentic selves. The ritualistic act of passing a hot comb through her hair, followed by immediate immersion in cold water, serves as a critique of the norms imposed on Black women's appearances. This poignant contrast functions as a visual metaphor for the resilience involved in embracing one's identity amid external pressures. Pilar's challenge to these expectations emerges as an empowering act that redefines beauty, dismantles conformity, and reclaims personal agency. Finally, attention turns to the compelling photograph titled *Llave maestra* or *Master Key*. In this image, Pilar's depiction of herself holding a machete carries profound symbolism, reflecting the complex historical context of Cuba.

The machete, historically associated with Cuba's fight for independence, is reimagined as a potent symbol of survival, resistance, and self-defense. Pilar's artistic manipulation of this emblem becomes a visual testament to the multifaceted strength of Afro-Cuban women. Through this piece, she skillfully blurs the lines between history and contemporary struggles, recontextualizing a symbol of revolution to reflect the ongoing fight for empowerment and dignity. As we traverse these three pieces, we are invited to navigate the intersections of art, history, and identity. Susana Pilar Delahante's work serves as a guiding thread, weaving together the silenced stories of Afro-Cuban women, amplifying their voices within a larger sociopolitical context. In light of the multifaceted exploration of Susana Pilar Delahante's transformative artistry, this chapter seeks to uncover the layers of significance and resonance that her work carries within the intricate contexts of Cuba's historical trajectory of the invisibility of the racialized woman body. Central to my analysis are the following research questions: How does Pilar's artistic navigation of disconnection, resilience, and reclamation provide a lens through which the experiences of Afro-Cuban women are both illuminated and challenged, within the backdrop of Cuba's sociopolitical fabric? Furthermore, to what extent does her evocative use of performance art and visual imagery transcend traditional representation, becoming conduits for dialogues about identity, history, and empowerment, particularly within the dynamic interplay of Cuba's historical past? Through the exploration of these questions, we endeavor to unravel the profound layers of Pilar's work and its contributions to the visibility, empowerment, and reclaiming of narratives that resonate with both local struggles and global discourses.

Susana Pilar, born in Havana, Cuba in 1984, currently resides and works in the same city. Her artistic focus revolves around the themes of the human body, gender, race, and social issues. The artist's personal experiences within her family have stimulated her interest in understanding the realities faced by women worldwide and the various forms of discrimination they encounter. This concern has led her to concentrate specifically on physical violence against Cuban women and the limited information available on this subject. During her creative process, she developed innovative approaches, such as constructing photographic scenes based on her memories, which became a formal and conceptual foundation for her subsequent works. Susana Pilar also developed an interest in death, exploring its symbolic interpretations and viewing it not as a definitive end but as a continuous thread. Additionally, she explores the physical history and processes of the human body, while actively engaging the public as participants in her artwork. A unifying element in all of Susana Pilar's artistic endeavors is her preoccupation with representing both the tangible reality and the constructed reality that society perpetuates. She recognizes that certain truths are obscured by societal mechanisms, limiting people's understanding, and thus employs art as a tool to access the essence of these hidden realities. Susana Pilar's educational background includes attending the José Antonio Díaz Peláez Elementary School and the San Alejandro Academy in Havana. She completed her studies in 2008, graduating from the Higher Institute of Art in Havana. From 2011 to 2013, she pursued postgraduate studies at the University of Arts and Design in Karlsruhe, Germany (HfG), with financial support from the DAAD. She has received numerous awards and artist residencies, including CAD+SR RESEARCH in Italy and Kenya (2019 to 2020); CIFO Grants and Commissions Program Award in Miami, US (2019); AIR of Fondazione Macc in Calasetta, Italy; AIR at the Academy of Fine Arts in Vienna, Austria (2017); El Reino de este mundo Scholarship from Asociación Hermanos Saíz in Havana, Cuba (2016); AIR Dance Hall Fire Hall in Calgary, Canada (2016); AIR Skövde in Skövde, Sweden (2016); Apexart Fellowship in New York, USA (2016); shared Maretti Award (2014); MAP Residency at ARTEZ in Enschede, Netherlands (2010 to 2011); Villa Waldberta in Munich, Germany (2010); Art Centre Darling Foundry in Montreal, Canada (2009); and Intermediae-Minbak at Matadero Madrid, Spain (2007). Susana Pilar's artwork has been showcased in various biennials and international art events, including the 14 Dakar Biennial in Senegal (2020); the Lubumbashi Biennial in the Democratic Republic of Congo (2019); the 12th and 13th Havana Biennial (2015, 2019); the 13 Biennial of Media Arts at Centro Nacional de Arte Contemporáneo Cerrillos in Santiago de Chile (2017); the New Talents Biennale 2016 in Cologne, Germany; the Cuban Pavilion at the Venice Biennial (2015); the International Biennale of Contemporary Art (BIAC) in Martinique (2013); the IV Bienal deformes de performance in Chile (2012); the III Biennale Arts Actuels Réunion in Reunion Island, France (2011); the International Photography Exhibition at the World Festival of Black Arts and Cultures in Dakar, Senegal (2010); and the 7th Gwangju Biennial in South Korea (2008).

As the examination of Susana Pilar's contemporary Afro-Cuban art unfolds, the recurring theme of migration prominently emerges. The estrangement from the African homeland is poignantly articulated in Pilar's work, especially in the performance piece *Dibujo intercontinental/*

Intercontinental Drawing (2017). In this evocative performance, Pilar conveys the trauma of separation by dragging a boat tethered to her waist. This act symbolizes not merely a desire for return but a profound quest for historical acknowledgment, capturing the complex emotions stemming from the division between two continents. According to the artist's official page, the performance is deeply rooted in her sense of carrying her family heritage. The boat symbolizes her African and Chinese ancestors who were forcibly transported to Cuba, and Pilar views herself as a product of this historical movement. This thematic resonance aligns with the previous chapter's analysis of María Magdalena Campos-Pons, particularly regarding the artistic symbolism associated with water, boats, and the legacy of slavery, as exemplified in Campos Pons's piece *De las dos aguas*.

In an interview by Roselin Rodríguez Espinosa in 2022, Pilar talks about how she sees her body as an archive of the forced displacement of people from Africa and Asia to Cuba, both ethnic groups that form her cultural heritage. Multiculturalism is then another element in common that we can find between Susana Pilar and the Afro-Cuban artist analyzed in the previous chapter, María Magdalena Campos Pons. The interviewer points out that if we consider a context like Cuba, where the policies of forgetting are systematic and determine daily life, reinventing memory, and the archive is an important key, even more so in the case of a migrant body like Pilar's. Then she proceeds to ask how Pilar developed that experience in her work with performance. To this question, Pilar responds as follows:

> Reinventing memory and the archive are super important in my research and artistic practice because some in power have erased the facts. My body, a descendant of forcibly displaced migrants from Asia and Africa to Cuba, is my archive and my memory. My family's oral narratives (since we were denied the right to write our History, and today we are reclaiming those rights) are my textbook. My ancestors inhabit my body and I generate actions that reclaim what we are.[3]

Susana Pilar's quote highlights the significance of memory and the archive within her artistic practice, particularly in response to the erasure of historical facts by those in positions of power. As an artist with a personal history rooted in the forced displacement of her ancestors from Asia and Africa to Cuba, Pilar sees her own body as an archive and repository of memory. Her family's oral narratives, passed down through generations, become her primary source of knowledge and understanding, a substitute for the written history that has been denied to her community. Pilar's assertion that her body is an archive carries a profound significance. It speaks to the idea that personal and collective memories are stored not only in written documents but also within lived experiences and the corporeal selves of individuals. By embodying the stories, struggles, and resilience of her ancestors, she reclaims and preserves their histories that have been marginalized or silenced. Furthermore, Pilar emphasizes the act of reinventing memory and the archive, suggesting that it is not enough to simply rely on existing historical narratives or institutional archives. Instead, she actively engages in the process of reconstructing and reimagining these narratives, drawing from her own lived experiences and family stories. This process of reinvention becomes a form of resistance and empowerment, enabling her to challenge dominant narratives and reclaim her own history. Pilar's understanding of her body as an archive and her family's oral narratives as her textbook reflects a deep connection to her ancestral roots and an affirmation of her identity. By integrating the stories and knowledge passed down through generations, she not only honors her ancestors but also generates actions that aim to reclaim what has been lost or suppressed.

It is also worth mentioning that the concept of body as an archive has been widely explored through history. In his work *The Archeology of Knowledge* (1972), Michel Foucault introduced a revolutionary perspective on the concept of the archive, framing it as the encompassing system responsible for the formation and transformation of statements (130). This innovative viewpoint signaled a departure from the conventional perception of the archive as a mere object or institutional repository, emphasizing instead its dynamic, procedural, and relational nature. Building on these foundations, subsequent scholars focused on this powerful concept, particularly in the sphere of performance arts and dance. For instance, Inge Baxmann, in her work "The Body as Archive: On the Difficult Relationship Between Movement and History" (2007), and later André Lepecki, in "The Body as Archive: Will to Re-Enact and the Afterlives of Dances" (2010), further solidified the significance of the dancing body as a repository of knowledge and memory, entrusted with the roles of preservation, transmission, and accessibility. The metaphorical conception of the "body as archive" or the "body archive" posits that the human body itself can be understood as a reservoir—a "storage place"—of corporeal documents, carrying within it a wealth of embodied knowledge. Through this lens, the body becomes a vessel that retains sensory, emotional, and cognitive experiences, accessible in the form of movements, gestures, patterns, and rhythms. The notion of the "body as archive" has profound implications for understanding the interplay between corporeal expression and intellectual comprehension. It reinforces the idea that the body, in its intricate movements and gestural vocabulary, encapsulates a holistic archive of lived experiences, emotions, and cognitive insights. By delving into this metaphor, we unveil the profound interconnectedness between the physical and the cognitive realms, recognizing the body as not merely a vessel for the creation of various forms of art, but as a living, dynamic repository that holds within it the power to perpetuate, communicate, and reimagine the multifaceted tapestry of human experiences.

Through her artistic practice, Pilar seeks to give voice to her community, asserting their agency, and demanding recognition and the right to tell their own stories. Susana Pilar's quote from her interview encapsulates her artistic approach of reinventing memory and the archive as a means of challenging historical erasure and reclaiming marginalized narratives. Her body becomes a vessel for memory, a site of resistance, and a source of empowerment. Through her work, she illuminates the significance of personal and collective memory in shaping our understanding of history and emphasizes the power of storytelling as a form of reclaiming agency and identity.

Another creative objective that Pilar highlights in her website is that of reclaiming the erased history of Afro-Cuban women. The narrative of the feminist movement in Cuba is a vibrant and dynamic tapestry, characterized by intricate subtleties that unveil a profound chronicle of relentless struggle and unwavering determination in the pursuit of fundamental rights for Cuban women. This historical journey is brimming with fervent episodes of empowerment, as women across the nation rallied to challenge traditional norms and societal constraints. Thankfully, the discipline of historiography has dutifully amassed an extensive array of accounts that encapsulate the essence of this pivotal movement. Scholars like González Pagés in 2006 and Stoner in 2003 have meticulously documented and analyzed various junctures within this transformative trajectory. Their scholarly endeavors have not only preserved the legacy of these trailblazing women but have also shed light on the multifaceted avenues through which change was catalyzed. From the early stages of this movement, where impassioned gatherings and grassroots initiatives were forged, to the later phases marked by strategic advocacy and legislative endeavors, the feminist movement in

Cuba has displayed an unyielding spirit. It has weathered societal prejudices, intersecting forms of discrimination, and formidable challenges, all
in pursuit of dismantling gender-based inequalities that had persisted for
generations. As these historical records depict, the feminist movement's
influence reverberated beyond mere political landscapes. It permeated
the realms of culture, education, and economics, propelling women to
the forefront of previously male-dominated spheres. The movement fostered a collective awakening, fostering a sense of unity among women
from diverse backgrounds who recognized the potency of their shared
aspirations. In essence, the history of the feminist movement in Cuba is
an intricate mosaic woven from the threads of perseverance, unity, and
transformation. Its significance transcends national boundaries, serving
as an emblem of resilience and a beacon of hope for ongoing struggles
toward gender parity worldwide. The scholarly endeavors of historians like
González Pagés and Stoner serve as invaluable testaments to this ongoing
journey, ensuring that the indomitable spirit of these pioneers remains an
enduring source of inspiration for generations to come.

To understand the sociopolitical and economic struggles that Pilar
brings forward with her art, especially the ones at the intersection of
race and gender in Cuba, it is helpful to review some of the fundamental
works that have been published on this topic, such as Almeida Junco
(2011), Alvarez Ramírez (2009), Barcia (1998, 2009), Castañeda (1993
to 94), Duharte Jiménez (1996), Faguada Iglesias (2009), Fuente (2000),
Helg (2000), and Keosha Brunson (2011). Due to the shade of their skin,
Afro-Cuban women endured the unfortunate legacy reminiscent of the
era of slavery. The myriad challenges they confronted were intricately
intertwined with the glaring deficiencies inherent in the prevailing racist ideologies that eroded Cuban society, as thoughtfully discussed by
Fernández Robaina (2009, 2012). The complexion-based experiences of
women led them to confront a spectrum of adversities rooted in historical
inequalities. These adversities not only stemmed from their gender but
were further compounded by the pervasive racial biases that permeated
society. The ramifications of slavery's legacy were inextricably linked
to their everyday lives, influencing their access to education, economic
opportunities, and social mobility. The struggles these women faced were
not isolated occurrences; rather, they emerged from a broader backdrop of
deeply ingrained racial prejudices. The societal landscape was marred by
prejudiced perceptions that cast a shadow over these women's aspirations
and prospects, limiting their agency and relegating them to the fringes of

power. It is within this context that Fernández Robaina's insightful analysis gains prominence. Her work delves into the intricacies of the historical tapestry, unraveling the ways in which the scars of slavery continued to impact women's lives long after its official abolition. Through meticulous research and critical examination, Fernández Robaina brings to light the interconnectedness of systemic racism and gender-based discrimination, highlighting the urgent need for a comprehensive understanding of the intersecting oppressions that shaped these women's realities. By acknowledging the profound implications of these historical dynamics, we are compelled to engage in a broader conversation about the lasting effects of structural inequalities. It becomes apparent that dismantling the entrenched prejudices and unequal power structures necessitates addressing not only gender disparities but also the deeply rooted racial biases that have endured through generations. The scholarship of Fernández Robaina serves as a poignant reminder that the struggle for equality must be multifaceted, encompassing the multifarious dimensions of identity that shape the experiences of marginalized individuals. In addition to Fernández Robaina's scholarship, Cuban essayist Roberto Zurbano Torres's works provide valuable insights into issues of equality and identity. Zurbano Torres is known for his critical analysis of race and racism in Cuba, particularly in his writings where he explores systemic racism and challenges Cuba's national narrative on racial equality. His perspectives on racial democracy critique the notion that racial harmony exists in Cuba, highlighting persistent racial inequalities and emphasizing the need for broader societal recognition and action. In particular, the documentary *Zurbano and His Racial Consciousness/Y su conciencia racial* (2022), directed and produced by Juanamaria Cordones-Cook, offers a testimonial on his personal journey and insights into racial issues in Cuba. From his modest origins in a small village, Zurbano eloquently traces the evolution of his intellectual and racial consciousness. He reflects deeply on the sociohistorical and cultural contributions of Black Cubans to the nation, critiquing the 1959 Cuban revolution for its failure to adequately address racism. Zurbano argues that racism and neoracism persist in Cuba yet remain largely absent from public discourse. The documentary, enriched with hip-hop music by Obsesión, provides a compelling exploration of these complex issues.

When analyzing the artistic practice of Susana Pilar, it is fundamental to discuss the constant element of visual self-narration[4] or visual autobiography that the artist consciously decides to utilize and display her own body to transmit her artistic message and tell her own story. As we observed in the previous chapter, this was also an artistic technique widely implemented by Afro-Cuban artist María Magdalena Campos Pons. A visual autobiography is a form of self-expression that communicates one's personal experiences and identity through visual art. It is a way of telling one's life story through images rather than words, using various mediums such as photography, painting, drawing, and sculpture. Visual autobiography allows individuals to reflect on their own lives, experiences, and emotions, exploring themes of identity, memory, and perception. This form of storytelling can be deeply personal and emotional, allowing the artist to communicate their innermost thoughts and feelings to others in a powerful and engaging way. It is a way of capturing and sharing one's unique perspective on the world and can serve as a means of empowerment and validation for marginalized or underrepresented groups. Photography has long been a powerful tool for representing the experiences of marginalized and underrepresented groups, including Afro-Cuban women. One of the most striking ways in which photographers have used this medium to represent these individuals has been through the use of black-and-white imagery as we will admire in the case of Susana Pilar.

Black-and-white photography has a timeless quality that can evoke a range of emotions and convey complex meanings with just a few simple tones. When applied to images of Black Latina women, this technique can serve as a powerful means of highlighting their beauty, strength, and resilience in the face of systemic oppression. In many cases, black-and-white imagery is used to create stark contrasts between light and dark, emphasizing the contours and textures of the subjects' bodies and features. This approach can be particularly impactful when applied to images of Afro-Cuban women, whose skin tones often fall outside of the normative range seen in mainstream media. By bringing these women's bodies to the forefront of the image and emphasizing the unique qualities of their skin, photographers can challenge dominant narratives that erase or minimize the experiences of Black Latina women. This approach can also serve as a means of claiming space and asserting the value of these women's bodies and experiences. In addition to these visual elements, artists who work in black and white photography, such as Susana Pilar, skillfully use this technique to create mood and atmosphere in their images. By using high contrast or deep shadows, photographers can create a sense of drama, tension, or mystery in their images, drawing viewers in and encouraging them to engage with the subject on a deeper level. The use of black-and-white photography is a powerful means of challenging dominant narratives and creating space for marginalized voices to be seen and heard. Through this technique, photographers can celebrate the resilience and strength of these women while also highlighting the injustices they continue to face in our society. Black-and-white photography has long been known for its ability to create powerful emotions in viewers. One way in which black-and-white photography achieves this is through the use of contrast. By using deep shadows and bright highlights, photographers can create a sense of drama and intensity in their images. This can be particularly effective in portraying dark or moody subjects, such as urban landscapes or portraits of people in difficult circumstances. Another way in which black-and-white photography evokes powerful emotions is through its ability to simplify complex scenes. By removing color, artists like Susana Pilar are able to focus on the lines, textures, and shapes within an image, creating a sense of harmony and balance. This can be particularly effective when photographing natural landscapes or architecture, as the absence of color allows the viewer to appreciate the beauty and structure of these elements in a new way. Black-and-white photography can evoke powerful emotions by tapping into our collective memory and cultural associations with the medium. Many people associate black-and-white photography with nostalgia, romanticism, or even melancholy, and these emotions can be powerful tools for creating a connection between the viewer and the subject. By using black-and-white photography to depict the experiences of marginalized communities, artists such as Susana Pilar can tap into these emotions to create a sense of empathy and understanding in their viewers.

Dibujo Intercontinental/Intercontinental Drawing

The art piece *Intercontinental Drawing* (figure 4.1) by Susana Pilar is a powerful representation of the transatlantic slave trade and the complex identity formation experienced by Afro-Cubans. Within the photograph, Susana Pilar is depicted with a cord tied to her waist, symbolizing the connection between her body and the boat that she is dragging. This boat represents the oppressive history of slavery and colonization and serves as a metaphor for the African diaspora and the forced migration of enslaved Africans across the Atlantic Ocean. The act of dragging the boat signifies the enduring legacy of this traumatic past and the ongoing struggles faced by Afro-descendant communities. The use of black-and-white photography further emphasizes the historical context of the transatlantic slave trade,

Figure 4.1. *Dibujo intercontinental*, Susana Pilar, 2017, performance, two hours. *Source:* Photo by Marnix van den Berg. Image courtesy of Artist and Galleria Continua.

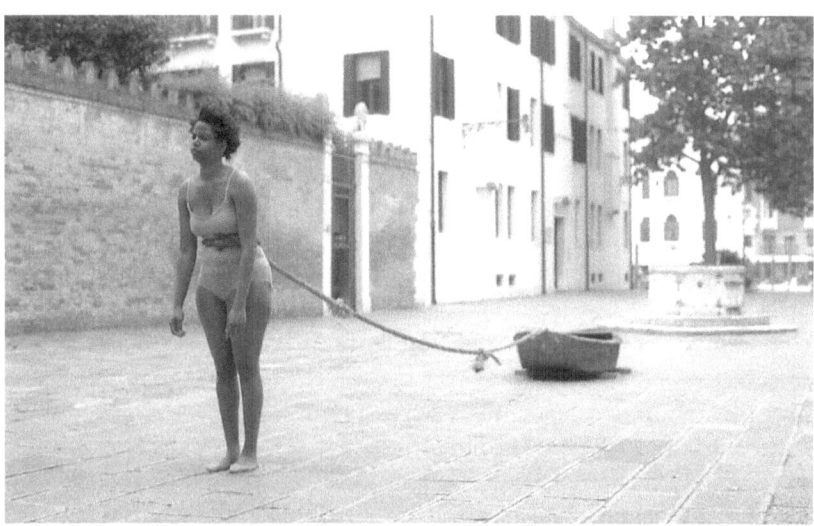

as well as the starkness and simplicity of the imagery. The absence of color also highlights the universal nature of the issues being addressed, transcending specific time periods and locations. The cord tied to Susana Pilar's waist suggests a physical and emotional connection to both Africa and the Americas. It reflects the tension and duality experienced by individuals of African descent who are simultaneously part of two continents, and the feelings of displacement and disconnection that arise from this dual identity. By visually representing this tension, Pilar invites viewers to explore the complexities of cultural hybridity and the psychological impact of the African diaspora.

Furthermore, the act of dragging the boat can be interpreted as an act of resistance and empowerment. It symbolizes the strength and resilience of Afro-Cuban people in reclaiming their history and asserting their agency. By acknowledging and confronting the painful legacy of slavery, Pilar challenges the dominant narratives that have silenced and marginalized Afro-descendant communities. *Intercontinental Drawing* is a profound exploration of the transatlantic slave trade, and the fractured identity experienced by Afro-Cubans. Through the symbolism of the cord, the boat, and the act of dragging, Pilar addresses the historical trauma of slavery, the complexities of cultural hybridity, and the ongoing struggles for recognition and equality. The use of black–and-white photography further enhances the impact of the piece, emphasizing its universal relevance and timeless significance. The symbol of the boat in this piece is significant in several ways. The boat represents the literal journey of enslaved Africans across the Atlantic during the transatlantic slave trade. This journey was marked by extreme hardship, suffering, and loss. By incorporating the boat into her artwork, Pilar brings attention to this history of forced migration and its enduring impact on Afro-descendant communities. Additionally, the act of dragging the boat can be seen as a metaphorical representation of the ongoing struggle for recognition, justice, and equality faced by Afro-Cubans and other Afro-descendant communities. It symbolizes their resilience and determination to reclaim their history and assert their agency in the face of systemic oppression and marginalization. The boat also serves as a powerful visual reminder of the cultural hybridity experienced by Afro-Cubans. It represents the blending of African, European, and Indigenous influences that have shaped their identity. By including this symbol, Pilar highlights the complexities and richness of Afro-Cuban culture and invites viewers to reflect on the interconnectedness of different cultures and histories. Overall, the symbol of the boat in *Intercontinental Drawing* encapsulates the historical trauma of the transatlantic slave trade, the ongoing struggles for recognition and equality, and the cultural hybridity experienced by Afro-descendant communities. Through this symbol, Pilar prompts viewers to engage with these complex themes and confront the painful legacies of slavery and colonialism. The fact that the boat is tied with a cord to Susana Pilar's waist adds another layer of symbolism to her artwork. It can be interpreted as representing the personal connection and responsibility that individuals have to their own histories and the legacies of forced migration and oppression. By physically attaching the boat to her waist, Pilar may be suggesting that these historical traumas are not something that can simply be detached or forgotten. They are deeply intertwined with her own identity and the identities of Afro-descendant communities. The cord could also symbolize the bonds of resilience and determination that connect these communities and their ongoing struggle for recognition and justice. Furthermore, the cord could be seen as a nod to the idea of intergenerational trauma, highlighting how the impact of the transatlantic slave trade and colonialism continues to reverberate through generations. By visually linking herself to the boat, Pilar emphasizes the personal and collective responsibility to confront and address these legacies. The cord attaching the boat to Susana Pilar's waist reinforces the themes of personal connection, responsibility, resilience, and intergenerational trauma within her artwork. The physical attachment of the boat to Susana Pilar's waist symbolizes the personal connection and responsibility individuals have to their own histories and legacies in several ways. First, it represents a tangible bond between Pilar and the history she is addressing. By physically attaching the boat to her waist, Pilar is visually demonstrating her personal connection to the historical events and experiences she is referencing. This attachment serves as a reminder that these histories are not distant or abstract, but deeply intertwined with her own identity. Second, the attachment implies a sense of burden and responsibility. Just as the boat is physically attached to Pilar, she is symbolically attached to the legacies and ongoing struggles of forced migration and oppression. This suggests that individuals have a responsibility to confront and acknowledge their own histories, as well as actively engage in the fight for justice and recognition for marginalized communities. Additionally, physical attachment highlights the idea that these histories cannot be easily detached or forgotten. They persist and continue to impact the present and future generations. By visually linking herself to the boat, Pilar emphasizes the lasting impact of historical traumas and the need to address them in order to create a more just and equitable society. The physical attachment of the boat to Susana Pilar's waist symbolizes the personal connection and responsibility individuals have to their own histories and legacies by visually demonstrating the bond, burden, and persistence of these histories.

Portraying this piece in black-and-white can have several benefits and this is another artistic aspect worth analyzing here. First, it can enhance the visual impact and intensity of the artwork. By removing color, the focus is placed solely on the forms, lines, and textures, allowing the viewer to fully engage with the composition and symbolism. Additionally, using black and white can evoke a timeless and universal quality. It eliminates the distraction of specific time periods or cultural contexts, allowing the artwork to resonate with people from different backgrounds and eras. This can make the piece more accessible and relatable to a wider audience. Black-and-white photography or artwork also often carries a sense of nostalgia or vintage aesthetic. This can create a sense of history and invoke a certain mood or atmosphere that aligns with the themes and subject matter of the artwork. Furthermore, choosing to depict the piece in black and white may also be a deliberate artistic choice to convey a sense of contrast or emphasis. By stripping away color, the artist may be highlighting certain elements or symbols within the artwork, drawing attention to specific details or narratives. Portraying this piece in black and white can enhance its visual impact, create a sense of timelessness and universality, evoke a specific mood or atmosphere, and allow for deliberate emphasis or focus on certain elements. Moreover, the title of the artwork, *Intercontinental Drawing*, suggests that the artist is exploring the concept of connection and exchange between continents, specifically Africa and the Americas. It implies that the artwork will depict or symbolize the interconnectedness of these two regions, particularly in relation to the transatlantic slave trade. The use of the term *drawing* indicates that this exploration will be visual in nature, possibly through the depiction of imagery or symbols related to the historical and cultural connections between Africa and the Americas.

Overall, the title sets the stage for a thoughtful examination of the transatlantic slave trade and its impact on identity and history. The title also suggests that the artwork may involve a depiction of movement or travel between continents. This could symbolize the forced migration of enslaved Africans across the Atlantic Ocean during the transatlantic slave trade. The word *intercontinental* further emphasizes the connection between two distinct regions, highlighting the historical and cultural exchanges that occurred because of this trade. The term *drawing* may also imply that the artist is using a medium or technique that involves lines, shapes, and forms to convey their message. This could suggest that the artwork will utilize visual elements to communicate the complex emotions and experiences associated with the transatlantic slave trade. By choosing to use the medium of drawing, the artist may have intentionally invoked a sense of intimacy and immediacy, allowing viewers to engage more directly with the subject matter. The title of the artwork provides insights into the artist's intentions and suggests that the piece will explore themes of connection, movement, and history. It invites viewers to contemplate the lasting impact of the transatlantic slave trade and the continued relevance of these historical events in contemporary society. The title also offers an invitation for viewers to engage in a dialogue about the intersections of identity and history. By using the term *intercontinental*, the artist acknowledges the interconnectedness of different regions and cultures, reminding us that the consequences of the transatlantic slave trade reverberate across continents to this day.

Drawing allows for a level of abstraction and interpretation, enabling the artist to convey complex emotions and ideas in a nuanced way. This choice of medium could indicate that the artwork aims to evoke a visceral response from viewers, encouraging them to reflect on their own emotions and experiences related to identity and history. Overall, the title *Intercontinental Drawing* encapsulates the multidimensional nature of the artwork and opens avenues for exploration and contemplation. It is a powerful starting point for engaging with the complexities of the transatlantic slave trade and its enduring legacies. The artist's use of the term *intercontinental* in the title emphasizes the global scope and interconnectedness of the transatlantic slave trade, inviting reflection on its far-reaching impact across diverse regions and cultures. The title suggests that the artwork is not limited to a specific geographical location but instead seeks to explore the transatlantic slave trade in a broader context. By using the term *intercontinental*, the artist acknowledges that the consequences of the transatlantic slave trade extend beyond the Americas and Africa. It recognizes that the impact of this trade reverberates across continents, affecting various regions and cultures in different ways. This concept is significant because it emphasizes the far-reaching and enduring legacies of slavery and reminds us that its effects are still felt today. Moreover, the term *intercontinental* suggests a connection or bridge between different parts of the world, symbolizing the need for dialogue and understanding among diverse communities. It encourages discussions about the shared history and experiences of people from various regions affected by the transatlantic slave trade, fostering empathy, and promoting a more comprehensive understanding of this complex issue. The artist's use of the term *intercontinental* in the title also expands the discourse surrounding the transatlantic slave trade, emphasizing its global impact, and encouraging viewers to consider the interconnectedness of different regions and cultures in relation to this historical event.

The concept of "intercontinental" broadens discussions about the legacies of slavery and its effects on different continents in several ways. First, it highlights the interconnectedness of various regions and cultures affected by the transatlantic slave trade. It encourages people to recognize that slavery was not confined to one specific area but had a global impact. This understanding fosters empathy and allows for a more comprehensive exploration of the diverse experiences of enslaved individuals and their descendants across different continents. Second, the concept of "intercontinental" prompts discussions about the shared history and experiences of people from different regions affected by slavery. It encourages dialogue and exchange of knowledge between communities, promoting a deeper understanding of the similarities and differences in how slavery impacted their lives. This can lead to the recognition of common struggles and the development of solidarity among diverse groups. Additionally, the concept of "intercontinental" brings attention to the enduring legacies of slavery. It reminds us that the consequences of this historical event are not limited to a particular time or place but continue to shape societies and cultures across continents today. By exploring these legacies, discussions can address issues such as systemic racism, economic inequalities, cultural assimilation, and the ongoing fight for justice and reparations. By emphasizing the intercontinental nature of the transatlantic slave trade, discussions can become more inclusive, comprehensive, and globally aware. This allows for a broader understanding of the impact of slavery and enables individuals to consider how its legacies continue to shape our world.

Moreover, in this piece the artist can be seen looking away from the camera or the viewer. This intentional act can have various effects on the viewer's interpretation and engagement with the artwork. The artist looking away from the camera and the viewer can then be interpreted in multiple ways. First, it can be seen as a deliberate act of defiance or resistance against being objectified or captured by the gaze of others. By avoiding direct eye contact, the artist may be asserting their agency and refusing to conform to societal expectations of how they should be seen or perceived. Additionally, the act of looking away can create a sense of mystery or intrigue, inviting the viewer to further engage with the artwork and its underlying concepts. It encourages the viewer to question why the artist is turning away and what significance this might hold within the context of the artwork. Furthermore, the artist looking away may also symbolize a form of introspection or inner reflection. By diverting their gaze inward, the artist could be conveying a deeper exploration of their own identity, experiences, and emotions. This introspective approach invites viewers to contemplate their own understanding of the themes presented in the artwork and encourages a more personal and introspective interpretation. The artist's decision to look away from the camera and the viewer adds layers of complexity and depth to the artwork. It challenges traditional notions of perspective and engagement, prompting viewers to actively participate in the interpretation and meaning-making process.

El tanque

Art has always been a powerful medium for expressing complex themes and stimulating thought-provoking conversations. In Susana Pilar's performance art piece titled *El tanque* (figure 4.2), the artist explores an intricate web of issues surrounding race, identity, power dynamics, and conformity. By using her own body as a canvas, Pilar delivers a compelling narrative that challenges conventional beauty standards and questions the impact of societal expectations on individual self-perception. The performance piece titled *El tanque* was produced in collaboration with Asunción Matienzo Serra. As stated on the artist's official website, the action is directed toward sacrifice and pain as a means of achieving a canon of aesthetic beauty—canons that differ significantly from those naturally possessed by Afro-Cuban individuals. The transformation of the body to follow a general canon that gives them public acceptance is the neuralgic point of this action. The performance consists of passing the hot comb to smooth Pilar's hair and immediately after its completion, putting her head in a tank of cold water until all the effect of the treatment has gone and her hair returns to its original state. The performance of *El tanque* centers around a sequence of three pictures, each telling a poignant story. In the

Figure 4.2. *El tanque*, Susana Pilar, 2015, performance in collaboration with Asunción Matienzo Serra. *Source:* Photo by Ana Maria La Mastra. Image courtesy of Artist.

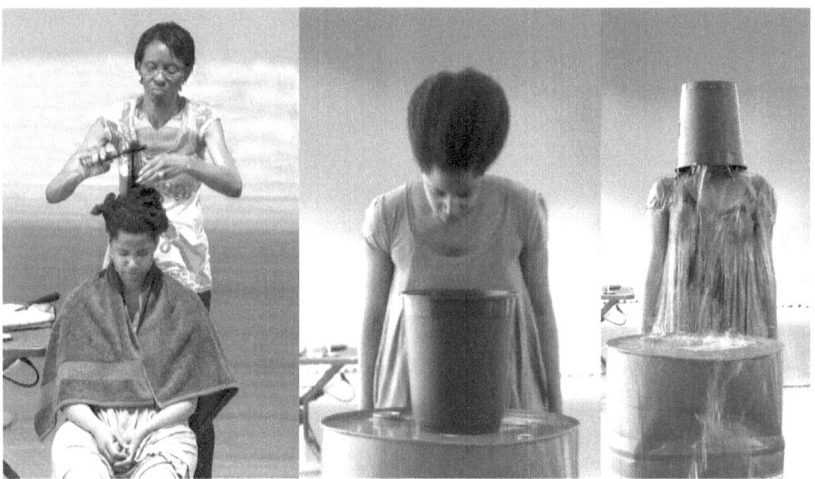

first image, we witness a Black woman passing a hot comb to smooth Susana Pilar's hair. This act holds significant symbolism as it delves into the intersectionality of race and identity. Hair texture has historically been associated with notions of beauty and cultural identity. By choosing to have a Black woman play a central role in this act, Pilar touches on the complex relationship between different racial and cultural groups and their interactions with one another. The presence of a Black woman manipulating the artist's hair also alludes to power dynamics. Throughout history, African people's hair has often been controlled or altered to conform to Eurocentric beauty standards, reflecting a broader context of power structures and privilege. The act of one person shaping another's hair subtly critiques the ways in which power is exerted and reinforces the need to question such dynamics within society. However, the narrative doesn't stop there. The second picture shows Susana Pilar approaching the tank of cold water, and in the third image she is immersing her head in the tank until the effect of the hot comb treatment has vanished, and her hair returns to its original state. This act is a powerful statement about self-expression versus conformity. It highlights the pressures individuals face to conform to societal beauty standards and the lengths to which they may go to fit in or temporarily alter their appearance. Pilar's decision to reverse the hair treatment asserts a message of empowerment, signaling the rejection of imposed beauty norms and embracing one's natural self. The theme of transformation is central to performance art, and *El tanque* is no exception. Throughout the sequence of images, the performance symbolizes metamorphosis and adaptation, emphasizing the fluidity of identity and the perpetual change individuals experience. Pilar's act of altering and then restoring her hair is a metaphorical representation of the ever-evolving nature of the self.

In the realm of artistic expression, titles play a pivotal role in guiding viewers toward the deeper meanings and intentions behind an artwork or performance. In the case of *El tanque* translating to "The Tank" in English, this title is rife with symbolic possibilities, carrying layers of significance and relevance that relate to the artwork's content. Through careful analysis, we can unravel the multidimensional interpretations and symbolic nuances associated with it. The word *tanque* in Spanish is commonly associated with confinement and containment. Tanks are closed containers used to store or transport liquids or gases, often restricting their flow and movement. In the context of the artwork described, the title *El tanque* might signify the artist's sense of being confined or restricted by societal norms and beauty standards. The act of putting the artist's head in a tank of cold water can metaphorically represent the struggle of an individual trying to break free from the restraints imposed by societal expectations. It could serve as a potent symbol of the pressures to conform and the quest for liberation. In certain contexts, *tanque* can be associated with military vehicles used in battles and conflicts. Consequently, *El tanque* could imply a personal battle or struggle within the artwork. It might reflect the artist's confrontation with societal norms, racism, or beauty standards. The performance could be interpreted as an act of resistance, urging society to address systemic issues and embrace diversity. The title itself invites viewers to contemplate the battle that the artist engages in, seeking societal transformation and positive change. A tank is also linked to the concept of transformation, as it contains substances that can undergo chemical changes. *El tanque* may therefore represent a symbolic vessel for the artist's transformational journey. In the context of the described performance, the act of reversing the hair treatment by immersing the head in a tank of water could symbolize the potential for change and the process of embracing one's natural state. It could be a statement of self-acceptance and liberation, challenging the imposed beauty standards and embracing individuality. Considering a tank as a container holding something valuable, *El tanque* could symbolize the artist's body as a metaphorical vessel for personal experiences, cultural identity, and resistance. The performance may act as an embodiment of the artist's thoughts, emotions, and experiences, pouring them into the artistic expression while simultaneously allowing viewers to immerse themselves in the narrative. The title, in this context, serves as a reminder of the richness and complexity that lies within the human form. Moreover, water in a tank is often cold, and the title *El tanque* may evoke a sense of rejection or discomfort. The act of submerging the head in cold water could symbolize the chilling effect of societal pressures on an individual's sense of identity and self-worth. It is an act of defiance, representing the artist's resilience against the cold and rigid expectations of society. Through this symbolic act, the artist communicates a message of strength and determination."El tanque" offers a plethora of symbolic interpretations, from themes of confinement and struggle to transformation and self-liberation. By exploring the depths of this evocative title, viewers can gain a better understanding of the nuanced expressions present in the artwork or performance, underscoring the enduring power of art to provoke reflection, challenge norms, and inspire change.

Now centering our attention on the element of hair in Afro-diasporic communities, we can refer to the work of Toyin Falola and his chapter titled "Yorúba Hair Art and the Agency of Women," in the book *Decolonizing*

African Knowledge. This chapter explores the powerful element of hair as art and a symbol for Afro-diasporic communities and more specifically women. Falola affirms that "by performing what Angela Rosenthal describes as "mediating between the natural and the cultural" human hair acquires centrality in the discourse of the body, connected to that which encompasses it. The natural and the cultural are rich metaphors of the environment and humans, respectively, which once again highlight the centrality of hair's role as medium" (374). The author explains that in traditional Yoruba, hair actively signifies gender (374), and it possesses a high level of expressivity with an extensive symbolic potentiality (375). Hair is a powerful agent that always communicates, and as Rosenthal argues "emerging from the flesh and thus both of, and without the body—at once corporeal and a mere lifeless extension" (1).

Rosenthal's perspective highlights the profound significance of hair as a potent form of communication, especially within Afro-diasporic communities. Hair has always held great cultural and historical significance among people of African descent, symbolizing identity, spirituality, and resistance against societal norms and discrimination. The connection between hair and communication is deeply rooted in the history of Afro-diasporic communities, where hairstyles and grooming practices have served as a means of expressing cultural pride, heritage, and resistance. The phrase "emerging from the flesh and thus both of, and without the body—at once corporeal and a mere lifeless extension" delves into the complex duality of hair as an extension of the physical body and a representation of something beyond the physical realm. For many in Afro-diasporic communities, hair carries immense cultural and spiritual significance, acting as an expression of connection to their roots and ancestors. It becomes a living testament to their heritage, a reminder of the journeys and struggles their communities have endured. At the same time, the quote suggests that hair, despite being physically attached to the body, transcends mere flesh. It becomes a canvas for storytelling, carrying historical and cultural narratives that may not be visible at first glance. Hair is a symbol of resilience, creativity, and adaptability, reflecting the diverse experiences and emotions of Afro-diasporic individuals throughout history. Moreover, the act of grooming and styling hair within Afro-diasporic communities can be a ritualistic and transformative experience. Hair care practices, such as braiding, locking, or styling into intricate patterns, are often imbued with cultural and spiritual meanings. Through these practices, individuals not only communicate their identity to the world but also connect with their roots, forging a link between the past, present, and future. In contemporary society, hair remains a powerful form of self-expression and resistance. Embracing natural hairstyles, such as Afros, braids, and dreadlocks, is an act of reclamation, challenging Eurocentric beauty standards and embracing one's authentic self. This act of defiance against societal norms is both a celebration of the corporeal body and a declaration of individuality beyond physicality. Yoruba's hair is a powerful identifier for spiritual, cultural, marital, gender, and physical status (Falola 2022, 376) and is therefore much more than a bodily extension: "Hair, as part of the body, is a site for cultural production, agency, and staging, and a gendered agent itself. All this occurs with the hair of Yoruba women" (376). Hair then becomes the physical framing of the self, what the Yoruba call *ará*[5] (377) and an index that carves out space for the "visuality of physiognomy" (Miller 2001, 187). As hair is one of the most powerful identity and culture signifier, Susana Pilar with her art stresses the importance of decolonizing it. As Kobena Mercer also points out "hair functions as a key 'ethnic signifier' because, compared with bodily shape or facial features, it can be changed more easily. by cultural practices" (248).

This quote by Kobena Mercer highlights the significant role of hair as an "ethnic signifier" within cultural contexts. Unlike bodily shape or facial features, hair is a malleable and versatile aspect of one's appearance that can be easily transformed through cultural practices. As such, hair becomes a powerful tool for expressing ethnic identity, heritage, and affiliation, particularly within diverse communities where cultural practices and traditions are cherished and celebrated. Throughout history, hair has played a crucial role in defining and communicating ethnic identity. Different ethnic groups have distinct hair textures, styles, and grooming practices that are passed down through generations, becoming emblematic of their cultural heritage. By altering their hairstyles, individuals can effectively communicate their affiliations, embracing and expressing their ethnicity, and engaging in a form of cultural self-representation. In the context of Afro-diasporic communities, hair has been a key ethnic signifier with profound historical and sociopolitical implications. During the era of transatlantic slavery, African hairstyles were suppressed and stigmatized by colonial powers seeking to erase cultural identities. As a result, hairstyles such as braids, dreadlocks, and Afros became powerful symbols of resistance and resilience. Despite attempts to suppress these cultural practices, they persisted and thrived, becoming enduring markers of ethnic pride and identity among Afro-diasporic individuals. In contemporary times, hair continues to serve as an ethnic signifier, even as societies become more diverse and interconnected. Hair care practices, including styles, textures, and adornments, are increasingly recognized as essential components of cultural heritage. From traditional ceremonies to everyday self-expression, individuals from diverse ethnic backgrounds use their hair to connect with their roots, preserve their cultural heritage, and celebrate their unique identity. Moreover, the quote points to the idea that hair is not fixed; it can be easily transformed through cultural practices. This flexibility reflects the fluidity of cultural identity, which evolves and adapts over time. People can use their hair as a dynamic canvas for expressing different aspects of their cultural identity, embracing hybridity and multiple influences while staying rooted in their heritage. Hair is strictly tied to racialized gender identity and knowing and embracing its cultural meaning is tied to regaining power and agency for marginalized communities. Susana Pilar fully embraces this need for ancestral knowledge and awareness when in her piece she decides to put her head in a tank full of cold water until her hair returns to its original state and the treatment effects cannot be noticed anymore. This reflects what Paulette Caldwell points out when she says, "I want to know my hair again, the way I knew it before I knew that my hair is me, before I lost the right to me, before I knew that the burden of beauty—or lack of it—for an entire race of people could be tied up with my hair and me" (275). At the end of the performance, in Pilar's *El tanque*, the artist's hair ends up being completely natural and undone and this aspect is also extremely powerful from a Yoruba perspective. As Falola clearly states, "a woman's hair undone signifies dangerous behavior, emotional discontent, and an inner state of distress or disengagement. It could be a show of dissent, a claim to power through the rejection of the standard, surrender to noncorporeal forces" (384). A woman's hair signifies her embrace of feminine wisdom and power. It becomes a powerful statement instructive of the sacredness of a person's essence (386). Hair is then an empowering medium and a vehicle of communication, and in Yoruba traditions it is also believed to have eyes. As Falola explains,

> It symbolizes the presence of an affecting feature, resituating the entire body as a site of visual appeal and enticing viewers who hold its gaze, commune with it, or dialogue with it. In this sense, hair can be said to have eyes, or even a face (one that possesses eyes and mouth—two powerful vehicles of

communication) calling out to passerby and intending for communicants to view it, and also relate it to its host. This reflects the Yoruba belief that "Ohun gbogdo ló lójú" (everything has eyes). It also references the popular idiom that "Ojú l'óró wá" (the eyes are where the matter lies). (389)

Falola's study delves into the profound symbolism and communicative power of hair, particularly in the context of Yoruba culture. It highlights how hair transcends its physical form, becoming an affecting feature that draws attention, captivates viewers, and initiates dialogue and connection. This analysis reveals the cultural significance of hair in Yoruba belief systems and its broader implications for human communication and self-expression. Falola suggests that hair symbolizes the presence of an affecting feature. This characterization emphasizes the visual appeal of hair, which goes beyond being a mere accessory or physical attribute. Instead, it becomes a powerful element that communicates, engages, and evokes emotions. The transformative nature of hair takes center stage, resituating the entire body as a site of visual and communicative allure. This concept resonates with the artistic and expressive aspects of hair within Yoruba culture, where intricate hairstyles and grooming practices hold deep cultural significance. Falola's quote introduces the idea that hair can be seen as possessing eyes and a face, imbuing it with a sense of sentience. This anthropomorphization of hair is crucial in understanding its role as a vehicle of communication. In Yoruba tradition, it is thought that everything has eyes, a concept that extends to hair and suggests a profound connection between human beings and their physical attributes. As hair seemingly gazes back at viewers, it calls for a mutual exchange and dialogue between the hair and the observer, reinforcing the idea that communication is not just one-way but interactive. The concept of "Ojú l'óró wá" (the eyes are where the matter lies) further reinforces the significance of visual communication. In Yoruba culture, the eyes are considered powerful vehicles of expression and communication. By attributing eyes and a face to hair, the quote suggests that hair possesses the same potential for expression and communication. This resonates with the notion that the physical attributes of a person can carry significant meaning and convey messages beyond words. In Yoruba culture, hair is an essential part of self-presentation and cultural identity. Different hairstyles and grooming practices reflect aspects of one's heritage, social status, and personal expression. The way hair is styled and adorned can convey messages about one's background, beliefs, and affiliations within the community. Moreover, hair is often intricately styled for special occasions and ceremonies, emphasizing its communicative role in cultural celebrations and rituals. By imbuing hair with eyes and a face, the quote underlines its capacity to engage viewers, initiate dialogue, and reflect the Yoruba belief that everything has eyes. The idea that hair possesses eyes aligns with the cultural importance of visual communication and the broader notion that physical attributes can convey deep meaning and messages. In essence, hair becomes a potent symbol of cultural expression and connection, reflecting the richness and complexity of Yoruba traditions.

Hair can also have a profound spiritual meaning, especially in connection to the Orisha Obatalá, the grand patron of the arts and the divine artist of creativity, who is known to mold humans from divine clay; it is believed that he molds the head, and therefore also the hair, first, attending to it with unequally care (Falola 2022, 394). After all these considerations, we "cannot deny the status of hair as art and woman as artist" (400). As Falola argues,

> The domain of hair, as made art, is public. It is made for public consumption, appreciation, use, and appeal. Knowledge of the public space's dynamic and functional structure is also instrumental to its creation. The *Onidirí* and the subject perform as societal beings in the heart of the public space, where women generally navigate the tides and tensions of public life. The salon, which is the home of the coiffeuse or *Onidirí*, naturally doubles as a place of creation and exhibition. In fact, it functions as an interconnecting space, supporting the fluidity of tradition and serving as the home of patronage, artistic influence, entrepreneurship, apprenticeship, and the place of power shifts. (400–1)

In this quote by Toyin Falola, the author delves into the domain of hair, particularly as an art form in the context of African societies. The passage sheds light on the multifaceted role of hair and the salon, emphasizing its significance as a public space where cultural dynamics and social interactions converge. Falola argues that the art of hair extends beyond mere personal expression, becoming a public spectacle for consumption, appreciation, and appeal. Hair, when styled and adorned, transcends individual aesthetics and takes on a social dimension. It becomes a means of communication, conveying cultural identity, and reflecting societal norms and values. The *onidirí*, or coiffeuse, and the subject receiving the hair treatment, both take on roles as societal beings within the public space. This notion highlights the salon's significance as a communal gathering place, where women navigate the complexities of public life. It becomes a space of camaraderie, exchange, and collective experience, where shared cultural practices and traditions find expression. The salon serves as not only a place for hairstyling but also a space for creativity and exhibition. It becomes a canvas for the coiffeuse's artistic skills and vision, displaying a repertoire of techniques and styles that are deeply embedded in cultural heritage. Moreover, the salon operates as an interconnecting hub, facilitating the fluidity of tradition and acting as a nexus for various social interactions. The salon functions as an interconnecting space that supports the fluidity of tradition and serves multiple purposes. It becomes a place for creativity and exhibition, where unique hairstyles are crafted and showcased, reflecting the individuality and cultural diversity of the community.

Additionally, the salon acts as a center for patronage, where clients seek the services of skilled coiffeuses who hold expertise in the art of hairstyling. Beyond mere hairstyling, the salon becomes a hub for artistic influence and entrepreneurship. Coiffeuses often innovate and create new hairstyles, drawing from both traditional and contemporary inspirations, contributing to the evolution of hairdressing as an art form. Entrepreneurship thrives within the salon as coiffeuses run their businesses, fostering economic independence and financial empowerment for themselves and their communities. The salon also serves as a place of apprenticeship, where younger individuals learn the skills and techniques of hairdressing from experienced coiffeuses, ensuring the preservation and transmission of this artistic tradition from one generation to another. Finally, the salon is a place where power dynamics may shift, as talented coiffeuses can gain prominence and respect within their communities, becoming influential figures and leaders. Additionally, the salon plays an essential role in economic empowerment and social mobility. It becomes a site of patronage, where clients invest in their appearances, contributing to the livelihood of the coiffeuse and her apprentices. Moreover, it fosters entrepreneurship, providing opportunities for women to establish and grow their businesses. The salon also serves as a place of knowledge transmission and power dynamics. It becomes a space for apprenticeship, where young individuals learn the art of hairstyling and the cultural significance behind each technique. Additionally, it acts as a platform for the exchange of ideas

and artistic influence, shaping the evolution of hairstyles and their societal meanings. Toyin Falola's analysis delves into the domain of hair as a
form of public art in African societies and helps us understand its value
in Susana Pilar's art. It emphasizes the salon's role as a space of cultural
expression, creativity, and social interaction. The salon becomes a nexus
where women navigate public life, exchange ideas, and uphold traditions,
while also serving as a place of entrepreneurship, knowledge transmission,
and artistic influence. Hair, in this context, transcends individuality and
becomes a powerful medium for communal identity and societal dynamics.
Falola also asserts that: "Contrary to modern culture, hair is never linked
solely to femininity or notions of attractiveness; it is highly symbolic of
social order, historical details, lineage architecture, spirituality, mythology,
class, gender, ethnicity, and many other things. It is hard to deny the
power that works through hair" (405). We can then see how the author
challenges the simplistic and superficial understanding of hair in modern
culture. Contrary to popular belief, hair is not merely linked to femininity
or notions of attractiveness. Instead, it holds a profound and multifaceted
symbolism that encompasses a wide range of social, historical, and cultural
aspects. First, hair is seen as a powerful symbol of social order. In many
societies, hairstyles can communicate one's social status, role, or position
within the community. Different hairstyles may indicate membership in
a particular group, such as royalty or a specific profession, signifying the
complex hierarchical structures of societies. Second, hair carries historical
details and lineage architecture. In some cultures, ancestral hairstyles are
passed down through generations, preserving a family's history and connecting individuals to their heritage. This tradition of preserving historical
hairstyles can provide valuable insights into a community's identity and
evolution over time. Third, hair is deeply intertwined with spirituality
and mythology. In various cultures, hair holds spiritual significance and
is regarded as a conduit to the divine. It may play a role in religious ceremonies, rituals, or acts of devotion. Additionally, hair is often associated
with mythical creatures or gods, representing their power or attributes.
Moreover, hair can signify class, gender, and ethnicity. Different hairstyles
may denote one's social class, and certain hairstyles can be specific to
particular genders or ethnic groups. Hair becomes a visual marker of identity, contributing to the diversity and richness of cultural expressions. By
emphasizing the diverse symbolism of hair, Falola highlights its intrinsic
importance as an expression of human identity and culture. Hair holds
immense power as a bearer of cultural heritage and a communicator of

intricate social nuances. Its significance goes beyond surface-level aesthetics and extends into the realms of tradition, spirituality, and individual and collective identity. This reflection serves as a reminder of the depth and complexity embedded in the symbolism of hair. It encourages us to move beyond simplistic associations and recognize the profound cultural, historical, and spiritual meanings woven into hairstyles. By acknowledging the multiple dimensions through which hair operates, we gain a deeper appreciation for its role in shaping the fabric of societies and the intricate tapestry of human experiences.

The fact that Susana Pilar intentionally decided to display herself with undone hair, speaks to her desire to disrupt Western standardized norms and colonized conceptions of beauty. As Falola explains, in Yoruba traditions, "these hairstyles are not manifestations of beauty, but their beauty-opposing and repudiating states manifest the symbolic power of their anti-aesthetics" (409). The author also recognizes that unmade hair is also linked to something sacred as the beginning of all creations.

> Apart from unmade hair serving in anti-aesthetic capacities, it also renders and refers to the symbolic cycle of birth and rebirth. In Yorùbá ontology and cosmology, life is believed to have come from chaos. Olódùmarè spoke the world into existence, mandating the Òrìsà to create the earth in a space that was previously void and filled with water. Beautiful hair is a finished product created from something more unrefined and chaotic—the unmade hair. Proceeding from the metaphor of the phoenix rising from ashes, well-styled hair is a beautiful thing that has grown and received life from the disheveled hair. In this context, the unmade hair is neither anti-aesthetic nor a signifier of a troubled state; it is the first stage of creation for a thing that will be aesthetically pleasing. (409)

In relation to the artistic piece of Susana Pilar analyzed here and her choice to return to undone, natural hair, Falola also comments on the symbolic significance of unmade hair, challenging the perception of unstyled hair as merely anti-aesthetic or a sign of a troubled state. Instead, he presents unmade hair as a representation of the cyclical process of birth and rebirth, drawing on Yorùbá ontology and cosmology to explore its deeper meaning. The quote above begins by acknowledging that unmade hair is often associated with being unkempt or lacking aesthetic appeal.

However, Falola shifts the narrative by presenting unmade hair as more than just its initial state. He connects it to the Yorùbá belief in the origin of life, where chaos precedes creation. In Yorùbá cosmology, Olódùmarè is the supreme being, who spoke the world into existence, and the Òrìṣà (deities) were tasked with shaping the earth out of a previously formless and watery space. Drawing from this cosmological concept, Falola draws a parallel between the process of creation and the state of unmade hair. Just as the world emerged from chaos, beautiful hair is the result of a transformation from the initial unrefined and chaotic state of unmade hair. This transformation is likened to the metaphor of the phoenix rising from ashes, where well-styled hair symbolizes a beautiful product that has grown and received life from the disheveled state of unmade hair. By making this connection, Falola challenges the perception that unmade hair is inherently undesirable. Instead, he imbues it with a profound sense of significance and potential. Unmade hair becomes the first stage of creation, the raw material from which beauty emerges. It is a representation of the cyclicality of life, where disorder and chaos are essential elements in the process of transformation and creation. In this context, unmade hair in Susana Pilar's piece becomes a symbol of the inherent beauty and potential that lies within all things, even in their seemingly disordered or unrefined states. It reminds us that beauty is not solely defined by societal standards but is a multifaceted concept that includes the natural and unadorned aspects of life. Embracing the concept of unmade hair as a stage in the cycle of creation challenges conventional beauty norms and encourages a deeper appreciation for the beauty that exists in the raw and unrefined elements of existence. Falola's analysis of unmade hair offers a profound perspective on its symbolic significance, rooted in Yorùbá ontology and cosmology. By connecting unmade hair to the cyclicality of creation, the author and Susana Pilar challenge the notion that it is inherently anti-aesthetic or indicative of a troubled state. Instead, unmade hair becomes a powerful symbol of beauty in its raw and unadorned state, representing the potential for transformation and the cyclical nature of life. This perspective invites us to reconsider our preconceived notions of beauty and embrace the inherent beauty that lies within all things, even in their most unrefined and chaotic forms.

Another critical aspect worth analyzing is the employment of different shades of pink as background color in this performance piece. The use of different shades of pink as the only recognizable color throughout the three images raises intriguing questions about its employment and underlying symbology. By exploring the significance of this color choice, we can aim to delve into the deeper meanings and messages conveyed by the artist's unique artistic expression. As we now know, in the performance, a Black woman passes a hot comb through Susana Pilar's hair, symbolizing a form of racial assimilation and the imposition of Eurocentric beauty standards. Immediately after this process, Pilar submerges her head in a tank of cold water until her hair returns to its natural state. Throughout the performance, the artist uses different shades of pink, which becomes the sole recognizable color. Pink has traditionally been associated with femininity, softness, and innocence. In the context of *El tanque*, its use can be seen as a subversion of these traditional associations. By employing pink in the context of a performance that challenges beauty standards and explores the complexities of race and identity, Susana Pilar challenges preconceived notions of femininity and invites viewers to question societal norms.

The use of different shades of pink can also be interpreted as a symbol of cultural and racial identity. As the artist undergoes the hot combing process, her hair is temporarily straightened, representing a relinquishing of her natural identity to conform to imposed standards. The varying shades of pink might signify the multifaceted nature of identity, implying that one's true identity cannot be reduced to a single color or stereotype. Within the Afro-descendant community, colorism remains a significant issue, with lighter skin tones often being favored over darker ones. The use of pink may be a poignant way to symbolize colorism and challenge the hierarchy of skin tones perpetuated by society. It confronts the viewer with the idea that even in a monochrome world, the differentiation of shades persists, reminding us of the complexities of racial dynamics. Despite the societal pressure to conform to Eurocentric beauty standards, the artist's act of submerging her head in cold water, causing her hair to return to its original state, embodies resilience and empowerment. This act symbolizes a reclamation of identity and the rejection of imposed beauty ideals. The color pink derives its name from the flowers known as "pinks," which are flowering plants belonging to the genus dianthus (Cornett 1998). The term *pinks* originates from the characteristic frilled or serrated edge of these flowers, which gives them a distinctive and delicate appearance. The delicate and soft hues of these flowers, ranging from pale blush to vibrant fuchsia, have been associated with the color pink, inspiring its naming and evoking a sense of tenderness and femininity. Throughout history, the color pink has been linked to various symbolic meanings, often reflecting notions of sweetness, love, and affection. Its association with the gentle and romantic qualities of flowers, such as roses and cherry blossoms, has contributed to its depiction as a color of love and beauty. Additionally, the playful and youthful connotations of pink have made it a popular choice for children's toys, clothing, and decor.[6] Public opinion surveys conducted in Europe and the United States reveal that pink is widely regarded as the color most closely associated with a range of positive attributes. These include charm, politeness, sensitivity, tenderness, sweetness, softness, childhood, femininity, and romance. The color pink consistently evokes sentiments of gentleness, warmth, and affection, making it a beloved hue that resonates with various aspects of human emotion and experience (Heller 2009, 179–85). In both Europe and the United States, pink has traditionally been linked to girls, while blue has been associated with boys. The practice of using these colors as gender signifiers began just before World War I, without a strict association to either gender. However, it was in the 1940s when pink was firmly established as a female gender signifier. Since then, these color associations have become deeply ingrained in societal norms, but it's important to recognize that they are relatively recent historical developments and not inherent to the colors themselves (Paoletti 2012, 87). Since 2008, numerous feminist groups and Breast Cancer Awareness Month campaigns have adopted the color pink as a symbol of women's empowerment. Breast cancer charities worldwide also utilize the color to represent support for individuals battling breast cancer and to raise awareness about the disease. The color pink has become a powerful emblem, signifying solidarity, strength, and advocacy for women's health and rights (Mitchell & Reid-Walsh 2022, 47). However, it is crucial to acknowledge that the significance of the color pink to femininity is a Western phenomenon. While pink is associated with masculinity in Japan and symbolizes a welcoming embrace in India, its gender associations vary across cultures. This demonstrates how color symbolism is culturally contingent and can hold different meanings and connotations in diverse societies. Then, the pink hues throughout the performance could represent the fluidity of identity, the ability to resist, and the power of self-determination. Therefore, the use of different shades of pink as the only recognizable color offers a multilayered and symbolic narrative. By subverting traditional associations, symbolizing cultural and racial identity, confronting colorism, and portraying resilience and empowerment, the artist employs pink to challenge viewers' perceptions and foster a deeper understanding of the complexities surrounding race, beauty, and identity. Through this evocative use of color, Pilar invites us to engage in a meaningful dialogue about social constructs and the journey to self-acceptance and self-empowerment.

Susana Pilar's performance art piece, *El tanque*, offers a thought-provoking and multilayered exploration of race, identity, power dynamics, conformity, and self-expression. By employing her body as a canvas for storytelling, Pilar confronts societal beauty norms and challenges viewers to question their assumptions and biases. The act of manipulating and then reversing the hair treatment serves as a powerful metaphor for empowerment, liberation, and the celebration of one's authentic self. Through this performance, Pilar prompts a broader dialogue about the complexities of human experience and the role of art in reflecting and challenging social constructs. *El tanque* stands as a testament to the enduring power of art as a means of critical inquiry and introspection.

The Symbolism of Survival: *Llave maestra/Master Key*

In the realms of art and symbolism, certain images can captivate and evoke profound emotional responses, while conveying layers of complex meaning. The third image analyzed in this chapter, the evocative photograph titled *Llave maestra* or *Master Key* (figure 4.3) demonstrates this capacity through its exploration of Cuban women's narratives. In this work, Afro-Cuban artist Susana Pilar wields a machete with a resolute grip, reinterpreting this iconic symbol of Cuban independence as a representation of resilience and self-defense. This section of the book is dedicated to an in-depth analysis of the profound symbolism inherent in the artwork, drawing connections to Audre Lorde's concept of "master's tools" and exploring the empowering narratives it embodies. Through a careful examination of the image and its contextual framework, this analysis aims to elucidate the rich tapestry of meaning embedded within Pilar's work and its broader sociocultural implications. To fully comprehend the symbolism encapsulated in *Llave maestra/Master Key*, it is crucial to first address the historical and cultural significance of the machete. Historically, the machete has been a symbol of Cuban independence and resistance against colonial domination, functioning as a tool wielded by revolutionaries in the struggle for liberation.

Desch-Obi (2009) explains that for centuries, the machete served as a crucial tool for agriculture and warfare in West and Central Africa. Its significance persisted during slavery in the Caribbean, where it kept its potential as a weapon. Prior to their enslavement, Africans in Biafra (now

Figure 4.3. *Llave maestra (Master Key)*, Susana Pilar, 2010 to 2012. Print on aluminum, 200 cm × 150 cm. *Source:* Photo by Susana Pilar. Image courtesy of Bruno Devos.

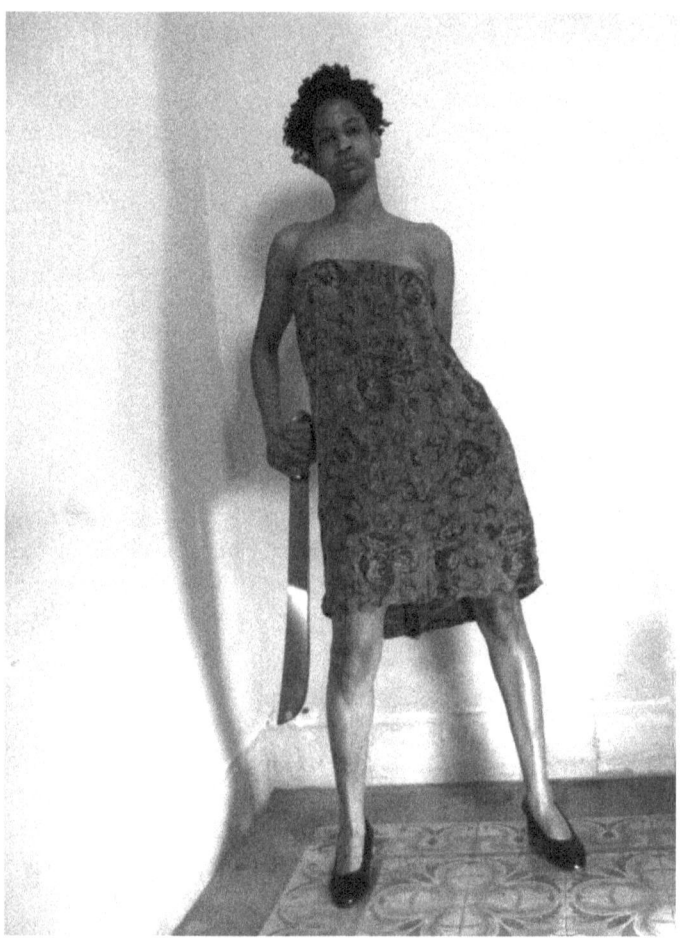

southeastern Nigeria) employed the machete as their primary tool in times of war. During periods of relative peace, they showcased their mastery of this weapon through sportive contests involving fighting sticks or wooden machetes known as *abariba*. Additionally, among Catholic Kongolese, the machete represented Saint James the conqueror, while for many in the Bight of Benin, it remained an emblem of the war deity, Ogun. Enslaved Africans carried these spiritual associations with them into the bonds of

American slavery, perpetuating them through various religious traditions in the Circum-Caribbean. However, within the larger secular and oppressive social context of racial slavery, the machete may have assumed a more ambiguous significance for many Caribbean enslaved individuals. Some may have viewed it as an instrument of oppression, symbolizing their subjugation and servile status. Machetes continued to hold a significant position during the Cuban Wars of Independence. Within these battles for liberation, Afro-Cuban soldiers frequently occupied prominent positions within the ranks (Ada Ferrer 1999). It is also fundamental to point out that the utilization of machetes by Black troops in Cuba was what instilled the most fear in Spanish soldiers (Martel 1946). John Lawrence Tone also suggests that "the machete was elevated to a central place in Cuban iconography not because it won battles, but because it was unmatched as a symbol of national unity, first against Spain and later against the United States" (8). Pilar, however, takes this symbol and recontextualizes it, shifting its significance from the struggle for independence to one of survival and defense. The machete, in Pilar's hands, becomes a tool of self-defense and protection. It embodies strength, resilience, and agency. By gripping the machete firmly, Pilar asserts her power and challenges societal expectations placed on Cuban women. It subverts traditional gender roles and confronts stereotypes, allowing for the reclamation of power and autonomy through physicality and symbolism. *Llave maestra/ Master Key* provides a transformative portrayal of Cuban women, high-lighting their strength and resilience. Pilar's exploration of the image seeks to challenge existing stereotypes and empower Afro-Cuban women. In a society often plagued by racial and gender inequalities, Pilar confronts the complexities of intersectionality and Afro-Cuban identity, shedding light on the experiences and struggles faced by these women. The photograph signifies a departure from victimhood, offering a narrative of empower-ment and agency. It presents Cuban women as active participants in their own stories, reclaiming their history and identity. By visualizing herself gripping the machete, Pilar showcases the ability to reshape the power dynamics within society and assert her place in history.

The above photograph is one of the three images in the series *Llave maestra/Master Key* (2012). On her website, the artist explains that these photos are an actual exploration she was doing trying to represent the actual image, condition, and attitude of many Cuban women. The machete as a symbol of Cuban independence is turned here as a symbol of surviv-ing defense. Moreover, the imagery in *Llave maestra/Master Key* bears a profound connection to Audre Lorde's concept of "master's tools" (1984). Lorde's work explores the limitations imposed by using the tools of the master's design, which perpetuate oppressive structures. Pilar's reimagining of the machete subverts these structures, transforming it from a symbol of dominance and control into a tool of survival and resistance. Audre Lorde's concept of "master's tools" is rooted in her examination of power dynamics and systems of oppression. In her essay "The Master's Tools Will Never Dismantle the Master's House," Lorde argues that utilizing the tools provided by the dominant culture or oppressive systems does not lead to true liberation or the dismantling of those systems. Instead, she calls for the creation and utilization of alternative tools that challenge and subvert oppressive structures. The term *master's tools* refers to the established systems, frameworks, and methods that maintain the status quo and perpetuate inequality and injustice.

These tools are inherently designed to serve the interests of those in power, marginalizing and silencing the voices of marginalized communities. Lorde contends that attempting to effect change using the very tools that maintain the existing power structure will only perpetuate the cycle of oppression. Connecting Lorde's theory to Susana Pilar's work, we can observe how Pilar reimagines and subverts the master's tools to challenge oppressive systems and empower marginalized communities, specifically Afro-Cuban women. Through her artwork, Pilar engages with symbols, such as the machete, which historically represented power and dominance within the context of Cuban independence. However, she transforms these symbols, imbuing them with new meaning and reclaiming them as tools of survival, resistance, and empowerment. By utilizing the machete, Pilar repurposes a symbol that was once synonymous with the master's tools and dominance and redefines it as a tool of personal agency and collective empowerment. In doing so, she exemplifies Lorde's call for the creation and utilization of alternative tools that challenge the oppressive structures. Furthermore, Pilar's approach aligns with Lorde's emphasis on the importance of centering the voices and experiences of marginalized communities in shaping their own narratives. Pilar's work elevates the stories, struggles, and resilience of Afro-Cuban women, highlighting their agency and reclaiming their place in history. In this way, she rejects the limitations imposed by the master's tools and crafts a new narrative, one that empowers and amplifies the voices of those who have been marginalized and silenced. Pilar's artistic practice embodies the essence of Lorde's concept by going beyond the mere use of the master's tools and actively reimagining and repurposing them to challenge existing power structures. Through her transformative approach, Pilar exemplifies the potential for alternative tools to create meaningful change, disrupt dominant narratives, and empower marginalized communities. Audre Lorde's concept of "master's tools" emphasizes the need to create alternative tools that challenge oppressive systems rather than relying on the tools provided by those systems. Susana Pilar's work aligns with this theory as she reimagines and subverts symbols associated with the master's tools, such as the machete, to empower marginalized communities, particularly Afro-Cuban women. Pilar's artistic practice exemplifies the transformative potential of alternative tools to challenge dominant narratives, reshape power dynamics, and amplify the voices and experiences of those who have been historically silenced.

Through her artwork, Pilar exemplifies the transformative potential of reappropriating symbols and asserting agency on one's own terms. The machete, once a tool of the oppressor, becomes a means of empowerment for Afro-Cuban women. It embodies the resilience to survive and thrive within a society that attempts to suppress their voices. At its core, *Llave maestra/Master Key* serves as a vehicle for subverting dominant narratives. Pilar challenges preconceived notions of power and agency, encouraging viewers to question existing power structures. The photograph encourages a shift from victimhood to empowerment, prompting a collective recognition and celebration of the strength, resilience, and autonomy inherent in marginalized communities. Through the reclamation of history and identity, Pilar wields the machete as a metaphorical "master key" to unlock hidden narratives. She asserts the right of Cuban women to tell their own stories, reshaping historical narratives that have long ignored or silenced their voices. In doing so, Pilar advocates for the recognition and amplification of silenced voices, reclaiming agency through symbols of survival.

Susana Pilar's *Llave maestra/Master Key* stands as a visual declaration of empowerment, challenging conventional notions of power and identity. Through her reimagined symbolism of the machete, Pilar empowers Afro-Cuban women, offering a fresh perspective on their strength and resilience. The photograph not only subverts dominant narratives but also draws inspiration from Audre Lorde's concept of "master's tools," highlighting the transformative potential of reappropriation. As viewers engage with *Llave maestra/Master Key*, they bear witness to a resounding message of empowerment and the reclamation of agency. Pilar's artwork celebrates the power, resilience, and autonomy within marginalized communities. It is a powerful reminder of the transformative potential of art to challenge existing power structures and rewrite historical narratives. Through this symbolically charged photograph, Pilar invites us to reflect on our own role in reshaping narratives, empowering voices, and embracing the power of resilience in the face of adversity.

Conclusion

In the exploration of Susana Pilar Delahante's captivating artistic pieces, a profound tapestry of themes unfolds, weaving together the threads of disconnection, resilience, and reclamation. Through her performances and images, Pilar does more than merely reflect the struggles of Afro-Cuban women; she embodies their narratives, evoking a visceral understanding of the complexities they face. This chapter's journey through her work underscores the power of art as a means to confront historical traumas, challenge societal norms, and reshape symbols to reflect contemporary struggles. The disconnection from the African homeland, a central motif in Pilar's oeuvre, serves as a resonant foundation on which her art stands. By invoking the trauma of separation in *Dibujo intercontinental/ Intercontinental Drawing*, she transforms history into a tangible, emotive experience, prompting viewers to grapple with the emotions of displacement and longing. Pilar's performances transcend mere representation; they immerse audiences in the struggle of being torn between continents, creating empathy for the complex identities of the diaspora. Pilar's work also engages with the themes of resilience and reclamation, shining a spotlight on the Afro-Cuban women's experience of negotiating beauty standards, identity, and survival. In *El tanque*, she ingeniously subverts societal norms by challenging the expectations placed on women's appearances. Through the juxtaposition of the hot comb and the tank of cold water, she redefines beauty as an individual's assertion of self, undoing the binds of conformity. This act of reclamation echoes in *Llave maestra*, where Pilar transforms the machete into a symbol of empowerment, reminding us that historical symbols can be reimagined to empower contemporary struggles. The importance of Susana Pilar's work for the visibility of Afro-Cuban women cannot be overstated. In a society often characterized by historical erasure and silenced narratives, her art becomes an invaluable instrument of empowerment. By daring to confront the intersection of gender, race, and identity, Pilar creates a platform that thrusts the experiences of Afro-Cuban women into the spotlight. Her work resonates beyond gallery walls, forging connections across borders and resonating with women whose stories have long been overlooked. In a world where visibility remains a battleground, Pilar's art takes on a role far beyond aesthetics. It becomes a vehicle for representation, a megaphone for unheard stories, and a catalyst for dialogue. Her art doesn't just seek to reflect reality; it seeks to redefine it. As we conclude this exploration of her work, we are reminded of the power of art to transform perspectives and rewrite narratives. Susana Pilar Delahante's art is not just a celebration of Afro-Cuban women; it's a transformative force that challenges us to see, feel, and understand the world through their eyes.

In a world where cultural narratives and historical representations have often marginalized and silenced certain voices, the significance of Susana Pilar Delahante's artistic contributions reverberates far beyond the canvas. In a society where Afro-Cuban women's stories have been relegated to the peripheries of discourse, Pilar's work takes center stage, carving out a space for their narratives to flourish. Her art doesn't merely exist within the realm of aesthetics; it transcends into the realm of activism, advocacy, and empowerment. At the heart of Pilar's artistic endeavors lies a profound commitment to visibility. She doesn't merely illustrate or depict the lives of Afro-Cuban women; she holds a mirror up to society, forcing it to confront the realities and complexities of their experiences. Her performances, photographs, and visual explorations confront historical erasure and the absence of diverse representation head-on. They fill a void that has been perpetuated by systemic biases and societal structures, ensuring that Afro-Cuban women are not just acknowledged, but celebrated for their unique stories. In a global landscape that continues to grapple with the legacies of colonialism, racism, and gender discrimination, Pilar's work operates as a beacon of resilience and resistance. Through her performances, she defies the limitations imposed by historical injustices, inviting audiences to share in the raw emotions of trauma, separation, and longing. In doing so, she creates a universal bridge that connects individuals across cultures and backgrounds, fostering empathy and understanding. We saw how Pilar's exploration of resilience extends to her reimagining of beauty standards and identity in *El tanque*. This provocative piece not only questions societal norms but also empowers Afro-Cuban women to embrace their authentic selves. By reclaiming agency over their appearances, Pilar's work becomes a testament to the power of individuality and self-assertion, challenging the often oppressive standards that have dictated women's lives for far too long. Perhaps the most powerful testament to Pilar's impact lies in *Llave maestra*, where she transforms the machete, a symbol of Cuba's fight for independence, into an emblem of contemporary empowerment. By grasping this symbol with unyielding determination, she taps into the reservoir of strength that has sustained Afro-Cuban women through generations of adversity. This transformation underscores the resilience ingrained in their history and reveals the enduring spirit of survival.

In the context of Cuba, Susana Pilar Delahante's artistic endeavors take on a heightened significance that transcends the confines of aesthetics. Her work resonates deeply within the complex tapestry of Cuba's history, politics, and its intricate relationship with the United States. Through her performances and images, Pilar not only navigates the struggles of Afro-Cuban women but also contributes to a larger narrative that challenges dominant discourses and fosters dialogue within a shifting sociopolitical landscape. Cuba's history is rife with colonization, slavery, and revolution, all of which have left indelible imprints on its societal fabric. Pilar's evocative pieces, particularly *Dibujo intercontinental/Intercontinental Drawing*, provide a visceral link to the historical trauma of displacement and disconnection. In a country that has been marked by the complexities of colonial exploitation and the enduring impact of enslavement, Pilar's art serves as a conduit for remembering, acknowledging, and healing. It urges Cubans to grapple with the echoes of history and confront the wounds that still reverberate today. Additionally, the relationship between the United States and Cuba has been a constantly evolving one, punctuated by political tension, economic embargo, and periods of thaw. Pilar's work takes on an added layer of importance within this dynamic. Her exploration of identity and resilience provides a counternarrative to dominant narratives that have often been shaped by external perspectives. Her performances become a space where the Afro-Cuban experience can be articulated on its own terms, independent of the geopolitical pressures that have influenced the narrative surrounding Cuba. In the context of the United States, where cultural misunderstandings and historical oversights have often characterized perceptions of Cuba, Pilar's art serves as a bridge. By delving into the lived experiences of Afro-Cuban women, she facilitates a deeper understanding of the nuances and complexities of Cuban identity. Her work resists facile categorizations, offering an alternative lens through which to view the country, one that acknowledges its historical struggles while celebrating its tenacity and cultural richness.

Furthermore, her reimagining of symbols, such as the machete in *Llave maestra*, resonates with Cuba's history of revolution and resistance against imperial forces. In a landscape shaped by these historical narratives, Pilar's reinterpretation becomes a poignant reminder of the ongoing struggle for empowerment and self-determination. Her art invites reflection on the shared histories and aspirations that bind Cuba and its diaspora, despite the geopolitical barriers that have often sought to divide them. Her art operates as a conduit for healing historical wounds, reclaiming identities, and fostering understanding across borders. By amplifying the voices of Afro-Cuban women, she challenges dominant narratives, urging us to engage with the complexities of history, culture, and identity that continue to shape the island and its people. In a world marked by geopolitical shifts, Pilar's art is a unifying force that bridges the gaps and offers a vision of resilience and unity that transcends the confines of politics.

In conclusion, Susana Pilar Delahante's artistic journey transcends the boundaries of her medium, the confines of her nation, and the limitations of her identity. Her work serves as a clarion call for inclusivity, representation, and acknowledgment. Through her performances and images, she becomes a conduit for the voiceless, an advocate for the marginalized, and a harbinger of change. In a world that is ever more conscious of the need for diverse narratives, Pilar's art provides not only a mirror but a roadmap for a future where the experiences of Afro-Cuban women and other marginalized groups are not just recognized but integral to the fabric of our collective understanding. Her work isn't just a testament to the past; it's a guiding light toward a more equitable and just future.

Chapter 5

Unveiling Symbolic Silence

Cultural Syncretism and Archetypal Allegory in Belkis Ayón's Visual Expression

Belkis Ayón's presence in the canon of Afro-Cuban art is not merely a testament to her exceptional skill but also to her profound ability to transcend the temporal limits of her life. Though Ayón passed away in 1999, her influence continues to ripple through contemporary Afro-Cuban art, making her an indelible figure whose contributions extend far beyond the years she lived. Dedicating this chapter to Ayón, the only deceased artist discussed in this book, serves not just to honor her legacy but also to reflect on the enduring power of art to survive its maker and speak across generations. Her life and work offer a poignant meditation on mortality, spiritual connection, and the ways in which art allows for both personal and collective memory to persist. Ayón's focus on the Abakuá society, a male-dominated Afro-Cuban spiritual tradition, and her reimagining of its mythologies underscore her unique place in Afro-Cuban visual expression. In centering her narrative, this chapter seeks to acknowledge the temporal dimension of legacy, where Ayón's work—though cut short by her untimely death—continues to resonate as a critical point of reference for Afro-Cuban women's artistic contributions. Her art, rich with spiritual symbolism and profound emotional depth, transcends the physical absence of the artist, cementing her as a figure who remains very much alive in the cultural imagination. In honoring Ayón, we begin to understand the significance of ancestral lineage not only in the Afro-Cuban spiritual traditions she depicted, but also in the broader arc of Decolonial AfroARTivism, where artists engage with both the past and future through their visual storytelling. Ayón's death reminds us of the impermanence of life, yet her work reaffirms art's capacity to preserve and perpetuate narratives that might otherwise be forgotten.

Few artists in modern and contemporary art have left as profound a legacy as Belkis Ayón. Her career, though tragically brief, stands as a powerful testament to the ability of art to engage deeply with themes of culture and identity. Ayón was a Cuban printmaker whose creations broke through artistic boundaries and continue to captivate audiences worldwide. Born in Havana in 1967, Ayón's early exposure to art through her father, a painter, shaped her path. While her education at the esteemed San Alejandro Academy sharpened her technical skills, it was her deep connection to Afro-Cuban culture that became the defining feature of her work. Ayón's chosen medium, collography,[1] allowed her to craft intricate, monochromatic works that brimmed with symbolism and texture. Her exploration of the Abakúa Brotherhood, a secret and traditionally all-male Afro-Cuban society, was groundbreaking. Despite the societal and gender barriers she faced, Ayón managed to gain unparalleled access to their rituals, symbols, and narratives, weaving them into her art with a rare depth and sensitivity. In this chapter, I delve into the themes that permeate Ayón's work: gender, identity, oppression, and the rich tapestry of Afro-Cuban culture. I dissect the symbolism of Sikán, the mythological figure who recurs in Ayón's prints, and discover the layers of meaning that make her art so compelling. Belkis Ayón's legacy is not confined to her prints; it extends to the countless hearts and minds her art has touched. Her work has been exhibited on the global stage, and her influence on contemporary art is immeasurable. Yet her life was marked by personal struggles, which tragically culminated in her untimely passing by committing suicide in 1999. Her art, however, remains an enduring testament to the power of creativity and its ability to transcend boundaries, challenge norms, and shed light on the profound complexities of culture and identity. In this chapter, I attempt to unravel the layers of meaning within her prints, peer into the world of the Abakúa Brotherhood, and witness the indomitable spirit of an artist whose work continues to inspire, provoke, and ignite the imagination. In a 1997 interview with David Mateo for *La Gaceta de Cuba* magazine, Ayón speaks about the Abakuá's influence in her art stating that "I have always been distant from the Abakuá mythology because my position is rather that of an observer. The distance in fact is the perspective in which I find myself to establish the analogies and to incorporate any universal experience in the specific logic of the myth." Her perspective reflects a unique approach to incorporating cultural and mythological elements into her work. Ayón expresses that she has always maintained a certain distance from the Abakuá mythology. This distancing can be interpreted as a deliberate choice to avoid becoming too immersed or personally entangled in the myth's intricacies. By maintaining this distance, Ayón positions herself as an observer rather than a direct participant or active participant in the mythology. This perspective allows her to maintain a level of objectivity and critical engagement. Ayón highlights the importance of distance as a means to establish analogies. By stepping back and observing from a distance, she gains a unique perspective that enables her to draw connections between the Abakuá mythology and broader, universal human experiences. This process of finding analogies suggests that Ayón seeks to uncover shared themes, emotions, or narratives that transcend the specific cultural context of the myth. Ayón's intention to incorporate universal experiences within the specific logic of the myth demonstrates her artistic intention to bridge the gap between cultural specificity and global human themes. She recognizes that myths hold the potential to communicate fundamental human truths and emotions, and her art becomes a medium for intertwining these universal aspects with the cultural nuances of the Abakuá mythology. She acknowledges that each myth possesses its own unique logic and narrative structure. By acknowledging the "specific logic" of the Abakuá myth, she shows an appreciation for the myth's inherent structure and storytelling patterns. Her art then becomes a means of engaging with and expanding on this logic while also drawing connections to wider human experiences. Her approach of maintaining a distance while still seeking to find points of connection between the myth's specific logic and universal human experiences underscores the power of art to bridge cultural divides and foster meaningful dialogue between different narratives and histories.

Belkis Ayón's artistic practice has been the subject of extensive scholarly research, highlighting her unique contributions to Afro-Cuban art and her profound engagement with themes of cultural identity, gender, and mythology. This section reviews some of the most significant studies on Ayón's work, providing a comprehensive understanding of her impact and the critical discourse surrounding her art. Barreto's paper (2006) offers a comparative analysis of three prominent Cuban women artists: Ana Mendieta, Belkis Ayón, and Sandra Ramos. By examining their works in the context of the *Unbroken Ties: Dialogues in Cuban Art* exhibit, Barreto highlights the shared themes of cultural and personal identity, self-representation, and the body. The study notes that despite the varied media used by these artists, their works collectively engage with the social, political, and cultural issues of their time. Barreto's analysis situates Ayón's art within a broader feminist discourse, recognizing her exploration of gender dynamics and the representation of women within the sociopolitical landscape of Cuba. This comparative approach enriches the understanding of Ayón's artistic practice by positioning it alongside the works of her contemporaries. Menéndez's study (2017) focuses on the cultural significance of Afro-Cuban plastic arts, emphasizing the influence of African heritage on Cuban art. The author explores how Afro-Cuban artists like Belkis Ayón incorporate themes of Black identity and social marginalization into their works. Menéndez's analysis is crucial in understanding Ayón's position within the broader context of Afro-Cuban art, particularly in relation to her peers, Manuel Mendive and Ana Mendieta. The article underscores Ayón's engagement with African-derived spiritual practices and her use of these elements to address issues of identity and marginalization. Menéndez's work provides a foundational context for examining Ayón's oeuvre within the continuum of Afro-Cuban artistic traditions. Pease (2022) delves into the mythological and psychological dimensions of Ayón's work, particularly her identification with the legendary figure of Sikán from the Abakuá secret society. The study argues that Ayón's art transgresses traditional boundaries by revealing the secret knowledge of the Abakuá, a domain traditionally reserved for men. Pease suggests that Ayón's work embodies a state of paradox, invoking feelings of confusion, fear, and trance to achieve a sense of sublimity. This analysis highlights Ayón's innovative approach to mythological narratives, portraying her as a transgressive figure who challenges established norms. Pease's exploration of the psychological and affective dimensions of Ayón's art provides a deeper insight into the emotional and conceptual complexity of her work. In her book chapter, Noël (2022) examines two of Ayón's works from 1998, focusing on how they engage with the concept of invisibility and challenge the traditional paradigm of the Abakuá secret society. Noël argues that Ayón's art recognizes the power of invisibility and uses it to disrupt the male-dominated mythology of the Abakuá. By doing so, Ayón not only critiques the exclusion of women from this secret society but also redefines the notion of power and visibility. Noël's analysis is instrumental in understanding Ayón's subversive use of mythological themes to address issues of gender and power, highlighting her role as a pioneering feminist artist within the Afro-Cuban context. The scholarly studies reviewed in this section collectively illuminate the multifaceted nature of Belkis Ayón's artistic practice. Through diverse analytical lenses, these works explore Ayón's engagement with themes of cultural identity, gender, mythology, and the psychological dimensions of her art. Menéndez's cultural analysis, Barreto's comparative feminist perspective, Pease's mythological and psychological exploration, and Noël's focus on invisibility and power collectively contribute to a nuanced understanding of Ayón's contributions to contemporary art.

In the artistic world of Belkis Ayón, the mythological character Sikán, rooted in the Abakúa tradition, plays a pivotal role, imbuing her creations with profound symbolism and depth. Sikán represents a multifaceted exploration of themes within Ayón's work. She embodies the defiance of traditional gender norms and the quest for identity within the male-dominated Abakúa Brotherhood (Olmos, 101; Torres Zayas, 39). Simultaneously, Sikán occupies dual roles, as an outsider infiltrating the Brotherhood's secrets and as an insider gaining access to their sacred knowledge, symbolizing the tension between belonging and challenging established boundaries. Her narrative revolves around rebellion and sacrifice, metaphorically highlighting the sacrifices individuals make to embrace their true selves. Furthermore, Sikán embodies the broader theme of cultural syncretism, bridging African and Cuban traditions, while her deliberately complex character encourages contemplation of the fluidity of identity and cultural boundaries. Sikán ultimately stands as a symbol of resistance and empowerment, challenging established norms and highlighting the individual's capacity for self-assertion and change, even in the face of adversity. Through Ayón's intricate collography prints, Sikán's enduring significance continues to provoke thought and inspire conversation, cementing her as a compelling and timeless symbol in contemporary art. On theme of women empowerment and reading her art pieces as feminist, the artist commented on her position in an interview with David Mateo for *La Gaceta de Cuba* magazine in 1997, asserting the following:

> I have never thought of my work as feminist. I have never had such built-in vocation. The first person who attempted to draw attention to that aspect was the critic Eugenio Valdés, and perhaps there is some degree of truth that my work induces certain femininity, since it reflects my own existential uncertainty; but I have not conceptualized it like that. Sikán's legend is a theme that I have been working within my prints

since I was in San Alejandro and what has always called my
attention is the female character's status as a victim, but rather
from a generic position, considering the connotations and the
analogies that could be derived from such situation.

In this excerpt from the 1997 interview, Ayón discusses her perspective
on the feminist interpretation of her art and the themes she explores. Her
comments shed light on her approach to her work and her reaction to
the feminist label. Ayón begins by stating that she has never intentionally
thought of her work as feminist or harbored a built-in feminist vocation.
This suggests that her artistic focus hasn't been motivated by a deliberate
desire to convey feminist ideas or perspectives. Instead, she seems to prioritize themes that resonate with her personal experiences and inquiries,
allowing her work to emerge from a more organic place. Ayón acknowledges that the first person to bring attention to the feminist aspect of her
work was the critic, Eugenio Valdés. This implies that while she may not
have explicitly aimed for a feminist interpretation, others have identified
elements within her art that resonate with feminist themes or sensibilities.
This recognition might be based on the way she addresses certain issues
or the lens through which she portrays characters and narratives. Ayón
mentions that there might be some degree of truth to her work inducing
a certain femininity. This could be attributed to her art reflecting her
own existential uncertainty, suggesting that her personal experiences and
emotions inform her creative expression. It's important to note that she
doesn't define femininity in traditional or stereotypical terms; rather, she
links it to her own introspection and emotions. The artist reveals that
she has been working with the theme of Sikán's legend in her prints since
her time at San Alejandro, an art school in Havana. Sikán's legend is a
recurring theme in her work, and she points out that her fascination lies
in the female character's status as a victim. However, she emphasizes that
she views this from a generic position, suggesting a broader perspective
that considers the thematic implications and analogies. By focusing on
the female character's victimhood from a generic position, Ayón seems to
be suggesting that she's interested in exploring the broader implications
of such themes beyond specific feminist interpretations. Her interest lies
in examining the connotations and analogies that stem from this status
rather than solely adhering to a feminist lens. In this excerpt, Belkis Ayón's
approach to her art appears to be driven by personal exploration and an
interest in broader thematic implications. While she acknowledges the

recognition of feminist elements in her work, she maintains a nuanced and open perspective that transcends traditional labels, allowing her art to resonate on multiple levels.

The original story of Princess Sikán is deeply rooted in the Abakúa tradition, an Afro-Cuban secret society with origins in the Calabar region of Nigeria. The Abakúa tradition is known for its rituals, codes, and mythology, which have been passed down through generations. Princess Sikán is a significant figure in this mythological narrative. In Abakúa mythology, Sikán was a beautiful and enigmatic princess, the daughter of a powerful king. She lived in a village by the sea, where her father ruled. Sikán's story revolves around her transgression of the Abakúa code of secrecy, which is one of the central tenets of society. One day, out of curiosity and a desire to understand the secret rituals of the Abakúa Brotherhood, Sikán disguised herself as a man and managed to infiltrate their sacred gatherings. This act of defiance was considered a grave breach of the Brotherhood's code, as it was traditionally an all-male society, and revealing its secrets to outsiders was strictly forbidden. As Sikán became increasingly involved in the Abakúa rituals and ceremonies, she gained knowledge of their sacred chants, dances, and symbols. Her presence among the Brotherhood went unnoticed for a considerable time, and she became a trusted member, participating in their gatherings and even leading their songs.

However, the secret could not remain hidden forever, and eventually, Sikán's true identity was discovered. Her breach of the Abakúa code was considered a severe transgression, and the penalty for such an offense was death. Sikán was sentenced to be executed for her actions. The story of Princess Sikán's execution is one of tragedy and sacrifice. Despite her transgression, Sikán's actions were driven by a desire to understand and participate in the sacred rituals of the Brotherhood. Her story has since become a symbol of defiance, gender identity, and the consequences of challenging societal norms within the Abakúa tradition. Belkis Ayón's artistic interpretations of Sikán draw from this original narrative, weaving elements of gender identity, cultural syncretism, and sacrifice into her prints. Through her art, Ayón invites viewers to contemplate the complexities of Sikán's story and the broader themes it represents within the context of Afro-Cuban culture and identity. It is also worth pointing out that there are many versions of Sikán's story. As the Calabar women[2] were strong, thrifty, energetic and independent, hardworking, enterprising and took and left husbands as they pleased, it is said that they were free and sold their bodies the riverbank (Cabrera 2005, 97). Men feared independent women and they feared Sikán, although now they adore her and invoke her in every ceremony where the goat that is sacrificed is an evocation of her sacrifice, just as the Eucharist is the evocation of the sacrifice of Christ (González Gómez 2016, 114). She is also described as a traitor, similarly to La Malinche, because she supposedly betrayed her tribe when it is said that she divulged the secret of the Efo to the Efik, her tribe. They say that after what happened in the river, she went to Efik[3] land to betray the Efo and that for being a traitor they killed her. It is said that she was a gossip girl, and that like all women, she didn't know how to keep secrets (González Gómez 2016, 114). In Cuba, the term *brikamos* refers to the members or leaders within the Abakuá secret society, a mutual aid organization rooted in Afro-Cuban traditions. They bestowed upon her the title of "Ntenyenebón," meaning "the one who has the power to reach the depths of the Abakuá religion," as she was recognized for her discovery of the Mystery (Cabrera 1988, 409). On the contrary the Efik defended her and refer to her as "Akuarumina," which means spirit, and they said she was killed because she knew a lot (Cabrera 2005, 151). As González Gómez points out,

> It is true that the Abakuá Society is known for silencing the female voice in its affairs, justifying itself in Sikán's betrayal, but precisely because of this rule, the stories about the founding myth of Sikán arouse curiosity. In Cuba, a well-known plastic artist associated with Abakuá mythology is Belkis Ayón. Belkis Ayón approached the myth of Sikán with respect. She has been an artist who recreates and visually reconstructs Sikanékue, not only because she identifies with her, but because her story includes the woman of the sacrifice.[4] (121)

This quote by González Gómez sheds light on the complex dynamics surrounding the Abakuá Society's treatment of women's voices and its connection to the myth of Sikán. The Abakuá Society is recognized for its historical tendency to marginalize and exclude women from its affairs, which it justifies by referencing Sikán's perceived betrayal. This practice has resulted in an environment where the narratives of female perspectives within the society are largely suppressed. However, this suppression has ironically fueled intrigue and curiosity about the foundational myth of Sikán, ultimately emphasizing the significance of her story. Sikán, as a central figure in Abakuá mythology, holds a pivotal role that elicits fascination due to her association with both the society's silencing of women and her foundational importance. Her story serves as a point of entry into the discussion about the complex gender dynamics within the society and highlights the consequences of this gendered exclusion. The reference to Belkis Ayón by the author underscores a different approach to engaging with Sikán's myth. Ayón's artistic exploration of the Sikán narrative is characterized by respect and sensitivity. She approaches Sikán's story as a means of re-creating and visually reconstructing the character of Sikanékue, which reflects her deep connection to the myth and her identification with Sikán's story. This approach challenges the society's historical tendency to silence the female voice, as Ayón's artistic expression becomes a platform for reclaiming and celebrating the silenced narrative of the woman in the myth. Gómez's perspective emphasizes that the retelling of Sikán's myth is a way to reintroduce the woman's perspective and significance, countering the historical pattern of exclusion. This not only pays tribute to the importance of Sikán's role in the mythology but also draws attention to the broader issue of gender representation and recognition within the Abakuá Society. Through artistic expression and exploration, individuals like Belkis Ayón challenge and reshape the narrative, offering a new lens through which to view Sikán's role and impact.

The act of Princess Sikán disguising herself as a man within the context of the Abakúa tradition holds significant connections to queer theory and the concept of transvestism, shedding light on the complex interplay between gender identity, cultural norms, and personal agency. Sikán's decision to disguise herself as a man is a clear challenge to the traditional gender norms and roles within the Abakúa Brotherhood. The Brotherhood, like many secret societies, operated within a strict gender binary, with membership and participation limited to men. Sikán's act of cross-dressing to gain access to the sacred rituals represents a form of gender nonconformity and challenges the established boundaries of male and female roles in her society. Sikán's actions align with the concept of gender as performative, a central idea in queer theory. The notion that gender identity is not an inherent trait but rather a social construct that individuals perform aligns with Sikán's deliberate performance of a male identity. Her actions highlight how societal expectations and rituals can shape one's perception of gender identity. Sikán's disguise as a man can also be seen as a subversion of heteronormativity, which assumes a binary and complementary relationship between men and women. Her act challenges the conventional expectations of how men and women should

behave within the Abakúa context, disrupting the notion of what constitutes "appropriate" gender roles and behavior. Travestism, often associated
with cross-dressing and gender performance, is relevant in understanding
Sikán's actions. Her disguise as a man aligns with the concept of travestism, which involves intentionally adopting the clothing, mannerisms, or
roles typically associated with the opposite gender. Travestism can be an
expression of gender fluidity and a challenge to rigid gender norms. Sikán's
story also illustrates the intersectionality of identity. She navigated not only
the complexities of gender identity but also cultural and religious identity
as a member of the Abakúa Brotherhood. Her actions challenge not only
gender norms but also the boundaries of religious and cultural identity
within her community. Incorporating the narrative of Princess Sikán into
discussions of queer theory and travestism offers a valuable perspective
on how gender identity and cultural norms intersect and interact within
specific cultural contexts. It underscores the importance of recognizing the
agency of individuals who challenge normative gender roles and highlights
the ways in which gender identity is socially constructed and performed.
Sikán's story serves as a compelling example of how art and folklore can
provide insights into complex discussions surrounding gender and identity
within diverse cultural traditions.

La Cena

In Ayón's art, Sikán emerges as a powerful symbol, challenging societal
norms and embracing a complex identity that defies easy categorization.
Through Sikán, Ayón not only portrays the struggle for gender equality
and personal identity but also addresses the broader theme of cultural
syncretism. *La Cena*, 1991 (figure 5.1) is a compelling example of Ayón's
work that offers a profound interpretation of Sikán's symbolism. In this
print, we see Sikán, rendered with exquisite detail and texture, seated at
a table reminiscent of Leonardo da Vinci's *The Last Supper*. The choice of
this iconic setting is symbolic in itself. It suggests Sikán's role as a bridge
between different cultural and spiritual worlds, much like how da Vinci's
painting represents a pivotal moment in Christian history. Around Sikán,
there are various elements that tell a deeper story. She holds an Abakúa
drum, an essential part of the Brotherhood's rituals. This suggests that
Sikán has not only infiltrated this male-dominated society but has become
an integral part of it, challenging the notion of traditional gender roles.

Figure 5.1. *La cena (The Supper)*, Belkis Ayón, 1991, collograph, 54³/₈ × 118¹/₈ in. *Source:* Photography by Alejandro González. Courtesy and Copyright © Belkis Ayón Estate, Havana, Cuba.

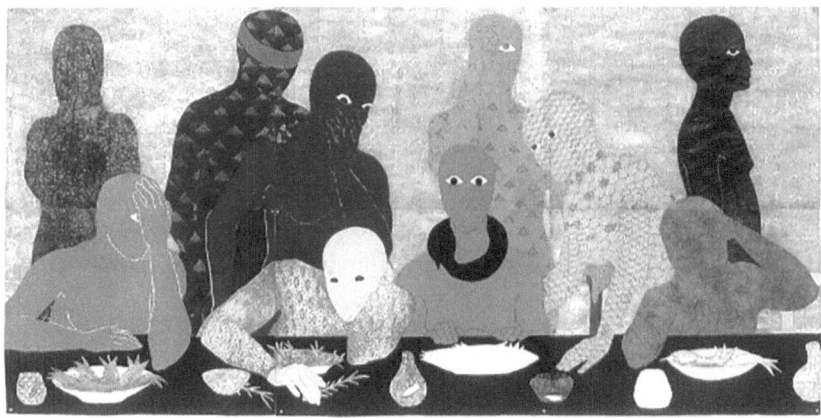

The table itself is laden with symbolic items: a rooster, a fish, and a bowl of water. In Abakúa symbolism, these elements represent deep spiritual and cultural significance. The rooster can be seen as a representation of Eleguá, a deity in the Yoruba religion, while the fish may allude to Olokun, another Yoruba deity associated with the sea. The bowl of water signifies purification. Together, these elements suggest a profound synthesis of Abakúa and Yoruba spiritual elements, underscoring the theme of cultural syncretism. The faces of the individuals surrounding Sikán are obscured, perhaps indicating the anonymity of those who have also ventured into this world of cultural blending. They are part of a collective, emphasizing the idea that Sikán's journey is not isolated; it represents a broader movement toward cultural fusion and transformation. In *La Cena* Belkis Ayón invites viewers to contemplate the complex interplay of gender, culture, and spirituality. Sikán, as the central figure, embodies the power of individual agency to challenge established norms and to bridge the divide between cultures and beliefs. Ayón's meticulous collography technique brings this symbolism to life, emphasizing the depth and texture of Sikán's character and the rich tapestry of cultural influences at work. Through this interpretation of *La Cena* we gain insight into how Belkis Ayón's art serves as a visual language, inviting us to explore the multifaceted dimensions of human experience and the profound impact of individuals who dare to defy boundaries and embrace the complexities of identity and culture.

In *La Cena* by Belkis Ayón, there is indeed a deliberate and thought-provoking parallelism drawn between the death of Jesus in *The Last Supper* and the demise of Princess Sikán within the context of the Abakúa mythology. This parallelism serves as a powerful artistic device to convey deeper themes and ideas within Ayón's work. The most immediate parallel is the setting itself. Ayón intentionally mirrors the iconic tableau of Leonardo da Vinci's *The Last Supper*. The use of this recognizable scene immediately draws viewers into a narrative that resonates with Christian religious symbolism, setting the stage for contemplation. In both depictions, there is a central figure, Jesus in *The Last Supper* and Sikán in Ayón's print, who holds a position of significance. This centrality highlights their pivotal roles in their respective narratives. Both narratives involve a sense of sacrifice. In the Christian tradition, *The Last Supper* is a prelude to Jesus's crucifixion, representing the sacrifice for the salvation of humanity. In the Abakúa tradition, Sikán's story also involves transgression and eventual sacrifice, symbolizing her defiance and the potential consequences of her actions. Various symbolic elements are at play in both scenes. In *La Cena*, Sikán holds an Abakúa drum and is surrounded by significant items like the rooster, fish, and bowl of water, each carrying deep spiritual symbolism within the Abakúa tradition. In *The Last Supper*, elements like the bread and wine symbolize the body and blood of Christ. These symbols imbue both scenes with layers of meaning and significance. Belkis Ayón's decision to create a parallel between these two narratives is a deliberate artistic choice that invites viewers to contemplate the universality of certain themes—sacrifice, defiance, and transcendence—across different cultural contexts. By referencing *The Last Supper*, Ayón underscores the idea that stories of sacrifice and spiritual significance are not unique to one culture or religion. Moreover, this parallelism highlights Sikán's significance as a transformative figure within the Abakúa tradition, echoing the transformative role that Jesus played in Christian theology. Sikán becomes a symbol of defiance and change, challenging established norms within her cultural context, much like how Jesus challenged societal and religious norms in his time. In *La Cena*, Belkis Ayón uses this parallelism to explore complex themes of sacrifice, gender, identity, and cultural syncretism, inviting viewers to reflect on the universal aspects of these themes and the enduring power of individual agency to challenge and reshape cultural narratives. The piece serves as a bridge between different cultural and religious worldviews, encouraging dialogue and contemplation about the common threads that connect human experiences across diverse traditions.

The omission of mouths and noses in the depiction of figures holds a significant artistic purpose. This artistic choice, prominent in Belkis Ayón's works, serves to convey a complex interplay of cultural, spiritual, and symbolic elements. While numerous pieces of Cuban art celebrate Afro-Cuban heritage by intertwining various religious practices, Ayón's creations stand out due to their ability to transcend mere representation of race, identity, and mythology. One of Ayón's pivotal works, *La Cena*, is particularly noteworthy in catalyzing a transformative shift in twentieth-century Cuban engraving. This masterpiece symbolizes a watershed moment, altering the trajectory of artistic expression in the country. It seamlessly merges the visual language of the Abakuá tradition with Christian symbolism. The conventional portrayal of the Christian "Last Supper," a quintessential image in Western art, is ingeniously reimagined by substituting Jesus, the central figure, with the princess Sikanekué. This substitution evokes intricate interconnections between religious and cultural narratives, shedding light on the syncretic nature of belief systems and their capacity to coexist harmoniously. The absence of mouths and noses in Ayón's figures emerges as a potent visual motif. This deliberate omission accentuates the universality of the themes she explores. The choice to exclude these facial features seemingly renders the characters voiceless and odorless, transcending mere individuality and emphasizing a collective consciousness. This approach underscores the idea that the messages conveyed in her works are not limited to a specific time, place, or person. The figures become vessels of archetypal significance, encapsulating broader human experiences and emotions that transcend cultural boundaries. Ayón's iconography is rich with symbolism drawn from Afro-Cuban traditions. Eyes without mouths reflect a distinctive form of communication—an emphasis on sight and perception over vocal expression. Fish, snakes, roosters, and goats, all common in her engravings, carry layers of allegorical meaning deeply rooted in Afro-Cuban cosmology. Fish can symbolize spirituality and transformation, snakes may represent hidden wisdom, roosters often signify protection, and goats can connote fertility and strength. Ayón masterfully weaves these symbols into her compositions, infusing her works with a multilayered visual language that requires viewers to engage on both surface and deeper levels. The exclusion of mouths and noses in Ayón's artistic representations goes beyond stylistic choice; it is a vehicle for profound storytelling and universal expression. Through this deliberate omission, Ayón invites viewers to explore the intricate tapestry of cultural syncretism, spiritual significance, and archetypal narratives. *La Cena* stands as a pivotal work that redefines Cuban engraving while her broader body of work challenges conventional boundaries and beckons us to contemplate the nuanced interplay between visual representation and the boundless realms of meaning.

In addition to its portrayal of Abakuá brotherhood symbols, the artwork of Belkis Ayón stands out for its incorporation of androgynous[5] figures, serving as a representation of the marginalized female presence within the Abakuá society. Curiously, it was through a female artist, Ayón herself, that the traditionally male-exclusive Abakuá secret society gained widespread international acknowledgment. The deliberate inclusion of androgynous figures in Ayón's creations adds a layer of complexity to her artistic narrative. By blurring the conventional boundaries of gender, these figures not only challenge societal norms but also offer a visual metaphor for the obscured female voices within the Abakuá brotherhood. Androgynous individuals might possess a well-rounded sense of self that encompasses the positive qualities traditionally associated with both genders. They tend to detach tasks from any societal or physical gender assignments. Those who embrace an androgynous identity generally pay little heed to traits that are artificially linked to males or females in a given culture. Instead, they concentrate on behaviors that prove most advantageous within a given situation (Woodhill & Samuels, 15). This artistic choice serves to unveil the multifaceted dimensions of a society that has historically favored a male-centric perspective. Ayón's art manages to paradoxically bridge a gap between historical exclusivity and contemporary inclusivity. Through her work, a secret society that was once characterized by its strict gender limitations finds itself resonating with a broader audience, transcending its own limitations. This transformation can be attributed to Ayón's unique position as a female artist delving into a traditionally male-dominated realm. In essence, Ayón's artistic contribution becomes an act of empowerment and reclamation.

By giving visual representation to the silent and marginalized female presence within the Abakuá brotherhood, she not only challenges the gender norms of the society but also contributes to a more comprehensive and inclusive understanding of its traditions. The recognition that the Abakuá society achieved on an international scale, paradoxically facilitated by Ayón, reflects the profound impact of her art in reshaping perceptions and breaking down long-standing barriers. Sikán clearly subverts the social construction of gender. In the field of sociology, the concept of the social construction of gender delves into how gender perceptions and expressions arise from cultural influences. It examines the ways in which gender roles develop within interpersonal and group interactions. More precisely, this theory asserts that gender roles are not inherent but rather something individuals attain as a "status" within a social setting. This status involves both implicit and explicit categorization of individuals, which in turn influences their social behaviors (Lindsey 2015, 4). Belkis Ayón's artistic repertoire ingeniously incorporates the enigmatic presence of androgynous figures, creating a multilayered narrative that delves into the intricacies of gender roles within the Abakuá society. This artistic endeavor becomes a poignant exploration of historical dynamics and the silenced voices of women within a traditionally male-centric environment. It is a paradoxical twist that elevates the status of the all-male Abakuá secret society to international recognition, facilitated by the hands of a woman artist. The deliberate use of androgynous figures in Ayón's compositions becomes a compelling visual strategy that challenges societal norms and prompts a contemplation of gender fluidity. By blurring the lines between masculine and feminine characteristics, she offers a profound commentary on the rigid gender distinctions that often underscore cultural traditions. These figures serve as intricate metaphors, embodying the presence of women who historically remained hidden and unheard within the Abakuá brotherhood. The choice to render these figures androgynous underscores the complexity of the subject matter, highlighting the multifaceted nature of identity and social roles. Ayón's art carries within it a paradoxical duality—a remarkable convergence of historical exclusivity and contemporary inclusivity. It's a paradox born out of the fact that a society once bound by strict gender divisions finds itself echoing in the diverse voices and perspectives of a global audience. This transformation isn't solely attributed to the artwork itself, but also to the artist's unique position. As a woman engaging with and interpreting the male-oriented Abakuá tradition, Ayón introduces a fresh vantage point that challenges preconceived notions and enriches the understanding of this secretive society. Her artistic contributions extend beyond the canvas; they represent an act of empowerment and reclamation. Through the visual manifestation of the silenced and marginalized female presence, Ayón restructures the narrative landscape. She doesn't merely create art; she becomes a catalyst for change, shedding light on the unspoken stories and overlooked individuals that history often forgets. Her work carves a space for these silent voices to resonate, demanding recognition and understanding. The global recognition achieved by the traditionally secluded Abakuá society, paradoxically spurred by Ayón's creations, amplifies the impact of her art. It signifies a broader transformation wherein art becomes a bridge between historical authenticity and contemporary relevance. The society's acknowledgment on an international stage highlights the universal nature of Ayón's message—a message that transcends cultural and gender-specific boundaries. Belkis Ayón's art emerges as a powerful vehicle for story-telling, reclamation, and transformation. Through the incorporation of androgynous figures, she navigates the complex tapestry of gender roles within the Abakuá society, simultaneously giving voice to the historically muted female presence. This paradoxical narrative resonates on a global scale, elevating the Abakuá brotherhood to a level of recognition it had not experienced before, all thanks to the paradoxical interplay of historical authenticity and contemporary inclusivity fostered by Ayón's remarkable artistic vision.

It is fundamental to point out a fundamental artistic practice that Belkis Ayón has in common with Afro-Cuban artist Harmonia Rosales, explored in the first chapter of this book. Belkis Ayón and Harmonia Rosales, two Afro-Cuban artists of distinct generations, engage in a thought-provoking parallelism through their intentional reimaginings of classical artworks rooted in Christianity and Western spirituality. This approach not only underscores their shared endeavor to reshape narratives but also emphasizes their individual voices within the broader discourse of art, culture, and identity. Both Ayón and Rosales employ the act of reinterpretation to challenge and recontextualize conventional artistic representations. Ayón, notably in works like *La Cena*, elegantly synthe-sizes Abakuá and Christian symbolism to construct a dialogue between religious and cultural narratives. In her choice to replace the central figure of Jesus with the princess Sikanekué, she simultaneously pays homage to tradition and introduces a fresh perspective. This parallelism between spiritual iconography and Abakuá heritage offers a unique lens through which to explore syncretism, opening space for deeper conversations on the intersections of belief systems. Rosales, on the other hand, extends this tradition of reinterpretation by introducing her own perspectives into classical artworks. Her acclaimed painting *The Creation of God* subverts Michelangelo's renowned *The Creation of Adam* by depicting an empowered Black Eve cradling a seemingly more vulnerable Adam. This intentional inversion challenges the historical power dynamics within the narrative and reflects Rosales's commitment to representing marginalized perspectives in art. Just as Ayón reshapes the Last Supper, Rosales reimagines the moment of Creation, both interventions serving to foster inclusivity and reinterpret established narratives from a modern perspective. The intentional decision by both artists to recontextualize classical Christian and Western themes speaks to their shared commitment to confronting historical and cultural imbalances. Through this parallel, they assert their presence within artistic canons that have often marginalized voices like theirs. While Ayón's and Rosales's approaches differ in style and execution, they share a resounding thematic resonance. By reimagining classical artworks, these artists actively participate in reshaping the narratives that have dominated cultural and spiritual discourse. Their interventions amplify the presence and perspectives of historically marginalized groups, thus rewriting art history to reflect the rich complexity of their identities. In this parallelism, we witness a shared commitment to art as a transformative force, capable of dismantling traditional power structures and fostering a more inclusive visual landscape.

This shared approach becomes a profound statement on the power of art to reshape narratives, challenge historical imbalances, and amplify the voices of the marginalized. Ayón's artistic exploration, epitomized by her iconic work *La Cena*, ingeniously fuses elements of Abakuá symbolism with the Christian narrative of the Last Supper. This fusion serves as a bridge between divergent belief systems, creating a visual dialogue that defies strict categorization. By replacing Jesus with the figure of the princess Sikanekué, Ayón not only honors her Afro-Cuban heritage but also questions the universality of religious imagery. This deliberate intervention not only asserts Ayón's artistic voice but also echoes her conviction that historical narratives can be reshaped to accommodate diverse cultural perspectives. In a similar vein, Harmonia Rosales demonstrates her artistic prowess through the bold reimagining of Michelangelo's *The Creation of Adam* in her work *The Creation of God*. Here, Rosales flips the power dynamics, replacing the iconic image of God reaching out to Adam with an empowered Black Eve reaching toward a seemingly vulnerable Adam. This inversion challenges centuries of patriarchal representations and underscores Rosales's determination to center the marginalized within canonical narratives. The parallel with Ayón's interventions is evident as both artists assert themselves within established artistic canons, infusing their reinterpretations with contemporary sensibilities. This parallelism extends beyond mere artistic technique, delving into a shared thematic resonance.

Ayón and Rosales, though distinct in style, unite in their mission to address historical and cultural imbalances through their art. By recontextualizing classical artworks, they confront the lack of representation and agency that marginalized groups have historically faced. Their deliberate interventions become a form of reclamation, a way to rewrite art history and imbue it with their own identities and experiences. Through this parallelism, a common thread emerges: the transformative potential of art. Ayón and Rosales wield their creativity as a tool for challenging norms, fostering inclusivity, and amplifying the voices of those who have been overlooked. They become advocates for cultural dialogue and social change, simultaneously engaging with tradition and reshaping it for contemporary relevance. The parallel artistic journeys of Belkis Ayón and Harmonia Rosales exemplify the remarkable power of reinterpretation. By purposefully reimagining classical artworks rooted in Christian and Western spirituality, they assert their identities, challenge historical imbalances, and contribute to a more inclusive artistic narrative. Their art serves as a testament to the capacity of creative expression to bridge gaps, ignite conversations, and reshape the way we perceive both art and the world around us.

Moreover, Belkis Ayón and Harmonia Rosales, share a powerful artistic approach that involves deliberately subverting the traditional gender roles ingrained in classical artworks. They ingeniously reimagine iconic pieces where male figures typically held prominence, infusing them with femininity and women figures to challenge and reshape conventional narratives. This intentional inversion becomes a profound commentary on gender dynamics, representation, and the reclamation of historical narratives. Ayón's artistic journey, epitomized by her captivating work *La Cena*, challenges the male-centric portrayal of religious and historical figures. By replacing Jesus with the enigmatic princess Sikanekué in the depiction of the Last Supper, Ayón not only nods to her Afro-Cuban heritage but also introduces a remarkable twist by celebrating the feminine presence. This audacious gesture disrupts the established gender hierarchy, allowing women to take center stage within narratives where they were previously marginalized. By incorporating the princess as a pivotal figure, Ayón's art confronts the historical exclusion of women, making a bold statement about their agency and significance within cultural and spiritual contexts. Similarly, Harmonia Rosales showcases her artistic prowess by reimagining well-known classical pieces, such as *The Creation of Adam*, in ways that amplify feminine perspectives. In her rendition, *The Creation of God*, Rosales shifts the focus to an empowered Black Eve, altering the traditional power dynamics. This intentional transformation not only reclaims the feminine within the creation narrative but also challenges deeply entrenched notions of hierarchy and control. Rosales's art serves as an affirmation of the strength and importance of women, simultaneously critiquing the historical erasure of their agency and representation. Both Ayón and Rosales contribute to a broader artistic movement that seeks to disrupt traditional norms and ideologies. By placing women at the forefront of narratives where men once dominated, they emphasize the multifaceted dimensions of femininity and the necessity of acknowledging women's historical contributions. This deliberate inversion is an act of empowerment, prompting viewers to reevaluate their preconceptions and consider the narratives that have historically shaped society's understanding of gender. Moreover, the intentional incorporation of femininity and women figures enriches the artistic discourse surrounding diversity and inclusivity. Ayón's and Rosales's interventions go beyond mere visual transformation; they initiate conversations about the intersections of culture, gender, and identity. Through their reinterpretations, they challenge viewers to examine the stories they've been told and question who has been left out of these narratives. In essence, Ayón and Rosales navigate the realms of gender and representation with incredible nuance and intention. Their shared commitment to subverting traditional gender roles in art not only reshapes the way we perceive classical pieces but also revitalizes conversations about equality, agency, and historical authenticity. Their art becomes a potent tool for rewriting history, celebrating diversity, and offering a platform for the stories that have long been silenced.

Sikán con chivo

Sin título (Sikán con chivo) or *Untitled (Sikán with Goat)*, 1993 (figure 5.2) is a notable artwork created by Belkis Ayón in 1993. This piece is a collograph print, a technique Ayón often employed to create intricate and visually compelling works that draw from Afro-Cuban mythology and culture. This particular artwork exemplifies Ayón's ability to infuse her prints with layered symbolism, cultural references, and a sense of mystique. The imagery in *Sin título (Sikán con chivo)* revolves around two central

Figure 5.2. *Sin título (Sikán con chivo)/Untitled (Sikán with Goat)*, Belkis Ayón, 1993, collograph, 35 × 27³/₄. *Source:* Photography by Alejandro González. Courtesy and Copyright © Belkis Ayón Estate, Havana, Cuba.

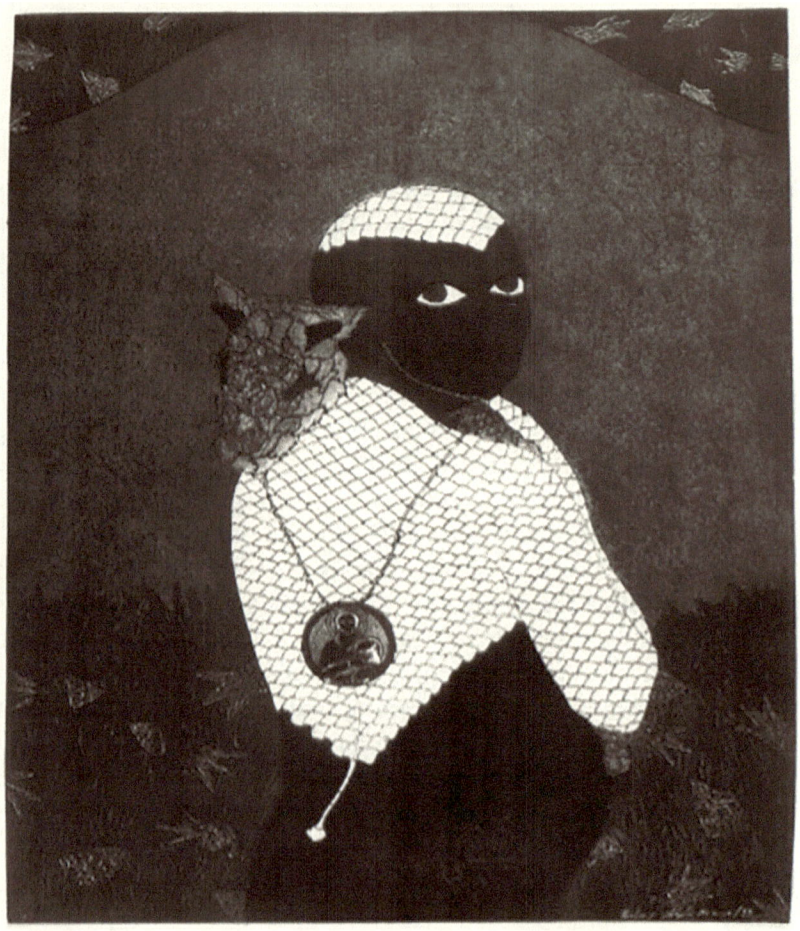

figures: Sikán, a prominent character in the Abakuá mythology, and a goat. Belkis Ayón's masterpiece created in 1993, stands as a 31-by-26-inch single-sheet print that invites viewers into a rich tapestry of symbolism, cultural fusion, and layered storytelling. This artwork not only show-cases Ayón's technical prowess in printmaking but also exemplifies her remarkable ability to amalgamate disparate traditions into a harmonious visual narrative. At the heart of the composition is the enigmatic figure of

Sikán, an iconic character within Afro-Cuban mythology. In this portrayal, Sikán's pregnant form is depicted from behind, a choice that prompts the viewer to engage with the essence of her identity beyond mere physical attributes. Holding a goat with its head resting on her left shoulder, Sikán's gaze meets ours over her right shoulder, establishing a connection that transcends time and space. This connection is intensified by the chain that falls down her back, culminating in a medallion—a representation of either Jesus or a saint cradling a lamb. This juxtaposition of the sacred and the earthly emphasizes Sikán's role as a conduit between realms, bridging the divine and the mortal within her being. As we venture farther down the artwork, the lower portion of the print is adorned with depictions of the magical fish, the source of the sacred knowledge Sikán bestowed on her people. These images of the fish echo the layers of mysticism and spirituality that pervade Afro-Cuban traditions. The interplay between Sikán, the goat, the medallion, and the fish create a harmonious visual symphony, each element contributing to the resonance of the narrative. The image of the goat and the act of sacrificing a goat holds significant cultural and religious symbolism within Afro-Cuban religious practices, particularly in Santería. In Santería, animals like goats are seen as intermediaries between the spiritual and physical worlds. The act of sacrifice is believed to establish a connection with the Orishas, the deities of the Yoruba pantheon, who are revered and honored through various rituals. Sacrifices are offered to appease the Orishas, seek their guidance, and gain their protection. Goats, among other animals, hold symbolic meanings associated with specific deities and their attributes (Mason 2002; Lammoglia 2007; Palmié 2013 & Morales 1990). The artwork *Sikán con chivo* likely draws on these Afro-Cuban religious practices and the symbolism of the goat within them. The title itself, which translates to "Sikán with goat," hints at a deeper narrative. *Sikán* could refer to a person's name or a representation of a spiritual figure, and the goat might symbolize the act of sacrifice or the connection with the divine. The artwork explores the duality and interconnectedness between the physical and spiritual realms. The goat could represent both the sacrificial nature of Santería[6] rituals and the embodiment of the divine in the material world. The artist might be commenting on the complex interplay between traditional religious practices and contemporary artistic expression, highlighting the continued significance of these rituals in Afro-Cuban culture. The use of the goat in *Sikán con chivo* could serve as a bridge between the religious and artistic dimensions, inviting viewers to contemplate the intricate relationship between cultural heritage, spirituality, and artistic representation. It could also be a commentary on how traditional symbols and practices persist and evolve in modern contexts, retaining their essence while taking on new meanings and interpretations.

Orlando Hernandez, former curator of the Museo Nacional de Bellas Artes in Havana, offers a compelling insight into Ayón's representation of Sikán. He reveals that Ayón based the portrayal of Sikán on her own body and face, thereby imbuing the figure with a personal and intimate dimension. The choice to depict Sikán as pregnant is particularly poignant. It speaks to Ayón's agency as a creator, a bearer of knowledge even in the face of oppressive circumstances. Sikán's pregnancy becomes a metaphor for the artist's own creative process, where she gives birth to narratives that resonate with themes of heritage, identity, and resistance. *Sin título (Sikán con chivo)* is not merely a representation of Abakuá mythology; it is a multilayered narrative that invites viewers to delve deeper and unravel its complexities. Ayón's artistry extends beyond the surface, engaging with themes of power, creation, and the human spirit's enduring capacity for transcendence. Through this artwork, Ayón masterfully blurs the lines between different cultural traditions, inviting us to contemplate the interconnectedness of humanity's shared narratives and the ever-evolving role of art in shaping our understanding of the world.

The image of the goat in this Belkis Ayón's artwork holds a significant place within the composition, contributing to the multifaceted symbolism and narrative layers of the piece. As a central element juxtaposed with the figure of Sikán, the goat brings forth a range of interpretations and enriches the artwork's exploration of Afro-Cuban mythology, spirituality, and cultural amalgamation. The positioning of the goat in the artwork alludes to its potential role in sacrificial and ritualistic practices. In many cultures, goats have been used as offerings in religious ceremonies to invoke blessings or communicate with spiritual entities. The goat's presence near Sikán could symbolize a connection to sacred rituals, underscoring the spiritual significance of Sikán's role in conveying sacred knowledge to her people. In various belief systems, goats are seen as creatures that bridge the gap between the earthly and the spiritual realms. Their agility and adaptability make them symbols of connections to higher forces. The goat's presence alongside Sikán, who serves as a mediator between realms, reinforces the idea that Sikán possesses a unique spiritual connection and the ability to traverse different dimensions. The goat's connection to femininity and fertility aligns with Sikán's role as a symbol of feminine energy and creativity. The goat's associations with vitality and reproduction complement Sikán's pregnant form, reinforcing the idea of creation and the interconnectedness of life forces. Ayón's deliberate inclusion of the goat reflects her adeptness at merging disparate cultural elements. In Afro-Cuban traditions, the goat carries its own symbolism, but Ayón's reinterpretation within the context of Sikán's narrative showcases her ability to fuse distinct cultural motifs into a cohesive whole. This amalgamation resonates with the syncretic nature of Afro-Cuban beliefs. The goat's symbolism can extend to themes of transformation and metamorphosis. Just as the goat can adapt to various environments, Sikán's role as a carrier of sacred knowledge speaks to the transformative power of wisdom and the potential for personal growth. In essence, the image of the goat in *Sin título (Sikán con chivo)* serves as a vital component in the artwork's intricate narrative. Its presence complements Sikán's figure and narrative role, creating a visually compelling dialogue between sacred and earthly realms. The goat's symbolism resonates with themes of sacrifice, spirituality, and cultural synthesis, inviting viewers to contemplate the layers of meaning embedded within the artwork and the enduring significance of Afro-Cuban mythologies within a contemporary context.

The symbolism of pregnancy in Belkis Ayón's artwork *Sin título (Sikán con chivo)* adds a profound layer of meaning to the composition, enriching the narrative with themes of creation, empowerment, and the endurance of cultural heritage. The pregnant form of Sikán serves as a potent visual metaphor that resonates deeply within the context of the artwork. Sikán's pregnancy is a direct representation of the creative power of the feminine. Pregnancy, a process of nurturing and bringing new life into the world, is often associated with the idea of creation and transformation. In the context of the artwork, Sikán's pregnancy symbolizes her role as a conduit of knowledge, bringing forth sacred wisdom and cultural significance that nourishes her people's spirits. The portrayal of Sikán as pregnant empowers her as a symbol of agency and influence. Despite the societal constraints and oppressive circumstances that may surround her, Sikán stands as a representation of strength and resilience. Her pregnancy becomes a metaphor for the artist's own ability to shape narratives and create meaningful expressions even within challenging environments. The pregnant form of Sikán also suggests the continuation of cultural heritage and traditions. Just as a mother carries forth her lineage through pregnancy, Sikán carries the weight of ancestral wisdom and knowledge that she imparts to her people. Her pregnancy becomes a metaphorical bridge between generations, highlighting the importance of preserving cultural legacies. Sikán's pregnant figure blurs the boundaries between the physical and the spiritual, the tangible and the mystical. This interplay underscores her role as a spiritual intermediary and emphasizes the interconnectedness of human experiences. The pregnant form becomes a conduit for spiritual energy, bridging the realms of the material and the divine. Sikán's pregnancy is reminiscent of mythological archetypes that often portray goddesses or revered figures as pregnant symbols of fertility, creation, and wisdom. This allusion enhances the depth of Sikán's significance within the Afro-Cuban mythos and situates her as a figure of reverence and guidance. In *Sin título (Sikán con chivo)*, the symbolism of pregnancy is a powerful narrative device that encapsulates layers of meaning within a single visual representation. It evokes notions of creation, empowerment, continuity, and spirituality, intertwining with the broader themes of cultural synthesis and mythology that define Ayón's artistic vision. The pregnant Sikán becomes a beacon of strength, cultural significance, and the enduring capacity of stories to transcend time and space. It is also fundamental to point out its prominent historical symbolism in relation to Cuban feminist movements. The most vocal proponents of feminism in Cuba were the radical activists, who emerged as the driving force behind the women's movement leading up to the formulation of the 1940 Constitution. Despite being a minority in terms of their numbers, radicalized Marxist feminists like Mariblanca Sabas Aloma[7] and Ofelia Dominguez wielded significant influence over publications that highlighted issues related to women's rights. Their articles were featured in prominent magazines such as *Carteles* and *Bohemia*, where they played a pivotal role in shaping the discourse on Cuban feminism and served as the intellectual frontrunners of the feminist cause. Through their writings, they facilitated a vibrant exchange of ideas surrounding various subjects, including the societal roles of women in Cuba, their positions as moral custodians, their participation in religious contexts, and their roles within the family unit. However, a prevailing and unifying theme consistently ran through their works: a steadfast admiration for the institution of motherhood. Within this ideological framework, Sabas Aloma and her fellow radical feminists perceived motherhood not merely as a biological process, but as a potent vehicle for advancing women's progress and achieving their emancipation (Stoner 89).

This perspective held that motherhood was integral to the broader struggle for gender equality and social transformation. It was seen as a platform through which women could assert their influence and agency, not only within the private sphere of the family but also within the larger societal landscape. In this view, motherhood was not confined to its traditional roles of child-rearing and domestic responsibilities; rather, it became a source of empowerment and an avenue for women to participate actively in reshaping the cultural, political, and economic contours of Cuban society. By assigning deep significance to motherhood, these radical feminists aimed to challenge and reshape prevailing societal norms, positioning women as active agents of change rather than passive recipients of existing gender roles. This ideology of empowering motherhood underscored their vision of achieving substantive equality and liberation for women in Cuba, ultimately leaving an indelible mark on the feminist movement of the time. Before the Cuban Revolution, figures like Sabas Aloma and Dominguez, who were at the forefront of the radical feminist movement, recognized that true progress in feminism necessitated a profound shift in moral awareness. They held a profound belief that the transformation of society's moral fabric was foundational to the success of the feminist cause. For them, the role of motherhood stood as a cornerstone in this process of moral evolution. Consequently, they linked the reverence for motherhood with the advancement of the women's movement. Their perspective rested on the notion that motherhood possessed the potential to serve as a catalyst for moral and societal change. This perspective finds a resonance in the art piece *Sikán con chivo*, where the portrayal of Sikán as a pregnant woman echoes the significance attributed to motherhood. Sikán's pregnant form embodies the idea of transformation, growth, and the nurturing of new life. Just as Sabas Aloma and her contemporaries believed, the representation of Sikán as a pregnant figure might symbolize the potential for moral and societal renewal that motherhood encapsulates. This could be interpreted as an ode to the profound influence that mothers and motherhood possess in shaping the moral landscape of society. However, the landscape shifted drastically after the Cuban Revolution of 1959. The revolutionary rhetoric of leaders like Castro and Espin took a divergent course, stigmatizing motherhood as a hindrance to women's advancement. Their reform campaigns framed motherhood as an impediment to women's progress, representing a stark departure from the prerevolutionary feminist stance. This shift essentially disregarded the importance of motherhood in the women's movement and within Cuban society as a whole. This departure from the earlier feminist ideals could be seen as a betrayal of the efforts undertaken by feminist trailblazers like Sabas Aloma and Dominguez.

Furthermore, the postrevolutionary climate brought about a significant change in women's choices and autonomy. The state's push to institutionalize motherhood meant that women were no longer given the agency to choose between family responsibilities and self-determination. The pressure to dedicate children entirely to the revolution dismantled the role of mothers as moral guides, which had been a significant aspect of their influence prior to the revolution. In the context of the art piece *Sikán con chivo*, this transformation could be mirrored in the symbolic imagery of Sikán's pregnancy. Just as motherhood was institutionalized and its influence diluted in the broader revolutionary goals, the image of Sikán's pregnancy might be seen as a reflection of the fading empowerment and agency associated with motherhood. Ultimately, this shift allowed the feminist movement to be co-opted by the overarching male-controlled revolution. The ideals of prerevolutionary feminist leaders, including their reverence for motherhood as a transformative force, were overshadowed by the dominant political agenda. The narrative of women's progress became subservient to the broader revolution's aims, illustrating a paradox where the revolution itself contributed to the curtailment of women's agency and empowerment.

In *Sin título (Sikán con chivo)*, the symbolism of pregnancy further amplifies the artwork's exploration of gender dynamics, spirituality, and the artist's creative agency. As Sikán's pregnant form takes center stage, a profound resonance emerges between the artistic representation and the broader cultural context it encapsulates. The pregnant figure of Sikán elevates the feminine to a position of prominence. In a cultural landscape often dominated by masculine narratives, Ayón's portrayal of a pregnant woman challenges traditional representations and emphasizes the power of the feminine in shaping narratives and identities. This elevation speaks to the importance of embracing diverse expressions of strength and wisdom. The portrayal of Sikán as pregnant subverts conventional expectations. Rather than relegating her to a passive role, the pregnancy becomes an emblem of empowerment. This subversion challenges societal norms that might limit women's agency and underscores the idea that motherhood and creative authority can coexist harmoniously. Sikán's pregnant form can be seen as a transcendent response to oppressive circumstances. By embodying creation and wisdom, she defies the limitations placed on her and her people. This defiance mirrors the resilience of the Afro-Cuban community in the face of historical adversity, suggesting that cultural identity and strength can flourish even under duress. The symbolism of pregnancy resonates on both a personal and universal level. While Sikán's pregnancy is a specific representation, it also becomes a universal metaphor for the birthing of ideas, knowledge, and stories. This duality underscores the artwork's ability to bridge the individual and the collective, inviting viewers to find connections between their own experiences and the broader human narrative. The pregnant Sikán extends an invitation to delve deeper into the layers of her story. Beyond her role in Abakuá mythology, she becomes a conduit for conversations about agency, heritage, and the enduring spirit of creativity. Her pregnancy prompts us to explore the narratives that are woven within our own lives and cultures, sparking contemplation on the cyclical nature of creation and rebirth. The symbolism of pregnancy in *Sin título (Sikán con chivo)* is a resonant thread that runs through the artwork's intricate tapestry. Through the pregnant figure of Sikán, Belkis Ayón engages with themes of femininity, empowerment, cultural continuity, and defiance against oppression. This symbolism serves as a vessel for Ayón's creative agency and for the broader narratives of Afro-Cuban mythology and heritage. As viewers engage with this artwork, they are invited to partake in a dialogue that transcends time and space, connecting them to the timeless power of creation and the enduring spirit of human expression.

La Familia

Belkis Ayón's artwork *La Familia/The Family*, 1991 (figure 5.3) is a masterful composition that delves into themes of transformation, cultural syncretism, and archetypal allegory. This piece offers a striking visual narrative that invites viewers to explore the depths of symbolic significance embedded within its intricate details. Through the portrayal of Sikán, the incorporation of Tanze, the sacrificial goat, the rooster, Mokongo, and the overall composition, Ayón constructs a multilayered tapestry of meaning that resonates with the artist's larger body of work and the Afro-Cuban cultural context. At the heart of *La Familia* is Sikán, depicted in a pivotal moment of metamorphosis. Seated with an air of contemplation, Sikán's connection to the sacred fish, Tanze, becomes apparent as it rests in her lap or womb. This portrayal serves as a visual embodiment of transformation, where Sikán is in the process of becoming "other." The symbolism here hints at spiritual rebirth and the fusion of human and mystical realms. Sikán's complexion, not yet "ghostly white," suggests her transition, aligning

Figure 5.3. *La familia (The Family)*, Belkis Ayón, 1991, collagraph. *Source:* Photography by Alejandro González. Courtesy and Copyright © Belkis Ayón Estate, Havana, Cuba.

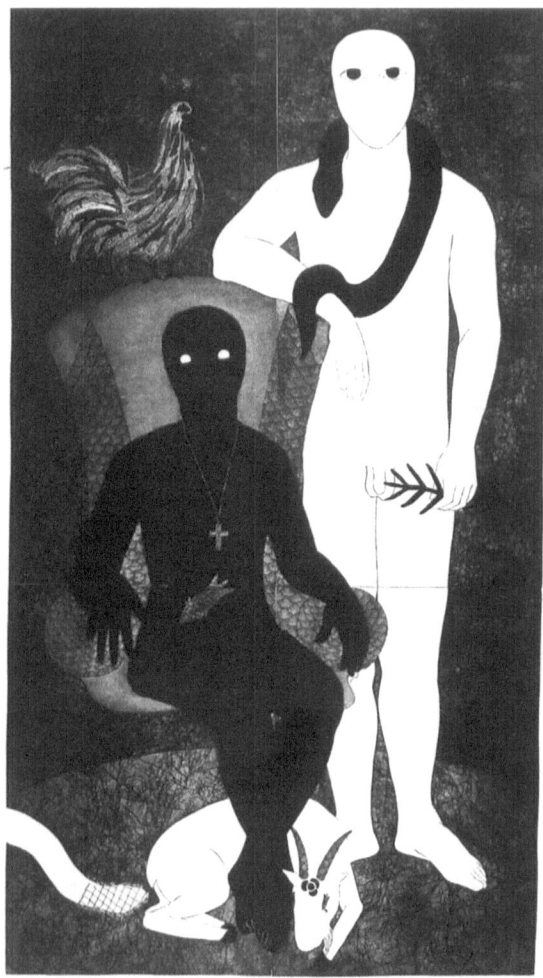

with the idea of liminality often present in rites of passage. Ayón's portrayal captures a sense of suspended time, allowing the viewer to witness the profound transformation Sikán undergoes as she moves closer to a transcendent state. Surrounding Sikán are several archetypal figures that contribute to the tapestry of symbolism. The sacrificial goat, an emblematic image in Afro-Cuban religious practices, holds layers of meaning.

It embodies notions of sacrifice, offering, and ritual purity. The rooster, symbolizing courage and spiritual awakening, perches behind Sikán, adding an element of transformation and rebirth to the composition. Mokongo's presence introduces an intriguing dynamic. As Sikán's fiancé, he takes on a role of agency and influence. His control over the snake underscores the duality inherent in many symbolic narratives—the snake being a symbol of both danger and transformation. Mokongo's involvement hints at the external forces shaping Sikán's journey, both on a personal level and within the cultural context. The hovering of Sikán's "provisional throne" serves as a visual manifestation of the ethereal and transformative nature of her journey. The levitation effect creates an otherworldly atmosphere, emphasizing the liminal space Sikán occupies—a threshold between the known and the transcendent. This levitation echoes Ayón's exploration of numinous maturation, where Sikán's spiritual growth is mirrored in her physical and symbolic levitation. *La Familia* is emblematic of Belkis Ayón's broader body of work, where her exploration of myth, identity, and spirituality through Afro-Cuban cultural lenses is vividly expressed. The incorporation of Afro-Cuban religious symbols—such as the sacrificial goat, the rooster, and the snake—ties *La Familia* to Ayón's exploration of syncretic belief systems and the preservation of cultural heritage. This Belkis Ayón's artwork is a multidimensional tableau of symbolism, transformation, and archetypal allegory. Through Sikán's journey, the presence of Tanze, the archetypal figures, the levitating throne, and the broader context of Ayón's oeuvre, the piece offers a profound exploration of liminality, cultural syncretism, and the numinous maturation of the human spirit. As viewers engage with the intricate details and layers of meaning, they are invited to traverse the threshold of Sikán's transformation and reflect on their own journeys of becoming "other."

The symbol of the fish Tanze in Belkis Ayón's artwork holds a profound significance, intricately tied to the artist's extensive research into Abakuá history and its central figure, Princess Sikán. This symbol not only enriches the narrative of Ayón's artwork but also serves as a bridge between cultural mythology, historical context, and the themes of transformation and sacrifice. Ayón's intensive research into the Abakuá tradition underscores her dedication to capturing the essence of its beliefs and myths. Within this tradition, Princess Sikán, as we saw, emerges as a pivotal figure, and the story of Tanze adds layers of meaning to Ayón's visual narrative. The central myth surrounding Tanze is crucial in understanding its symbolism. According to Abakuá tradition, Princess Sikán inadvertently captures the enchanted fish, Tanze. This fish is not just any aquatic creature; its significance lies in its voice, which imparts extraordinary power to those who hear it. The resonance between Tanze's voice and the concept of spiritual empowerment or transformation is evident, as the fish serves as a conduit between the material and mystical worlds. The cautionary aspect of the myth cannot be ignored. Sikán's transgression of breaking her father's warning and sharing the secret with her fiancé, a leader of an enemy tribe, results in a devastating consequence: a death sentence for both Sikán and Tanze (González Gómez, 117). This emphasizes the high stakes associated with this secret knowledge and the sacredness of Tanze's voice. In *La Familia*, Ayón's portrayal of Sikán cradling Tanze in her lap or womb infuses the narrative with layers of symbolism. Tanze's presence within Sikán represents the potential for transformative power, echoing the Abakuá belief in the fish's voice as a source of great strength. Sikán's engagement with Tanze signifies a journey of self-discovery and empowerment, aligning with the myth's narrative of attaining exceptional abilities through connection with the mystical. The fate of both Sikán and Tanze offers a powerful allegory. Sikan's ultimate sacrifice due to her indiscretion mirrors the theme of sacrifice and transformation prevalent in many mythologies. Her willingness to divulge the secret to her beloved, even if it costs her life, speaks to the complexities of human relationships, loyalty, and the pursuit of personal or collective empowerment. In Ayón's *La Familia*, Tanze's incorporation is a masterful convergence of myth, history, and artistic expression. Its presence magnifies the artwork's exploration of spiritual transformation, the consequences of divulging sacred knowledge, and the intricate interplay between power and sacrifice. The symbolism of Tanze enhances the depth of Sikán's journey within the artwork, reflecting the broader human quest for understanding, empowerment, and connection to the mystical and sacred.

The myth also includes other interesting details. The tale of Sikán, the chief's daughter, teaches us that while she was collecting water from the river, inadvertently caught a fish housing the spirit of Tanze, a deceased king known for his prophetic abilities. Her actions led to her being labeled a traitor and subsequently sacrificed to the rhythmic beat of the Ekwe drum, which was believed to produce the voice or soul of Tanze (Cano 2022, 1). The image of Tanze in this myth carries profound symbolic and cultural significance, offering insights into the beliefs, values, and practices of the community in which the legend originates. Tanze is portrayed as a deceased king who possessed remarkable prophetic abilities. This highlights his elevated status within the community during his lifetime. Prophets or individuals with the ability to foresee future events are often held in high regard in many cultures, as they are seen as conduits to the divine or as wise leaders. Tanze's prophetic talents underscore his importance and influence. The fact that Tanze's spirit resides within a fish adds a layer of mysticism to the narrative. Fish can have various symbolic meanings in different cultures, often representing fertility, transformation, or spirituality. In this context, the fish becomes a vessel for the remnants of Tanze's spiritual power, connecting the earthly realm with the supernatural. The encounter between Sikán and the fish housing Tanze's spirit is accidental, emphasizing the unpredictable nature of fate. This element suggests that divine or supernatural forces can enter one's life unexpectedly, with significant consequences. It underscores the idea that individuals may not have full control over the spiritual or mystical aspects of their existence. Sikán's role as the one who inadvertently captures Tanze's spirit highlights the concept of destiny or preordained roles within the community. Her actions, though unintentional, lead to her being labeled a traitor. This underscores the idea that individuals may be assigned specific roles or destinies within their social and cultural contexts, whether they actively choose them or not. The sacrifice of Sikán to the rhythmic beat of the Ekwe drum reveals the community's strong beliefs in ritual and spirituality. The drum, believed to produce the voice or soul of Tanze, serves as a powerful symbol of the connection between the living and the spiritual realm. The act of sacrifice itself reflects the community's dedication to preserving its cultural traditions and maintaining a connection with the supernatural.

The title, *La Familia*, can be also read as having a profound meaning, especially if taking in consideration historical feminist efforts in Cuba in relation to the constitution of the family and the role of women in society. During a gathering of women leaders from socialist nations in Havana in 1989, Vilma Espín,[8] a Cuban revolutionary, feminist, and chemical engineer, made a thought-provoking declaration regarding the intricate relationship between the prevailing social structures and the modes of production within a specific historical context and geographical location: "The social institution under which men at a definite historical epoch and of a definite country live are conditioned by both kinds of production: by the stage of development of labor on one hand and of the family, on the other" (68). In her statement, Espín emphasized that these social institutions are intricately linked to two fundamental facets: the stage of labor development and the state of the family structure. Espín's viewpoint suggests that these two elements, labor development and family structure, are inextricably intertwined and influence one another. She posited that for a truly socialist society to thrive, it is imperative that all members of the family, without exception, including mothers and their offspring, become fully integrated into the revolutionary cause. Furthermore, Espín argued that the concepts of self-definition, self-worth, and self-purpose should find their meaning within the context of serving the interests of the revolutionary state. In her view, the individual's identity and sense of value should be deeply rooted in their contribution to the collective goals and progress of the socialist society. This perspective reflects a collectivist ethos, where personal aspirations and objectives are secondary to the broader objectives of the state and its revolutionary agenda. Vilma Espín's statement underscores the interplay between the socioeconomic structures of a given era, the family unit, and the role of individuals within a socialist society. She advocates for the complete alignment of individual identity and purpose with the overarching goals of the revolutionary state, emphasizing a commitment to the collective over individual pursuits. This perspective offers valuable insights into the ideological foundations of socialist movements and the complex dynamics of family and labor within such societies.

The passage about Vilma Espín's perspective on family and the art piece *La Familia* both touch on the themes of transformation and the blending of human and mystical elements, although in different contexts and mediums. In Vilma Espín's view, family members, including mothers like Sikán, must be fully integrated into the revolutionary state, aligning their self-identity and purpose with the collective goals of the socialist society. This perspective emphasizes the subordination of individual pursuits to the broader revolutionary cause and highlights the importance of aligning oneself with the collective. In *La Familia* by Ayón, the artwork portrays Sikán in a moment of contemplation, cradling the sacred fish, Tanze, in her lap or womb. This imagery symbolizes a profound transformation in progress, where Sikán is in the process of becoming something different or "other." The connection between Sikán and Tanze represents a fusion of human and mystical realms, akin to a spiritual rebirth. The common thread between these two concepts is the idea of transformation and the transcendence of individual identity for a higher purpose. Vilma Espín's perspective emphasizes this transformation in the context of a socialist society, where individuals are expected to align themselves with the state's objectives. In contrast, Belkis Ayón's artwork presents this transformation as a mystical and spiritual journey, where Sikán's connection with Tanze signifies a transition beyond the human experience. Both perspectives invite us to contemplate the complexities of transformation, whether in the context of ideological revolutions or spiritual and mystical experiences. They underscore the idea that individuals can undergo profound changes, whether for collective or spiritual reasons, and that these transformations often involve a fusion of the human and the mystical, blurring the boundaries between them. The legend of Sikán, who was sacrificed to the sound of the Ekwe drum, and Vilma Espín's advocacy for women's equality both revolve around the theme of women's voices and their roles in patriarchal societies. These two narratives intersect in their exploration of the challenges women face in societies where their voices and agency are often suppressed. In the legend of Sikán, her fate is sealed when she inadvertently captures the spirit of Tanze. Her voice and her agency are effectively silenced as she is labeled a traitor and sacrificed. This narrative reflects the historical reality of many women in patriarchal societies who were denied a voice and autonomy over their lives. Vilma Espín was a staunch advocate for women's rights and gender equality within the context of socialist Cuba. She recognized that women in many societies, including Cuba, had been marginalized and denied equal opportunities due to deeply ingrained patriarchal norms. Espín's work aimed to empower women's voices and encourage their active participation in the revolutionary cause. She believed that women, like men, had a crucial role to play in building a socialist society and should have equal opportunities in education, employment, and politics. The themes of voicelessness and women's empowerment in both narratives align. Sikán's voice is silenced by the oppressive norms of her society, while Espín fought against such norms to ensure that women's voices were heard and valued in the revolutionary context. Both Sikán's legend and Vilma Espín's activism highlight the broader quest for gender equality and the need to challenge patriarchal structures that limit women's opportunities and agency. In essence, the legend of Sikán and Vilma Espín's advocacy converge in their shared concern for women's rights and their struggle for a more equitable society in Cuba. While Sikán's story serves as a cautionary tale of the consequences of silencing women's voices, Espín's work exemplifies the fight to empower women, amplify their voices, and create a society where gender equality is a reality rather than a myth. Espín highlighted constantly in her work and activism the social inequalities of sexes in Cuba. The revolutionary and feminist figure asserted that: "the monogamous family, from its very origin, implied the social inequality of sexes. Women were excluded from social production and confined to bearing children of proven paternity, raising and educating children as useful members of society, as well as being responsible for the small-scale domestic economy. . . . women were lowered to that 'productive species' as Engels called the production of man himself" (Espín 68). Vilma Espín's quote offers a profound analysis of the historical and social implications of monogamous family structures, particularly in the context of gender inequality. Her statement reflects her deep commitment to women's rights and her critical perspective on traditional family dynamics. Espín begins by asserting that the monogamous family, even from its inception, has been intertwined with social inequality between the sexes. This observation acknowledges that gender disparities have deep historical roots, and the family structure itself has played a role in perpetuating such inequality. She highlights a key aspect of this inequality, which is the exclusion of women from social production. In many historical societies, women were often relegated to domestic roles while men were primarily engaged in economic and public activities. This division of labor resulted in unequal power dynamics within the family unit. Espín underscores the traditional roles assigned to women within the monogamous family, emphasizing their primary functions as bearers of children with proven paternity and as caregivers responsible for raising and educating children to become productive members of society. This role limitation confined women to specific domestic duties, limiting their opportunities for economic and social participation. The quote references Friedrich Engels's concept of women's role in "the production of man himself." This concept suggests that women's primary function was to ensure the reproduction and upbringing of the next generation, reinforcing their subordination within the family structure. It's important to note that Vilma Espín's perspective is situated within the broader context of socialist ideology and the struggle for gender equality during the Cuban Revolution. Her critique of the monogamous family aligns with the broader goals of the revolution, which sought to dismantle traditional gender roles and empower women in all aspects of society. Vilma Espín's perspective offers a critical analysis of how traditional monogamous family structures have historically contributed to the subordination of women and their exclusion from broader social and economic participation. Her perspective reflects a commitment to challenging gender inequality and advocating for women's rights within the framework of socialist principles. Her words serve as a reminder of the complex interplay between family structures and societal norms in shaping gender roles and inequalities.

Sikán as portrayed in *La Familia* and in others Ayón's pieces such as *Sikán con chivo*, the art piece analyzed in an earlier section of this chapter, make us also reflect on the role of motherhood in Cuba. In this context, it is also beneficial to turn to Espín perspective on Revolutionary Motherhood in the context of Cuba. Vilma Espín's concept of Revolutionary Motherhood, which mandates that mothers step out of their domestic roles and engage in the public sphere to promote the Revolution, closely aligns with the principles outlined by Friedrich Engels in his influential work, *The Origin of the Family, Private Property, and the State*. Espín refers to Engels often in her work. Both Espín and Engels emphasize key objectives that underline women's rights and gender equality. Engels and Espín share a common vision of ending the economic dependence of women on their husbands. In traditional family structures, women were often financially reliant on their spouses, which limited their autonomy and decision-making power. Both thinkers advocate for economic independence as a means of empowering women. Another shared objective is the inclusion of women in the workforce and the removal of the barriers that confined them to the home. Engels and Espín recognize that women's isolation within the domestic sphere hindered their ability to participate in public life, pursue careers, and contribute to society's progress. Their respective ideologies promote breaking down these barriers (Engels 2001). Engels and Espín both advocate for the socialization of household chores traditionally assigned to women. This entails the establishment of public facilities such as laundries, cafeterias, day-care centers, schools, and other communal services. By shifting these responsibilities to the public sphere, they aim to relieve women of the disproportionate burden of domestic work and allow them to engage more fully in public life.

Expanding on this connection, it's important to note that both Espín and Engels were proponents of socialist ideals. Espín's vision of Revolutionary Motherhood was a core component of the Cuban Revolution's broader goal of achieving gender equality within a socialist framework. Engels, on the other hand, laid the theoretical foundation for understanding the intersection of the family, private property, and the state within a historical and economic context. In essence, Espín's concept of Revolutionary Motherhood can be seen as a practical application of Engels's theoretical framework, aiming to transform gender roles and achieve greater gender equality by addressing economic dependency, women's isolation, and the socialization of domestic labor. This alignment underscores the enduring relevance of Engels's ideas and their practical implications in the pursuit of women's rights and gender equality, particularly within socialist movements. The art piece *La Familia* resonates with the concepts discussed in the context of Vilma Espín's Revolutionary Motherhood and Friedrich Engels's ideas about the transformation of the family structure. While the artwork does not directly illustrate these concepts, it provides a visual representation of the complexities of family, identity, and transformation that are relevant to these discussions. Both Vilma Espín and Friedrich Engels advocated for women breaking free from traditional roles within the family and society. In *La Familia*, Sikán's contemplation and her connection with Tanze may symbolize a departure from conventional gender roles and expectations, reflecting the idea of women stepping out of their traditional roles to pursue greater independence and participation in public life. The artwork hints at shifting family dynamics and the interplay between the individual and the collective. Just as Vilma Espín's vision of Revolutionary Motherhood sought to challenge traditional family structures, *La Familia* suggests a transformative process within the family unit, where individual identities may evolve to align with broader societal changes. In both the concepts of Revolutionary Motherhood and the themes explored in *La Familia*, there is an underlying tension between the individual and the collective. Espín's vision called for women to align their roles with the collective goals of the Revolution, while *La Familia* portrays an individual (Sikán) on the cusp of a transformation that may impact her collective identity. *La Familia* serves as a visually compelling representation of transformation, identity, and the complexities of family dynamics, which intersect with the concepts of women's roles, gender equality, and societal transformation discussed in the context of Vilma Espín's ideas and Friedrich Engels's theories. While the artwork does not directly illustrate these concepts, it invites viewers to contemplate the dynamic interplay between the individual and the collective within the family unit and society at large.

Conclusion

The intricate and evocative works of Belkis Ayón discussed in this chapter— *La Cena, Sin título (Sikán con chivo), and La Familia/The Family*—reveal a transformative exploration of Cuban culture, Afro-Cuban mythology, and the profound symbolism inherent in each piece. Collectively, these masterpieces stand as a testament to Ayón's exceptional artistic vision and her capacity to transcend temporal, cultural, and narrative boundaries. In

La Cena, the deliberate parallelism between the Abakúa myth of Princess Sikán and the iconic scene of Jesus at the Last Supper facilitates an examination of themes such as spirituality, sacrifice, and the enduring resonance of symbolic storytelling. Through Ayón's astute integration of these narratives, the roles of transformative figures and the significance of their respective journeys are brought into contemplation. *Sin título (Sikán con chivo)* immerses the viewer in the depths of Afro-Cuban culture, where Sikán's representation transcends mere physicality and delves into the core of her identity. The inclusion of the goat, the enigmatic interaction between Sikán and the observer, and the seamless integration of cultural traditions contribute to a multifaceted narrative. Ayón's technical brilliance and her skillful synthesis of diverse elements underscore the profound depth of her artistic prowess.

In *La Familia/The Family*, Ayón invites us to witness a profound moment of transformation and cultural syncretism. Sikán's metamorphosis, her connection with Tanze, and the symbolism of spiritual rebirth all beckon us to contemplate the intersection of the human and mystical realms. It is essential to continue the visibility and recognition of artists like Belkis Ayón for several compelling reasons. Ayón's work is a reflection of Afro-Cuban culture and its rich heritage. By keeping her art visible, we preserve and celebrate an integral part of Cuba's cultural tapestry, ensuring that it is not forgotten or overlooked. Ayón's art amplifies the voices and stories of marginalized and underrepresented communities, particularly Afro-Cuban women. Visibility for her work serves as a platform for these voices, empowering them to be heard and understood on a broader scale. Ayón's art challenges stereotypes and misconceptions about Afro-Cuban culture and its complex history. By continuing to showcase her work, we actively counter stereotypes and encourage a more nuanced understanding of the Afro-Cuban experience. Belkis Ayón's contribution to the world of art is undeniable. Her unique printmaking techniques and compelling narratives have left an indelible mark. By keeping her art visible, we ensure that her artistic legacy continues to inspire and influence future generations of artists and art enthusiasts. Ayón's art invites viewers to engage in dialogue about culture, identity, spirituality, and transformation. By continuing to promote her work, we foster meaningful conversations and a deeper appreciation for the themes she explored. Moreover, Ayón's art has a global resonance, transcending borders and cultures. It offers a unique perspective on universal themes. By making her art more visible, we encourage cross-cultural dialogue and appreciation. Ayón's work adds to the growing recognition of women artists who have historically been underrepresented in the art world. Her visibility contributes to the broader movement of acknowledging and celebrating women's contributions to the arts. Through intricate composition and the language of symbolism, Ayón provokes reflection on liminality and the rites of passage that define our existence.

Collectively, these three masterpieces by Belkis Ayón stand as a testament to the power of art to transcend boundaries and connect diverse traditions. They challenge us to delve deeper into the narratives, symbolism, and layers of meaning, echoing the complex tapestry of Cuban history and Afro-Cuban heritage. Ayón's work serves as an enduring reminder of the profound role that culture and mythology play in our collective human experience. Nevertheless, Belkis Ayón's artistry serves as a bridge between the past and the present, between cultural traditions and contemporary contemplation. Her masterpieces are not mere depictions but portals into the depths of our shared humanity, where transformation, spirituality, and cultural syncretism intersect. Through her art, Ayón continues to inspire us to explore the profound narratives that shape our world and to embrace the enduring power of visual storytelling.

Chapter 6

Empowering Through Art, Shaping Cultural Narratives, and Celebrating Afro-Cuban Heritage

An Interview with Harmonia Rosales

I had the honor of meeting Harmonia Rosales in person on Thursday, August 17, 2023, after years of studying her artistic practice. We had an illuminating conversation in front of her captivating masterpiece *The Birth of Oshun*. This is the powerful artwork that graces the cover of my book. We met during the VIP preview and private reception of her current exhibition titled *Master Narrative* at Spelman College Museum of Fine Art in Atlanta, that ran run from August 18 to December 2, 2023. Harmonia Rosales's *Master Narrative* is an extraordinary exhibition featuring a collection of twenty meticulously crafted paintings. Born in the vibrant city of Chicago in 1984, and now based in the creative hub of Los Angeles, Rosales is a visionary artist who possesses the remarkable ability to interweave the rich tapestry of Afro-Cuban Lucumí religion, the enchanting lore of Greco-Roman mythology, and the profound symbolism of Christianity. With each stroke of her brush, Rosales embarks on a daring artistic expedition that defies conventional boundaries. Her work challenges the very notion of the master narrative, creating a bridge that spans the depths of time, collapses millennia, and traverses the widest of oceans. Within her canvases, tales and characters from disparate traditions converge, inviting viewers to explore the intersections of cultures and belief systems. At its core, *Master Narrative* invites us to question the divisions that have historically separated humanity. Rosales deftly guides us through a thought-provoking exploration of fundamental themes—creation, tragedy, survival, and resilience—all through the unique lens of the Black Cuban diaspora. In doing so, she prompts us to reconsider the universality of these profound human experiences, urging us to recognize the shared threads that connect us all. For Harmonia Rosales, the act of storytelling transcends the realm of mere artistic expression. It is a deeply personal journey, a voyage of self-discovery, and a powerful means of reclaiming one's cultural identity. In a world where identity is often defined by external forces, Rosales encourages us to embark on a journey of rediscovery, reconnecting with our roots as a means not only of survival but of flourishing. The interview to the artist that follows was in written format and invites readers to explore the intricate narratives, vivid imagery, and profound concepts that define her artistry.

In the world of contemporary art, there are those who create, and then there are those whose creations transcend the canvas, speaking to the soul and sparking conversations that resonate far beyond the gallery walls. Harmonia Rosales is unquestionably among the latter—an artist whose work has not only captivated audiences worldwide but has also ignited crucial dialogues about culture, feminism, representation, and empowerment. It is with great honor and profound appreciation that I present this exclusive interview with Harmonia Rosales. Her unique artistic vision and unwavering commitment to addressing critical issues through her art have not only inspired countless individuals but have also challenged societal norms and enriched our collective understanding of history, identity, and spirituality. Through this interview, we gain insight into her perspective on art as empowerment, her journey to embracing natural beauty, and her dedication to reshaping the narrative of Black women in art. Moreover, we uncover the deep influence of Afro-Cuban culture on her work and her visionary aspirations for the future of her art. This conversation with Harmonia Rosales is an invitation to embark on a transformative journey through the world of art, culture, and spirituality—a journey that promises to leave an indelible mark on your perception of art's potential to empower, educate, and inspire.

Interview

First and foremost, I'd like to extend my heartfelt gratitude to Harmonia Rosales for taking the time to do this interview for my book. Harmonia,

Figure 6.1. On the left, artist Harmonia Rosales; on the right, the author of this book, during their meeting in front of Rosales's masterpiece *The Birth of Oshun*. *Source:* Courtesy of Author.

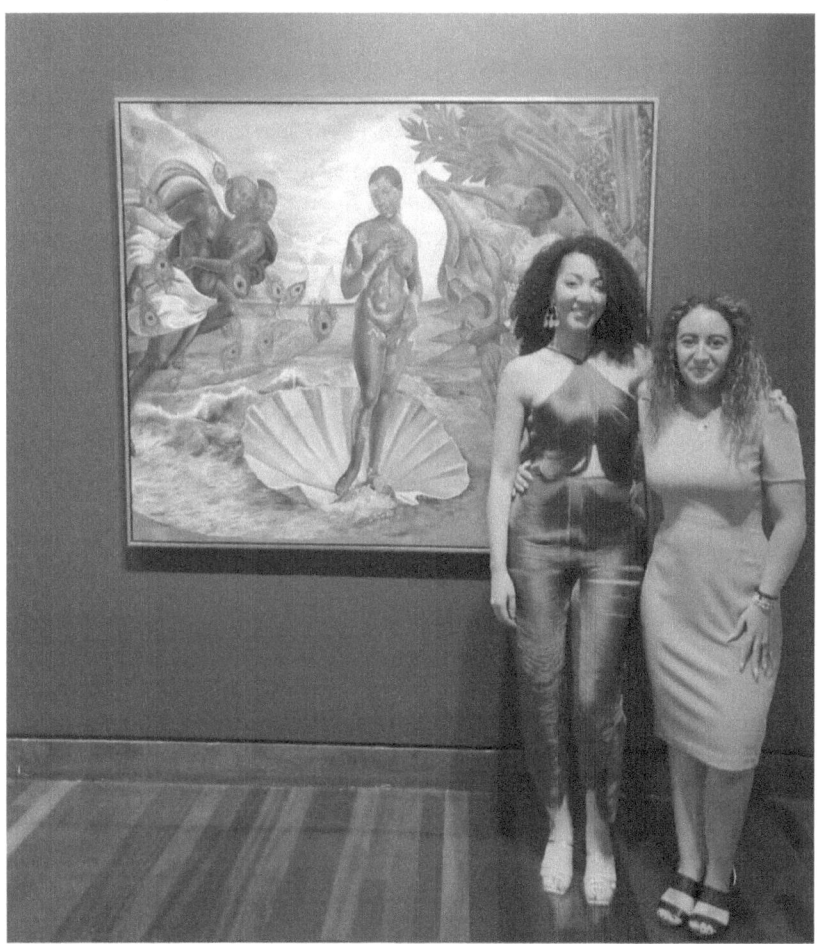

your work as an artist has not only captivated audiences around the world but has also sparked important conversations about culture, feminism, and representation. Your creative vision and commitment to addressing critical issues through your art are truly inspiring. Thank you for sharing your insights and experiences with us.

∾

Rosita Scerbo: Your art highlights the strength and resilience of Black women. In this regard, do you perceive your cultural and artistic expression as a form of political resistance? If so, could you elaborate on how your art serves this purpose?

Harmonia Rosales: Political resistance typically implies a structured opposition against an established government or foreign power, aiming to disrupt societal order and stability. My art, however, does not seek to cause such disruption, except perhaps in the minds of those who have yet to confront their own unhealed wounds. Instead, my art looks to challenge a mentality that has long kept us in metaphorical chains.

I create pieces that narrate ancient tales rich with historical context and factual information. My intent is not to resist, but to enlighten, to empower. My brush strokes aim to weave the narratives of the African diaspora into the broader tapestry of human history. Therefore, I view my art as a powerful tool for empowerment, an instrument for inclusivity—not a medium for political resistance.

RS: Do you consider your art to be Afro-feminist, and if so, could you share what that term means to you and how it influences your creative process and themes in your work?

HR: While I resonate with certain aspects of Afro-feminism, I don't fully identify myself within its framework. In my view, Afro-feminism is about asserting our significance and articulating the necessity of our visibility in society. However, my personal approach leans more toward fostering self-recognition of our worth among ourselves. I believe that when we, as a community, acknowledge and embrace our own power, it creates an undeniable radiance that inevitably draws recognition from others. So, while I may not be an Afro-feminist in the traditional sense, my aim remains steadfast—to empower us from within, so no one can overlook our brilliance.

RS: In many of your paintings, the Black women you portray have dark skin complexions. What message or commentary do you believe this conveys about colorism within our own community, and how does it fit into your artistic vision?

HR: My artwork primarily features Black skin, which is a deliberate choice made to challenge and combat the pervasive colorism within our society.

The magnificence of Black skin is undeniable, yet societal narratives have historically painted a different picture, suggesting that darker hues are less desirable or signify negative connotations. These misleading narratives permeate various aspects of life, from religion to socioeconomic status, often associating darkness with negativity and whiteness with purity or success.

However, the reality is far from these misconceptions. Just as light embodies all colors in its spectrum, so does dark skin encompass an array of shades, each one radiant and beautiful. Through my art, I incorporate this multitude of colors to showcase the luminosity, beauty, and royal essence inherent in Black skin.

Therefore, while every color holds its own unique beauty, my focus on painting the darkest shades of skin is a conscious effort to reiterate to people of color that Black is not just beautiful, but also symbolic of wealth and divinity. By doing so, I aim to rewrite the narrative and affirm the truth: Black is indeed beautiful, affluent, and divine.

RS: Many of the Black women in your artwork are depicted with short and natural hair. Can you discuss the significance of this choice and what it might tell us about challenging gender normativity and embracing natural beauty in your work?

HR: The decision to portray women with short hair in my paintings is deeply personal, stemming from my own journey toward self-discovery and acceptance. I had been using hair relaxers since first grade, conforming to societal expectations of beauty. However, a pivotal moment in my life led me to renounce many such preconceptions, including the notion that straightened hair was a prerequisite for acceptance.

My hair was severely damaged due to years of chemical treatments and weaves, leading me to make the drastic choice of "the big chop" when I decided to embrace my natural hair. The decision was daunting, accompanied by feelings of vulnerability. Yet, once I stepped out into the world, I felt liberated and self-assured.

This newfound confidence was jolted when a man questioned my decision to cut my hair, insinuating that my beauty was diminished without long hair and further suggesting that a man must have influenced my decision. This encounter was a stark reminder of the gender normativity that pervades our society, where a woman's beauty is often defined by her physical attributes and men's perceived preferences.

However, I firmly believe that beauty transcends hair length or texture. It lies within the individual, in their unique features, and their authentic selves. Through my art, I strive to challenge these conventional norms and celebrate natural beauty. I aim to depict the raw and individualized splendor that resides in each one of us, unmasked by makeup or hidden behind long tresses. My paintings are a testament to the inherent beauty of women, regardless of societal expectations or standards.

RS: In your opinion, what are some of the most important changes that you would like to see in the art world, particularly in relation to representation, diversity, and the recognition of underrepresented voices and artists?

HR: I believe that there is a tendency in the art world to celebrate representations of us primarily in contexts of victimhood or poverty. This seems to motivate artists to persistently depict us in narratives of slavery, violence, financial struggle, or materialistic success.

What I would like to see is a significant shift in this narrative. I envision artwork that can inspire and empower us, where our authentic identities are portrayed in all their richness and complexity. I yearn for art that elevates us and expands our imaginative horizons.

RS: Your work often addresses issues of race, identity, and empowerment. How do you hope your art contributes to discussions about these topics, and what impact do you aspire to achieve through your work?

HR: My ultimate aspiration is to facilitate a cultural shift where African deities are recognized, celebrated, and integrated into mainstream discourse. Imagine a world where upcoming generations learn about Zeus and Shango concurrently, or Venus and Oshun with equal reverence. The potential impact on the minds of future creative leaders would be profound. Inspired by these diverse narratives, they might pen stories or create films that reflect this rich cultural heritage.

Consider the ripple effect this would have on audiences who engage with these works. They would have the opportunity to appreciate the beauty and richness of these cultures—our culture—in a new light. This kind of transformation could lead to true societal change. My deepest hope is to witness this inclusive understanding and appreciation within my lifetime. Through my art, I aim to contribute to these conversations about race, identity, and empowerment, and inspire this great shift.

RS: Afro-Cuban culture plays a significant role in your art. Could you talk about your personal connection to this culture and how it influences your creative expression?

HR: My early years were significantly shaped by my Afro-Cuban heritage, primarily through the influence of my grandmother who introduced me to Lukumi—the Cuban interpretation of the Yoruba religion. Central to this belief system is the idea of heeding your inner voice and pursuing your destined path, a philosophy that was further reinforced by my parents.

However, it wasn't until the birth of my daughter that I truly began to resonate with these teachings. A sense of curiosity emerged, leading me to question why such rich cultural narratives were absent from our educational curriculums. This prompted a personal quest for answers, unraveling layers of unexplored knowledge. Each story unearthed a piece of history, each historical account unveiled resilience and strength.

This journey led me toward a deeper understanding of myself. Now, each artwork I create and each story I narrate through my paintings unveils a facet of my identity, reflecting my true essence. In this way, my Afro-Cuban upbringing has profoundly shaped my artistic expression and creative process.

RS: Your paintings often feature strong and empowered female figures. What significance do these representations hold for you, and how do they relate to broader conversations about gender and empowerment?

HR: Growing up in a culture that prioritized male narratives and perspectives, I found myself living a life heavily influenced by these norms. The expectation was to marry and have children, with little emphasis on personal growth.

When my marriage ended, leaving me as a single mother, I was at a crossroads. Despite societal and familial pressures to remarry, I chose a different path.

I wanted to demonstrate that I could be financially independent and didn't need to rely on a man for stability. This experience led me to question the origins of these deeply ingrained beliefs about gender roles and power dynamics. It all traced back to religious narratives, where "God"—the ultimate symbol of power—is typically portrayed as male, relegating everyone else to secondary status.

In response to these traditional narratives, I decided to challenge this hierarchy in my artwork. My paintings often portray women as empowered figures, not superior to men, but their equals. This reflects the principles of the Yoruba religion, which emphasizes the necessity of both male and female elements for the creation of life. Through my art, I aim to promote a narrative of equality.

RS: Your work has garnered attention and acclaim worldwide. What advice do you have for emerging artists of color, especially Black and Latina women, who aspire to have their voices heard and their art recognized on a larger scale?

HR: I would advise budding artists of color, particularly Black and Latina women, to create art that is a true reflection of their unique identities. Don't be swayed by what you perceive others might want to see. Instead, focus on creating art that resonates with your personal experiences, passions, and perspectives.

The reality is, when you infuse your work with your own identity, you're essentially creating for yourself. You'll find that this authenticity will resonate with many others who identify with your experiences and viewpoints.

By staying true to yourself in your art, you will inevitably find that your voice reverberates powerfully, reaching those who need and appreciate your unique perspective. Your art will not only be recognized on a larger scale but will also make a profound impact.

RS: Your art incorporates elements of Afro-diasporic spirituality, drawing inspiration from the Orishas and the Lucumí religion. Could you share how these spiritual and cultural aspects influence your creative process, and what significance they hold in your artwork?

HR: Afro-diasporic spirituality and elements from the Orishas and the Lucumí religion permeate every stroke of my brush—it's the core of my artwork, the very essence of what I create. I find myself irresistibly drawn to these themes; they fill a deep void within me, and I can hardly envision painting anything else.

This is more than just a religion to me. It's our history, our struggles, and our resilience. It's how we've managed to preserve our stories and pass them down through generations.

These narratives have been instrumental in shaping my identity, empowering me to explore my roots and express my unique perspective through art. My hope is that my artwork, steeped in these spiritual and cultural aspects, will resonate with others, empowering them in the same way it has empowered me. The significance they hold in my artwork is profound—they are not just themes but the lifeblood of my creative process—my artist DNA.

RS: In what ways do you envision your art evolving in the future, both in terms of style and the messages you want to convey?

HR: Predicting the evolution of my art is a challenge, as I often allow the creativity to lead me. However, I do make a conscious effort to pause occasionally and reflect on my journey and the milestones I've achieved. This retrospection enables me to recognize the growth in all facets of my life—my skills, storytelling capabilities, and personal development.

While my style and techniques may evolve over time, the core message that's rooted in my work remains constant—to empower and heal. This purpose will continue to guide my artistic journey, no matter how my art transforms in the future.

RS: Are there any upcoming projects or exhibitions you'd like to share with your audience?

HR: At present, my creative energies are largely channeled into my forthcoming series titled *Transformations*, slated for release in 2025. This collection seeks to continue with the endless stories of the Orishas and how they shaped our lives.

Simultaneously, I'm also penning a book that will serve as a companion piece to the art series. The book will weave together the myriad stories of the Orishas that have profoundly influenced my life.

My overarching aim with these projects is not only to showcase the beauty and power of the Orishas but also to ensure the longevity of this ancient religion. By sharing these stories and my artwork with the world, I hope to contribute to preserving this spiritual tradition for future generations in a way where everyone can have it in their home.

Chapter 7

Transcending Boundaries

Art, Activism, and Afro-Cuban Identity:
An Interview with Diarenis Calderón Tartabull

In the ever-changing tapestry of contemporary art, voices like that of Diarenis Calderón Tartabull stand as poignant reminders of the depth and complexity of human experience. This September 2023, I was graced with the opportunity to delve into an enriching conversation with Diarenis, a luminary in the Afro-Cuban art scene, whose impactful work transcends canvases to foster cultural enrichment and community activism. In this interview, originally conducted in Spanish and now offered with an English translation, we traverse a gamut of subjects that are as diverse as they are interconnected. Diarenis, with her innate artistry, mirrors the intricate blend of history, resistance, and celebration that characterizes the Afro-Cuban heritage. She generously shares her journey, shedding light on the foundations of her artistic philosophy, which is deeply rooted in Afro-feminism. As we navigate through her thoughts, readers will gain a glimpse into her steadfast commitment to initiating dialogues that challenge and redefine the notions of identity and gender equity. Beyond her artwork, Diarenis stands as a pillar in her community, tirelessly working to uplift and empower Afro-descendant communities through various initiatives and projects. These endeavors seek not only to carve out spaces for representation but also to foster a greater sense of belonging and recognition, rekindling a profound respect for ancestry and heritage. As you immerse yourself in this conversation, anticipate an exploration into the heart of a woman whose life and art are a vibrant testament to the beauty and resilience of the Afro-Cuban spirit. This interview offers not merely a glimpse into the world of a remarkable artist but serves as a bridge, connecting readers to the pulsating rhythms of a culture rich with history, struggle, and an unyielding hope for a more inclusive and just future.

Interview

Dear Diarenis Calderón Tartabull,

It is an honor to have the opportunity to conduct this written interview with you and explore your incredible journey as an Afro-Cuban artist, activist, and cultural promoter. I want to express my sincere gratitude for taking the time to share your experiences and perspectives with me. Your commitment to promoting Afro-descendant culture, inclusion, and social justice is inspiring, and I am eager to learn more about your approaches, projects, and visions through this conversation. Your contribution to the empowerment and visibility of marginalized communities is invaluable, and I am excited to have the opportunity to highlight your work in my book. Thank you once again for your generosity in sharing your knowledge and perspective.

ROSITA SCERBO: You started off with a degree in religious studies. How does this background influence your artistic approach and your activities as a community educator and cultural promoter?

DIARENIS CALDERÓN TARTABULL: Really, in a chronological analysis, first there was cultural promotion, which over time evolved into being a curator of visual/plastic arts. Then came community education, and finally, a degree in religious studies. Starting in cultural promotion was a beautiful moment, full of light and exploration, allowing me to connect with the art world, from communities to institutions, encompassing many expressions, aesthetic components, and the individuals who bring them to life.

The role of cultural promoters as agents of change and transformation within community spheres, sciences, and educational environments is vital to strengthening cultural values, considering traditions, the future, the present, and popular wisdom. A promoter must have a vocation for culture, be a creative communicator, respectful, and understand everyone holistically from a horizontal perspective and through bilateral dialogue;

encouraging collective interest and dynamics of social responsibility with sociocultural projects. They must also be a researcher who recognizes the work of groups bearing cultural traditions and artists, stimulating knowledge and creative learning without ableist tendencies. Curatorship has the mission of preserving, exhibiting, and reshaping works of art, as well as facilitating dialogue between institutions, creators, and recipients. From my personal vision, it is the continuity of the promotion and dissemination of artwork, always dignifying the voices of individuals themselves, in interaction or articulation with the surrounding world. As a community educator, it is basic to be willing to learn and unlearn, to consciously connect all your experiences for the benefit of others, and to grow spiritually and be part of the changes that life needs, in the political, economic, social spheres, and beyond. Empowering yourself and others with practices and theories that enrich social organization and each of its involved structures. The conception and methodology of community education are nourished by educational work, playfulness, a plurality of knowledge, participatory diagnoses, inductive methodology; all of which forms a counterhegemonic strategy of high political value.

It is very important to say that I am not an active practitioner of any religious denomination, but I do believe that religions exist and have the power to transform the context in which they operate. I also recognize the potential of faith circles to accompany individuals both in their conflicts, social inequalities, aspirations, as well as in their socio-theological contexts (whatever they may be). I find it hard to relate to the ideas that the religious empire uses to manipulate and harm other populations they deem subordinate or oppressed, keeping them focused on selfishness and pain, building myths, stigmas, and professing the law of fundamentalist god above empathy, compassion, and generosity.

Following the formative order, arriving at studies of the sciences of religions allowed me to understand more about the individuals I worked with and their diverse religious and creative vocations, supporting my conception of collectivity, identities, and community. Recognizing who we are and where we are going, and for whom we work is visible and viable in the world of art and religion; what changes is the perception, the historical circumstances, and the adherence to establishing taboos or fundamentalisms that exclude honest participation. Connected with the practice of freedom, my role is more like a connecting bridge of experiences between creative individuals and their recipients. The universe and its holistic sources.

RS: As the founder of *mirArte diaDía* [a community-focused initiative that promotes art as a tool for social change and cultural awareness], you have been involved in a wide range of roles, from activist to curator. How do you find the balance between these responsibilities and how do they complement each other in your work?

DCT: *MirArte diaDía* was a powerful and supercreative time. I was constantly thinking about what more we could do to socialize with artists and their works. Sharing roles was a beautiful transition that complemented the study of arts and the power of listening.

Listening to people creating or visiting the foundational moment of an idea, eating together, reading—we practiced constantly sitting in debate circles to analyze the daily and historical processes of antiracist struggles, gender, the Black community, its contemporary narratives as a living source of culture and thought, and the result was used as a driving force for artistic discourse. . . . I had and still have a strong commitment to Afro-descendant populations (all of them) and my transition desire is to feel how the conflicts and joys experienced traverse art. Recognizing and promoting the work and projects of less favored artists by the institutions was the mission of *mirArte diaDía*, achieving visibility-legitimacy as neo-African art. We turned that dialogue into theoretical works, murals, exhibitions, or performances, which brought us back to community antiracist and gender activism with forms and colors. We linked the origins and history of art with an Afro-centered view, questioned the Eurocentric teaching models from the art institutions. We initiated a balanced process of reconstructing the Caribbean Black subject, validating the features in Cuban pictorial and poetry; we gave talks in communities of children and youth, proudly showing our Afro-diasporic perspective. We took trips to the rest of the country, focusing on artists with whom we would later start a creative space in Havana and Santiago de Cuba. Finding the balance is a hard job, I recognize, and the attempt to approach and respect the voices executing an artistic work, I believe, is the most real thing.

RS: You have organized community cultural events like the *NaturArte Festival* and International Community Classroom. How do you believe these events contribute to the promotion of Afro-Cuban culture and the empowerment of the community?

DCT: Working in *NaturArte* and the community classroom has an international symbolic charge, produced and conceived by young members of the antiracist and artistic movement in Havana, Brazil, Colombia, and the USA, so it is multidisciplinary, multicultural, and multiethnic—factors to consider when contributing to the promotion of cultural heritage. Two different moments with diverse people (generations, formations, legal status, and gender identity, artistic projections, and interpretation of contexts), all of the above makes any path of creation more controversial and enriched, being a pattern and reference for other people in the communities. We participants value the power of love for art, the pride of feeling and identifying as Afro-diasporic, as demands with which we work on a marronage cultural proposal, political, unique, we intended to recognize racism in all its categories and its penetration into contemporary artistic society, showing boundaries for survival. Boundaries to access the large circles of artistic power (to the large galleries, theater centers, to the music record labels, or to execute megaconcerts).

The fight against the ways we are represented by the entertainment companies and the low wages related to misogyny and gentrification were also discussed. Ahh not to forget the defense to validate the production of knowledge from Black communities, for example, capoeira, hip-hop, performance, and oral narration. These exercises to decolonize language and mass media totally correspond with the community because in both spaces we invite the community to participate and dialogue in addition to artivist subjects with the purpose of cocreating a balanced space between managers and beneficiaries, we all are parts. Each encounter is important as we question the past and present, working to subvert the fear of the Black, highlighting their labors, contributions, and merits having the art platform.

RS: Your work as a popular educator covers topics such as inclusion, diversity, and social communication. How do you use the arts and alternative education to address these issues and promote empowerment in your community?

DCT: We always start from enriched diagnoses made together with real community actors who dominate the environment and the theme we are going to address. We use the most adjustable artistic manifestation to that diagnosis, and we structure a script with those elements that is submitted for approval. Then, with practice, we verify the next point and involve groups of people essentially from various backgrounds, identities, and ages to attend. Meetings, workshops, film debates, exhibitions, games, and theatrical tableaux can be organized to encourage the contribution of all voices and expressions that interact, including the coordination (I never do it alone). Learning spaces with communicational meaning are a dialectical, collective process, where educator-learner immerse themselves in a common adventure of learning, organized in a space-time that considers the needs of the attendees and considers their roles. We can take a sculptural piece or a film and integrate what is already known (which is not definitive, nor a mandate) with what the attending group contributes and these terms, regardless of our will, create other conceptions, concepts, and paths worthy of listening to and analyzing. These methods foster trust and facilitate the critical appropriation of thought in the function of empowerment. As a curator, you have been involved in organizing sixteen exhibitions related to raciality and the Cuban Afro-descendant community. How do you choose the themes and artists for these exhibitions and what is the message you hope to convey through them?

Well, concretely, the messages are of unity, love, pride, self-representativeness, interactions, and social, religious, and historical conflicts related to raciality. The artists are almost always the same ones we have been in contact with for a long time, although new faces and experiences are added. I always meet new people through personal exhibitions that I visit, trying to learn about other forms and styles of doing. The vision is that they enjoy participating from their autonomy and consider the collective space as their own stage to show their artistic and intersectional worth. Also, that they are respectful and inclusive and value the maximum of their power to fluidly carry out positive work. I always share a maxim of Popular Education "No one knows everything, no one ignores everything." I consider that art is a vehicle of thought, it is self-expression, we can achieve transformations toward the individual that become a greater goal and involve the receivers. I work with Black women, people from the LGBTQ+ community, girls, boys and children, people with different (nonnormative) abilities, young people and adults (elderly).

The themes are connected in two ways: When I create an event, I design it by reflecting on themes of empowerment and human existence—universal conflicts that resonate with anyone, regardless of their background. To shake up and face the silence that we have lived for centuries in neglected communities. It is a me-you-community relationship, reconquering the right to speech, action, and poetic courage; a balanced dialogue in positive demands of emotion. I work on the environment with repercussions in affirmative actions from our experiences as racialized subjects living in peripheral areas to argue together what world we have and which we deserve.

The second theme almost always used is the "Capture of Freedom" as a concept, the openness to conceiving Africa, who we are and wish to be as subjects who have faith in their racial consciousness, self-esteem, worldviews, and philosophies. (Will Africa be a feminine vision?) It is a constant in my curatorial works also to assume Africa as a continent with the totality of creative forces that it is and not as a country.

Hope is not for those who sit with crossed arms; it is for those who talk about deep and constant changes that influence the receivers in a visit to the show and invite them to know the artist they have in front of them. Freedom is greater than us, but it is our responsibility to achieve it. The opposite is injustice.

RS: In 2018, you launched the Afro-feminist platform "Nosotrxs," which seeks to empower and make visible the Afro-descendant community in Cuba. What inspired you to create this platform and what have been its impacts so far?

DCT: Well, several motivations come together.

- The desire to take action with two Afroqueer creators and activists. The poet Afibola Sifunola. The engraver and painter Nancy Cepero (now recognized as Cyann).

- Conflict: the lack of physical spaces for the enjoyment, pride, and sharing of dialogue of the Afroqueer community through art.

- The important organizational triangle of women, politics, and power. Our individualities, coupled with all that experiential outbreak that we are, found ourselves facing a conflict.

- The prevailing sexism, misogyny, prejudices, phobias, and lack of empathy within antiracist circles.

- Afro-feminisms with their various facets and modalities. As antiracist fighters and Afroqueer artivists, we recognize the challenges of confronting the colonial and patriarchal systems that persist in the twenty-first century, which underscores the need for self-organization as nonbinary individuals to foster debates and practices centered on self-esteem, self-care, and combating racism, homo/lesbi/transphobia within artistic spaces, while also analyzing the Afroqueer community's belonging to transparent, political, private, and public spaces as crucial arenas for dismantling exclusion.

We have had five years of path obstacles and achievements.

Achievements:

- Always celebrating ourselves with pride, sharing spaces with vegetarian-vegan food. Building a creative comfort-zone community.

- Supporting Black and diverse women and their descendants (artists or not). Integrating and forming alliances with other creators and artivists for the rights of the LGBTQ+ and Afro community.

- Being visible. Accompanying personal and political processes of other collectives or of the nation within the community (discussing the family code and the constitution of the republic as an Afroqueer collective).

- Assuming the role of support agents during the COVID-19 pandemic, providing many people with medical, food, and emotional supplies.

- Surviving the COVID-19 pandemic.

- Educating our daughters, sons, and children. Learning and unlearning from all the processes.

Obstacles:

- Not having concrete ways to maintain a circular, solid, sustainable economy and the wear and tear it produces on "Nosotrxs."

- Not receiving all the supports (financial and access to general information) necessary to better manage our work.

- The growing social inequality in Cuba and the planet, gender violence.

- The gradual increase in environmental damage, the over-exploitation of nature by capitalism, and its impact on Afro-descendant populations.

- Absence of a gender-differential approach in the country.

RS: You have been part of networks of lesbian and bisexual women, as well as of Black and Latin American women. How has your membership in these networks influenced your art and your approach to promoting diversity and inclusion?

DCT: Being a part of these networks has given me the opportunity to start early on a journey toward sisterhood, to grow and enjoy a militant sorority and solidarity, which I assume positively and powerfully. These networks guided the path to resonate with art that is coherent and serves our people, not elitist or whitewashed but organic and questioning. It allowed me to reinforce the feeling of cooperation and completeness. Understanding our places of enunciation, discussing them, advocating for the need for laws and decrees that stop femicides and legalize abortion, viewing the main lines and contributions to the debate on survival, race, education from a decolonizing, community-based, socio-theological, lesbian, theoretical perspective, is a journey of deep passion. A group of both national and international individuals, comprised of urban and rural women, artists, anthropologists, and leaders, have come together to insert our emancipatory and libertarian tradition, understanding justice, the history of Caribbean and Latin American art, and its social mobilization as a pattern toward a transnational entity that is autonomous, plural, and complex, which works with those values on me and the approach of enhancing artistic knowledge and promoting diversity and inclusion, of dissident bodies.

RS: In your community work with girls and teenagers, how do you address sensitive topics such as violence, self-harm, and self-care, and how do you think art can be an effective tool to address these issues?

DCT: Generally, we approach it through art (photography, drawing, and music). We have created a technique of identification with a mirror to discuss how we are and how others see us. Here we work on self-esteem and self-care, inviting them to draw themselves or take a photograph (selfie) to express how they feel. It is important to see how racism has operated in the early stages of life, how it scrutinizes your story; I have testimonies and drawings where Black children and adolescents paint themselves with straight and blond hair. At that point, it is necessary to emphasize skin color, features, heritage, love for ancestors, and the presence of white supremacy and domination, all with simple, concrete, and transparent words. Words that allow the person to return home safely, especially emphasizing strengthening their true essence and instilling a sense of belonging and pride both intellectually and within the family.

When it comes to the topic of violence, it is more complex because it requires an ethical and respectful discourse that approaches a some-times-painful palpable reality. There are types of violence that are difficult to identify at an early age, and our contribution is to show them the types of violence and the collateral damage they leave on everyone—that its reproduction can turn us into undesirable, nonadmirable people. We pay a lot of attention to the real context where the subjects exist, to the events they narrate; we go through the theoretical context and construct, with collective feedback, drawings or art books or photographic exhibitions that analyze in depth new stances and/or critical relationships with violence. It's neither easy nor achievable in the short term.

RS: In a global context, how do you see the role of art in promoting equality, empowerment, and social justice, especially in relation to Afro-descendant communities?

DCT: I find it difficult to see it in a comprehensive and respectful way with affirmative actions or public policies dedicated to empowerment. It is assumed in an extractivist way, for example, Africa and its artistic references are not part of the curriculum in Cuba and other places. Generally, one learns about culture and the history of Eurocentric art. It is thought of as primitive, animistic art with a pejorative discourse, alien in the study programs. From that perspective, there will be no justice or equality.

RS: You have had a significant impact on cultural promotion and community activism. Could you share some projects or initiatives that you are currently working on or plan to develop in the future?

DCT: Yes, I have had a significant tangible impact within the circle of creators and in some communities. First, having their works recognized by institutions and decision makers. The powerful act of linking creators from different latitudes and the result of these alliances. Personal dreams (of the artists) fulfilled after influencing a hard work of promotion. The impact of exhibitions or invitations to other territories and the fact that the act of knowledge goes from theory to practice and finally to establish references is very significant.

There have been opportunities offered for joint work between generations of artists for an international memorial, and we will have talented and beautiful people from Cuba working to achieve it. I have cherished an initiative for a long time, seeking places and supports in the idea of having a personal gallery (still a dream) that helps to recover the ethics, politics, philosophy, music, pictorial discourses of neo-African art, its influences, and its legacies that are the foundation and pride of Afro-descendant people.

RS: In addition, your work covers important themes of identity and social justice. Considering your commitment to the Afro-descendant community, I would like to know how you define your artistic approach. Do you believe that your art can be categorized as Afro-feminist? If so, how do you think your work contributes to the broader conversation about Afro-feminist empowerment and gender equity?

DCT: I hope that now we refer to the art that I produce. If so, I will say that it is something very new. It has emerged from all the questions and reflections I have about life and its dialectic; it goes through the conception and structuring of consciousness from my crossroads and intersections to the purest act of knowledge, which is creating. The sense of my images, textures, and worldviews are very close to the respect for existence, my forms travel from dissident bodies to forests; they are amorphous, often colorless, made with pencil, of fluid or nonbinary gender, with large breasts. Multiheaded, they are mutant being's half plant, half human, plants crossed with the inclemencies of the weather, in short.

I consider myself Afro-feminist. I use my figurations to visualize my thoughts on Afro-feminism of trans women, queer people, non-binary, fluid gender, etcetera. Women with nonnormative abilities, urban women, rural women, ecological perspective, religious diversity, among others.

My contribution is directed toward the conversations or conferences I have with young artists or students of international university programs. I am also concerned that the current issues—geopolitical issues that cross the Caribbean and the island of Cuba—are changing to accelerate poverty, marginalization, inequality, exploitation, child violence, domestic violence, vicarious violence, gender-based violence, cyberbullying, migration, exclusion of Afro-descendant peoples, micromachismos, and the new faces of private/public violence from the structures of racism and heteropatriarchal power.

Conclusion

Resonating Echoes: Toward a Liberated Aesthetic Future

Throughout *Gendered Aesthetics of Blackness*, I analyzed the world of Afro-Cuban women artists and their transformative role in redefining the narrative of Black femininity. As I explored their artistry, I uncovered a dynamic and profound conversation that speaks not only to Afro-Cuban identity but to the broader discourse on Blackness, identity, and social justice. The vibrancy of Cuba's cultural history served as my unique lens through which I delved into the visual expressions of its Afro-Cuban women. The evolving identity of Black Cubans, marked by moments of triumphant resurgence amid periods of oppression, formed the backdrop against which I examined their indomitable spirit and artistic brilliance. In the opening chapters, I explored the historical backdrop of Cuba, setting the stage for a comprehensive exploration of Afro-Cuban women's visual expressions. The intricate dance between Black identity and Afro-feminism emerged as a poignant testimony to the resilience, creativity, and activism of Black women. It became evident that these visual expressions were not only reflective of their identity and struggles but also instrumental in shaping the larger narrative of Afro-feminism in Cuba. As I analyzed the artistry of Afro-Cuban women, I encountered and examined four remarkable artists—Harmonia Rosales, María Magdalena Campos-Pons, Susana Pilar, and Belkis Ayón. Each of these artists offered a unique perspective and approach, enriching our understanding of the multifaceted experiences of Black Cuban women. Harmonia Rosales boldly reimagined classical works of art, challenging traditional representations of Black women and transforming them into embodiments of nobility, strength, and divinity. Maria Magdalena Campos-Pons skillfully merged history, memory, and identity, presenting a layered portrayal of Black femininity that transcends stereotypes. Susana Pilar courageously confronted history through her body as a platform, reclaiming the narrative and promoting discourse that dismantles prejudices. Belkis Ayón's monochromatic prints ventured into Afro-Cuban mythology, elevating Black women to powerful figures and rejecting limiting representations. The concluding interviews with Harmonia Rosales and Diarenis Calderón Tartabull provided a personal touch, grounding the analytical discussions in the lived experiences of these trailblazing Afro-Cuban women. The inclusion of two interviews with Harmonia Rosales and Diarenis Calderón Tartabull within this comprehensive examination of Afro-Cuban women's artistry served as a deliberate and strategic extension of the analytical discourse presented in the preceding four chapters. The decision to intersperse these interviews amid the more formal and structured analytical discussions is underpinned by the recognition of the profound importance of lived experiences in contextualizing and enriching the academic exploration of artistic expressions. In tandem with the preceding analytical chapters, the interviews operate as complementary components, contributing a distinctive layer of depth to the overarching narrative. Harmonia Rosales and Diarenis Calderon Tartabull, both pivotal figures in the Afro-Cuban art scene, bring forth a nuanced and personal dimension to the scholarly inquiry. Their insights, reflections, and responses serve to humanize the academic discourse, infusing it with the palpable realities of artistic creation and identity negotiation. Harmonia Rosales, through her reimagining of classical artworks, challenges and reshapes established visual canons, offering a unique perspective on the empowerment and divinity of Black women. The interview with Rosales provides a direct line to the motivations, inspirations, and challenges she confronts in her artistic practice, elucidating the intentional choices she makes in her creative process. In essence, the inclusion of these interviews in conjunction with the analytical chapters is predicated on the belief that the academic exploration of visual expressions necessitates an integration of both formal analysis and personal narratives. By doing so, the research not only endeavors to dissect and interpret the artistic contributions of Afro-Cuban women but also acknowledges the invaluable insights that emerge when these women are actively engaged as stakeholders in the scholarly dialogue. The interviews, therefore, function as a methodological and epistemological bridge, ensuring that the multifaceted experiences and intentions of the artists themselves are intrinsic to the academic discourse surrounding their work.

It is noteworthy that several books on visual arts in Latin America and women artists already exist, such as *Radical Women: Latin American Art, 1960–1985* by Cecilia Fajardo Hill, Andrea Giunta, Rodrigo Alonso, Julia Antivilo, and Connie Butler (Prestel 2017); *Latin American Women Artists of the United States: The Works of 33 Twentieth-Century Women* by Robert Henkes (McFarland 2008); and more specific works such as *Women Street Artists of Latin America: Art Without Fear* by Rachel Cassandra and Lauren Gucik (2015), among others. Some volumes aim to reassess the role of Latin American women artists in historical movements such as Modernism, previously overlooked. However, there remains a notable absence of academic texts focusing on Black Cuban women artists and no comprehensive compilation of works addressing the representation of race and gender by Black women artists in Cuba, the diaspora, and as second-generation Latinas. Therefore, this book represents a significant contribution as it brings attention to the understudied realm of Black Latinx artists, particularly Black Latinx women, whose artistic endeavors are frequently marginalized. Even within artistic circles and movements of Black Cubans, such as visual arts and cinema, Black Cuban women and their creative productions remain largely invisible. Furthermore, this book explored how themes of race and gender are visually represented across different generations, backgrounds, and geographical contexts linked to the island of Cuba. This comparative approach is pivotal for understanding Cuba's racial and gender dynamics from diverse perspectives. By examining visual representations of race and gender, this book created a space to reexamine the island's history, including its connections to the United States, through a critical lens. Such an approach is crucial in the study of Cuba, offering a transversal analysis that broadens the discourse on these pressing issues.

Afro-Cuban women visual expressions echo the transformative power of art as a tool for fostering inclusivity and respect in the discourse surrounding Black women's representation. The creative perspectives and visual mediums employed by these artists has been instrumental in effecting a paradigmatic shift, facilitating a profound reevaluation of the representation of Black Cuban women. These artistic interventions, rooted in a meticulous deconstruction of prevailing tropes, offer a critical interrogation of historical narratives and power structures that have historically marginalized Black Cuban women. This transformative process, as illuminated by the artistic analyses conducted, signifies more than a mere aesthetic evolution; it encapsulates a conscientious scholarly endeavor to dismantle entrenched stereotypes. By delving into the intricacies of the visual narratives, we discern the deliberate endeavors of the artists to disrupt conventional norms, challenging the viewer to confront ingrained biases and assumptions. The analytical journey undertaken herein echoes a broader scholarly imperative—one that challenges the status quo, advocates for epistemological inclusivity, and underscores the profound impact of visual narratives in shaping nuanced, truthful representations of marginalized identities.

Black artists in Latin America and the Caribbean use their art to explore and assert their identities, challenging stereotypes and reclaiming their narratives (Harney 1999). They depict the complexities and nuances of the Afro-Latin experience, highlighting the intersections of race, ethnicity, and culture (Mitchell et al. 2022). Through their art, Black artists contribute to the visibility and recognition of Afro–Latin American communities, promoting self-acceptance and empowerment (Dache et al. 2019). In this context, *Gendered Aesthetics of Blackness* explored how art produced by Afro-Cuban women can be considered a form of decolonial aesthetics in several ways, giving shape to an original and unique form of AfroARTivism. Their art challenges and disrupts colonial power structures by centering the experiences, perspectives, and cultural expressions of Black women (Collins 1992). It provides a platform for reclaiming and asserting their identities, histories, and narratives, which have often been marginalized or erased. Through their art, Afro-Cuban women challenge Eurocentric beauty standards and celebrate the beauty and diversity of Black bodies, promoting self-acceptance and self-love (D'Agostino & Dobke 2017). Moreover, their art engages with intersectionality and identity politics, exploring the intersections of race, gender, ethnicity, and culture (Figueroa 2020). It challenges monolithic representations and embraces the complexities and nuances of Black diasporic identities (Bardwell-Jones & McLaren 2020). By doing so, their art disrupts dominant narratives and offers alternative ways of knowing and being that challenge colonial and neocolonial forms of power (Figueroa 2020). Afro-Cuban women's art also serves as a form of resistance and activism, addressing social justice issues and advocating for change (Keys 2021). It raises awareness about racial inequality, discrimination, and social injustices faced by Afro-descendant communities (Reyes 2019). Through their art, Afro-Cuban women contribute to broader movements for social change and challenge dominant systems of oppression (Ashdown-Franks & Joseph 2021). Through the different chapters, it was evident how the art of Afro-descendant women draws on cultural traditions, oral histories, and ancestral knowledge, connecting with decolonial frameworks that seek to challenge Western epistemologies and center alternative ways of knowing (Oslender 2007). Their visual expression embraces embodied spirituality, sonic aesthetics, and social dimensions, offering insurgent practices that reformulate notions of decoloniality and Afro-diasporic studies (Figueroa 2020). Ultimately, the art produced by Afro-Cuban women can be seen as a form of decolonial aesthetics as it challenges colonial power structures, centers marginalized voices and experiences, disrupts dominant narratives, promotes self-acceptance and self-love, engages with intersectionality and identity politics, serves as a form of resistance and activism, and draws on cultural traditions and alternative ways of knowing.

A notable strength of *Gendered Aesthetics of Blackness* lies in its transnational focus, which expands the narrative beyond the geographical boundaries of Cuba and delves into the experiences of Afro-Cuban women artists living in the United States. This dynamic perspective adds a layer of complexity to the book, allowing for a deeper exploration of the histories of exile, immigration, and the transnational identities of artists like Maria Magdalena Campos-Pons and Harmonia Rosales. By examining the lives and works of artists who have crossed borders and made homes in the US, we gained insight into the rich tapestry of Afro-Cuban women's experiences, both within their home country and in the diaspora. This transnational lens allows us to explore how these artists navigate questions of identity, belonging, and activism across two distinct cultural and social landscapes. The inclusion of artists who have experienced exile and immigration broadens the scope of the book. It highlights the impact of historical and political events on the lives and creative expressions of Afro-Cuban women. Artists like Maria Magdalena Campos-Pons and Harmonia Rosales bring with them unique perspectives forged by their journeys, and their work reflects the confluence of multiple cultures and histories. Afro-Cuban women residing in the United States often inhabit transnational identities. Their experiences straddle two or more cultural spheres, resulting in a complex negotiation of selfhood. By analyzing their art, we gained insight into how they navigate the intersections of their Afro-Cuban heritage and their experiences in the US. This provided a more nuanced understanding of identity and belonging. Moreover, the transnational focus of the book speaks to the global impact of Afro-Cuban women artists. Their works resonate with audiences worldwide and contribute to broader conversations about race, gender, and art. The reach of these artists extends beyond national borders, making them influential figures in the Afro-Latinx and broader African diaspora artistic communities. By examining the works of Afro-Cuban women artists in both Cuba and the US, *Gendered Aesthetics of Blackness* allowed for a comparative analysis of how geographical location and cultural context shape their artistry. This comparative approach offers a deeper understanding of the complexities of their visual expressions. The inclusion of artists in exile amplifies the voices of those who are part of the Afro-Cuban diaspora. It sheds light on the ways in which art becomes a tool for preserving cultural memory, bridging the gap between the homeland and the diaspora, and advocating for social justice in both contexts. Their artistry, situated in both Cuba and the US, forms a bridge between different worlds and challenges us to think critically about the complexities of identity, heritage, and activism within a transnational framework.

Gendered Aesthetics of Blackness offered a significant contribution to the field of Afro-Cuban women's visual culture. By examining the works of prominent artists, I unraveled the transformative power of art as a tool for challenging and reshaping the representation of Black femininity. The analysis of these artists' creations demonstrated their critical role in advancing the field, as they redefined traditional artistic boundaries and liberated Black women's identities from oppressive stereotypes. The implications were profound, encouraging scholars, artists, and audiences alike to engage in a deeper and more inclusive discourse about the representation of Afro-Cuban women in visual arts. The implications of this research extended to the broader context of art, gender studies, and racial representation. By portraying Black women as figures of strength, nobility, and divinity, these Afro-Cuban women artists challenged deeply ingrained stereotypes that had pervaded art and society for centuries. They redefined the narrative of Black femininity, emphasizing the multifaceted experiences of Black women and rejecting limiting representations. In doing so, they paved the way for a more inclusive and nuanced understanding of Black women's identities. The insights garnered from this exploration were not confined to academic circles. They had the potential to inspire activism, dialogue, and a greater sense of social justice. The courage of these artists to confront history and oppressive narratives served as a powerful example of using art as a platform for change. Their messages resonated with audiences globally, and their activism fostered inclusivity and respect in the discourse surrounding Black women's representation. By shedding light on the transformative work of these Afro-Cuban women artists, this research invites further exploration and analysis. It encourages scholars and artists to delve deeper into the themes of Black femininity, identity, and decolonial aesthetics in visual culture. The implications of this work extended into future research endeavors, offering a solid foundation for subsequent studies and artistic creations that sought to redefine and empower the representation of Black Latina women. The implications of this research were far-reaching. By focusing on the artistic expressions of Afro-Cuban women, we challenged stereotypes, promoted inclusivity, and inspired change. The narrative of Black femininity was being rewritten, and these artists served as the vanguards of this transformation. It is my hope that this research continues to influence and inspire, fostering a future where the representation of Black Cuban women is rich, nuanced, and truly reflective of their diverse experiences and indomitable spirit.

Another remarkable attribute of *Gendered Aesthetics of Blackness* is its dedication to shedding light on the works of Black Cuban artists who have remained unexamined in academic publications. Artists like Diarenis Calderon Tartabull, Harmonia Rosales, and Susana Pilar emerge as pivotal figures in the Afro-Cuban artistic landscape, and this book offers them the recognition and scholarly attention they were still missing. Diarenis Calderon Tartabull, Harmonia Rosales, and Susana Pilar are significant artists whose contributions to Afro-Cuban visual culture have been overlooked in the academic sphere. *Gendered Aesthetics of Blackness* brings their notable work to the forefront, providing a platform for in-depth analysis and appreciation. Each of these artists has a unique and innovative approach to their craft: Diarenis Calderon Tartabull's activism and upbringing, beautifully explored in her interview; Harmonia Rosales'S reinterpretation of classical art through painting; and Susana Pilar's thought-provoking installations and performances all enrich the book's content with a diverse range of artistic practices. By including these understudied artists, this book offers fresh and compelling perspectives on Afro-Cuban art and its intersections with Black femininity, identity, and activism. The inclusion of these artists contributes to their visibility on a global platform. Their artistry and insights offer readers a unique opportunity to engage with previously unexplored narratives, experiences, and representations of Blackness and womanhood in Cuba. These women represent the diversity of voices within the Afro-Cuban community. Their distinct backgrounds, artistic expressions, and experiences broaden the scope of the manuscript, providing a multifaceted exploration of Black Cuban women's visual culture. The focus on underrepresented artists is a testament to the book's commitment to inclusivity and its dedication to enriching the scholarly landscape.

While *Gendered Aesthetics of Blackness* offered valuable insights and contributions to the field of Afro-Cuban women's visual culture, it is essential to acknowledge some of its limitations. The book focused on a specific selection of Afro-Cuban women artists, namely, Harmonia Rosales, Maria Magdalena Campos-Pons, Susana Pilar, Belkis Ayón, and Diarenis Calderon Tartabull. While these artists are influential and groundbreaking, there are more Afro-Cuban women artists whose works could provide additional perspectives. Furthermore, throughout *Gendered Aesthetics of Blackness*, I've undertaken a comprehensive exploration of the artistry and visual expressions of Afro-Cuban women through the specific mediums of paintings, photography, and performance. These visual mediums have allowed me to delve deeply into nuanced narratives, reimagined identities, and powerful challenges to historical stereotypes. However, it is essential to acknowledge that these are not the sole visual mediums through which Afro-Cuban women express their experiences, and future research should continue to broaden the scope. Therefore, one omission from this research is the analysis of other visual mediums such as cinema, documentaries, and music videos. These mediums offer unique opportunities to explore the multifaceted identities, stories, and struggles of Afro-Cuban women. Future research should consider these further methods of visual expression. For instance, the world of cinema presents a captivating avenue for the visual representation of Afro-Cuban women. Exploring films directed by Afro-Cuban women or featuring their narratives can provide insights into the cinematic artistry and the themes of identity, race, and gender within the context of Cuba. Analyzing the portrayal of Afro-Cuban women in various cinematic works and their impact on both the Cuban and international audience is a rich field for future exploration. The representation and experiences of Afro-Cuban women in cinema have not been the subject of many scholarly exploration. Some references provide valuable insights into the roles, representations, and cultural significance of Cuban women in cinema but not focus on the unique experiences of Afro-descendant women. For instance, Benamou (1994) examined the threshold of gender in Cuban cinema, shedding light on the representation and portrayal of women in Cuban films. Tierney (2014) discussed the work of Marvin D'Lugo, Catherine, and Julianne Burton-Carvajal, among others, who have analyzed Cuban films and their diverse representations of women. Films such as *Lucía*, *Retrato de Teresa*, *De cierta manera*, and *Lejanía* have been examined for their portrayal of women and their experiences. Other works have focused on male filmmakers or on Afro-Cuban cinema without considering the intersection of race and gender. Yero (2022) historicized the issue of appropriation and explores Afro-Cubans' discussions about the nationalization of their culture. This reference could provide insights into the broader cultural context in which Afro-Cuban women's experiences are situated. Wood (2009) discussed the work of Tomás Gutiérrez Alea, a prominent Cuban filmmaker, and his contribution to Cuban cinema. This reference provided then just a broader understanding of the Cuban cinematic landscape and its key figures. In conclusion, the literature on Afro-Cuban women in cinema is limited but growing. Further research is needed to explore this topic in more depth and to amplify the voices and perspectives of Afro-Cuban women in the cinematic landscape. However, it is worth mentioning that the cinema of Afro-Cuban filmmakers such as Sara Gómez and Gloria Rolando has been the subject of scholarly exploration. Nonetheless, the literature is still lacking a manuscript entirely centered on this topic. By way of example, Hackett (2021) discussed the work of Sara Gómez, particularly her revolutionary classic *De cierta manera* (*One Way or Another*). The author explored the impact of Gómez's body of work on subsequent generations of Cuban filmmakers who continue her mission to critique the Revolution through an antiracist and feminist lens. Ramos (2013) presented an interview with Gloria Rolando, offering insights into her perspective as a filmmaker. The interview provided valuable information about Rolando's approach to filmmaking, her inspirations, and her experiences as an Afro-Cuban filmmaker. Quesada (2021) focused on Gloria Rolando's film *Raíces de mi corazón* (*Roots of My Heart*) and examined the dual biopolitics present in the film. The author analyzed the ways in which Rolando explores issues of power, politics, and gender in her work. Nevertheless, further research is needed to explore their works in more depth and to amplify the voices and perspectives of these important filmmakers. Future research should also consider the intersection of these visual mediums. For example, analyzing how a painting may relate to a performance or how a documentary may incorporate photography. The interplay between different mediums can offer a deeper understanding of the complexity of Afro-Cuban women's visual expressions. While *Gendered Aesthetics of Blackness* has provided a detailed exploration of the visual expressions of Afro-Cuban women artists in the realms of paintings, photography, and performance, there remains a rich landscape of uncharted territory. Future research that encompasses a broader array of visual mediums will ensure a more comprehensive understanding of the multifaceted stories, artistry, and activism of Afro-Cuban women. These mediums have the power to create a vibrant tapestry of representation, one that reflects the diversity, resilience, and creative agency of Afro-Cuban women both in Cuba and on the global stage.

In closing, Afro-Cuban women artists have not only created historically valuable art pieces but also become the agents of a transformative visual narrative. They have challenged, deconstructed, and transcended stereotypes, offering an enduring testament to their strength, creativity, and activism. Through their art, these women have become critical voices in the ongoing global discourse on Blackness, identity, and social justice. The journey continues as they inspire and encourage us to explore, question, and redefine our understanding of Black femininity and the power of art in driving social change. The culmination of this extensive inquiry into the visual expressions of Afro-Cuban women underscored the imperative nature of this research within the broader academic landscape. The exigency of this undertaking lies in the critical lacunae existing within scholarly discourses, wherein the artistic contributions of Afro-Cuban women have been historically marginalized and underrepresented. By systematically examining and interpreting the multifaceted visual narratives crafted by these artists, this research endeavored to rectify the historical oversight that has persistently obscured their invaluable contributions to both the artistic milieu and the broader sociocultural fabric. The overarching significance of this research can be discerned in its redemptive function, as it endeavors to reclaim and amplify the voices of Afro-Cuban women within academic spheres. Through a meticulous examination of their visual expressions, this study not only elucidated the diverse and nuanced experiences of these women but also served as a methodological template for future inquiries into the intersectionality of gender, race, and artistic production. By amplifying these narratives, this research not only enriches the academic discourse surrounding Afro-Cuban art but also contributes to a broader global dialogue on the intersectional identities and narratives often relegated to the peripheries of scholarly attention. In essence, the necessity of this research lies in its capacity to rectify historical oversights, amplify marginalized voices, and inaugurate a more inclusive and comprehensive understanding of Afro-Cuban women's contributions to the visual arts.

Notes

Introduction

1. Extract from the poem "Mujer Negra/Black Woman" by Nancy Morejon, the best known and most widely translated woman poet of postrevolutionary Cuba. The poem is found in *Where the Island Sleeps Like a Wing*, trans. Kathleen Weaver (Black Scholar Press, 1985), 87.

2. Black feminism is a feminist movement and theoretical framework that centers the experiences, perspectives, and liberation of Black women. It recognizes that gender oppression intersects with race, class, sexuality, and other social categories, leading to unique forms of marginalization and discrimination faced by Black women. Black feminism challenges and expands on mainstream feminist theories by addressing the intersecting systems of power and oppression that affect Black women's lives. Some of the main theorists associated with Black feminism include bell hooks, a renowned feminist author and scholar who has made significant contributions to Black feminism. Her works, such as *Ain't I a Woman? Black Women and Feminism* (2015) and *Feminist Theory: From Margin to Center* (1984), explore the intersections of race, gender, and class, and critiques the exclusion of Black women from mainstream feminist discourse. Audre Lorde was a poet, essayist, and civil rights activist whose writings focused on intersectionality, racism, sexism, and homophobia. Her works, including *Sister Outsider: Essays and Speeches* (1984) and *Zami: A New Spelling of My Name* (1982), emphasize the importance of embracing all aspects of one's identity and the need for coalition building among marginalized communities. Patricia Hill Collins is a sociologist and author known for her groundbreaking book *Black Feminist Thought: Knowledge, Consciousness, and the Politics of Empowerment* (1990). Her work explores the intersecting dynamics of race, gender, and class and the importance of Black women's voices in challenging systemic oppression. Angela Davis is a political activist, scholar, and author whose work addresses issues of racism, feminism, and abolition. Her book *Women, Race, and Class* (1983) examines the intersections of race, gender, and class in the context of women's struggles for liberation.

These theorists, among others, have contributed significantly to the development of Black feminism as a critical framework. They have challenged dominant feminist narratives, advocated for the inclusion of Black women's experiences, and emphasized the importance of intersectionality in understanding and addressing systems of oppression. Black feminism continues to evolve and inspire activism, scholarship, and social change, centering the voices and experiences of Black women and promoting justice and liberation for all.

3. Decolonial theory is a critical framework that emerged in response to the ongoing legacies of colonialism and imperialism. It seeks to challenge and dismantle the structures of power, knowledge, and cultural dominance that have been imposed by colonial forces. Decolonial theorists in Latin America have made significant contributions to this field, with specific attention to the experiences and perspectives of Indigenous and Afro-descendant women. To better understand this theoretical perspective, see some of the principal theorists and concepts within decolonial theory in Latin America, such as: Aníbal Quijano (2010), a Peruvian sociologist, who developed the concept of "coloniality of power" to describe how colonialism's hierarchical and racialized power structures persist even after formal colonization has ended. He emphasizes the need to decolonize political and economic systems, knowledge production, and cultural practices. María Lugones (2006) is another pioneer in this field. She is an Argentine philosopher and feminist theorist, who introduced the concept of "coloniality of gender" to analyze how gender relations have been shaped by colonialism. She explores the intersections of gender, race, and colonial power dynamics, highlighting the unique experiences of women of color. Sylvia Marcos (2010) is another theorist worth mentioning. She is a Mexican anthropologist and feminist thinker; Marcos focuses on Indigenous women's perspectives within decolonial theory. She emphasizes the importance of Indigenous worldviews, spirituality, and knowledge systems as vital sources of resistance against colonial domination. Yuderkys Espinosa Miñoso (2014) is an Afro-Dominican scholar who contributes to decolonial theory through her exploration of Afro-descendant women's experiences and agency. She highlights the intersections of race, gender, and coloniality, examining the ways in which Afro-descendant women challenge and transform oppressive structures. These are just a few examples of the principal theorists and concepts within decolonial theory in Latin America, with a specific focus on the perspectives and experiences of Indigenous and Afro-descendant women. Decolonial theory in the region aims to challenge dominant narratives, center marginalized voices, and promote social justice and equality by addressing the ongoing effects of colonialism and coloniality.

4. Traditional representations of Black femininity vary across different cultures and historical contexts. Here are some broad categories and examples of traditional representations of Black femininity.

Mammy/Servant: In the era of slavery and its aftermath, Black women were often portrayed as maids, caregivers, or "mammies" in popular media. These representations depicted Black women as subservient, nurturing, and dedicated to serving white families. Examples include the character Mammy in the film *Gone with the Wind* (1939).

Jezebel/Seductress: This stereotype portrays Black women as overly sexualized, promiscuous, and seductive. It perpetuates the idea that Black women are hypersexual beings and objectifies their bodies. Examples can be found in various films, music videos, and literature throughout history.

Strong/Independent Woman: In response to negative stereotypes, there is a tradition of depicting Black women as resilient, strong, and independent. This representation emphasizes their strength, intelligence, and ability to overcome adversity. Examples include characters like Celie in Alice Walker's novel *The Color Purple* (1982) and Shuri in the film *Black Panther* (2018).

Matriarch/Community Leader: Black women have often been portrayed as the backbone of their communities, taking on leadership roles and guiding their families through difficult times. This representation highlights their strength, wisdom, and nurturing qualities. Examples can be seen in films like *Sounder* (1972) and *Hidden Figures* (2016).

Natural/Unapologetic: In recent years, there has been a growing movement celebrating Black women's natural beauty and promoting self-acceptance. This representation emphasizes embracing natural hair, body shapes, and cultural heritage. The natural hair movement and the popularity of figures like Lupita Nyong'o have contributed to this representation.

It's important to note that these representations are not exhaustive, and there is significant diversity within the experiences and identities of Black women. Contemporary media and activism have challenged and expanded these traditional representations, creating space for more nuanced and multifaceted portrayals of Black femininity.

5. Mythology encompasses a collection of narratives and stories that hold deep cultural and spiritual meanings. By drawing inspiration from Afro-Cuban mythology, Ayón, Campos-Pons, and Pérez Bravo infuse their artwork with narratives that connect to ancestral wisdom, historical events, and collective memory. These references create a bridge between the past and the present, allowing viewers to explore the intricate layers of Afro-Cuban cultural identity and the interplay between spirituality and everyday life.

6. Visual storytelling refers to the practice of conveying narratives, ideas, and experiences through visual mediums such as photography, film, painting, illustration, or any other visual art form. It involves using images, symbols, colors, and composition to communicate messages, evoke emotions, and engage the viewer in a narrative or concept. Visual storytelling holds significant importance in feminist Indigenous and Afro-descendant communities for several reasons, such as: amplifying marginalized voices, cultural preservation and revitalization, resistance, and empowerment, and as a form of intersectional feminism.

7. Syncretism refers to the blending of African religious practices with elements of Catholicism and other belief systems, which is a characteristic feature of Afro-Cuban spirituality. By incorporating these ritual elements and objects, the artists not only pay homage to their cultural heritage but also invite viewers to engage with the rich symbolism and spiritual significance associated with Afro-Cuban religious practices.

8. See Alejandro de la Fuente, *A Nation for All: Race, Inequality, and Politics Century Cuba* (University of North Carolina Press, 2001); Alejandro Campos. "Agenda and Public Policy Against Racism (1959–2008)," in *Changing Cuba/Changing Mauricio A. Font* (Bildner Center for Western Hemisphere Studies, 2008), 375–92.

Chapter 1

1. For a comprehensive list of Afro-Cuban women and their inestimable contributions refer to *The AfroCubanas Directory*, a digital tool that compiles files of Afro-descendant Cuban women, who have contributed significantly to national culture and history. In each file you can find information in various formats: texts, videos, audios, images, and so on. You can download the sheet in PDF format using the Print Friendly tab at the end of each sheet. The platform can be accessed here: https://directoriodeafrocubanas.com/category/artistas-plasticas/.

Chapter 2

1. Chicana/x feminists are individuals who identify as Chicana or Chicano and engage in feminist thought, activism, and advocacy. The term Chicana emerged during the Chicano Movement of the 1960s and 1970s to describe Mexican American women who asserted their unique identities and experiences as both women and members of the Chicano community. Chicana/x feminists aim to challenge and dismantle intersecting systems of oppression based on race, gender, class, and more, while also centering the specific experiences and struggles of Chicanas and other Latinx women. Chicana/x feminism encompasses a range of perspectives, but some common themes and goals include Intersectionality: Chicana/x feminists emphasize the importance of intersectionality, recognizing that the experiences of Chicanas are shaped by multiple intersecting identities, such as race, gender, class, and immigration status. They seek to understand and address the unique challenges faced by Chicana women within the broader feminist movement. Cultural Identity and Self-Determination: Chicana/x feminists emphasize the importance of reclaiming and celebrating their cultural heritage and identities. They challenge assimilationist narratives and work toward empowering

Chicanas to assert their cultural pride and self-determination. Social Justice and Activism: Chicana/x feminists are committed to social justice and advocate for the rights and well-being of Chicanas and other marginalized communities. They engage in activism and community organizing to challenge systemic inequalities, promote equitable representation, and fight against discrimination and violence. Education and Empowerment: Chicana/x feminists place significant emphasis on education as a tool for empowerment and liberation. They advocate for access to quality education for all, seek to decolonize educational curricula, and promote critical consciousness and knowledge of Chicana history and contributions. Health and Reproductive Justice: Chicana/x feminists address issues related to women's health and reproductive rights from a perspective that recognizes the challenges faced by Chicanas and Latinx women. They advocate for comprehensive health care, reproductive autonomy, and culturally sensitive approaches to health-care provision. Prominent Chicana/x feminists include Gloria Anzaldúa: Anzaldúa was a scholar, writer, and activist who explored the intersections of gender, race, and sexuality in her influential work *Borderlands/La Frontera: The New Mestiza*. She emphasized the importance of embracing multiple identities and the concept of "nepantla," a state of in-betweenness. Cherríe Moraga: Moraga is a playwright, poet, and essayist known for her contributions to Chicana feminism. Her works, such as *This Bridge Called My Back: Writings by Radical Women of Color* (coedited with Gloria Anzaldúa), explore themes of identity, queerness, and the complexities of being a Chicana feminist.

Ana Castillo: Castillo is a writer, poet, and scholar who has explored issues of race, gender, and sexuality in her works. She addresses topics such as cultural hybridity, immigration, and the experiences of Chicanas in the United States. Dolores Huerta: While not explicitly identifying as a feminist, Huerta is a prominent activist and labor leader who has fought for the rights of farmworkers and has been a powerful advocate for social justice. Her work intersects with feminist principles of equity and justice.

2. Colonialism and coloniality are related concepts, but they refer to distinct aspects of the same historical and ongoing processes of domination and control. While colonialism refers to the physical occupation and control of territories by external powers, coloniality refers to the enduring legacy and system of power that persists even after formal colonialism has ended. Colonialism refers to the practice of one nation or group establishing and maintaining political, economic, and cultural control over another territory or people. It involves the direct colonization and exploitation of resources, labor, and land. Colonialism typically entails the imposition of new political structures, legal systems, and cultural norms on the colonized population. The process often involves violence, displacement, and the subjugation of Indigenous cultures and knowledge systems. Coloniality, on the other hand, refers to the long-lasting social, economic, and cultural structures that persist even after the formal end of colonial rule. It encompasses

the continued dominance and subordination of certain groups based on racial, cultural, and socioeconomic hierarchies established during colonialism. Coloniality operates through institutions, ideologies, and power dynamics that perpetuate the marginalization, exploitation, and devaluation of certain populations. Coloniality extends beyond the physical presence of colonial powers and encompasses the systemic and deep-rooted inequalities that persist in postcolonial societies. It is characterized by ongoing forms of oppression, such as racism, Eurocentrism, and the marginalization of indigenous knowledge and cultural practices. Coloniality influences various aspects of society, including education, economic systems, governance, language, and cultural norms.

3. The Orishas are deities or divine forces worshiped in the traditional African religions of the Yoruba people, primarily originating from present-day Nigeria and Benin. They form an integral part of the Yoruba spiritual and cultural worldview. The term Orisha can be translated as "deity" or "sacred force," and each Orisha is associated with specific natural elements, phenomena, and aspects of human life. In Yoruba cosmology, it is believed that the Supreme Being, Olodumare, created the Orishas to govern and influence different aspects of the world. The Orishas are considered intermediaries between humans and Olodumare, facilitating communication, blessings, and protection. They possess their own distinct personalities, characteristics, and domains. Each Orisha is associated with attributes and symbols, such as colors, animals, plants, and rituals. They encompass a wide range of aspects of human existence, including fertility, love, war, healing, wisdom, and abundance. For example, Oshun is associated with sweet waters, love, beauty, and fertility, while Shango is associated with thunder, fire, justice, and leadership. Orisha worship involves rituals, ceremonies, prayers, and offerings to honor and seek the blessings of these divine forces. Devotees often establish personal relationships with specific Orishas based on their individual needs, challenges, and aspirations. The practices and beliefs surrounding Orisha worship have also been carried to various parts of the African diaspora, particularly through Afro-Caribbean and Afro-Latinx religions such as Santeria, Candomble, and Vodou.

4. Yoruba refers to both an ethnic group and a language predominantly found in southwestern Nigeria, as well as in parts of Benin and Togo. The Yoruba people have a rich cultural heritage and are one of the largest ethnic groups in Africa, numbering over forty million individuals. Yoruba religion, also known as Ifa or Orisa tradition, is the Indigenous religious and spiritual practice of the Yoruba people. It is a complex system of beliefs, rituals, and customs that encompasses various deities (Orishas), ancestral reverence, divination, and healing practices. Yoruba religion is characterized by its deep connection to nature, the spiritual realm, and the principles of balance and harmony. The Yoruba religion has also had a significant influence on various diasporic religions in the Americas, such

as Santeria in Cuba, Candomble in Brazil, and Vodou in Haiti. These syncretic practices blend Yoruba beliefs with elements of Christianity and Indigenous traditions. Yoruba religion serves not only as a spiritual system but also as a framework for cultural identity, moral values, and social cohesion within Yoruba communities. It continues to be practiced and celebrated by millions of people, both in its traditional form in Nigeria and in various adaptations across the diaspora.

5. Afrofuturist imagery refers to artistic, cultural, and literary representations that combine elements of African diasporic culture, history, and aesthetics with futuristic and science fiction themes. It is a creative expression that envisions alternative and empowering futures for people of African descent, challenging mainstream narratives and reimagining the possibilities of Black existence. Afrofuturism emerged as a cultural movement in the late twentieth century, influenced by science fiction, fantasy, speculative fiction, and various art forms. It encompasses a wide range of mediums, including literature, music, visual arts, fashion, film, and digital media. Afrofuturist imagery often combines elements of traditional African cosmologies, folklore, and spirituality with futuristic technologies, outer space, and futuristic landscapes. This aesthetic often portrays Black people as protagonists in narratives that explore themes of identity, liberation, social justice, and cultural empowerment. Afrofuturist imagery challenges the historical erasure and marginalization of Black people and offers a counternarrative that affirms their presence, agency, and resilience. Examples of Afrofuturist imagery can be found in the works of artists such as Sun Ra, Octavia Butler, Janelle Monáe, Wangechi Mutu, and Jean-Michel Basquiat. Their creations incorporate elements of Afrocentric symbolism, cosmic themes, futuristic fashion, and technological advancements. Afrofuturist literature, such as Octavia Butler's *Parable of the Sower* and Nnedi Okorafor's Binti series, imagines alternative worlds and futures that explore social and political issues from a Black perspective.

6. Western depictions of beauty refer to the prevailing standards and ideals of physical attractiveness that have been historically promoted and perpetuated within Western societies. These standards are subjective and have evolved over time, influenced by cultural, social, and historical factors. It is important to note that Western beauty standards are not fixed or universally embraced. They vary across time, cultures, and individual perspectives. Furthermore, there has been an increasing recognition of the limitations and harmful effects of narrow beauty ideals. Contemporary movements advocate for greater diversity and inclusivity, challenging Western beauty norms and promoting a broader understanding of beauty that embraces different racial, ethnic, body size, and age diversity. Critics argue that Western beauty standards can reinforce harmful social hierarchies, perpetuate inequalities, and contribute to body image issues, low self-esteem, and the marginalization of individuals who do not conform to these ideals. Efforts are being made to challenge and redefine beauty standards to promote body

positivity, self-acceptance, and a more inclusive notion of beauty that embraces the diversity of human appearances.

7. In the Lucumí faith, which is a syncretic religion that evolved among enslaved Africans in the Caribbean, who melded their Yoruba religious traditions with elements of Catholicism, a "pataki" refers to a type of religious narrative or mythological story. These stories often serve as foundational texts, narrating the experiences, attributes, and interactions of the Orishas—the revered deities in the Lucumí belief system, as well as explaining natural phenomena, moral lessons, and the origins of rituals and ceremonies. Patakís function as both spiritual guidance and historical accounts, weaving the rich tapestry of traditions, wisdom, and cultural practices that form the Lucumí religious framework. They are often recounted through oral tradition, passed down from generation to generation, serving as a vital tool in the preservation of the culture and its complex web of mythological narratives. Through these stories, devotees find not only religious instructions but also an understanding of the universe's intricate dynamics, the human condition, and the deeper nuances of their faith. These narratives imbue the rituals, dances, and music of the Lucumí religion with a deeper symbolic significance, offering a rich and profound spiritual experience to its followers.

8. In the Yoruba religion and its diasporic derivatives like the Lucumí faith, Olodumare is considered the supreme deity, the ultimate source and ruler of all that exists. Often perceived as a transcendental entity, Olodumare embodies an omnipotent, omniscient, and omnipresent force that governs the cosmos. Olodumare is believed to be the primal force of existence, transcending time and space. This deity has neither beginning nor end, embodying eternity and the infinite nature of the universe. It is the ultimate representation of the unmanifested, the unseen force that underpins all creation and the cycle of life and death. In the cosmology of the Yoruba religion, *Ashe* is a vital life force, a kind of spiritual energy that pervades everything in the universe. Olodumare is considered the central reservoir and distributor of this divine energy. The deity bestows *ashe* on the universe, giving life, power, and dynamism to both living beings and inanimate objects. Olodumare is hailed as a benevolent creator, a deity responsible for the creation of the earth and all its inhabitants. The deity designed the cosmos with a well-structured order, establishing a balance and harmony that allows life to flourish. This deity's compassion and wisdom are reflected in the beauty and complexity of the natural world.

9. *Aché* is believed to be bestowed by the deities or Orishas, who are considered the source and embodiment of this spiritual power. Through rituals, offerings, and devotion, practitioners seek to connect with and receive *aché* from the Orishas, enhancing their spiritual well-being and bringing harmony into their lives. The concept of *aché* also emphasizes the interconnectedness of all living beings and the natural world. It recognizes that individuals are not separate entities

but part of a larger cosmic web. By aligning oneself with the flow of *aché*, one can cultivate a sense of harmony, balance, and alignment with the divine forces and the rhythms of life. In addition to its spiritual connotations, *aché* can also be seen as a moral and ethical principle. It encompasses notions of integrity, righteousness, and acting in alignment with divine principles. Practitioners strive to cultivate *aché* within themselves by leading virtuous lives, upholding moral values, and making positive contributions to their communities.

10. The colonial imposition of Christianity refers to the historical process by which European colonial powers, particularly during the era of European imperialism, forcefully introduced and promoted Christianity in colonized territories. This imposition was a key aspect of the broader project of colonization, which aimed to assert political, economic, and cultural dominance over indigenous peoples and their lands. Christianity was often used as a tool for colonization, serving as a means to justify and legitimize the subjugation and exploitation of Indigenous populations. European colonial powers, such as Spain, Portugal, France, and Britain, viewed the spread of Christianity as a mission of "civilizing" and "saving" the "heathen" or "primitive" peoples they encountered in colonized territories. The imposition of Christianity involved various methods, including forced conversion, destruction of indigenous spiritual practices, suppression of indigenous languages and cultural expressions, and the establishment of Christian institutions such as churches, schools, and missions. Indigenous religions and spiritual beliefs were often labeled as "pagan," "savage," or "superstitious," and were actively discouraged or prohibited.

Colonial powers often employed missionaries as agents of conversion, who played a significant role in spreading Christianity and undermining indigenous cultures. Missionaries, backed by the colonial powers, sought to erase or marginalize Indigenous religious practices, rituals, and belief systems, portraying them as backward or sinful. The colonial imposition of Christianity had profound and lasting impacts on Indigenous communities. It disrupted traditional social, cultural, and spiritual structures, causing the loss of Indigenous languages, knowledge systems, and cultural practices. Indigenous peoples were often forced to abandon their ancestral beliefs and adopt the religious and cultural norms of the colonizers, leading to the erasure or suppression of their own cultural identities. The process of colonial imposition of Christianity also had political and economic ramifications. European powers used Christianity as a means of control, seeking to convert and assimilate Indigenous populations into the colonial order. Indigenous resistance to conversion was often met with violence, punishment, and marginalization.

11. Women in Christian iconography have been depicted in various ways throughout history, often reflecting cultural and religious beliefs, as well as societal norms and values. These depictions range from biblical figures and saints to representations of female virtues and archetypes. The portrayal of women in

Christian iconography has been a subject of study and analysis by various theorists and scholars. One prominent theorist in this field is Thurston Bonnie, whose work focuses on the representation of women in Christian art and iconography. In her book *Women in the New Testament: Questions and Commentary* (2004), she examines the diverse roles and representations of women in biblical narratives and their significance in shaping Christian iconography. Another influential scholar is Mattes Mark who explores the gendered dimensions of religious art in her work *Image and Spirit: Finding Meaning in Visual Art* (2005). He analyzes the portrayal of women in Christian art, including their roles as biblical figures, saints, and symbols of virtue, discussing the ways in which gender ideologies are manifested in visual representations. The representation of women in Christian iconography has evolved over time, reflecting cultural and societal shifts. In medieval Christian art, for example, the Virgin Mary was often depicted as the idealized and virtuous mother figure, embodying qualities of purity, humility, and obedience. However, feminist theologians and scholars have critiqued these representations for perpetuating limiting and stereotypical gender roles. In the context of contemporary Christian art in the United States, there is a growing movement to challenge and expand the representation of women. Artists such as Janet McKenzie and Sandra Bowden explore alternative and inclusive depictions of biblical women and female spiritual figures, emphasizing their strength, diversity, and individuality. Moreover, feminist theology has called for the inclusion of women's voices and experiences in interpreting and shaping Christian iconography. It advocates for a more inclusive and egalitarian understanding of Christianity that affirms the full humanity and spiritual agency of women.

12. Colorism refers to a form of discrimination or prejudice based on skin color, typically within the same racial or ethnic group. It involves the privileging or favoritism of individuals with lighter skin tones over those with darker skin tones, leading to differential treatment and opportunities based on perceived color hierarchy. Colorism can manifest in various aspects of society, including employment, education, media representation, beauty standards, and interpersonal relationships. To learn more about colorism and "gendered colorism" see M. E. Hill (2002); A. M. Landor, L. G. Simons, R. L. Simons, G. H. Brody, C. M. Bryant, F. X. Gibbons, and J. N. Melby (2013); M. Hunter (2007); M. S. Thompson and V. M. Keith (2001); E. N. Glenn (2008); M. Hughes and B. R. Hertel (1990); and V. M. Keith and C. Herring (1991).

Chapter 3

1. The Yoruba people worship many deities or Orishas and ancestors. These deities are specific to certain regions of Nigeria where the Yoruba reside. We can count 401 deities or Orishas in the Yoruba belief system. They have

often been compared with the Greek Pantheon. However, the Yoruba have their own distinct divination system that predates Greek mythology and is practiced throughout the world today.

2. Dr. Fu-Kiau Kia Bunseki, one of the most distinguished scholars of African culture, was Born in Minianga, Democratic Republic of Congo.

3. Bakongo or Kongo people are a Bantu ethnic group that speaks the Kikongo language. There are many theories as to how the Kongo people got their name. Some believe the name is derived from the word N'kongo, which means "hunter," but others believe it is meant to mean "mountains" in the Bantu language.

4. The Middle Passage refers to the infamous and brutal stage of the transatlantic slave trade during which enslaved Africans were forcibly transported across the Atlantic Ocean from Africa to the Americas. It is characterized by its dehumanizing conditions, high mortality rates, and the immense suffering endured by the enslaved individuals during the journey. Numerous theorists and scholars have explored and written about the Middle Passage, shedding light on its historical significance and its profound impact on African diaspora communities. Some notable works and theorists include Olaudah Equiano: Equiano was an enslaved African who wrote a compelling autobiography titled *The Interesting Narrative of the Life of Olaudah Equiano* (1789). His narrative vividly describes his experiences during the Middle Passage, providing firsthand insights into the inhumane conditions and atrocities endured by enslaved Africans. Paul Gilroy: In his influential work *The Black Atlantic: Modernity and Double Consciousness* (1993), Gilroy examines the cultural and intellectual connections between Africa, the Americas, and Europe, emphasizing the significance of the Middle Passage in shaping black identity, resistance, and cultural exchange. Saidiya Hartman: Hartman's book *Lose Your Mother: A Journey Along the Atlantic Slave Route* (2007) combines historical research with personal reflection to explore the fragmented history of the Middle Passage. She delves into the experiences of enslaved Africans, the erasure of their narratives, and the lasting impact on contemporary African diaspora communities. Marcus Rediker: Rediker's work *The Slave Ship: A Human History* (2007) provides a comprehensive examination of the transatlantic slave trade, including a detailed analysis of the Middle Passage. Through extensive research, Rediker explores the economic, social, and psychological dimensions of this tragic chapter in history. Stuart Hall: Hall, a cultural theorist, explores the Middle Passage in the context of diaspora and cultural identity in his essay "Cultural Identity and Diaspora" (1990). He examines the role of history, memory, and displacement in shaping the experiences of African diaspora communities, connecting them to the traumatic legacy of the Middle Passage. These works and theorists have contributed significantly to our understanding of the Middle Passage, offering critical perspectives on its historical significance, the experiences of enslaved Africans, and the enduring impact on contemporary society. Through their scholarship, they illuminate the horrors of this chapter in history while also

emphasizing the resilience, cultural creativity, and ongoing struggles for justice within African diaspora communities.

5. The transatlantic slave trade, also known as the Atlantic slave trade, was a brutal system of human trafficking and forced labor that took place between the sixteenth and nineteenth centuries. It involved the enslavement and transportation of African people from their homelands in West and Central Africa to the Americas, primarily to European colonies in North and South America and the Caribbean. The slave trade was driven by the economic interests of European powers, who sought to exploit the labor-intensive industries of their colonies, such as sugar plantations, tobacco farms, and mines. African men, women, and children were captured or purchased by European slave traders, often through violence and coercion, and then transported across the Atlantic Ocean in extremely harsh conditions. The middle passage was the journey from Africa to the Americas, and it was marked by extreme suffering and death for many enslaved individuals. The enslaved Africans were packed tightly into the cargo holds of ships, enduring cramped and unsanitary conditions. They faced disease, starvation, physical abuse, and the psychological trauma of being forcibly separated from their families and communities. Upon arrival in the Americas, the enslaved Africans were sold at slave markets to plantation owners and other buyers. They were subjected to a lifetime of brutal labor, often working under oppressive and inhumane conditions. Slavery was a deeply entrenched institution that denied enslaved people their basic human rights, treating them as property to be bought, sold, and exploited. The transatlantic slave trade had profound and lasting effects on both Africa and the Americas. It contributed to the wealth and development of European powers while devastating African societies, as millions of people were taken from their homelands. It also shaped the racial dynamics of the Americas, with systems of racial discrimination and oppression persisting long after slavery was officially abolished. Abolitionist movements and changing economic realities eventually led to the end of the transatlantic slave trade in the nineteenth century. However, its legacy continues to impact societies and discussions about race, justice, and reparations to this day.

6. In chapter 7 of *Pedagogies of Crossing: Meditations on Feminism, Sexual Politics, Memory, and the Sacred*, M. Jacqui Alexander invokes Spirit, and particularly the spirit of Kitsimba, one of her ancestors from the Mayombe region of Central Africa, who is remembering the symbolic and real violence of "the Crossing" that brought her to the "New World" and bestowed her plantation slave name "Thisbe."

Chapter 4

1. Black femininity refers to the multifaceted and diverse expression of femininity within the context of Black women's experiences and identities. It

encompasses the array of ways in which Black women navigate, express, and negotiate their gender identity within the intersections of race, culture, history, and social dynamics. Black femininity challenges monolithic notions of womanhood by recognizing the complexity and uniqueness of Black women's experiences and identities. Black femininity is shaped by historical legacies, cultural traditions, social expectations, and personal agency. It can encompass both traditional and nontraditional expressions of femininity, embracing a range of appearances, behaviors, roles, and attitudes that reflect the diverse backgrounds and life experiences of Black women. Black femininity can be characterized by strength, resilience, creativity, and a sense of community, often in response to historical and contemporary challenges faced by Black women. However, it's important to note that Black femininity is not a singular or fixed concept; it's fluid and evolving. Different Black women may express their femininity in various ways that resonate with their personal identities and experiences. As with any concept of femininity, Black femininity is deeply individual, shaped by intersectional factors, and should be understood within a context that acknowledges and respects the diversity of Black women's lives and perspectives.

2. Artists frequently incorporate their own bodies as a central element in their art pieces, a practice that holds significant meaning and artistic potential. This approach, known as "body art" or "performance art," involves the artist using their own physical presence and actions as a medium of expression, often blurring the lines between the artist's body, the artwork, and the audience's experience. By using their own body, artists can engage with themes such as identity, vulnerability, social issues, and personal experiences in a uniquely impactful way. This form of self-inclusion in the artwork allows for a deep exploration of the artist's own emotional landscape and can create a powerful connection with the viewer. Additionally, this embodiment of the artwork can challenge traditional artistic boundaries and norms, pushing the boundaries of what art can be and how it can be experienced. Using their own body as a canvas, artists can convey complex narratives, question societal norms, and evoke visceral emotions. This deeply personal form of expression often invites viewers to confront their own emotions, perceptions, and biases, fostering a more intimate and introspective engagement with the art. Throughout art history, numerous artists, including Frida Kahlo, Marina Abramović, and Ana Mendieta, have used their bodies as a canvas to communicate their ideas, experiences, and activism. The body becomes a tool for storytelling, and the artist's physical presence serves as a bridge between the internal and external worlds, inviting viewers to witness, contemplate, and engage with the artwork in a profoundly visceral and thought-provoking manner.

3. Entire interview can be reviewed here: https://contemporaryand.com/magazines/susana-pilar-delahante-reclaiming-space-through-performance/.

4. Visual self-narration refers to the process of using visual mediums, such as art, photography, or other visual representations, to tell a personal story or

communicate aspects of one's identity, experiences, emotions, and perspectives. It involves creating visual artifacts that reflect an individual's unique journey, thoughts, and emotions, allowing them to share their narrative in a way that goes beyond words alone. This concept recognizes the power of images and visual symbols in conveying complex ideas and feelings. Visual self-narration enables individuals to communicate their lived experiences, cultural background, challenges, triumphs, and aspirations through a creative and often symbolic visual language. It offers a means to explore and express one's identity, emotions, and worldview while inviting others to engage with and understand their personal narrative on a deeper level.

5. In Yoruba, *ará* (also written as *ara*) translates to *body* in English. The word *ará* is commonly used to refer to the physical body of a person or any living being. In Yoruba culture and language, the body is considered an essential aspect of one's existence, and it holds significant importance in various rituals, ceremonies, and everyday expressions. The term *ará* is an integral part of Yoruba vocabulary and reflects the cultural understanding of the physical self as a fundamental element of individual identity and spirituality.

6. Beyond its visual appeal, the color pink has also been embraced by various social and cultural movements. In the early twentieth century, pink became associated with femininity and girlhood, leading to the tradition of dressing baby girls in pink attire. However, it is essential to note that color associations can be culturally contingent and have evolved over time. In recent years, pink has been reappropriated and embraced as a symbol of empowerment and advocacy for causes such as breast cancer awareness and LGBTQ+ rights. In contemporary art and design, pink continues to captivate creators for its versatility and emotive qualities. From soft pastel tones to bold neon shades, pink has found its place in diverse artistic expressions, representing a spectrum of emotions and themes, from innocence and purity to rebellion and subversion.

Chapter 5

1. Collography is an artistic printmaking technique that involves creating a textured printing plate by adhering various materials to a rigid surface. These materials can include fabric, paper, cardboard, string, and other found objects. The plate is then inked and pressed onto paper or another printing surface to transfer the textures and patterns onto the paper, resulting in a unique and visually rich print. The process of creating a collograph involves several steps: An artist starts by selecting a rigid surface as the base for their printing plate, often using materials like cardboard or wood. They then glue or attach various materials onto this surface to create textures, patterns, and relief elements. The plate is often sealed and primed with a varnish or adhesive to prevent excessive absorption of

ink and to protect the adhered materials. The plate is inked by applying printing ink or paint onto its textured surface. The ink is pushed into the recessed areas and textures created by the attached materials.

Wiping: Excess ink is carefully wiped off the raised surfaces, leaving the ink within the recessed areas and textures intact. A sheet of paper is then placed over the inked plate, and pressure is applied through a printing press or other manual means. The paper absorbs the ink from the plate's textured surfaces, resulting in a print that captures the intricate patterns and textures. Artists can experiment with inking techniques, layering, and combining different materials to create a wide range of visual effects and outcomes. Collography allows artists to explore the interplay between texture, shape, and color in their prints. The variety of materials used for the collaged plate can result in highly expressive and unique prints, with each impression often having subtle variations due to the manual nature of the printing process. This technique encourages experimentation and can yield a wide array of visual results, making it a versatile and captivating method within the realm of printmaking and artistic expression.

2. The term Calabar women historically refers to a group of African women who were captured, enslaved, and transported to the Americas, particularly during the transatlantic slave trade era. Calabar, in this context, refers to the region in what is now southeastern Nigeria. The women from this region were known for their strength, resilience, and cultural contributions even in the face of extreme hardship and oppression. The "Calabar women" were part of the larger group of African slaves who were forcibly taken from various regions of Africa and brought to the Americas to work on plantations, in mines, and in various other labor-intensive industries. These women were subjected to unimaginable suffering, including the brutalities of the Middle Passage, the voyage across the Atlantic Ocean under horrific conditions. Despite their circumstances, many Calabar women and other enslaved individuals managed to retain elements of their culture, traditions, and identity. They often found ways to resist and maintain connections to their African heritage, even within the confines of slavery. This might include preserving traditional knowledge, practicing religious and spiritual rituals, and using various forms of communication to pass down their stories and traditions. It's important to note that while the term Calabar women highlights the origin of some enslaved African women, the experiences of enslaved individuals were diverse, and they came from a wide range of backgrounds across the African continent. The term serves as a reminder of the resilience and cultural strength of those who endured the atrocities of the transatlantic slave trade and contributed to shaping the cultural landscape of the Americas, often in ways that might not be immediately apparent due to the erasure of their voices and histories. In modern contexts, discussions about the Calabar women often center on acknowledging and honoring the contributions and legacies of African diasporic cultures in

the Americas and recognizing the ongoing impact of historical trauma on these communities. For more information on this topic see Randy J. Sparks (2004), J. C. Cotton (1905), or Efiong U. Aye (1967).

3. The Efik people are an ethnic group indigenous to the southeastern region of Nigeria, particularly in the Cross River State. They also inhabit parts of the neighboring Akwa Ibom State. The Efik people have a rich cultural heritage and history that sets them apart as a distinct group within Nigeria. The Efik people have a vibrant cultural identity that includes traditional ceremonies, festivals, art, music, and dance. Their cultural practices are often characterized by intricate rituals and symbolism. The Efik language, also known as Efik-Ibibio or Calabar, is spoken by the Efik people. It has different dialects and variations, but it remains an important element of their cultural identity. The Efik people, like many other ethnic groups in West Africa, were significantly affected by the transatlantic slave trade. The Efik region, particularly around the city of Calabar, played a notable role in this trade due to its coastal location and established trade networks. See Efiong U. Aye (2000), Stephen D. Behrendt; Eric J. Graham (2003), Kannan K. Nair (1972), and Donald C. Simmons (1958).

4. My translation from Spanish of the original source.

5. *Androgynous* refers to a state of having both masculine and feminine qualities or characteristics, or a blending of gender traits that transcends traditional notions of male and female identities. An androgynous person or depiction typically lacks distinct or exaggerated gender markers, making it difficult to easily assign them to a specific gender category. Androgyny challenges the binary understanding of gender by embracing a more fluid and encompassing perspective, recognizing that individuals can possess a diverse range of physical, emotional, and behavioral traits that may not conform to conventional gender norms. The exploration of androgynous figures and themes is a common practice in art, spanning various time periods and cultures. Artists often use androgyny to challenge societal norms, question traditional gender roles, and explore the complexity of human identity. We can mention some examples from art history around the world, such as Leonardo da Vinci's *Vitruvian Man*. This iconic drawing from the Renaissance era depicts a figure with both arms and legs outstretched, fitting within both a square and a circle. The image symbolizes the harmonious relationship between the human body and geometry. The androgynous qualities of the figure reflect the idea of balance and universality, transcending the confines of traditional gender representations. In Greek mythology, Hermaphroditus was the child of Hermes and Aphrodite, possessing both male and female attributes. This mythological figure has been depicted in various art forms, including sculptures and paintings, as a symbol of duality and the blurring of gender boundaries. The Austrian Expressionist Egon Schiele often painted androgynous figures, emphasizing elongated limbs and distorted features. His portraits challenge conventional beauty standards and explore the fluidity of gender identity. Catherine Opie's

Self-Portrait/Cutting is another great example. This contemporary photograph by Catherine Opie shows the artist with her back exposed, revealing a carving of the word *pervert*. The androgynous figure and provocative imagery challenge societal expectations and confront issues related to identity and sexuality. Japanese artist Yasumasa Morimura is known for his self-portraits in which he dresses as iconic figures from art history, literature, and pop culture. Through these gender-bending performances, Morimura explores questions of identity, representation, and cultural context. These examples demonstrate that androgynous themes have been prevalent across different artistic movements and cultures, serving as a means of artistic expression, social commentary, and exploration of the fluidity of human identity.

6. Santería is a syncretic religion that originated in Cuba, blending elements of Yoruba spirituality brought by African enslaved people with Catholicism introduced by Spanish colonizers. It is a complex and multifaceted belief system that fuses African and Catholic traditions to create a unique spiritual practice. In Santería, practitioners venerate deities known as Orishas, which are derived from the Yoruba pantheon of West Africa. Each Orisha is associated with specific attributes, natural forces, and aspects of life. These Orishas are often syncretized with Catholic saints, allowing for a covert continuation of African religious practices under the guise of Catholicism during the period of colonization and slavery. Central to Santería are rituals, ceremonies, and divination practices that seek to establish a connection between the material and spiritual realms. Animal sacrifices, drumming, dancing, and chanting play important roles in these rituals, helping practitioners communicate with the Orishas, seek guidance, and maintain balance between the physical and spiritual worlds. Santería emphasizes personal growth, healing, and guidance through its interaction with the Orishas. It is often practiced within a community setting and may involve initiations into different levels of understanding and involvement. See Bascom 1950, Hagedorn 2001, Wirtz 2007, and Pasquali 1994.

7. Mariblanca Sabas Aloma, a fervent feminist journalist and writer during the prerevolutionary era, found herself deeply influenced by the momentous Russian Revolution of 1917. Her literary contributions bore the imprints of this revolutionary spirit, as she envisioned the realm of domestic life as a potent tool for combating both political inequities and the prevailing "machismo" culture. In her writings, Sabas Aloma championed the idea that the private sphere held the key to dismantling societal disparities. A notable aspect of Sabas Aloma's critique centered on the interpersonal dynamics among Cuban women. She scrutinized their penchant for gossip and their tendencies toward unkindness, which, in her view, fostered an atmosphere of mutual mistrust. This lack of solidarity among women, she contended, permeated into broader Cuban society and functioned as the linchpin behind social injustice. In her analysis, she attributed a significant portion of societal issues to the distrust propagated by women's interactions. Sabas Aloma placed a profound responsibility on women for Cuba's societal challenges,

particularly concerning gender relations and social inequality. She postulated that mothers, as the primary nurturers of future generations, possessed the extraordinary power to reshape society's trajectory. Her argument rested on the premise that transformation could be ignited by altering the way children were raised, ultimately dissuading them from adopting behaviors and beliefs that perpetuated betrayal and mistrust. Furthermore, Sabas Aloma was emblematic of the radicalized feminist movement that emerged in the early twentieth century. Her prominence in feminist journalism earned her the moniker of the "Red Feminist," distinguishing her as one of the most radical voices within the feminist movement, particularly for her socialist inclinations. She was a notable member of the Grupo Minorista, a collective of young intellectuals who rallied around Marxism as their intellectual foundation. This association underscores her alignment with broader radical ideologies of her time, mirroring the revolutionary fervor that characterized her era (Stoner 2003, 88). Mariblanca Sabas Aloma's contributions as a radical feminist journalist were deeply shaped by her exposure to revolutionary ideals and Marxist thought. She envisioned the transformation of society through the reimagining of the domestic sphere and believed that women, especially mothers, held the potential to reshape societal values. Her position within the broader radical feminist movement and her role in the Grupo Minorista further solidify her place as a pivotal figure in Cuba's prerevolutionary feminist landscape.

8. Vilma Espín Guillois (1930 to 2007) was a prominent Cuban revolutionary and political figure. She played a significant role in the Cuban Revolution alongside Fidel Castro, and later married his brother, Raúl Castro. Vilma Espín was recognized for her advocacy of women's rights and gender equality in Cuba. She was an active participant in the Cuban Revolution, which culminated in the overthrow of the Batista regime in 1959. She was part of the 26th of July Movement, led by Fidel Castro, and played a role in the armed struggle against the Batista government. After the revolution, Vilma Espín became a strong advocate for women's rights and gender equality in Cuba. She worked to dismantle gender-based discrimination and promoted policies and initiatives that aimed to empower women in various aspects of society, including education, employment, and politics. Founder of the Cuban Federation of Women (FMC): In 1960, Vilma Espín cofounded the Cuban Federation of Women (Federación de Mujeres Cubanas or FMC), an organization dedicated to advancing women's rights and gender equality. The FMC has played a significant role in advocating for women's issues in Cuba. Vilma Espín's dedication to gender equality and her contributions to the Cuban Revolution made her a respected figure both in Cuba and internationally. Her work continues to be recognized as an important aspect of Cuba's history and the broader struggle for women's rights in Latin America.

Bibliography

Adamovsky, Ezequiel. "Race and Class Through the Visual Culture of Peronism." In *Rethinking Race in Modern Argentina*, edited by Paulina Alberto and Eduardo Elena. Cambridge University Press, 2016, 155–83.

Aimes, Hubert H. S. *A History of Slavery in Cuba, 1511 to 1868*. G. P. Putnam's, 1907.

Alexander, M. Jacqui. *Pedagogies of Crossing: Meditations on Feminism, Sexual Politics, Memory, and the Sacred*. Duke University Press, 2005.

Allahar, Anton L. "Slaves, Slave Merchants and Slave Owners in 19th Century Cuba." *Caribbean Studies* 21, no. 1 (1988): 158–91.

Almeida Junco, Yulexis. "Género y racialidad: Una reflexión obligada en la Cuba de hoy." In *Afrocubanas: Historia, pensamiento y prácticas culturales*, edited by Daysi Rubiera Castillo and Inés María Martiatu Terry. Editorial de Ciencias Sociales, 2011, 133–49.

Álvarez Ramírez, Sandra. "De cierta manera feminista de filmar." In *La memoria y el olvido. Syllabus afrocubano*, edited by Juan F. Benemelis. La Ceiba, 2009, 286–98.

Alves, Miriam, and Carolyn Richardson Durham, eds. *Enfim . . . Nós/Finally Us: Escritoras Negras Brasileiras Contemporaneas/Contemporary Black Brazilian Women Writers*. Three Continents, 1994.

Andrews, George Reid. *Afro-Latin America (1800–2000)*. Oxford University Press, 2004.

Bucholtz, M. *The Afro-Argentines of Buenos Aires, 1800–1900*. University of Wisconsin Press, 1980.

Bucholtz, M. *Afro-Latin America: Black Lives, 1600–2000*. Harvard University Press, 2016.

Bucholtz, M. *Blackness in the White Nation a History of Afro-Uruguay*, 1st ed. University of North Carolina Press, 2010.

Bucholtz, M. *Blacks & Whites in São Paulo, Brazil, 1888–1988*. University of Wisconsin Press, 1991.

Bucholtz, M. *Identity and Interaction: A Sociocultural Linguistic Approach*. London: Sage Publications, 2005.Anzaldúa, Gloria. *Borderlands/La frontera: The New Mestiza*. Aunt Lute Press, 1987.

Arnedo-Gomez, Miguel. "Uniting Blacks in a Raceless Nation: Afro-Cuban Reformulations of Afrocubanismo and Mestizaje in 1930s Cuba." *Journal of Iberian and Latin American Studies* 18, no. 1 (2012): 33–59.

Arrelucea Barrantes, Maribel, and Joseph P. Sánchez, Angelica Sánchez-Clark, and Larry D. Miller (trans). "Slavery, Writing, and Female Resistance: Black Women Litigants in Lima's Late Colonial Tribunals of the 1780s." In *Afro-Latino Voices: Narratives from the Early Modern Ibero-Atlantic World, 1550–1812*, edited by Kathryn Joy McKnight and Leo J. Garofalo. Hackett, 2009, 285–301.

Arriaga, Eduard, and Andrés Villar, eds. *Afro-Latinx Digital Connections*. University of Florida Press, 2021.

Ashdown-Franks, Garcia, and Janelle Joseph. " 'Mind Your Business and Leave My Rolls Alone': A Case Study of Fat Black Women Runners' Decolonial Resistance." *Societies* 11, no. 3 (2021): 95.

Aye, Efiong U. *The Efik People*. Glad Tidings Press, 2000.

Aye, Efiong U. *Old Calabar Through the Centuries*. Hope Waddell Press, 1967.

Ayón, Belkis. Interview with David Mateo. *La Gaceta de Cuba Magazine*, 1997.

Babb, Florence E."Theorizing Gender, Race, and Cultural Tourism in Latin America." *Women's Place in the Andes*, 2018, 183–99.

Bardwell-Jones, Celia, and Margaret McLaren. "Introduction to Indigenizing and Decolonizing Feminist Philosophy." *Hypatia* 35, no. 1 (2020): 2–17.

Ball, Erica L., Tatiana Seijas, and Terri L. Snyder, eds. *As If She Were Free: A Collective Biography of Women and Emancipation in the Americas*. Cambridge University Press, 2020.

Barcia, María del Carmen and Fernando Carr Parúas. *Mujeres al margen de la historia*. Editorial de Ciencias Sociales, 2009.

Barreto, Reina. "Gender and identity in the Art of Ana Mendieta, Belkis Ayón, and Sandra Ramos." *Proceedings of the Pacific Coast Council on Latin American Studies* 23, no. 1 (2006).

Bascom, William R. "The Focus of Cuban Santería." *Southwestern Journal of Anthropology* 6, no. 1 (1950): 64–68.

Baxmann, Inge. "The Body as Archive: On the Difficult Relationship Between Movement and History." In *Knowledge in Motion: Perspectives Artistic and Scientific Research in Dance*, edited by Sabine Gehm, Pirkko Husemann, and Katharina von Wilcke. Bielefeld transcript Verlag, 2007, 207–16.

Beckenstein, Joyce. "Zilia Sánchez, María Magdalena Campos-Pons, and Glenda León: Three Cuban Artists, Three Generations, Three Perspectives." *Woman's Art Journal* 37, no. 2 (October 2016): 20–28.

Behrendt, Stephen D., and Graham, Eric J. "African Merchants, Notables and the Slave Trade at Old Calabar, 1720: Evidence from the National Archives of Scotland." *History in Africa* 30, no. 1 (2003): 37–61.

Benamou, Catherine L. "Cuban Cinema: On the Threshold of Gender." *Frontiers: A Journal of Women Studies* 15, no. 1 (1994): 51.

Benítez-Rojo, Antonio, *The Repeating Island: The Caribbean and the Postmodern Perspective*. Duke University Press, 1996.

Bennett, Herman L. *Colonial Blackness: A History of Afro-Mexico*. Indiana University Press, 2009.

Berger, Sally. "Maria Magdalena Campos-Pons: 1990–2001." In *Authentic Ex-Centric: Conceptualism in Contemporary African Art*, edited by Salah Hassan and Olu Oguibe. Prince Claus Fund Library, 2001.

Bishell, Ellen R. "Cuban Music, Global Screen: Hypervisibility, Identity Politics, and Resistance in Seidy 'la niña' carrera's tumbao." *Comparative American Studies an International Journal* 18, no. 3 (2021): 413–29.

Bostoen, Koen, and Inge Brinkman. *The Kongo Kingdom: The Origins, Dynamics and Cosmopolitan Culture of an African Polity*. Cambridge University Press, 2018.

Braham, Persephone. *African Diaspora in the Cultures of Latin America, the Caribbean, and the United States*. Rowman & Littlefield, 2014.

Branche, Jerome, ed. *Black Writing, Culture, and the State in Latin America*. Vanderbilt University Press, 2015.

Busey, C., and Cruz, B. "A Shared Heritage: Afro-Latin@s and Black History." *Social Studies* 106, no. 1 (2015): 293–300. https://doi.org/10.1080/0037799 6.2015.1085824.

Cabrera, Lydia. *La lengua sagrada de los ñáñigos*. Ediciones Universal, 1988.

Cabrera, Lydia. *La sociedad secreta Abakuá. Narrada por viejos adeptos*. 3rd ed., Ediciones Universal, 2005.

Cabrera, Lydia. *Yemayá y Ochún*. Ediciones Universal, 1996.

Caldwell, P. M. "A Hair Piece: Perspectives on the Intersection of Race and Gender." In *Critical Race Theory: The Cutting Edge*, edited by Richard Delgado and Jean Stefancic. Temple University Press, 2000, 275–85.

Campos, Alejandro. "Agenda and Public Policy Against Racism (1959–2008)." In *Changing Cuba/Changing*, edited by Mauricio A. Font. Bildner Center for Western Hemisphere Studies, 2008, 175–92.

Campos-Pons, María Magdalena, and William Luis. "Art and Diaspora: A Conversation with María Magdalena Campos-Pons." *Afro-Hispanic Review* 30, no. 2 (October 2011): 155–66.

Campos-Pons, María Magdalena, and William Luis. "Feminist Artist Statement." Brooklyn Museum, 2023. https://www.brooklynmuseum.org/eascfa/about/feminist_art_base/maria-magdalena-campos-pons.

Cannella, Gino. "#BlackIsBeautiful: The Radical Politics of Black Hair," *Visual Studies*35, no. 2–3 (2020): 273–84.

Cano, Regina. "The Abakua Sect in Cuba." *Havana Times, Open Minded Writing*, 2022, 1. https://havanatimes.org/diaries/regina/the-abakua-sect-in-cuba/.

Carby, Hazel. "White Woman Listen! Black Feminism and the Boundaries of Sisterhood." In *CCCS Selected Working Papers*, edited by Ann Gray, Jan Campbell, Mark Erickson, Stuart Hanson, and Helen Wood. Routledge, 2007, 753–74.

Casamayor-Cisneros, Odette. *Utopía, distopía e ingravidez: Reconfiguraciones cosmológicas en la narrativa postnacional del siglo XXI*. Iberoamericana/Vervuert, 2013.

Casamayor-Cisneros, Odette. "Cuando Las Negras Se Desnudan: La Experiencia Inasible del Cuerpo Caribeño y Afro-Diaspórico en la Creación Plástica de María Magdalena Campos-Pons y la Narrativa de Mayra Santos Febres." *Revista Iberoamericana* 77, no. 236 (2011): 873–88.

Cassandra, Rachel, and Gucik, Lauren. *Women Street Artists of Latin America: Art Without Fear*. Manic D Press, 2015.

Castañeda Fuertes, Digna. "La mujer esclava en Cuba durante la primera mitad del siglo xix," *Anales del Caribe* 13, no. 1 (1993–1994): 53–69.

Cheryl, Finley, and Salah M. Hassan. *Diaspora Memory Place: David Hammons, Maria Magdalena Campos-Pons and Pamela Z*. Prestel, 2008.

Chwalkowski, Farrin. *Symbols in Arts, Religion and Culture: The Soul of Nature*. Cambridge Scholars Publishing, 2016.

Cleveland, Christena. *God Is a Black Woman*. HarperOne, 2022.

Cohen, Theodore W. *Finding Afro-Mexico: Race and Nation After the Revolution*. Cambridge University Press, 2020.

Collins, Patricia Hill. *Black Feminist Thought: Knowledge, Consciousness, and the Politics of Empowerment*. 2d ed. Routledge, 2000a.

Collins, Patricia Hill. "Gender, Black Feminism, and Black Political Economy." *Annals of the American Academy of Political and Social Science* 568, no. 1 (2000b): 41–53.

Combahee River Collective. "A Black Feminist Statement." *Women's Studies Quarterly* 42, no. 3/4 (2014): 271–80.

Cooper, A. J. *A Voice from the South: Xenia*. Aldine Printing House, 1892.

Coplan, Amy, and Goldie Peter. *Empathy: Philosophical and Psychological Perspectives*. Oxford University Press, 2011.

Cordones-Cook, Juanamaría. "Zurbano and His Racial Consciousness/y su conciencia racial," (2022).

Cornett. Peggy, "Pinks, Gilliflowers, & Carnations." *The Exalted Flowers | Thomas Jefferson's Monticello*, January 1998. www.monticello.org. Retrieved March 8, 2023.

Cotton, J. C. "The People of Old Calabar." *Journal of the Royal African Society* 4, no. 15 (1905): 302–6.

Crenshaw, Kimberle. "Mapping the Margins: Intersectionality, Identity Politics, and Violence Against Women of Color." *Stanford Law Review* 43, no. 1 (1991): 1241–99.

Cruz-Janzen, Marta I. 2001. "Latinegras." *Frontiers* 22, no. 3 (2001).

Cuervo Hewitt, Julia. *Voices Out of Africa in Twentieth Century Spanish Caribbean Literature.* Bucknell University Press, 2009.

Curiel, Ochy. "Crítica poscolonial desde las practices del feminism antirracista." *Nómadas* 26, no. 1 (2007): 92–101.

Curiel, Ochy. "Hacia la construcción de un feminismo descolonizado: A propósito de la realización del Encuentro Feminista Autónomo: Haciendo Comunidad en la Casa de las Diferencias." In *Feminismos en el Abya Yala: Miradas Críticas y Diálogos en Tiempos de Luchas por la Descolonización*, edited by María Jesús Martínez Alonso et al. Editorial Universidad de Granada, 2019.

Curiel, Ochy. "Identidades esencialistas o construcción de identidades políticas: El dilemma de las feministas afroodescendientes." *Otras Miradas* 2, no. 2 (2005): 96–13.

Curiel, Ochy. "Los aportes de las afrodescendientes a la teoría y la práctica feminista: Desuniversalizando el sujeto mujeres." In *Perfiles del feminismo iberoamericano*, edited by María Luisa Femenías. Buenos Aires: Catálogos, 2007, 159–76.

Dache, Amalia, Mariana Fuentes, Cheryl Matias, Cristina Morales, and Tracie Léost. "A Badge of Honor Not Shame: An AfroLatina Theory of Black-Imiento for U.S. Higher Education Research." *Journal of Negro Education* 88, no. 2 (2019): 130–45.

Davis, Angela. *Women, Race & Class.* 1st Vintage Books edition. Vintage Books, 1983.

Dazed. "Harmonia Rosales Repaints Classic Artworks to Show God Is a Black Woman." 2018. https://www.dazeddigital.com/art-photography/article/41202/1/harmonia-rosales-repaints-classic-artworks-god-is-a-black-woman-rjd-gallery.

DeCosta-Willis, Miriam, eds. *Daughters of the Diaspora: Afra-Hispanic Writers.* Ian Randle, 2003.

de la Fuente, Alejandro. "Mitos de 'Democracia Racial': Cuba 1900–1912." In *Espacios, silencios y los sentidos de la libertad: Cuba entre 1878 y 1912*, edited by Fernando Martínez Heredia, Rebecca J. Scott, and Orlando García Martínez. Unión, 2001, 235–69.

de la Fuente, Alejandro. *A Nation for All: Race, Inequality, and Politics Century Cuba.* University of North Carolina Press, 2001.

de la Fuente, Alejandro. "Slave Law and Claims-Making in Cuba: The Tannenbaum Debate Revisited." *Law and History Review* 22, no. 2 (2004): 339–69.

de la Fuente, Alejandro. "Tengo una raza oscura y discriminada' El movimiento afrocubano: hacia un programa consensuado." *Nueva Sociedad* 242, no. 1 (2012): 92–105.

de la Fuente, Alejandro. *Una nación para todos. Raza, desigualdad y política en Cuba 1900–2000.* Colibrí, 2000.

Desch-Obi, T. J. "Peinillas and Popular Participation: Machete Fighting in Haiti, Cuba, and Colombia." *Revista Digital de Historia y Arqueología desde el Caribe* 1, no. XI (2009).

Duany, J. "Neither White nor Black: The Representation of Racial Identity Among Puerto Ricans on the Island and in the U.S. Mainland. In *Neither Enemies nor Friends*, edited by A. Dzidzienya and S. Oboler. Palgrave Macmillan, 2005, 173–88.

Du Bois, W. E. B. *The Souls of Black Folk.* Barnes and Noble Books, 2003.

Duharte Jiménez, Rafael. "Tres mujeres cubanas hablan de prejuicios raciales," *América Negra, Bogotá* 12, no. 1, 1996, 159–72.

Duke, Dawn. *Literary Passion, Ideological Commitment Toward a Legacy of Afro-Cuban and Afro-Brazilian Women Writers.* Bucknell University Press, 2008.

Economic Commission for Latin America and the Caribbean. *Afrodescendants and the Matrix of Social Inequality in Latin America: Challenges for Inclusion,* 2021. http://hdl.handle.net/11362/46871.

Eltis, David, Stanley L. Engerman, K. R. Bradley, Paul Cartledge, Craig Perry, David Richardson, and Seymour Drescher, eds. *The Cambridge World History of Slavery.* Cambridge University Press, 2011.

Engels, Friedrich. *The Origin of the Family, Private Property, and of the State.* Electric Book Company, 2001.

Espín, Vilma. "A Revolution Within a Revolution." Interview by Deborah Shnookal, September 1988. Reprinted in *Cuban Women Confront the Future*, edited by Deborah Shnookal and Mirta Yáñez. Ocean Press, 1991, 7–14.

Espinosa Miñoso, Yuderkys, Gómez Diana, and Ochoa Karina, eds. *Tejiendo de Otro Modo: Feminismo, epistemología y apuestas descoloniales en Abya Yala.* Editorial de la Universidad del Cauca, 2014.

Equiano, Olaudah. *The Interesting Narrative of the Life of Olaudah Equiano, or, Gustavus Vassa, the African.* Broadview Press, 2001.

Fabricant, Nicole, and Nancy Postero. "Contested Bodies, Contested States: Performance, Emotions, and New Forms of Regional Governance in Santa Cruz, Bolivia." *Journal of Latin American and Caribbean Anthropology* 18, no. 2 (2013): 187–21.

Facio, Elisa, and Irene Lara, eds. *Fleshing the Spirit: Spirituality and Activism in Chicana, Latina, and Indigenous Women's Lives.* University of Arizona Press, 2014.

Faguada Iglesias, María Elena. "La mujer afrocubana." In *La memoria y el olvido: Syllabus afrocubano*, edited by Juan F. Benemelis. La Ceiba, 2009, 250–66.

Fajardo-Hill, Cecilia, Andrea Giunta, and Marcela Guerrero. *Radical Women: Latin American Art, 1960–1985*. Prestel, 2017.

Falola, Toyin. *Decolonizing African Knowledge: Autoethnigraphy and African Epistemologies*. Cambridge University Press, 2022.

Fanon, Frantz. *The Black Skin, White Masks and the Wretched of the Earth as Visionary Apprehensions of Reality*. Trans. Chester J. Fontenot. University of California Press, 1952.

Fernández Robaina, Tomás. *El negro en Cuba. Colonia, república, revolución*. Editorial de Ciencias Sociales, 2012.

Fernández Robaina, Tomás. "El término 'afrocubano': Una contribución olvidada de Fernando Ortiz." In *Identidad afrocubana: Cultura y nacionalidad*, edited by Lourdes Canabal Antúnez and Mario Castillo Santana. Editorial Oriente, 2009, 73–84.

Ferrer, Ada. *Insurgent Cuba: Race, Nation, and Revolution, 1868–1898*. University of North Carolina Press, 1999.

Figueroa-Vázquez, Yomaira C. "After the Hurricane: Afro-Latina Decolonial Feminisms and Destierro." *Hypatia* 35, no. 1 (2020): 220–29.

Figueroa-Vázquez, Yomaira C. *Decolonial Diasporas: Radical Mappings of Afro-Atlantic Literatures*. Northwestern University Press, 2021.

FitzPatrick Sifford, Elena. "A Fly in Milk: Fear and Black (In)visbility in New Spanish Painting." In *Emotions, Art, and Christianity in the Transatlantic World, 1450–1800*, edited by Heather Graham and Lauren G. Kilroy-Ewbank. Brill, 2021, 345–73.

Flores, Juan, and Miriam Jiménez Román. *The Afro-Latin@ Reader: History and Culture in the United States*. Duke University Press, 2010.

Franklin, Sarah L. *Women and Slavery in Nineteenth-Century Colonial Cuba*. University Rochester Press, 2012.

Foucault, Michel. *The Archeology of Knowledge*. Translated from the French by A. M. Sheridan Smith. Pantheon, 1972.

Freire, G., Diaz-Bonilla, C., Orellana, S., Lopez, J., and Carbonari, F. *Afro-Descendants in Latin America: Toward a Framework of Inclusion*. World Bank, 2018.

Fusco, Coco. *The Bodies That Were Not Ours: And Other Writings*. Routledge, 2001.

Glenn, E. N. "Yearning for Lightness: Transnational Circuits in the Marketing and Consumption of Skin Lighteners." *Gender & Society* 22: 2008: 281–302.

Godreau, I., Reyes Cruz, M., Franco Ortiz, M., and Cuadrado, S. "The Lessons of Slavery: Discourses of Slavery, Mestizaje, and Blanqueamiento in an Elementary School in Puerto Rico." *American Ethnologist* 35, no. 1 (2008): 115–35.

Gómez, Shirley. "First Look at Celia Cruz US Quarter Coin." *Hola.com*, July 26, 2023. Accessed September 16, 2023. https://www.hola.com/us/celebrities/20230726348471/first-look-at-celia-cruzs-us-quarter-coin/.

Gonzalez, Anita. *Afro-Mexico Dancing Between Myth and Reality*. 1st ed. University of Texas Press, 2010.

Gonzalez-Barrera, A. "Hispanics with Darker Skin Are More Likely to Experience Discrimination than Those with Lighter Skin." *Pew Research Center*, 2019. https://www.pewresearch.org/fact-tank/2019/07/02/hispanics-with-darker-skin-are-more-likely-to-experience-discrimination-than-those-with-lighter-skin.

Gonzalez-Barrera A., and López G. "Afro-Latino: A Deeply Rooted Identity Among US Hispanics." *Pew Research Center*, 2016. http://www.pewresearch.org/fact-tank/2016/03/01/afro-latino-a-deeply-rooted-identity-among-u-s-hispanics/.

González Gómez, Cásseres. "Sikanékue, mujer fundacional en Abakuá." *Afro-Hispanic Review* 35 (2016): 111–23.

González Mandri, Flora. *Guarding Cultural Memory: Afro-Cuban Women in Literature and the Arts*. University of Virginia Press, 2006.

González Pagés, Julio César. *En busca de un espacio: Historia de mujeres en Cuba*. Editorial de Ciencias Sociales, 2006.

Guerra, Lillian. *Visions of Power in Cuba: Revolution, Redemption, and Resistance, 1959–1971*. University of North Carolina Press, 2012.

Gutman, H. *The Black Family in Slavery and Freedom, 1750–1925*. Pantheon Books, 1976.

Hall, Gwendolyn Midlo. *Slavery and African Ethnicities in the Americas: Restoring the Links*. University of North Carolina Press, 2005.

Hackett, Susanne, Isabel C. Millán, Ana M. López, and Santiago Ochoa. "A Re-Visionist Her-Story of *De cierta manera* ([1974] 1977): Reading Yoruba Myth in Sara Gómez's Revolutionary Classic." *Studies in Spanish & Latin American Cinemas* 18, no. 2 (2021): 195–210.

Hagedorn, Katherine J. *Divine Utterances: The Performance of Afro-Cuban Santería*. Smithsonian Institution Press, 2001.

Hall, Stuart. "Cultural Identity and Diaspora." In *Identity: Community, Culture, Difference*, edited by J. Rutherford. Lawrence & Wishart, 1990, 222–37.

Hall, Stuart. "The Spectacle of the 'Other.'" In *Representation: Cultural Representations and Signifying Practices*, edited by Stuart Hall, SAGE Publications, 1997, 223–79.

Hammons, David, Maria Magdalena Campos-Pons, and Pamela Z. *Diaspora Memory Place: David Hammons, Maria Magdalena Campos-Pons, Pamela Z.* Prestel, 2008.

Harney, Elizabeth, Salah M. Hassan, and Kobena Mercer. "Black Art and Culture in the 20th Century." *Nka: Journal of Contemporary African Art*, no. 10 (1999): 69.

Harris, A. "From Color Line to Color Chart: Racism and Colorism in the New Century." *Berkeley Journal of African American Law and Policy* 10, no. 1 (2008): 52–64.

Harris, Michael D. "Meanwhile the Girls Were Playing: Maria Magdalena Campos-Pons." *Nka: Journal of Contemporary African Art* 13, no. 1 (July 2011): 48–55.

Hartman, Saidiya V. *Lose Your Mother: A Journey Along the Atlantic Slave Route.* Macmillan, 2008.

Hassan, Salah. "Maria Magdalena Campos-Pons: Interiority or Hill-Sided Moon." *Nka: Journal of Contemporary African Art*, no. 19 (2004): 94–96.

Helg, Aline. *Lo que nos corresponde. La lucha de los negros y mulatos por la igualdad en Cuba 1886–1912.* Imagen Contemporánea, 2000.

Heller, Eva. *Psicología del Color: Efectos y Símbolos.* Pirámide, 2009.

Henkes, Robert. *Latin American Women Artists of the United States: The Works of 33 Twentieth-Century Women.* McFarland, 2008.

Hernández, T. "Too Black to Be Latino/a: Blackness and Blacks as Foreigners in Latino Studies." *Latino Studies* 1, no. 1 (2003): 152–61.

Heywood, Linda M. *Njinga of Angola: Africa's Warrior Queen.* Harvard University Press, 2017.

Heywood, Linda M., and Luis Madureira (trans.). "Queen Njinga Mbandi Ana de Sousa of Ndongo/Matamba: African Leadership, Diplomacy, and Ideology, 1620s–1650s." In *Afro-Latino Voices: Narratives from the Early Modern Ibero-Atlantic World, 1550–1812*, edited by Kathryn Joy McKnight and Leo J. Garofalo, 38–51. Hackett, 2009.

Hill Collins, Patricia. *Black Feminist Thought: Knowledge, Consciousness, and the Politics of Empowerment.* Unwin Hyman, 1990.

Hill, M. E. "Skin Color and the Perception of Attractiveness Among African Americans: Does Gender Make a Difference?" *Social Psychology Quarterly* 65 (2002): 77–91.

Hoetink, Harmannus. *Slavery and Race Relations in the Americas: Comparative Notes on Their Nature and Nexus.* Harper & Row, 1973.

Holder, Michelle, and Alan A. Aja. *Afro-Latinos in the U.S. Economy.* Lexington Books, 2021.

hooks, bell. *Ain't I a Woman: Black Women and Feminism.* Routledge, Taylor & Francis, 2015.

hooks, bell. *Black Looks: Race and Representation.* South End Press, 1992a.

hooks, bell. *Feminist Theory: From Margin to Center.* South End Press, 1984.

hooks, bell. "The Oppositional Gaze: Black Female Spectators." In *Black Looks: Race and Representation.* South End Press, 1992b, 115–31.

hooks, bell. "Straightening Our Hair." *Z Magazine*, 2007. https://znetwork.org/zmagazine/straightening-our-hair-by-bell-hooks/.

Hordge-Freeman, E., and Veras, E. "Out of the Shadows, Into the Dark: Ethnoracial Dissonance and Identity Formation Among Afro-Latinxs." *Sociology of Race and Ethnicity* 6, no. 2 (2020): 146–60.

Hughes M., and Hertel B. R. "The Significance of Color Remains: A Study of Life Chances, Mate Selection, and Ethnic Consciousness Among Black Americans." *Social Forces* 68 (1990): 1105–20.

Hull, Alasha Gloria. *Soul Talk: The New Spirituality of African American Women.* Inner Traditions, 2001.

Hunt, P. "Swathed in Cloth: The Headwraps of Some African American Women in Georgia and South Carolina During the Late Nineteenth and Early Twentieth Centuries." *Dress: The Journal of the Costume Society of America* 21, no. 1 (1994): 30–38.

Hunter, M. *Gender, Race, and the Politics of Skin Tone.* New York: Routledge, 2005.Hunter, M. "The Persistent Problem of Colorism: Skin Tone, Status, and Inequality." *Sociology Compass* 1 (2007): 237–54.

Jacobs-Huey, L. *From the Kitchen to the Parlor: Language and Becoming in African American Women's Hair Care.* Oxford University Press, 2006.

James, Conrad, ed. *Writing the Afro-Hispanic: Essays on Africa and Africans in the Spanish Caribbean.* Adonis & Abbey, 2012.

Jewell, K. Sue. *From Mammy to Miss America and Beyond: Cultural Images and the Shaping of U.S. Social Policy.* Routledge, 1993.

Jiménez Román, Miriam. "Allá y Acá: Locating Puerto Ricans in the Diaspora(s)." *Diálogo* 5, no. 1 (2001): 10–13.

Jiménez Román, Miriam. "Looking at that Middle Ground: Racial Mixing as Panacea?" *A Companion to Latina/o Studies*, edited by Juan Flores and Renato Rosaldo. Blackwell, 2007, 325–36.

Jorge, Angela. "The Black Puerto Rican Woman in Contemporary American Society." *The Afro-Latin@ Reader*, edited by Miriam Jiménez Román and Juan Flores. Duke University Press, 2010, 269–75.

Keith, V. M., and Herring C. "Skin Tone and Stratification in the Black Community." *American Journal of Sociology* 97 (1991): 760–78.

Keosha Brunson, Takkara. "Constructing Afro-Cuban Womanhood: Race, Gender and Citizenship in Republica-Era Cuba 1902–1958." PhD diss., University of Austin Texas, 2011.

Keys, Domale D., Moya Bailey, and Alexis Pauline Gumbs. "Black Women's Lives Matter: Social Movements and Storytelling Against Sexual and Gender-Based Violence in the US." *Feminist Review* 128, no. 1 (2021): 163–68.

Klein, Herbert S., and Ben Vinson III. *African Slavery in Latin America and the Caribbean.* Oxford University Press, 2007.

Lammoglia, Jose A. "Legal Aspects of Animal Sacrifice Within the Context of Afro-Caribbean Religions." *St. Thomas Law Review* 20, no. 1 (2007).

Landor A. M., L. G. Simons, R. L. Simons, et al. "Exploring the Impact of Skin Tone on Family Dynamics and Race-Related Outcomes." *Journal of Family Psychology*27 (2013): 817–26.

Laó-Montes, Agustín. "Afro-Latin American Feminisms at the Cutting Edge of Emerging Political-Epistemic Movements." *Meridians: Feminism, Race, Transnationalism* 4, no. 2 (2016): 1–24.

Lawal, Babatunde. "Reclaiming the Past: Yoruba Elements in African American Arts." In *The Yoruba Diaspora in the Atlantic World*, edited by Toyin Falola and Matt D. Childs, 291–324. Indiana University Press, 2004.

Lefrançois, Frédéric. "Decolonizing Trans-American Skin Memory." *NaKaN: A Journal of Cultural Studies* 1, no. 1 (2022).

Lepecki, André. "The Body as Archive: Will to Re-Enact and the Afterlives of Dances." *Dance Research Journal* 42, no. 2 (2010): 28–48.

Lindsey, Linda L. "The Sociology of Gender." In *Gender Roles: A Sociological Perspective*, edited by Claire M. Renzetti and Daniel J. Curran. Pearson, 2015.

Lisocka-Jaegermann, Bogumiła, Magdalena Rzeczkowska, and Magdalena Wróblewska. "Debates on Women and Femininity in Cuban Santería: Postcolonial Interpretations." *Studia Religiologica* 52, no. 3 (2019): 177–90.

López Oro, José. "Ni de aquí, ni de allá: Garífuna Subjectivities and the Politics of Diasporic Belonging." In *Afro-Latin@s in Movement: Critical Approaches to Blackness and Transnationalism in the Americas*, edited by Petra R. Rivera-Rideau, Jennifer A. Jones, and Tianna S. Paschel. Palgrave Macmillan, 2016.

López Oro, Paul Joseph. "Refashioning Afro-Latinidad: Garifuna New Yorkers in Diaspora." In *Critical Diálogos in Latina and Latino Studies*, edited by Ana Y. Ramos-Zayas and Mérida M. Rúa. New York University Press, 2021, 223–40.

Lorde, Audre. "Learning from the 60s." *SOS: Calling All Black People*, edited by John H. Bracey, Sonia Sanchez, and James Smethurst. University of Massachusetts Press, 2015.

Lorde, Audre. "The Master's Tools Will Never Dismantle the Master's House." In *Sister Outsider: Essays and Speeches*. Crossing Press, 2007, 110–14.

Lorde, Audre. *Sister Outsider: Essays and Speeches*. Crossing Press, 1984.

Lorde, Audre. *Zami, A New Spelling of My Name*. Crossing Press, 1982.

Louise, René. "The Great Conceptual Maroonism." In *Manifesto of Modern Maroonism: A Philosophy of Aesthetics*, edited by Kehinde Andrews and Jamal Torres. Yehkri, 2018.

Lugones, María. "Colonialidad y género: hacia un feminismo descolonial." In *Género y descolonialidad*, edited by Walter Mignolo. Ediciones del Signo, 2008, 13–54.

Lugones, María. "Heterosexualism and the Colonial/Modern Gender System." *Hypatia* 22, no. 11 (2006): 196.

Lugones, María. "Toward a Decolonial Feminism." *Hypatia* 1, no. 25 (2010): 742–59.

Maguire, Emily. *Escritura gráfica Kongo y otras narrativas del signo*. El Colegio de México, 2012.

Maguire, Emily. "The Eusebia Cosme Show: Translating an Afro-Antillean Identity." In *Writing the Afro-Hispanic: Essays on Africa and Africans in the Spanish Caribbean*, edited by Conrad James. Adonis & Abbey, 2012, 77–98.

Maguire, Emily. *Things That Cannot Be Seen Any Other Way: The Art of Manuel Mendive*. Frost Museum of Art, 2013.

Maldonado-Torres, Nelson. "Thinking Through the Decolonial Turn: Post-Continental Interventions in Theory, Philosophy, and Critique, an Introduction." *Transmodernity: Journal of Peripheral Cultural Production of the Luso-Hispanic World* 1, no. 2 (2011).

Marcos, Sylvia, ed. *Women and Indigenous Religions*. Praeger, 2010.

Martel, Manuel Piedra. *Campañas de Maceo en la última Guerra de Independencia*. Editorial Lex, 1946, 68–72.

Martín Sevillano, Ana Belén. "Crisscrossing Gender, Ethnicity, and Race: African Religious Legacy in Cuban Contemporary Women's Art." *Cuban Studies* 42, no. 1 (2011): 136–54.

Martínez-Ruiz, Bárbaro. "Ma kisi Nsi: L'art des habitants de région de Mbanza Kongo." In *Angola figures de pouvoir*, edited by Christiane Falgayrettes-Leveau, Musée Dapper, 2010, 2–39.

Martínez Toledo, Yanet, ed. *Emancipaciones feministas del siglo XXI*. Ruth Casa Editorial, 2010, 189–200.

Mason, Michael Atwood. *Living Santería: Rituals and Experiences in an Afro-Cuban Religion*. Smithsonian Institution, 2002.

Mattes, Mark C. "Image and Spirit: Finding Meaning in Visual Art." *Currents in Theology and Mission* 32, no. 5 (October 2005), 381.

May, Vivian M. *Pursuing Intersectionality: Unsettling Dominant Imaginaries*. Routledge, 2015.

McIver Lopes, Dominic. "An Empathic Eye." In *Empathy: Philosophical and Psychological Perspectives*, edited by Amy Coplan and Peter Goldie. Oxford University Press, 2011, 118–33.

McKnight, K., and Garofalo, L., eds. *Afro-Latino Voices: Narratives from the Early Modern Ibero-Atlantic World, 1550–1812*. Hackett Publishing, 2009.

Medeiros, Melanie A., and Perry Keisha-Khan Y., eds. *Black Women in Latin America and the Caribbean*. Rutgers University Press, 2023.

Menchaca, M. *Recovering History, Constructing Race: The Indian, Black, and White Roots of Mexican Americans*. University of Texas Press, 2001.

Méndez, María José. "'The River Told Me': Rethinking Intersectionality from the World of Berta Cáceres." *Capitalism Nature Socialism* 29, no. 1 (2018), 7–24.

Menéndez, Lázara. "Un Viaje a Través de Las Artes Plásticas . . . ¿afrocubanas?" *Afro-Hispanic Review* 36, no. 2 (September 2017), 163–79.

Mercer, K. "Black Hair/Style Politics." *New Formation* 3 (1987): 33–54.

Mercer, K. "Black Hair/Style Politics." In *Out There: Marginalization and Contemporary Cultures*, edited by Russell Ferguson, Martha Gever, Trinh T. Minh-ha, and Cornel West. New Museum of Contemporary Art, 1990, 247–64.

Miller, T. R. "Hair in African Art and Culture," *American Anthropologist* 103, no. 1 (2001): 182–88.

Mitchell, Claudia, and Jacqueline Reid-Walsh, eds. *Girl Culture* (2 volumes): *An Encyclopedia*. Greenwood, 2008.

Mitchell, Natalie A., Darrick J. Hamilton, Geraldine Rosa Henderson, and Sonya A. Grier. "Representation of Women of Color on the Covers of the Top Three Fashion Magazines: A Content Analysis." *Journal of Consumer Marketing* 40, no. 5 (2022): 597–608.

Montejo, Carmen. "Minerva: A Magazine for Women (and Men) of Color." In *Between Race and Empire: African-Americans and Cubans Before the Cuban Revolution*, edited by Lisa Brock and Digna Castañeda Fuertes. Philadelphia: Temple University Press, 1998, 33–49.

Moraga, Cherríe, and Gloria Anzaldúa. *This Bridge Called My Back: Writing by Radical Women of Color*. Women of Color Press, 1981.

Morales, Beatriz. "Afro-Cuban Religious Transformation: A Comparative Study of Lucumi Religion and the Tradition of Spirit Belief." PhD thesis, City University of New York, 1990.

Morales, Helen. "Harmonia Rosales: Entwined." *The AD&A Museum*, 2022, 1–20.

Moreno Vega, Marta, Marta Moreno-Vega, Marinieves Alba, and Yvette Modestin. *Women Warriors of the Afro-Latina Diaspora*. Arte Público Press, 2012.

Morgan, Nigel, Annette Pritchard, and Derek R. Hall. "Gender, Advertising and Ethics: Marketing Cuba." In *Tourism and Cuba*, edited by Nigel Morgan, Annette Pritchard, and Derek R. Hall, 119–36. Channel View Publications, 2020.

Morris, Margaret Lindsay. *The Afro-Latino Voice in World Literature*. Edwin Mellen Press, 2003.

Munanga, Kabengele. "Arte afro-brasileira: o que é, a final?" In *Mostra do redescobrimento: Arte afro-brasileira*, edited by Nelson Aguilar. Associação Brasil 500 Anos Artes Visuais, 2000, 98–111.

Murray, David. "The Slave Trade, Slavery and Cuban Independence." *Slavery and Abolition* 20, no. 3 (1999): 106–26.

Nair, Kannan K. *Politics and Society in South Eastern Nigeria, 1841–1906: A Study of Power, Diplomacy and Commerce in Old Calabar*. Frank Cass, 1972.

Noël, Samantha A. "Disrupting Subaltern Geographies: The Artistic Intersections of Belkis Ayón." *Transnational Belonging and Female Agency in the Arts*. Wayne State University Press, 2022, 161–78.

Oboler, Suzanne, and Anani Dzidzienyo, eds. *Neither Enemies nor Friends: Latinos, Blacks, Afro-Latinos*. Palgrave Macmillan, 2005.

Olmos, Margarite Fernández, and Lizabeth Paravisini-Gebert. "The Afro-Cuban Religious Traditions of Regla de Palo and the Abakuá Secret Society." *Creole Religions of the Caribbean*. 3rd ed. New York University Press, 2022, 101–29.

Ortíz, Fernando. *La Africanía de la musica folklorica de Cuba*. La Habana, 1950.

Ortíz, Fernando. *Hampa Afro-Cubana: Los Negros Esclavo; Estudio Sociológico y de Derecho Público*. Forgotten Books, 2015.

Oslender, Ulrich, Arturo Escobar, and Joanne Rappaport. "Revisiting the Hidden Transcript: Oral Tradition and Black Cultural Politics in the Colombian Pacific Coast Region." *Environment and Planning D: Society and Space* 25, no. 6 (2007): 1103–29.

Palmié, Stephan. *The Cooking of History: How Not to Study Afro-Cuban Religion*. University of Chicago Press, 2013.

Paoletti, Jo B. *Pink and Blue: Telling the Girls from the Boys in America*. Indiana University Press, 2012.

Paschel, T. "The Right to Difference: Explaining Colombia's Shift from Color Blindness to the Law of Black Communities. *American Journal of Sociology* 116, no. 3 (2010) 729–69.

Pasquali, Elaine Anne. "Santeria." *Journal of Holistic Nursing* 12, no. 4 (1994): 380–90.

Simmons, Donald C. *Analysis of the Reflection of Culture in Efik Folktales*. PhD diss., Yale University, 1958.

Patton, T. O. "Hey Girl, Am I More than My Hair? African American Women and Their Struggles with Beauty, Body Image, and Hair." *National Women's Studies Association Journal* 18, no. 2 (2006): 24–51.

Pease, Silvia Márquez, "Belkis Ayón: Fear, Confusion, Trance, Dignity, and the Sublime." Department of Art and Art History, 2022. https://digitalcommons.fiu.edu/art-art-history/.

Pérez, Louis A., Jr. *Cuba Under de Platt Amendment*. University of Pittsburgh Press, 1986.

Perez Lopez, Y. "Mestizaje Ideology as Color-Blind Racism: Students' Discourses of Colorism and Racism in Mexico." PhD diss., Syracuse University, 2017.

Pew Research Center. *Afro-Latino: A Deeply Rooted Identity Among U.S. Hispanics*, 2016. https://www.pewresearch.org/fact-tank/2016/03/01/afro-latino-a-deeply-rooted-identityamong-u-s-hispanics/.

Pichardo, Maikel Colón. "Racismo y Feminismo en Cuba: ¿Dos mitades y una misma naranja? Claves históricas para su estudio." *Boletín Americanista* 72, no. 1 (2016): 179–98.

Postma, J. *The Atlantic Slave Trade*. Greenwood Press, 2003.

Prieto, René. *Body of Writing: Figuring Desire in Spanish American Literature*. Duke University Press, 2000.

Quesada, Sarah, Vanessa K. Valdés, and Yolanda Martínez-San Miguel. "The Dual Biopolitics in the Cuban Postplantation of Gloria Rolando's *Raíces de mi corazón*." *Small Axe: A Caribbean Journal of Criticism* 25, no. 2 (2021): 50–68.

Quijano, Aníbal. "Coloniality and Modernity/Rationality." In *Globalization and the Decolonial Option*, edited by Walter Mignolo and Árturo Escobar. Routledge, 2010, 22–32.

Quinn, Rachel Afi. *Being La Dominicana: Race and Identity in the Visual Culture of Santo Domingo*. University of Illinois Press, 2021.

Rahier, Jean Muteba, and Mamyrah A. Dougé-Prosper. "Interview with María Alexandra Ocles Padilla, Former Minister, *Secretaría de Pueblos, Movimientos Sociales y Participación Ciudadana,* Ecuador." In *Black Social Movements in Latin America: From Monocultural Mestizaje to Multiculturalism,* edited by Jean Muteba Rahier, Palgrave Macmillan, 2012, 169–84.

Rahier, Jean Muteba, and Mamyrah A. Dougé-Prosper. "Interview with Maria *Inês* Barbosa, Former Vice-Minister, *Secretaria Especial de Políticas de* Promoção *da Igualdade Racial* (SEPPIR), Brazil." In *Black Social Movements in Latin America: From Monocultural Mestizaje to Multiculturalism,* edited by Jean Muteba Rahier. Palgrave Macmillan, 2012, 213–24.

Ramos, Julio, Esteban Luis Cárdenas Grant, and Zaira Zarza. "Um cinema afro-cubano? Conversa com Gloria Rolando/An Afro-Cuban Cinema? Chat with Gloria Rolando." *Revista Contracampo* (2013): 34–48.

Ramsay, Paulette A., and Antonio D. Tillis, eds. *The Afro-Hispanic Reader and Anthology.* Ian Randle Publishers, 2018.

Rawick, G. P., ed. *The American Slave: A Composite Autobiography.* Greenwood Press, 1972.

Ray, V. "A Theory of Racialized Organizations." *American Sociological Review* 84, no. 1 (2019): 26–53.

Rediker, Marcus Buford. *The Slave Ship: A Human History.* Viking, 2007.

Reyes, Castriela E., Edna Bonilla, and Aurora Vergara-Figueroa. "Black Women's Struggles Against Extractivism, Land Dispossession, and Marginalization in Colombia." *Latin American Perspectives* 46, no. 2 (2019): 217–34.

Ribando, C. *Afro-Latinos in Latin America and Considerations for U.S. Policy: CRS Report for Congress.* Congressional Research Service, Library of Congress, 2005.

Richardson, Jill Toliver. *The Afro-Latin@ Experience in Contemporary American Literature and Culture: Engaging Blackness.* Springer, 2016.

Rivero, Eliana. "Fronterisleña, Border Islander." *Michigan Quarterly Review* 33, no. 4 (1994): 669–74.

Rivera-Rideau, Petra R., Jennifer A Jones, and Tianna S. Paschel (eds.). *Afro-Latin@s in Movement: Critical Approaches to Blackness and Transnationalism in the Americas.* Palgrave Macmillan, 2016.

Rochin, R. "Latinos and Afro-Latino Legacy in the United States: History, Culture, and Issues of Identity." *Professional Agricultural Workers Journal* 3, no. 2 (2016). http://tuspubs.tuskegee.edu/pawj/vol3/iss2/2.

Rodríguez-Mangual, Edna M. *Lydia Cabrera and the Construction of an Afro-Cuban Cultural Identity.* University of North Carolina Press, 2004.

Román Jiménez, M., and Flores, J. *The Afro-Latin Reader.* Duke University Press, 2010.

Rout, Leslie B., Jr. *The African Experience in Spanish America: 1502 to the Present Day.* Markus Wiener, 2003.

Roselin Rodríguez Espinosa. *Susana Pilar Delahante: Reclaiming Space Through Performance* (interview). 12th Berlin Biennale, July 2022.

Rosenthal, A. "Raising Hair," *Eighteenth-Century Studies* 38, no. 1 (2004): 1–16.

Roth, Benita. "Second-Wave Black Feminism in the African Diaspora: News from New Scholarship."*Agenda: Empowering Women for Gender Equity*1, no. 58 (2003): 46–58.

Rubiera Castillo, Daisy. "Apuntes sobre la mujer negra cubana." *Cuban Studies* 42, no. 1 (2011): 176–85.

Rubiera, Daisy, and Maria Ines Martiatu, ed. *Afrocubanas: Historia, Pensamiento y Prácticas Culturales.* Ciencias Sociales, 2013.

Ruiz, Ada. "Harmonia Rosales: Black Femininity in Classical Artworks." *Los Angeles Academy of Figurative Art*, exhibition catalog, 2018.

Scerbo, Rosita. *The Afro-Descendant Woman in Latin American Diasporic Visual Art.* Routledge, 2024.

Scerbo, Rosita. "Bridging the Gap Between Literature and Visual Art: Reimagining Black Femininity Through an Ekphrastic Analysis of Harmonia Rosales' Decolonial Feminist Aesthetics," *Hispanic Journal* 44, no. 2 (2023): 125–47.

Scerbo, Rosita. "Centering Black Women, Challenging Latinidad: Harmonia Rosales' Black Decolonial Aesthetics and AfroARTivism." *Confluencia* 39, no. 2 (2024): 2–20.

Scerbo, Rosita. "El arte visual como práctica feminista decolonial: feminidad negra y ARTivismo afrocubano en las pinturas de Harmonia Rosales." *Perspectivas Afro: Journal of Afro Latin American and Afro Caribbean Studies* 3, no. 2 (January–June 2024): 385–404.

Scerbo, Rosita. "Reimagining Black Femininity: Afro-Latina's Decolonial Aesthetics and AfroARTivism." In *Introduction to Women's, Gender and Sexuality Studies: Interdisciplinary and Intersectional Approaches*, 3rd ed., edited by L. Ayu Saraswati, Barbara L. Shaw, and Heather Rellihan. Oxford University Press, forthcoming.

Scerbo, Rosita. "Reimagining Mythical Spaces: Spiritualized Afro-feminism and Decolonial Aesthetics in the Visual Expression of Afro-Cuban Painter Harmonia Rosales." In *The Afro-Descendant Woman in Latin American Diasporic Visual Art.* Routledge, 2024.

Scerbo, Rosita, and Concetta Bondi, eds. *AfroLatinas and LatiNegras: Culture, Identity, and Struggle from an Intersectional Perspective.* Rowman & Littlefield, Lexington Books, 2022.

Schildkrout, Enid. "Inscribing the Body." *Annual Review of Anthropology* 33, no. 1 (2004).

Scott, James. Decoding Subaltern Politics: Ideology, Disguise, and Resistance in Agrarian Politics. Routledge, 2012.

Seppälä, Tiina. "Feminizing Resistance, Decolonizing Solidarity: Contesting Neoliberal Development in the Global South." *Journal of Resistance Studies* 2, no. 1 (2016): 12–47.

Simmons, Kimberly Eison, and Bernd Reiter. *Afro-Descendants, Identity, and the Struggle for Development in the Americas*. Michigan State University Press, 2012.

Slavevoyages.org. "Trans-Atlantic Slave Trade Database." https://www.slavevoyages.org/voyage/database, accessed December 2, 2021.

Smith, M. "Four Steps to a Paradigm Shift: Employing Critical Perspectives to Improve Outreach to Low-SES African American and Latino Students and their Parents." *Journal of College Admission* 201, no. 1 (2008): 17–23.

Souza Caridad, and Cespedes L. Karina. "Dispatches from an Afro-Latinx Decolonial Feminism." *Chicana/Latina Studies: The Journal of Mujeres Activas en Letras y Cambio Social* 22, no. 1 (2022).

Sparks, Randy J. *The Two Princes of Calabar: An Eighteenth-Century Atlantic Odyssey*. Harvard University Press, 2004.

Spence Benson, Devyn ed. *Afrocubanas: History, Thought, and Cultural Practices*. Trans. Alma Karina. Rowman & Littlefield, Lexington Books, 2020.

Stoner, K. Lynn. *De la casa a la calle. El movimiento cubano de la mujer a favor de la reforma legal (1898–1940)*. Colibrí, 2003.

Stoner, K. Lynn. *From the House to the Streets: The Cuban Woman's Movement for Legal Reform, 1898–1940*. Duke University Press, 1991.

Stoner, K. Lynn, and González, Mario. *Minerva: Revista Quincenal Dedicada a la Mujer de Color*. Instituto de Historia de Cuba, 1998.

Synnott, A. "Shame and Glory: A Sociology of Hair." *British Journal of Sociology* 38, no. 3 (1987): 381–413.

Tannenbaum, Frank. *Slave and Citizen: The Negro in the Americas*. Knopf, 1947.

Telles, E. *Pigmentocracies: Ethnicity, Race, and Color in Latin America*. University of North Carolina Press, 2014.

Telles, E., Flores, R. D., and Urrea-Giraldo, F. "Pigmentocracies: Educational Inequality, Skin Color and Census Ethnoracial Identification in Eight Latin American Countries." *Research in Social Stratification and Mobility* 40, no. 1 (2015): 39–58.

Telles, E., and Garcia, D. "Mestizaje and Public Opinion in Latin America." *Latin American Research Review* 48, no. 3 (2013): 130–52.

Telles, Edward E., René D. Flores, and Fernando A. Limongi. "Who Is Black, White, or Mixed Race? How Skin Color, Status, and Nation Shape Racial Classification in Latin America." *American Journal of Sociology* 120, no. 3 (2014): 864–907.

Thompson, C. "Black Women, Beauty, and Hair as a Matter of Being." *Women's Studies* 38, no. 8 (2009): 831–56.

Thompson, Robert F. *The Four Moments of the Sun*. National Gallery of Art, 1981.

Thompson, Robert F. Flash of the Spirit: African and Afro-American Art and Philosophy. Random House, 1983.

Thompson M. S., and Keith V. M. "The Black the Berry: Gender, Skin Tone, Self-Esteem, and Self-Efficacy." *Gender & Society* 15 (2001): 336–57.

Thornton, John K., and Linda Heywood. "The Treason of Dom Pedro Nkanga a Mvemba Against Dom Diogo, King of Kongo, 1550." In *Afro-Latino Voices: Narratives from the Early Modern Ibero-Atlantic World, 1550–1812*, edited by Kathryn Joy McKnight and Leo J. Garofalo. Hackett, 2009, 2–29.

Thurston Bonnie. *Women in the New Testament: Questions and Commentary.* Wipf and Stock, 2004.

Tierney, Dolores. "Guy Baron, Gender in Cuban Cinema: From the Modern to the Postmodern. Peter Lang, 2011, vi, 326. *New West Indian Guide* 88, no. 3–4 (2014): 369–71.

Tone, John Lawrence. "The Machete and the Liberation of Cuba." *Journal of Military History* 62, no. 1 (January 1998): 7–28.

Torres Zayas, Ramón. *La sociedad Abakuá: Los hijos de Ékpé.* Ruth, 2018.

Truth, S. "Ain't I a Woman." Speech delivered at Women's Convention, Akron, Ohio, 1851.

Vega, Marta Moreno, Marinieves Alba, and Yvette. Modestin. *Women Warriors of the Afro-Latina Diaspora.* Arte Público Press, 2012.

Velázquez, María Elisa. "Experiencias de esclavitud femenina: africanas, afrodescendientes e indígenas en el México virreinal." In *Debates históricos contemporáneos: africanos y afrodescendientes en México y Centroamérica*, edited by María Elisa Velázquez. México: Instituto Nacional de Antropología e Historia, 2011, 243–66.

Verene, Shepherd, and Beckles, Hilaryeds. *Caribbean Slavery in the Atlantic World.* Ian Randle, 2000.

Vinson, Ben, and Greg Graves. "The Black Experience in Colonial Latin America." *Latin American Studies.* Oxford University Press, 2011.

Wade, Peter. *Race and Ethnicity in Latin America.* Pluto Press, 2010.

Wade, Peter. "'Race,' Nature and Culture." *Man* 28, no. 1 (1993): 17–34.

Wells, I. B. *Lynch Law in All Its Phases.* New York Age Print, 1892.

West-Durán, Alan. "Regla de Ocha and Ifá." In *Cuba*, edited by Alan West Durán. Charles Scribner's Sons-Gale, 2011.

West-Durán, Alan. "What the Water Brings and Takes Away: The Work of María Magdalena Campos Pons." In *Yemoja: Gender, Sexuality, and Creativity in the Latina/o and Afro-Atlantic Diasporas*, edited by Solimar Otero and Toyin Falola. State University of New York Press, 2013, 197–213.

White, D. G. *Ar'n't I a Woman? Female Slaves in the Plantation South.* rev. ed. Norton, 1999.

Willis, Deborah, and Carla Williams. *The Black Female Body: A Photographic History.* Temple University Press, 2002.

Wirtz, Kristina. *Ritual, Discourse, and Community in Cuban Santería: Speaking a Sacred World.* University Press of Florida, 2007.

Wood, David. "Tomás Gutiérrez Alea and the Art of Revolutionary Cinema." *Bulletin of Latin American Research* 28, no. 4 (2009): 512–26.

Woodhill, Brenda, and Samuels, Curtis. "Desirable and Undesirable Androgyny: A Prescription for the Twenty-First Century." *Journal of Gender Studies* 13, no. 1 (2004): 15–28.

Yero, Cary A. "To Whom It Belongs: The Aftermaths of Afrocubanismo and the Power over lo Negro in Cuban Arts, 1938–1958." *Latin American Research Review* 57, no. 1 (2022): 1–18.

Zamora Z., Omaris. "(Trance)forming AfroLatina Embodied Knowledges in Nelly Rosario's Song of the Water Saints." *Label Me Latina/o Special Issue: Afro-Latina/o Literature and Performance* 7, no. 1 (2017): 1–16.

Zeuske, Michael. "Marcas ocultas, secretos compartidos: Acerca de marcas raciales y construcción de razas en Cuba." *Debates Americanos* 2, no. 1 (2008): 101–20.

Index

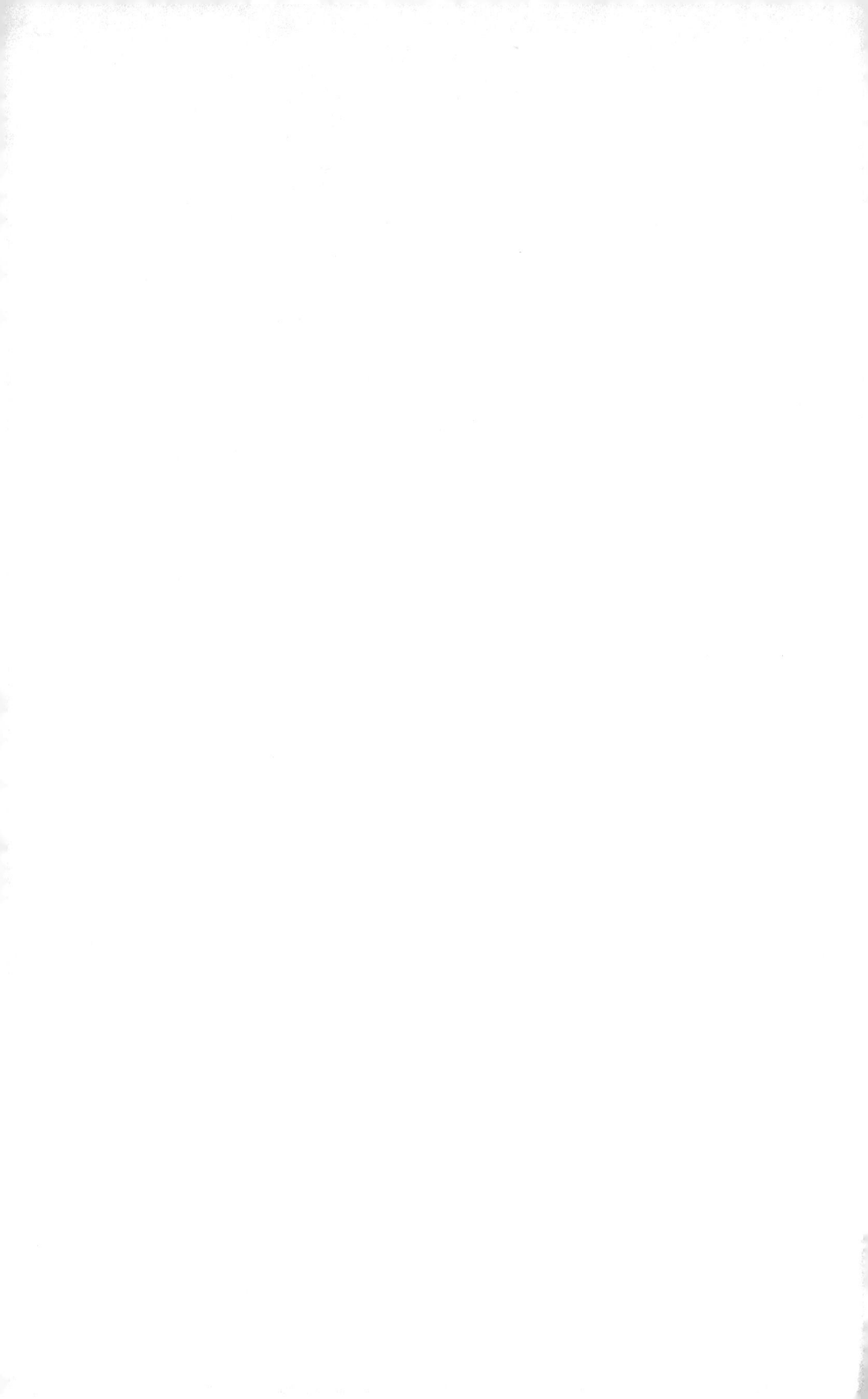

www.ingramcontent.com/pod-product-compliance
Lightning Source LLC
Chambersburg PA
CBHW050435290526
45786CB00006B/2040